Dear Brenda,

Merry Christmas!

Hope you enjoy this.

Love,

Sally, Al, A.J. & Bobby

SAN FRANCISCO
A LA CARTE

A COOKBOOK

SAN FRANCISCO
A LA CARTE

The Junior League of San Francisco

DOUBLEDAY

NEW YORK   LONDON   TORONTO   SYDNEY   AUCKLAND

Published by DOUBLEDAY, a division of Bantam Doubleday Dell Publishing
Group, Inc., 666 Fifth Avenue, New York, New York 10103.

DOUBLEDAY and the portrayal of an anchor with a dolphin are trademarks
of Doubleday, a division of Bantam Doubleday Dell Publishing Group, Inc.

Design by M Franklin-Plympton

Library of Congress Cataloging in Publication Data
Main entry under title:
San Francisco a la carte.
   1. Cookery, American—California.   2. San
Francisco—Social life and customs.   I. Junior
League of San Francisco.
TX715.S182   641.5
ISBN: 0-385-13545-9
Library of Congress Catalog Card Number 78–14702

20   22   24   26   27   25   23   21

OG

The purpose of the Junior League is exclusively educational and charitable; its aim is to promote voluntarism, to develop the potential of its members for voluntary participation in community affairs, and to demonstrate the effectiveness of trained volunteers.

The profit realized by the Junior League of San Francisco, Inc., from the sale of *San Francisco à la Carte* will be used to support community projects that we undertake in the San Francisco Bay Area. It is to this community program, and to the Junior League volunteers who serve that program so energetically, that we proudly dedicate this book.

Acknowledgments

The Junior League of San Francisco, Inc., would like to thank the many people who contributed to this book: members and friends who donated recipes; the test kitchens; the many people whose assistance, advice, and support were so vital; Mr. and Mrs. Robert T. Devlin for their wine expertise; the cookbook committee:

CHAIRPERSONS:	Patricia Wright Klitgaard
	Katherine Judd Shoen
EDITORS:	Becky Paterson Holbrook
	Bettie McGowin Studer
	Mary Scott Tilden
COMMITTEE MEMBERS:	Sandra Snyder Banks
	Joan Mayhew Beales
	Betsy Selby Bingham
	Coralie Davies Castle
	Nancy Barnes Crary
	Linda Guynup Dewey
	Elizabeth McNeill Ford
	Holly Romans Green
	Sallie Glassie Griffith
	Janet Saxton Hill
	Katherine Dibblee Kirkham
	Phoebe Allen Olcott
	Elisa Escamilla Schwartz
	Martha Lamason Sheaff
	Tracy Innes Stephenson
	Loulie Hyde Sutro
	Lila Hazelton Vultee
	Genevieve Molloy Wilson

Contents

Introduction

There's something special about San Francisco. Something that goes beyond cable cars and flower stalls, foghorns and the Golden Gate Bridge. Something more than quaint Victorian houses or spinnakers billowing on the bay. It's home. Home to people of almost every state, every nation. Home to people who brought with them many different cultures and traditions, appetites and expectations, blending together and yet retaining their individual identity.

Of these people some were so delighted to find an ideal climate for fruits and vegetables and vineyards that they spilled into the surrounding counties to develop an agricultural bounty unparalleled on the globe. Others found the open-minded social climate of San Francisco so ideal that they stayed to develop a unique city rich with diversity and personal freedom, a city pulsing with the ebb and flow of tide and man alike. A city alive with creativity. And of all the creations to which this marriage of man and nature gave birth, none is as loved or as well known as the superb cuisine San Francisco boasts today—a cuisine famous for its myriad combinations and sophistication.

Built on the abundant harvest of nearby field and sea, distilling the best from a huge variety of influences and culinary techniques, cooking and eating in San Francisco have become not only an art form but a civic preoccupation. In the city's first years, when the population was mostly male, living in boardinghouses and hotels, a favorite local pastime was eating and drinking. No doubt the fascination with creating unusual flavor combinations in the kitchen is a holdover from those beginnings. Our taste in food and wine alike is a reflection of that early day melting pot of Spanish missionary, forty-niner, Chinese laborer, and gold and silver baron.

It was the missionaries who started San Francisco's love affair with wine. They brought the root stock for wine grapes on the backs of their donkeys as they traveled north from Mexico and established the missions. Later, as the French and Italian settlers arrived on sailing ships

at the height of the gold rush, they added European know-how and ap-
preciation and planted the first commercial vineyards. Today the coun-
tryside is sprouting with family-owned wineries, seeking excellence in
their small but exquisite production while the large established wine
companies provide California wines to an ever-growing circle of ad-
mirers.

In this book we offer you a sampling of the best food anywhere
brought from everywhere by the extraordinary people who were and
are San Francisco. It is a book that, like our city, was created from both
old traditions and new ideas. We invite you to share and enjoy these old
and new, familiar and unusual, easy and elegant recipes.

CHAPTER I

MENUS

Civic Center

San Francisco's Civic Center is enshrined in classic architecture—a glorious symbol of its important place in a city given to democratic government, education, fine arts, entertainment, and commerce. These civic institutions are housed in and represented by a group of magnificent buildings surrounding a four-square-block plaza. City Hall, resplendent with gilt and marble, rising on the site of its predecessor, destroyed in the earthquake, dominates the assemblage with its enormous dome. In addition are the Main Library, the Civic Auditorium, and the State Building, and on Van Ness Avenue are the Opera House, the only municipally owned structure of its kind in the country, and the Veterans Memorial Building, housing the Museum of Modern Art. Together these structures comprise a multifaceted monument to the efforts of San Francisco's early citizens who brought culture and refinement and sculptured an orderly and lawful society from the mud of a restless gold rush town.

Here is an impressive cluster of man's finest architectural efforts. Here is the coming together of all the diversity of culture, where the separate ethnic groups become one citizenry before the law; here is the treasury of the past brought alive by books and letters, music and art; here is the hope for the future symbolized by the signing of the United Nations Charter in the Opera House in 1945; here is where imagination and organization work together with inspiration to create the heartbeat of the city; here is where planning and creativity combine to administer the work of the metropolis.

And so it is with the creative culinary arts—imagination and inspiration need menus, planning, and order to create banquets and buffets, suppers and brunches, parties and family meals. It is the administrative skill that brings together diverse flavors and contrasting textures to create the appropriate result.

Menus can be simple or elaborate, saved in a party book, or stashed in your head, but they are the framework for a successful effort.

We offer a few in the hope that they may be useful in stimulating your own creativity—*Bon Appétit!*

A special note:

Because the San Francisco Bay Area is the threshold of the wine capital of America, it seems appropriate to include some wine suggestions with these menus. The wines and wineries mentioned here are but a few of the many available. Ninety per cent of the fine quality domestic wines begin as grapes on vines that grow within a two-hour drive of San Francisco. As a consequence, most of the wines listed here come from the California wine region known broadly as the North Coast area. Included are samplings of the two types of California wine—generic and varietal. A generic wine is named for the style of wine by European wine districts such as Burgundy or Chablis and may contain a blend of several grapes. Varietal wines bear the name of a specific variety of grape and must contain a minimum 51 per cent of that grape. Some well-known varietals are Cabernet Sauvignon, Pinot Chardonnay and Pinot Noir. While these suggestions and comments may add to the enjoyment of wine tasting, the best way to learn about California wines is to tour a winery and share the results of two hundred years of the vintner's artistry and science.

BRUNCHES

The recipe for each item marked with an asterisk in the menus that follow can be found in the Index.

Easter Brunch

*King Fizzes
Fresh Melon Platter
*Breakfast Soufflé

Grilled Sausages
*Danish Loaf Cake

After-Tennis Brunch

*Rum Funky
*Cheese Pudding
*Upside-Down Pecan Rolls

Fresh Strawberries with
    Sour Cream and Brown
    Sugar

Brunch for a Crowd

*Baked Eggs in Mushroom
    Sauce
*Date Nut Muffins
Platter of Sliced Melon,
    Grapes, Pears, and
    Apples

*Swiss Nut Torte

Weekend Brunch

*Mushroom-Sausage Strudel
Sliced Tomatoes with
    *Creamy Basil Salad
    Dressing

*Strawberry Shortcake

LUNCHEONS

Ladies' Luncheon

*Cold Tomato Soup
*Green Noodle Casserole
*Molded Cucumber Mousse

*Nanaimo Bars

Beringer Vineyards
 Los Hermanos Chablis

Special Friend's Birthday Luncheon

*San Francisco Cocktail
*Crab Crepes with Oyster
  Sauce
Buttered Broccoli

*Cold Lemon Soufflé

Wente Brothers
 Sauvignon Blanc

Committee Meeting Luncheon

*Sam's "Famous Ramos"
  Gin Fizz
*Mexican Corn Bread
  Soufflé

*Brown Derby Salad
*Brazo de Jitano

Bridge Party Luncheon

Bloody Marys or Virgin
  Marys
*Pacific Avenue Casserole
*Semi-Caesar Salad

Parker House Rolls
*Cherry Torte

Wente Brothers
 Pinot Chardonnay

Patio Luncheon

*Chicken Livers Baked with
  Rice
*Green Bean Salad Proven-
  çal

*Cold Raspberry Soufflé
*Surprise Meringue Cookies

Alfresco Luncheon

*Cold Salmon Mousse with
  Cucumber Sauce
Stuffed Eggs

*English Muffin Bread
Sliced Pineapple with
    *Brown Sugar Rum
    Sauce

Sunday Dinner at Noon

Cold Asparagus with *Sour
  Cream Dressing
*Butterflied Leg of Lamb
*Lemon Dill Rice
*Sherried Broiled Tomatoes

*Amaretto Sauce and Fresh
  Fruit
*Sonoma Vineyards
  Pinot Noir*

Maytime Luncheon

*Frosted Cantaloupe Salad
*Stuffed Chicken Breasts
*Stir-Fried Asparagus

*Frozen Yogurt
*Pecan Lace Cookies

BARBEQUES—PICNICS

Labor Day Barbecue

*Marinated Prawns
*Marinated Chuck Roast
Corn on the Cob
*Korean Salad
Garlic French Bread

*Chocolate Rum Ice Cream
*Pecan Lace Cookies

*Louis Martini
Zinfandel*

Picnic Perfecto

*Summer Berry Soup
Cold Roast Game Hens in
    Foil
*Tabbouleh in Lettuce Cups
*Asparagus Vinaigrette
French Bread with Sweet
    Butter

Fruit with *Citrus Sauce for
    Fresh Fruit
*The World's Best Cookies

*Kenwood Vineyards
Chablis*

Wine Country Picnic

*Country Sausage Pâté
*Mission Gazpacho
*Orange-Lemon Chicken,
    cold
*Sweet and Sour Zucchini

*Cold Rice Salad
*Sour Cream Chocolate
    Cake

*Louis Martini
Mountain White Chablis*

COCKTAIL PARTIES—BUFFETS

All-out Hors D'Oeuvres Buffet

*Green Chile Frittata
*Curried Cheese Rounds
*Mini Quichettes
*Skewered Chicken
*Tiropites
*Banana Rumaki
*Caviar Pie

*Crab Delight
*Curry Almond Spread
*Deviled Shrimp
*Steak Tartare
Baked Ham and Turkey
Barbecued London Broil
*Refrigerator Rolls

Film Festival Buffet

*Blue Cheese Soufflé
*Shrimp Curry
Rice

*Spinach and Mushroom
   Salad
*Apricot Dacquoise

Tailgate Buffet

*Gravlax with Mustard
   Sauce
French Bread with Sweet
   Butter
*Boned Stuffed Chicken

*Marinated Cucumbers
*Brie Quiche
Fresh Apples and Pears

*Sebastiani Vineyards
   Chablis*

DINNERS AND SUPPERS

Never-on-Sunday Dinner

*Avgolemono Soup
*Spanakopita
*Moussaka
Tossed Greens with *Anchovy Salad Dressing

Fresh pears, apples, and grapes

Beaux Arts Dinner

*Crocked Beer Cheese on Crackers
*Jean Varda Chicken à la Beach
Tossed Salad with *Tarragon Dressing

*San Francisco Sourdough French Bread
Alice B. Toklas Brownies

Elegant Dinner

*Cannelloni
Standing Rib Roast with *Madeira Sauce
*Champignons de canne à l'escargot
Asparagus in Butter

*Butter Lettuce with spicy Vinaigrette Dressing
*Frozen Strawberry Soufflé

Sterling Vineyards Cabernet Sauvignon

Formal Dinner

*Smoked Salmon Spread
*Parsley Soup
*Filet de Boeuf Rôti with Béarnaise Sauce
*Sautéed Julienne Vegetables

Buttered New Potatoes
*Gâteau Ganache

Robert Mondavi Winery Cabernet Sauvignon

Dinner for Six

*Marinated Shrimp
*Filet of Beef in Filo Pastry
*Butter-Glazed Carrots
Hearts of Romaine Salad
    with *French Vinai-
    grette Dressing

*Rich Chocolate Cake
*Sutter Home Winery
    Zinfandel*

Teen-agers Dance

*Manicotti with Tomato
    Sauce
Tossed Green Salad

Toasted Garlic Bread
*Chocolate Cheesecake

Dinner and Dancing

*Crab Soufflé
*Veal Francisco
*Eggplant Parmigiana
Sautéed Green Beans
Sliced Tomatoes with
    Chopped Chives and
    Cracked Black Pepper

*Lemon Curd Tarts
*Beaulieu Vineyard
    Sauvignon Blanc*

After-Theater Supper

*Curried Spinach Salad
*Fondue Sandwiches

*Pears Roman Style

Black-Tie Dinner

*Shrimp alla Livornese
*Rack of Lamb Persillé
*Sautéed Cherry Tomatoes
Scalloped Potatoes
Butter Lettuce Salad with
    Walnuts

*Ice Cream Soufflé with Hot
    Strawberry Sauce
*Domaine Chandon
    Blanc de Noirs
    Sparkling wine (California
    Champagne)*

Festive Spring Dinner

*Cold Salmon Mousse
*Rack of Lamb Persillé
*Shredded Carrots
*Stuffed Onions

*Pavlova

*Beaulieu Vineyard
   Pinot Noir*

A Springtime Dinner

*Watercress Soup
*Broiled Salmon Steaks with
   Mustard Sauce
Rice

*Artichokes Jambon
Sliced Peaches with
   *Grand Marnier Sauce
*Surprise Meringue Cookies

Summer Dinner

*Baked Fish with Almond
   Stuffing
*Rice Soufflé
*Cherry Tomatoes in Cream

*Asparagus Vinaigrette
*Strawberry Tart

*Sterling Vineyards
   Pinot Chardonnay*

Cool Summer Supper

*Cold Pea Soup with Mint
*Chicken Breasts in Cham-
   pagne
Rice

*Sautéed Julienne Vegeta-
   bles
*Hearts of Palm Salad
*Frozen Strawberry Soufflé

Midsummer Dinner

*Yogurt Soup
*Fillet of Sole Gruyère
*Broccoli Sauté à la Niçoise

*Confetti Rice
*Semi-Caesar Salad
*Lemon Curd Tarts

Harvest Feast

*Fresh Vegetable Soup
*Marinated Chuck Roast
*Beets with Parsley Butter

*Boiled New Potatoes
*Peach Cobbler

Oktoberfest

*Zucchini Soup
*Chicken Paprika
*Mixed Noodles
*Crookneck Squash
Lettuce with
    *Old-Fashioned Boiled
    Salad Dressing

*Grand Marnier Pots de
    Crème

*Robert Mondavi Winery
    Zinfandel*

Midwinter German Dinner

*Celery Root Soup
*Wiener Schnitzel
*Schroeder's Potato Pan-
    cakes

*Beets with Parsley Butter
*Apple Tart

Ski Weekend Dinner

*Strasbourg Sauerkraut
New Potatoes

*Swedish Rye Bread
Beer
*Apple Dapple Cake

Fisherman's Wharf Supper

*Artichoke Frittata
*Shellfish Chowder
*Sourdough French Bread

*Curried Spinach Salad
*Frozen Lemon Torte

Northwest Salmon Dinner

*Curried Fresh Pea Soup
*Baked Salmon with Sour
　　Cream Sauce
Asparagus with Chopped
　　Egg and Melted Butter

*Refrigerator Rolls
*Freezer Strawberry Jam
*Coffee Toffee Pie

*Wente Brothers
　Pinot Blanc*

Country French Dinner

*Fresh Mushrooms Stuffed
　　with Snails
*Cassoulet
*Marinated Brussels Sprouts

Marinated Artichoke Hearts
　　with Cherry Tomatoes
Warm French Bread
*Crème Brûlée

A Normandy Feast

*Caviar Mold
*Carrot Soup
*Normandy Pork Roast
Buttered Egg Noodles with
　　Parsley

*Herbed Green Beans
*Steamed Cranberry Pud-
　　ding with Vanilla Sauce

*Concannon Vineyard
　Semillon*

North Beach Dinner

Antipasto
Linguine with *Calamari
　　Sauce for Pasta
*Chicken Marsala
*Sicilian Broccoli

*Frozen Orange Yogurt
*Almond Macaroons

*Sebastiani Vineyards
　Barbera*

Middle Eastern Dinner

*Eggplant Caviar
　　with Pita Bread
Crab Cocktail

*Bastila
*Tabbouleh Salad
*Carob and Honey Pie

Gung Hay Fat Choy Dinner

*Oriental Fresh Mushrooms
*Creamed Corn and Crab
    Soup
*Beef with Bok Choy
*Parchment Chicken

*Chinese Vegetables with
    Cashew Nuts
*Fried Rice
Fortune Cookies

Mexican Dinner

Sangria
*Nachos
*Ceviche
*Mexican Pork Stew

Boiled New Potatoes
Green Salad
*Chocolate Potato Cake
    with Fudge Sauce

A Family Get-together

*Chicken Curry
Rice
Condiments

*Mushroom Tomato Salad
*Orange Cake

Wedding Rehearsal Dinner

Crepes with Sour Cream and
    Caviar
Iced Vodka
*Steak au Poivre Vert
Sautéed Potatoes
*Broccoli Purée

Watercress and Endive Salad
    with *Lemon Mustard
    Dressing
*Mocha Mousse

*Schramsberg
    Blanc de Blanc,
    Napa Valley Champagne*

An Anniversary Dinner

*Artichoke Crab Meat
    Bisque
*Stuffed Flank Steak
*Baked Mushrooms
*Herbed Green Beans

*Celeriac Rémoulade
*Italian Meringue Torte

*Beaulieu Vineyard
    Private Reserve Cabernet
    Sauvignon*

Graduation Celebration

*Cold Tomato Soup
*Orange Lemon Chicken
*Barley and Pine Nut Casserole

Sautéed Spinach
*Blueberry Tart

After-Church Easter Dinner

*Shrimp Gazpacho or *Parsley Soup
Baked Ham
Broccoli with
  *Lemon Cream Sauce
*Onions Amandine

Corn Muffins
Green Salad
*Pashka

*Charles Krug Winery
  Chenin Blanc*

Independence Day Dinner

*Chilled Yellow Squash Soup
*Medallions of Pork Sauté
*Grits Soufflé
*Artichoke Medley

Lettuce with *Caraway Salad Dressing
*Strawberry Tart

*Mirassou Vineyards
  Gewürtztraminer*

Supper for Ghosts and Goblins

*Hot Mulled Cider
*Stuffed Pumpkin
Carrot and Celery Sticks

Buttered Noodles
*Carrot Cake

Thanksgiving Dinner

*Oyster Bisque
Roast Turkey
*Sweet Potato Casserole
*Herbed Scalloped Tomatoes

Fresh Peas
Romaine Lettuce with
  *Avocado Salad Dressing
*Pumpkin Date Torte

Gala Holiday Dinner

*Walnut Liver Pâté
Olympia Oysters with
    *Cocktail Sauce a la
    Ritz
Roast Turkey
*Gourmet Stuffing
*Artichoke Ring

Creamed Onions
*Cranberry Relish
*Steamed Persimmon Pud-
    ding with Brandy Sauce

*Domaine Chandon
    Brut Sparkling Wine
    (California Champagne)*

CHAPTER II

BEVERAGES

Golden Gate Park

The Japanese Tea Garden is a treasure from the past, part of an authentic Japanese village created in Golden Gate Park for the 1894 Midwinter International Fair, and so beloved that it was retained as a permanent feature.

Golden Gate Park is a lush thousand-acre emerald belt reaching into the city from the Pacific Ocean, created out of barren windswept sand dunes by John McLaren in the 1880s. Dotted with statuary, resplendent with all manner of flowers—azaleas, fuchsias, rhododendrons, crowned with grand public buildings, it offers respite from the urban pressures that surround it.

The Japanese Tea Garden is the epitome of escape, offering magical transport into a world of bonsai, ponds, arched bridges, and the soothing comfort of tea and quiet—a contrast to the wide variety of other beverages offered in this busy, bustling city. San Francisco is surrounded by vineyards great and small, bubbling with breweries and coffeehouses, overflowing with watering holes of every conceivable mood and décor, carrying on in a tradition of convivial imbibing.

Cheers!

SANGRIA

Makes 10 to 12 servings

1 orange, thinly sliced	2 bay leaves
1 lemon, thinly sliced	½ cup brandy
¼ cup superfine sugar	1 quart club soda
½ gallon red Burgundy	
½ cup orange-flavored liqueur	

Combine and marinate overnight the orange, lemon, sugar, red wine, liqueur, and bay leaves. Add the brandy. Just before serving, add the soda and some ice.

SANGRITA

Makes 8 to 10 Servings

16 ounces tomato juice
16 ounces orange juice
2 tablespoons fresh lime juice
4 ounces tequila
1 teaspoon Worcestershire
   sauce

Salt and pepper to taste
Tabasco sauce to taste
6 to 8 slices of lime for
   garnish

Mix all ingredients, except the lime slices, in a pitcher. Pour into glasses filled with ice cubes and garnish with lime slices. You may vary the proportion of tomato and orange juices to suit your own taste.

KING FIZZ

Serves 1

1½ ounces simple
   syrup (see recipe
   below)
1 ounce gin

1 ounce fresh lime juice (or
   bottled lime juice)
1 whole egg
1 dash Cointreau (optional)

Place all ingredients in a blender with lots of cracked ice and blend for 15 to 20 seconds until smooth.

Simple Syrup (Bar Syrup)

Mix 1 part water and 2 parts sugar and boil for 5 minutes. Keep in the refrigerator to sweeten drinks.

SAM'S "FAMOUS RAMOS" GIN FIZZ

Serves 1

1½ ounces gin or vodka
1 ounce lemon juice
1 tablespoon orange juice
1 teaspoon sugar

1 whole egg
2 ounces heavy cream
Dash of orange flower water
½ cup cracked ice

Pour all ingredients into a blender and blend well.

RUM FUNKY

Serves 1

2 ounces light rum
6 ounces fresh orange juice
Galliano liqueur

Pour the rum and orange juice over ice in a tall glass. Float a little Galliano on top.

SAN FRANCISCO COCKTAIL

Makes 12 to 14 servings

2 fifths of white port, chilled
1 cup light rum
½ cup fresh lemon juice

Strawberries or cherries for
garnish

In a large pitcher or punch bowl combine the port, rum, and lemon juice. Chill. Serve in stemmed glasses filled with crushed ice. Garnish with strawberries or cherries.

FROZEN DAIQUIRI

Makes 12 to 14 servings

1 6-ounce can frozen limeade
1 6-ounce can water
18 ounces light rum

1 quart carbonated
   grapefruit mix

Combine all ingredients and freeze until slushy. Stir briefly and spoon into small cocktail glasses.

RUM TROPICAL

Watch out for this! It is deliciously lethal and the longer it ages the smoother it gets. Falernum syrup is a liquor mix from Barbados; it can be found in good liquor stores.

Makes 14 to 16 servings

1 fifth of white or gold rum
1 quart unsweetened
   pineapple juice, fresh or
   canned

½ cup fresh lime juice,
   strained
¼ cup Falernum syrup or 3
   tablespoons fine sugar

In a large bowl, combine all ingredients and mix well. Transfer to two quart-size bottles. Store in the refrigerator for at least forty-eight hours. It can keep indefinitely. Serve in small glasses over crushed ice.

HOT BUTTERED RUM BATTER

Makes 3 cups

1 pound dark brown sugar
½ pound butter, softened
½ teaspoon nutmeg

½ teaspoon cinnamon
½ teaspoon ground cloves

Cream sugar and butter together and add seasonings. Refrigerate until ready to use. It will keep for several weeks.

TO SERVE: Place about 1 tablespoon of batter in an 8-ounce mug, add 6 ounces of boiling water and 1 ounce of dark rum.

BRAZILIAN COFFEE

Makes 4 to 5 servings

4 cups hot chocolate
1½ cups strong coffee
1 cup brandy or rum

½ cup heavy cream,
    whipped with 1
    teaspoon sugar

Heat the chocolate, coffee, and brandy or rum together. Fold in whipped cream (or place a spoonful on top of each serving).

DRUNKEN COFFEE

Serves 10 to 15

3 oranges
2 lemons
Whole cloves
¼ cup sugar
2 sticks cinnamon
¼ cup Grand Marnier
Additional Grand Marnier

Additional lemon juice
Superfine sugar
Hot coffee
Whipped cream
Freshly grated orange or
    lemon rind

Cut the peels of the oranges and lemons into strips 3 inches long and approximately ½ inch wide. Into each strip stick 2 cloves. Combine the juices and peels of the oranges and lemons, sugar, cinnamon, and ¼ cup Grand Marnier. Bring to a gentle boil and simmer until thickened. Mixture should be thick and peels should be translucent. Cool. Transfer to a decanter and add 1½ ounces Grand Marnier per person. Dip inverted wineglasses ½ inch down in additional lemon juice and then dip in superfine sugar. Pour 1½ ounces of the Grand Marnier and juice mixture and several peels into each glass. Add hot coffee and stir. Top with dollops of whipped cream and a sprinkling of grated orange or lemon rind.

RUSSIAN TEA

Makes 12 to 14 servings

2 tablespoons orange pekoe
    or Darjeeling tea leaves
2 sticks cinnamon
½ teaspoon whole cloves
½ teaspoon whole allspice
⅛ teaspoon freshly grated
    nutmeg

½ teaspoon freshly grated
    orange or lemon rind
1 gallon boiling water
1½ to 2 cups sugar
Juice of 4 oranges
Juice of 3 lemons

Place the tea leaves, cinnamon, cloves, allspice, nutmeg, and rind in a cheesecloth bag. Drop into the boiling water, add the sugar, and boil for 10 minutes. Remove the bag and add the orange and lemon juices. Adjust for sweetness and serve hot.

VIENNESE CHOCOLATE

Makes 10 to 12 servings

4 ounces semisweet
    chocolate
⅓ cup sugar
⅓ teaspoon salt

1⅓ cups boiling water
4 cups scalded milk
1 teaspoon vanilla extract
1 cup heavy cream, whipped

Melt the chocolate in the top of a double boiler over hot water. Stir in the sugar and salt and slowly add the boiling water, blending well. Add the scalded milk. Simmer the mixture for a few minutes and then beat with a whisk until frothy. Add the vanilla. Serve the chocolate from a heated coffee pot and use demitasse cups. Pass the whipped cream separately.

HOT MULLED CIDER

A great hot nonalcoholic drink for after skiing. Children love it!

Makes 10 servings

½ cup brown sugar
¼ teaspoon salt
2 quarts apple cider
1 teaspoon whole allspice
1 teaspoon whole cloves
3 inch stick of cinnamon

Dash of nutmeg
A cinnamon stick for each
    mug
An orange slice for each
    mug (optional)

Combine the first 7 ingredients and bring to a boil. Simmer for 20 minutes. Remove the spices. Serve in mugs with cinnamon sticks and with orange slice floaters if desired.

HOT SPICED CIDER

Makes 10 servings

2 quarts apple cider
3 cinnamon sticks
2 teaspoons nutmeg
2 teaspoons whole cloves

½ cup fresh lemon juice
2 cups fresh orange juice
Cinnamon sticks for stirring

Boil the cider and spices together for 15 minutes. Add the lemon and orange juices and simmer. Serve warm in mugs with a cinnamon stick in each for stirring.

DUBONNET PUNCH

Makes 18 to 20 servings

1 fifth of Dubonnet
1 pint gin
Juice of 6 limes or lemons

1 quart club soda, chilled
1 lime or lemon, sliced

Mix together the Dubonnet, gin, lime juice, and soda. Pour over a block of ice in a punch bowl and garnish with lime or lemon slices.

ON-THE-WAGON PUNCH

Perfect for a children's party or as a nonalcoholic refresher for adults.

Makes 30 servings

3 6-ounce cans frozen
    Hawaiian punch,
    defrosted
3 cups cold water
1 24-ounce can powdered
    lemonade mix

5 quarts soda water, chilled
2 quarts ginger ale, chilled
1 quart raspberry sherbet

In a large punch bowl, mix all the liquid ingredients well. Add the sherbet.

INGE-LISE HOLIDAY PUNCH

Makes 45 to 50 servings

1 quart vodka, chilled
2 fifths of dry white wine,
    chilled
4 ounces curaçao

2 quarts 7-up, chilled
2 fifths of brut champagne,
    chilled

Combine all ingredients in a punch bowl with ice. Stir and serve.

EGGNOG

Makes 25 to 30 servings

12 eggs, separated
2¼ cups sugar
4 cups Bourbon
2 cups dark rum

4 cups milk
4 cups heavy cream,
    whipped
Freshly grated nutmeg

Beat the egg yolks well, add the sugar and continue beating until
smooth and yellow-colored. Slowly stir in the Bourbon, rum, and milk.
Fold in the whipped cream. Whip the egg whites until stiff but not dry.
Fold into the nog mixture. Transfer to a punch bowl and sprinkle with
nutmeg.

CHAMPAGNE PUNCH WITH
A FROZEN FRUIT MOLD

This is a lovely punch for a spring or summer wedding reception or a ladies' luncheon. With ginger ale it could be spectacular at a party for any age group. The frozen mold keeps it icy cold as long as there is punch in the bowl.

Serves 40

3 cups sugar
6 cups water
2 6-ounce cans frozen orange
    juice concentrate
1 6-ounce can frozen lemon
    juice concentrate

1 46-ounce can unsweetened
    pineapple juice
4 bananas
4 bottles champagne or 4 to
    5 quarts ginger ale,
    chilled

In a large saucepan dissolve the sugar in the water. Add the orange, lemon, and pineapple juices. Place the bananas in a blender or food processor, add a small amount of the juices, and purée. Add this mixture to the juices, stir until well blended, and pour into a 16 cup size ring mold (or one of another shape). Freeze.

TO SERVE: remove the fruit mold from freezer about an hour before serving. Unmold and place in a large punch bowl. Pour over it champagne or ginger ale.

CHAPTER III

APPETIZERS

Montgomery Street

Montgomery Street—Wall Street of the West—was named for Captain John B. Montgomery, who claimed San Francisco for the United States in 1846. At that time the town was called Yerba Buena, or "good herb," for the wild mint that grew on the sand dunes that would later blossom into a metropolis.

Montgomery Street which fronted on the edge of the bay in the early years, was the financial center of the city. Interspersed among the banks and exchanges of the day were the gathering places for bankers, brokers, and businessmen—saloons. In these saloons, transactions of all kinds took place under the watchful eyes of saloonkeepers who, acting on tips, were often able to advance themselves into positions of wealth.

With names sounding more like businesses than bars, the saloons were often for men only. Steam beer, a locally made favorite so named because of its very frothy head, was a popular choice and is still available today. It could be found at the Bank Exchange Bar along with its specialty, Pisco Punch; the Mining Exchange served a free lunch of gargantuan proportions to their patrons from 4 P.M. to midnight.

Today on Montgomery Street nothing has changed but the height of the buildings and the pace of life on the street. It is still the center of financial activity, and its restaurants and bars are still the places where business transactions are made—all those office buildings notwithstanding. And happily the Happy Hour remains, with many establishments offering complementary hors d'oeuvres with their drinks—although hardly the groaning boards of yesteryear. Still, tempting aromas waft streetward, entrapping the not unwilling businessmen at the end of the day and offering such delectable delicacies as French-fried eggplant, chicken wings, tiny bite-sized pizzas, cocktail sausages wrapped in dough, meat balls, and artichoke *frittata*.

Here are some great beginnings.

STUFFED FRENCH BREAD

Serves 12 to 15

1 loaf French bread
8 ounces cheese spread
    (recipe given below) or
    an 8-ounce jar of
    commercial cheese
    spread

Mayonnaise to moisten
6 ounces crab meat
3 tablespoons chopped
    parsley

CHEESE SPREAD
8 ounces sharp Cheddar
    cheese, grated
1 tablespoon butter, softened

Place the grated cheese in a food processor or blender with the butter and blend until smooth.

Preheat oven to 350 degrees. Cut the loaf of French bread in half lengthwise. Remove some of the bread to make a shallow trench in each half. Cover each with cheese spread. Add the mayonnaise to the crab meat to moisten and spread over the cheese. Bake for 20 minutes or until bubbly. Sprinkle with chopped parsley. Cut into serving pieces and serve.

BANANA RUMAKI

Serves 8

8 to 10 bacon slices,
    cut in half
5 bananas, slightly underripe

½ cup brown sugar
1 tablespoon curry powder

Blanch bacon in boiling water for 10 minutes. Drain and dry thoroughly. Cut bananas into 1½-inch chunks and wrap in bacon, securing it closed with a toothpick. Combine brown sugar and curry powder and sprinkle on wrapped bananas. Bake on rack for about 10 minutes at 350 degrees until bacon is crisp and sugar is slightly caramelized.

DOLMADES

Makes about 50

½ cup olive oil
2 large onions, finely
    chopped
2 cups uncooked rice
1 pound ground beef
1½ teaspoons freshly
    ground black pepper
½ cup pine nuts
Juice of 1 lemon

2 tablespoons chopped fresh
    mint
2 tablespoons chopped
    parsley
1 jar grape leaves (about
    50), rinsed, then dried
    on paper towels
2 cups water

In a large skillet, sauté onions in oil until soft but not brown, then stir in rice and cook, stirring, until golden. Add beef, pepper, pine nuts, lemon juice, mint, and parsley. Sauté for about 5 minutes, stirring frequently. Stuff each grape leaf with 1 large tablespoon of filling, fold, and roll up. Place in a single layer, close together, rolled edge down, in a large skillet. Add water to cover. Place an ovenproof plate or lid directly on top of the dolmades so they won't open while cooking. Simmer slowly for about 45 minutes to 1 hour or until all water has been absorbed. Cool and serve at room temperature.

CHEESE PUFFS

Makes about 4 dozen

1 loaf unsliced white bread
½ cup butter
3 ounces cream cheese

¼ pound sharp Cheddar
    cheese, grated
2 egg whites, stiffly beaten

Trim crust from bread and cut loaf into 1-inch cubes. In the top of a double boiler over simmering water melt butter, cream cheese and Cheddar cheese, then beat until smooth. Fold in egg whites. Line a cookie sheet with foil. Dip bread cubes into cheese mixture and place on cookie sheet. Refrigerate overnight or freeze. Preheat oven to 400 degrees. Bake for 10 to 12 minutes or until browned. May be baked directly from the freezer.

CAVIAR PIE

Everything can be done ahead for this stunning hors d'oeuvre except for adding the sour cream. It serves a lot of people and is always very popular.

Serves 8 to 10

4 hard-cooked eggs
4 tablespoons butter,
  softened
1 medium onion, finely
  chopped
1 can flat anchovies, drained

1 tablespoon mayonnaise
2 tablespoons chopped
  parsley
1 4-ounce jar caviar
Juice of a half lemon
1 cup sour cream

Mash hard-cooked eggs and mix with butter and half of the chopped onion. Spread evenly on the bottom of a 9-inch pie plate and refrigerate for at least ½ hour. Mash anchovies and blend with mayonnaise and chopped parsley. Spread on top of egg mixture. Combine caviar and remaining chopped onion and add lemon juice. Spread on top of pie, then frost with sour cream just before serving. Serve with crackers or bread rounds.

ARTICHOKE FRITTATA

Serves 16

3 6-ounce jars marinated
  artichokes, drained and
  finely chopped
½ pound sharp Cheddar
  cheese, grated
1 medium onion, finely
  chopped

4 eggs, lightly beaten
6 single soda crackers, finely
  crushed
Dash of Tabasco sauce
Salt and pepper to taste

Preheat oven to 325 degrees. Mix ingredients well and pour into a buttered 8-inch-square baking pan. Bake at 325 degrees for 1 hour. Cut into 1-inch squares and serve hot. May also be served at room temperature.

STUFFED MUSHROOMS

The herb mixture used here, fines herbes, *is a classical French combination of equal parts of parsley, chives, tarragon, and chervil. You can mix your own or buy those of several well-known spice companies.*

Serves 8

1 pound medium-sized mushrooms	1 ounce blue cheese
2 tablespoons butter	2 tablespoons chopped onion
3 ounces cream cheese	¼ teaspoon *fines herbes*
	Paprika

Wash mushrooms. Remove stems, finely chop, and set aside. Melt butter in a heavy skillet, and when foaming begins to subside, add mushroom caps and sauté over medium heat for about 2 minutes. Combine cream cheese, blue cheese, mushroom stems, onion, and *fines herbes*. Mix well. Stuff mushroom caps with cheese mixture, dust with paprika, and broil until bubbly.

CHILI CHEESE APPETIZER

Makes approximately 2 dozen

1 small loaf French bread, thinly sliced	1 small clove garlic, pressed
4 tablespoons butter, softened	¼ pound Monterey Jack cheese, shredded
¼ cup chopped, seeded canned green chilies	Mayonnaise if needed to moisten (optional)

Toast one side of the bread slices under the broiler until just golden. Mix together the butter, green chilies, and garlic, and spread on the untoasted side of the bread slices. Top with cheese or cheese-mayonnaise mixture, spreading to edge of slices. Broil until browned and puffy. Serve hot. May be made ahead and refrigerated until ready to broil. May also be frozen, but for several days only.

CLAM PUFFS

Makes 18 to 20

1 8-ounce can minced clams,
    drained
3 ounces cream cheese,
    softened
1 teaspoon onion juice

18 to 20 1-inch bread
    rounds or squares
4 tablespoons butter
Paprika

Combine clams, cream cheese, and onion juice. Sauté one side of bread rounds or squares in butter, then spread clam mixture on unbuttered side. Broil until bubbly. Sprinkle with paprika before serving.

CHEESE FONDUE

The classic cheese fondue.

Serves 6

1 small loaf French bread,
    cubed so that each piece
    has a crust
½ pound Emmenthaler
    cheese, shredded
½ pound Gruyère cheese,
    shredded
2 tablespoons cornstarch
1 clove garlic, bruised

1 cup Rhine wine
2 tablespoons kirsch
1 tablespoon fresh lemon
    juice (optional)
⅛ teaspoon salt
⅛ teaspoon white pepper or
    cayenne
⅛ teaspoon freshly grated
    nutmeg

Allow bread cubes to dry slightly before preparing the fondue. Toss the cheeses with the cornstarch to coat well. Rub the inside of a chafing dish or fondue pot with garlic, pressing with a wooden spoon to allow the essence of the garlic to coat the chafing dish. Pour in the wine and, stirring constantly, heat over low heat without boiling. Slowly add the cheese until melted. Blend in remaining ingredients. Stir until smooth and keep warm over a candle or burner.

BROILED ONION TOAST

Very easy and very Good! Mixture can be prepared ahead, then put on the bread at the last minute. Also tasty with soup.

Serves 16

1 large Bermuda onion,
    finely chopped
3 tablespoons mayonnaise
Salt

Freshly ground black pepper
8 slices French bread or
    party rye, cut in half

To the onion add mayonnaise and salt and pepper to taste. Spread mixture on slices of bread and broil until bubbly and brown. Serve hot.

CAMEMBERT SAUTÉ

This cheese, with a good bottle of chilled white wine and some good crackers or French bread, is heaven. It could be the single hors d'oeuvre before an important dinner. Even for people who don't like Camembert, this will be a hit.

Serves 12

1 6-inch round Camembert
    cheese, medium soft
1 egg, beaten
1 cup fresh bread crumbs

4 tablespoons unsalted butter
½ cup chopped green onion
    tops

Dip the unskinned cheese round in the egg and then coat both sides with bread crumbs. Heat 2 tablespoons of the butter until it starts to brown. Over high heat brown cheese round on both sides. Remove to a heated serving plate and keep warm. Add the remaining butter to the skillet. When foamy, sauté the onions for 2 minutes. Pour over top of the cheese round and serve immediately with table water biscuits or plain crackers. The outside of the cheese should be crisp and the inside warm and runny. If the cheese is too ripe, it will melt when browning.

CHILI CON QUESO

Serves 20

2 large onions, chopped
¼ pound margarine or
butter
1 28-ounce can peeled whole
tomatoes, chopped and
well drained

1½ pounds sharp Cheddar
cheese, grated
1 7-ounce can green chili
peppers
Tabasco sauce to taste
Tortilla chips

Sauté onions in margarine or butter until transparent. Add tomatoes and simmer for 20 minutes or until thickened. Add cheese and cook and stir over low heat until cheese is melted. Drain chili peppers, discard seeds, and chop. Add to cheese mixture and season with Tabasco. Serve in a chafing dish with tortilla chips. Keep mixture warm.

LOG CABIN CHEESE STRAWS

Makes approximately 4 dozen straws

4 tablespoons butter,
softened
1 cup grated sharp Cheddar
cheese
¼ cup milk
¼ teaspoon salt
Dash Tabasco sauce
Dash paprika

Dash cayenne
¾ cup all-purpose white
flour
1½ cups fine soft French
bread crumbs
Coarse salt
Grated Parmesan cheese
Poppy or sesame seeds

Cream the butter and cheese, add the milk and seasonings, and stir until well blended. Add the flour and bread crumbs, and mix well. Divide into 2 portions, form into balls and wrap in waxed paper. Refrigerate for 1 hour. Preheat oven to 350 degrees. Working quickly, roll each portion between 2 sheets of wax paper until they are very thin, approximately ⅛ inch thick. Cut into strips 5 inches long and ¾ inch wide. Sprinkle with coarse salt, Parmesan cheese, and poppy or sesame seeds. Place on an ungreased cookie sheet and bake for 12 to 15 minutes.

CHEESE KRISPIES

This dough can be made up and frozen for a ready cheese cracker. Once made, they keep well in a covered tin.

Serves 25 to 30

½ pound butter, softened
1 pound Cheddar cheese,
   grated
1 teaspoon salt

· ¼ teaspoon cayenne pepper
2 cups flour
2 cups Rice Krispies

Preheat oven to 350 degrees. Mix together butter and cheese, add salt and pepper. Blend in flour and Rice Krispies. Form into balls the size of walnuts and place on an ungreased baking sheet. Dip a fork in water and flatten each ball. Refrigerate until chilled. Bake for 10 to 12 minutes. Do not brown. Serve warm or store in a tightly covered tin.

CURRIED OLIVE APPETIZER

These hors d'oeuvres are great for a large crowd. You can make them ahead and refrigerate them, then pop them under the broiler just before serving.

Serves 8

1 4½-ounce can chopped
   ripe olives
¼ cup diced green onion
¾ cup grated Cheddar
   cheese
4 tablespoons mayonnaise

Salt
Curry powder to taste
Small loaf French bread,
   sliced and lightly
   toasted on one side
Minced parsley

Mix together the olives, onion, cheese, mayonnaise, a pinch of salt, and curry powder. Spread on the untoasted side of French bread slices and broil until bubbly. Sprinkle with minced parsley.

CURRIED CHEESE ROUNDS

Makes approximately 40 rounds

¾ pound sharp Cheddar
　cheese, grated
3 green onions, chopped
3 to 4 teaspoons curry
　powder

½ cup mayonnaise, or as
　needed for spreading
　consistency
Salt to taste
1 loaf party-size rye bread

Combine cheese, onions, curry powder, mayonnaise, and salt. Chill for 1 hour. Toast the rye bread on one side. Spread the cheese mixture on the untoasted side of the rye bread and put on a cookie sheet under the broiler until cheese is melted. Serve immediately.

MINI QUICHETTES

These are so versatile and easy they should be in everyone's repertoire.

Serves 6 to 8

PASTRY
½ cup butter
3 ounces cream cheese
1 cup flour

Beat together the butter and cream cheese till smooth, add flour, and form into a ball. Wrap in wax paper and chill for 30 minutes or longer. The pastry can be made a day ahead. Make miniature pie shells by shaping the dough into 1-inch balls and pressing it into the bottom and sides of small muffin cups about 1½ to 2 inches in diameter.

FILLING
4 ounces small shrimp
1 medium onion, chopped
　and lightly sautéed
½ cup grated Swiss cheese
2 eggs, lightly beaten

½ cup milk
⅛ teaspoon nutmeg
Freshly ground pepper to
　taste

Preheat oven to 450 degrees. In each miniature pie shell place a few small shrimp, then a little sautéed onion, then a little grated cheese. Combine the eggs with the milk, nutmeg, and ground pepper, and pour into the cups. Bake for 10 minutes. Reduce heat to 350 degrees and continue baking for 15 minutes more. Serve immediately. These can be frozen after baking and reheated at 450 degrees for 10 minutes directly from the freezer. The filling in this recipe may be prepared by substituting one of the following for the shrimp: crab, canned clams, chopped cooked ham, sautéed chopped bacon.

DEVILED SHRIMP

These shrimp are beautiful served in a large bowl over cracked ice with long bamboo skewers for a big cocktail party. Or put the marinated shrimp on a platter and pour the reserved marinade in a small bowl for dipping.

Serves 8 to 10

2 pounds medium to large
    raw shrimp
1 lemon, thinly sliced
1 medium red onion, thinly
    sliced
1 cup pitted black olives,
    well drained
2 tablespoons chopped
    pimiento
¼ cup vegetable oil

2 cloves garlic, minced
1 tablespoon dry mustard
1 tablespoon salt
½ cup lemon juice
1 tablespoon red wine
    vinegar
1 bay leaf, crumbled
Dash of cayenne
Chopped parsley

Shell and devein shrimp. Bring 1 quart salted water to a boil, add the shrimp, and cook for a scant 3 minutes. Drain at once, rinse in cold water, drain, and set aside. In a bowl, combine lemon slices, onion, black olives, and pimiento, and toss well. Combine oil, garlic, dry mustard, salt, lemon juice, wine vinegar, bay leaf, cayenne, and parsley, and add to the bowl with the lemon mixture. Arrange shrimp on a serving dish and pour marinade over them. Cover and chill no longer than 3 hours. Serve with toothpicks.

MARINATED SHRIMP

Serves 8 to 12

MARINADE

1⅓ cups olive oil
⅔ cup tarragon vinegar
½ teaspoon salt
¼ teaspoon freshly ground
    black pepper
¼ teaspoon paprika
1 large onion, coarsely
    chopped
1 clove garlic, mashed

3 tablespoons Dijon mustard
1 tablespoon German style
    mustard
2 tablespoons prepared
    horseradish
1 tablespoon powdered
    thyme
1½ to 2 pounds jumbo
    shrimp

Place all ingredients except the shrimp in a blender or food processor. Blend until onion is finely minced. Cook the shrimp in boiling salted water about 3 minutes, then rinse under cold running water to stop the cooking process. Remove shells and chill in the marinade until icy cold. To serve, drain off the marinade and serve it separately as a dip for the shrimp.

MUSHROOM ROLLS

These are so easy to make ahead and have waiting in the freezer just to be brushed with butter and baked.

Makes 7 to 8 dozen

1 pound mushrooms, finely
    chopped
½ cup butter
6 tablespoons flour
1½ teaspoons salt
2 cups light cream

2 teaspoons lemon juice
1 teaspoon onion salt
1½ loaves sliced white
    sandwich bread
4 tablespoons melted butter

Preheat oven to 400 degrees. Sauté the mushrooms in the butter for 5 minutes. Remove from heat and cool slightly. Add the flour and blend well, then add the salt. Stir in the cream and cook, stirring constantly, until thick. Add the lemon juice and onion salt, and cool. Remove the crusts from the bread and roll slices very thin with a rolling pin. Spread some mushroom mixture on each slice of bread and roll up. Place on a baking sheet, seam side down. Place in the freezer for at least 10 minutes. Cut rolls into thirds, brush with melted butter, and bake for 15 to 20 minutes.

MARINATED MUSHROOMS STUFFED WITH CHICKEN

Serves 6 to 8

1 cup salad oil
1 tablespoon finely chopped onion
1 tablespoon finely chopped chive
1 tablespoon finely chopped parsley
1 bay leaf
3 cloves

¼ teaspoon black pepper
Dash of Tabasco sauce
½ teaspoon salt
1 clove garlic, peeled and halved
1 pound medium mushrooms of uniform size, stems removed

CHICKEN STUFFING
½ chicken breast, cooked
3 tablespoons mayonnaise
3 tablespoons chopped green onion

Pepper to taste
Salt to taste
Sour cream

In a large bowl, combine the oil, onion, chive, parsley, bay leaf, cloves, pepper, Tabasco, salt, and garlic. Add the mushrooms and marinate for 2 days, carefully stirring occasionally. Mix together the chicken, mayonnaise, green onion, pepper, salt, and enough sour cream to bind. Stuff mushrooms with chicken mixture and chill.

FRESH MUSHROOMS STUFFED WITH SNAILS

Serves 8

½ cup soft butter
1¼ teaspoons minced
    shallots
1 large clove garlic, finely
    minced
1½ tablespoons minced
    parsley

½ tablespoon grated celery
¼ teaspoon salt
Pepper to taste
16 large mushrooms,
    approximately 2 inches
    in diameter
16 canned snails, drained

Preheat oven to 375 degrees. Cream 6 tablespoons of the butter with the shallots, garlic, parsley, celery, salt, and pepper. Discard the stems of the mushrooms. With a sharp knife, hollow out a ¾-inch depression in the top of each cap. Sauté them in the remaining 2 tablespoons of butter for 5 minutes. Place a small amount of the herbed butter in each mushroom cap, then add a snail and a little more butter. Place in a baking pan and bake for 15 minutes.

EGGPLANT CAVIAR

Serves 8

1 medium eggplant
1 medium onion, finely
    minced
1 to 2 cloves garlic, finely
    minced
1 ripe tomato, peeled,
    seeded, and finely
    chopped

1 teaspoon sugar
3 tablespoons olive oil
2 tablespoons vinegar
Salt and freshly ground
    pepper to taste

Broil eggplant, 5 to 6 inches from heat turning often, for 45 minutes or until skin is black and blistered and pulp is very soft all the way through. Cool, peel, and chop finely. Blend well with remaining ingredients, cover, and refrigerate for at least 4 hours or overnight. Serve with pita bread or rye crackers. This dish may also be served on crisp Romaine lettuce leaves as a first course.

MARINATED BRUSSELS SPROUTS

When fresh Brussels sprouts are available, this is a lovely and different way to serve them.

Serves 8 to 12

1½ pounds small Brussels sprouts, trimmed
¾ cup white wine
6 tablespoons wine vinegar
1½ tablespoons firmly packed brown sugar
2 cloves garlic, crushed

Dash of Tabasco sauce
3 tablespoons chopped dill pickle
3 tablespoons chopped green onion
3 tablespoons chopped pimiento

Place sprouts, wine, vinegar, sugar, garlic, and Tabasco in a saucepan. Bring to boil, stirring to dissolve sugar. Lower heat and simmer, partially covered, until sprouts are just barely tender. They should remain crisp. Transfer to a bowl and add pickle, onion, and pimiento. Cover and refrigerate, stirring occasionally, for 24 or more hours. Serve with toothpicks.

NEW POTATO HORS D'OEUVRES

These are tasty, different, and just as delicious served cold or warm, good one-bite appetizers.

Serves 8 to 10

2 dozen new potatoes, tiniest size
½ cup sour cream

Chopped chives
Cooked, chopped bacon, or caviar

Cook potatoes with skins on in boiling salted water until done. When cool enough to handle, cut the potatoes in half and scoop out a small cavity with a spoon or melon baller. Fill the cavity with sour cream and top with chopped chives and bacon or with caviar.

NACHOS

A marvelous do-it-yourself hors d'oeuvre for an informal gathering. Jícama is a delicious, crunchy root vegetable of Mexican origin.

Serves 4

Tortilla chips
Jícama, peeled, sliced, and
　　cut into triangles
1 7-ounce can whole green
　　chilies, seeded and sliced
　　into bite-size pieces

8 ounces Monterey Jack
　　cheese, cut into wedges
Fresh coriander (cilantro)

On a large round platter, place tortilla chips, jícama slices, pieces of green chilies, and wedges of cheese. Place a large bunch of coriander in the center.

ORIENTAL FRESH MUSHROOMS

Serves 8

16 fresh mushrooms, 1 to
　　1½ inches in diameter
Fresh lemon juice
½ pound raw lean ground
　　pork
¼ cup minced water
　　chestnuts

¼ cup minced green onions
1 egg, lightly beaten
1 teaspoon soy sauce
¼ teaspoon garlic powder
¼ pound butter, melted
¼ cup untoasted sesame
　　seeds

Preheat oven to 350 degrees. Wash mushrooms and remove and reserve the stems. If prepared in advance, rub caps with lemon juice to keep them white. Chop the mushroom stems finely and combine with pork, water chestnuts, green onions, egg, soy sauce, and garlic powder. Stuff the caps with the mixture and coat bottoms of caps with butter. Top with sesame seeds. Put in a large ovenproof baking dish and bake for 30 to 40 minutes. Serve immediately.

SWEET AND SOUR BROCCOLI

A very tasty way to use the part of the broccoli that often gets thrown out.

Serves 4 to 6

1 pound broccoli stems
2 tablespoons white vinegar
2 tablespoons sugar

1 teaspoon salt
2 tablespoons sesame oil

Peel the broccoli stems and cut into diagonal slices $\frac{1}{8}$ to $\frac{1}{16}$ inch thick. Combine the vinegar, sugar, and salt in a large jar. Add the broccoli and shake to coat well. Cover and refrigerate overnight, shaking occasionally. Drain and place the broccoli in a serving dish. Pour sesame oil over the broccoli and serve with toothpicks.

CRUDITÉS WITH SEASONED SALT

These are the most versatile of hors d'oeuvres, and some of the most attractive when arranged on a wicker tray or basket. They make a great picnic course and can serve as a salad for a large crowd.

Cauliflower, broken into
    flowerets
White turnip, peeled, sliced
    into circles
Carrots
Celery
Cherry tomatoes
Broccoli, broken into
    flowerets

Radishes, whole or made
    into rosettes
Green onions, 6 inches long
Brussels sprouts
Snow peas
Green beans
Asparagus
Curly kale

SEASONED SALT
½ cup salt
1 teaspoon celery salt

¼ teaspoon white pepper
¼ teaspoon dried thyme

Use any combination of fresh raw vegetables. Wash them and soak in ice water to crisp. (You may wish to blanch Brussels sprouts, snow peas, green beans, and asparagus by plunging them into boiling water for a few minutes, then immediately removing them to a bowl of ice water. Drain, then chill.) Line a basket with curly kale. On the top of the kale arrange the raw vegetables attractively by contrasting colors. Serve with seasoned salt or your favorite dip. Adjust the amount and type of vegetables used to the number of people you wish to serve.

CHINESE POTSTICKERS

These make a good Sunday night family dinner or informal first course for a Chinese dinner.

Makes about 60 potstickers

MEAT FILLING

1½ pounds ground pork
6 tablespoons soy sauce
6 green onions, minced
2 tablespoons dried shrimp, soaked and minced (optional)
3 tablespoons shrimp water (optional)
1 tablespoon sesame oil

2 tablespoons peanut oil
½ teaspoon grated fresh ginger
1 egg
1 to 2 cloves garlic, minced
1- to 1½-pound Chinese cabbage
2 teaspoons salt

Mix together well the pork, soy sauce, green onions, dried shrimp, shrimp water, sesame oil, peanut oil, ginger, egg, and garlic. Set aside. Core the cabbage and chop it finely. Cover the cabbage with the salt and let sit for 1 hour. Press out the water and add the cabbage to the meat mixture. Set mixture aside until ready to assemble potstickers.

PASTRY

5 cups flour
2 cups water

Mix the flour and water. Keep it rather soft for ease in handling. Let it rest for 10 minutes. Cut or pull off walnut-size balls and roll each one out to the size of a 3-inch circle. The edges of the dough should be thinner than the middle. Fill each round with approximately 1 teaspoon of meat filling. Pinch together in the shape of a half moon.

COOKING AND SERVING

Peanut oil

½ cup water

Vinegar

Chinese hot oil (chili oil)

Soy sauce

Fresh coriander (cilantro), chopped

Heat about 2 tablespoons of peanut oil in a skillet and stand the pot-stickers up close together in the skillet with the seam side up. Sauté over medium heat for 2 to 3 minutes. Do not allow them to burn. Add ½ cup water, cover, and steam for 20 minutes. Serve immediately with vinegar, Chinese hot oil, soy sauce, and coriander.

WALNUT LIVER PÂTÉ

A delicious pâté that's easy to make, keeps well, and is a nice change from chicken livers.

Makes approximately 1 cup

2 ounces shelled walnuts

4 ounces cream cheese, softened

4 to 5 ounces liverwurst

2 tablespoons cognac

½ teaspoon crumbled dried tarragon

Finely chopped parsley

Preheat oven to 350 degrees. Boil walnuts, uncovered, for 3 minutes. Drain and, shaking pan often, roast at 350 degrees for 15 minutes. Cool and chop finely. Beat cream cheese and liverwurst and blend in cognac, tarragon, and walnuts, mixing well. Mound on a serving plate, cover with plastic wrap, and refrigerate. Encircle pâté with finely chopped parsley. Serve with toast points, crackers, or French bread.

COUNTRY SAUSAGE PÂTÉ

A perfect picnic pâté or elegant first course for a formal summer dinner. It freezes well and would be lovely served with a homemade brioche and wine.

Serves 12 to 16

2 pounds good bulk country style pork sausage
2 pounds fresh spinach, chopped and squeezed dry
2 teaspoons salt

½ teaspoon mace
½ teaspoon cinnamon
½ teaspoon thyme
1½ teaspoons minced fresh basil

Preheat oven to 375 degrees. Mix all ingredients well in a blender or food processor. Pack into a 9-inch loaf pan and bake for 45 minutes. Remove from oven and weigh down immediately with a brick wrapped in foil or with several heavy cans. Cool, wrap well, and refrigerate. When ready to serve, unmold on serving plate and scrape off any excess fat. Slice and serve with crackers. This keeps well refrigerated for 1 week, or frozen for 3 weeks. It may also be served as a first course on a lettuce leaf, garnished with cherry tomatoes and homemade bread.

BAKED PÂTÉ PATRICE

A beautiful pâté for a cocktail buffet. Easy to make and delicious.

Serves 20

1½ pounds chicken livers, diced
½ pound veal stew meat, diced
1 medium onion, chopped
4 tablespoons butter
1 clove garlic, minced
2 eggs

¼ cup all-purpose white flour
½ teaspoon powdered ginger
½ teaspoon allspice
Salt and pepper to taste
1 cup heavy cream

Preheat oven to 350 degrees. Sauté livers, veal, and onion in butter until meats are just rare and onion is softened. Cool slightly and coarsely purée livers, veal, onion and their juices with butter, garlic, eggs, flour, and seasonings in a blender or food processor. Blend in cream and adjust seasonings. Pour into a buttered and floured 1½-quart Pyrex meat-loaf pan, cover tightly with foil, and bake for 1½ hours. Remove foil, cool on a rack, cover, and chill. Turn out onto serving plate and serve with Melba rounds or plain crackers.

PÂTÉ IN ASPIC

Serves 16 to 18

ASPIC

3 envelopes unflavored gelatin	2 cans beef consommé
6 tablespoons cold water	2 tablespoons sherry

PÂTÉ

¾ pound liverwurst	6 ounces cream cheese
2 tablespoons Worcestershire sauce	2 tablespoons sherry
	1 small onion, grated

Dissolve the gelatin in the cold water. Heat the consommé and add the gelatin, then the sherry, stirring until all is blended. Cool. While the mixture is still liquid, pour it 1 inch deep into a round or oblong bowl or a lightly greased mold. Put this in the refrigerator to jell. Set aside the remaining consommé mixture. Meanwhile, place all pâté ingredients in a blender or food processor and blend until smooth. When the mixture in the mold is set, place the pâté in the center to about 1 inch from edge. Fill the sides and cover the top with the remaining consommé mixture. Chill until all is set. Unmold onto a chilled serving dish and serve with crackers.

MUSHROOM PÂTÉ

Serves 12 to 14

1 pound chicken livers
1 pound fresh mushrooms,
    washed and sliced
¾ pound butter, soft
½ cup chopped green
    onions

½ teaspoon thyme
½ teaspoon salt
⅛ teaspoon nutmeg
½ cup cognac
Parsley sprigs for garnish

In a large skillet, sauté chicken livers and mushrooms in ¼ pound of the butter until livers are no longer pink. With slotted spoon remove livers and mushrooms to a blender or food processor. Reduce liquid in skillet, then add to liver-mushroom mixture along with onions and remaining butter. Blend and add seasonings, then the cognac. Adjust seasonings, adding more cognac if desired. Blend until smooth and pour into a 3-cup mold that has been lightly oiled. Cover and chill until firm. Unmold, garnish with parsley, and serve with plain crackers or Melba rounds.

CRAB DELIGHT

Don't be offended by the idea of canned soup combined with crab meat. The blend of flavors is delectable, and this is an easy, attractive hors d'oeuvre to have ready in the refrigerator.

Serves 12

1 envelope unflavored
    gelatin
3 tablespoons cold water
1 can cream of mushroom
    soup
6 ounces cream cheese,
    softened

¾ cup mayonnaise
1 cup chopped celery
½ pound crab meat, fresh if
    possible
1 small onion, grated
Parsley

Soften the gelatin in the cold water. Warm the soup to simmering, add
the softened gelatin and cream cheese, and stir over medium heat until
dissolved, about 3 minutes. Remove from heat and add the mayonnaise,
celery, crab meat, and grated onion. Rinse a 4-cup mold with cold
water. Pour the mixture into the mold and refrigerate overnight. Unmold on a cold serving platter and garnish with parsley. Serve with
crackers.

SHRIMP MOUSSE

*This may also be served as a luncheon dish, for 4 to 6 people, or as a
first course in individual molds, for 8.*

Serves 12

1½ cups small shrimp
½ cup finely chopped celery
3 tablespoons fresh lemon
    juice
2 tablespoons white wine
    vinegar
1 teaspoon prepared
    horseradish
½ teaspoon freshly ground
    pepper

½ teaspoon salt
1 envelope unflavored
    gelatin
¼ cup cold water
½ cup heavy cream
1 cup mayonnaise
Cucumber slices
Avocado slices
8 large cooked shrimp

Combine shrimp, celery, lemon juice, vinegar, horseradish, pepper, and
salt. Marinate for 30 minutes. Soften gelatin in cold water and carefully
dissolve over low heat. In a large bowl whip the cream until stiff. Add
the mayonnaise, gelatin, the shrimp and their marinade, and adjust the
seasonings. Pour the mixture onto an 8-inch ring mold or fish mold that
has been oiled or has been rinsed in cold water. Stirring occasionally
until it starts to set, chill the mousse 4 to 5 hours or overnight. Unmold
onto a chilled serving platter and garnish with the cucumber and
avocado slices and the large shrimp. Serve with crackers.

INDIAN CHICKEN CURRY BALLS

A tasty way to use up that last bit of leftover chicken.

Serves 8

4 ounces cream cheese,
    softened
2 tablespoons mayonnaise
1 cup chopped cooked
    chicken
1 cup chopped roasted
    almonds

½ teaspoon salt
2 teaspoons curry powder
1 tablespoon chopped
    chutney
½ cup shredded coconut

Combine cream cheese and mayonnaise. Add chicken, almonds, salt, curry powder, and chutney. Refrigerate until firm. Form into small balls and roll in shredded coconut. Cover and chill. Refrigerate for at least 24 hours. Will keep up to 3 days.

SKEWERED CHICKEN

Serves 24

2 to 3 whole chicken breasts,
    boned
½ cup soy sauce
½ cup dry white wine or
    dry vermouth
½ teaspoon dry mustard
Freshly ground pepper to
    taste

2 tablespoons chopped
    parsley
1 medium onion, sliced or
    chopped
¼ cup peanut oil
Several slices fresh ginger
    root

Cut the chicken breasts along the grain into 3 or 4 strips each, then cut into bite-size cubes. Combine the soy sauce, wine, mustard, pepper, parsley, onion, oil, and ginger to make a marinade. Marinate the chicken for 1 hour at room temperature or up to 24 hours in the refrigerator. After marinating, place the chicken on skewers. Broil or barbecue for about 3 minutes per side. The chicken should be browned lightly and be juicy inside when cut. Depending on your heat source, the broiling time may vary. Do not overcook.

TIROPITES

These take time to make, but they are worth the effort. They freeze well. The phyllo used here is very thin, strudel-like pastry that can be bought in Greek and Middle Eastern specialty shops. It is also available in the frozen food sections of some large supermarkets.

Makes 4 dozen

FILLING

2 tablespoons butter
4 tablespoons flour
1 cup milk
4 eggs
½ pound Kefalotyi or
    Kasseri cheese, grated
½ pound feta cheese,
    crumbled
2 to 3 tablespoons finely
    chopped green onion,
    including tops
2 to 3 tablespoons finely
    chopped parsley
¼ teaspoon nutmeg

In a heavy saucepan melt the butter and slowly stir in the flour to make a thick roux. Stir in the milk, then add the eggs, one at a time. Remove from the stove and add the cheeses, the green onion, parsley, and nutmeg.

PASTRY

1 pound fresh phyllo pastry (about 60 sheets or layers)
Melted butter

Separate each piece of phyllo and brush with melted butter. Cut each piece lengthwise into 4 strips. Each strip will be approximately 2 inches wide. Butter only 4 pieces of phyllo at a time and keep the remaining phyllo covered at all times, as it will otherwise dry out very quickly.

To assemble: Put a tablespoon of filling at one end of each phyllo strip and roll up by folding over and over in a triangular shape.

To cook: Place the tiropites on a cookie sheet and bake at 425 degrees for approximately 8 minutes. Watch for burning corners. If they cook too fast, lower the oven temperature. These freeze very well. Brush the finished tiropites with melted butter before freezing. Bake directly from the freezer at 425 degrees for 15 minutes. If they defrost, keep them covered with a damp cloth before baking.

STEAK TARTARE

The classic of hearty hors d'oeuvres.

Serves 8

1 egg yolk, lightly beaten
1 pound ground round, best
    quality, ground 3 times
3 tablespoons melted butter
Dash cayenne pepper
1 tablespoon salt
Freshly ground pepper
1 tablespoon cognac

¼ cup grated onion
1 tablespoon chopped
    parsley
1 tablespoon Worcestershire
    sauce
¼ cup capers
2 hard-cooked eggs

Gently mix the egg yolk into the meat. Add the butter, cayenne, salt, pepper, cognac, grated onion, parsley, and Worcestershire sauce. Mix with hands just until the ingredients are blended. Mound the mixture in the center of a serving plate (not silver). Stud the tartare with capers. Chop the hard-cooked egg yolks and whites separately. Make a circle of the egg yolks around the beef, then a circle of chopped egg whites. Serve with rye rounds.

HERBED CHEESE

This cheese is delicious, and the amount of garlic and herbs can be adjusted to suit the cook's taste.

Makes about 1 cup

8 ounces cream cheese,
    softened
2 cloves garlic, pressed

1 tablespoon *fines herbes*
Chopped parsley

Using a blender or food processor, mix together the cream cheese, garlic, and *fines herbes*. Chill overnight to blend flavors. To serve, form the mixture in a ball and roll in freshly chopped parsley. Serve with crackers.

BLUE CHEESE SOUFFLÉ

This is a glorious dip that is so very attractive. The cheese taste is quite sharp, and it goes well with drinks. Who would ever expect a soufflé with cocktails? Well worth the time and effort.

Serves 12

1 envelope unflavored
    gelatin
2 tablespoons cool water
4 tablespoons sweet butter,
    softened
4 ounces cream cheese,
    softened

4 ounces blue cheese,
    softened
1 egg, separated
1 teaspoon Dijon mustard
½ cup heavy cream,
    whipped

Soften gelatin in cool water, then gently stir over low heat to dissolve. Using a food processor or electric mixer, beat together butter and cheeses, adding egg yolk, mustard, and gelatin. Beat egg white until stiff but not dry, and gently fold into mixture. Then fold in whipped cream. Prepare a 1-cup soufflé dish with a collar of oiled waxed paper or foil. Tie to the dish with string. Spoon mixture into the dish so that it comes up over the sides and up to the top of the collar. Chill for several hours or overnight. Remove the collar and serve with crackers or raw vegetables.

CHEESE SPREAD

Serves 8

¼ pound unsalted butter,
    softened
½ pound Gorgonzola
    cheese, softened
¼ pound Camembert
    cheese, softened

¼ cup brandy
1 to 2 cloves garlic, finely
    minced

Combine all ingredients thoroughly and pack into a 1½-cup crock. Cover and refrigerate. Before serving bring to room temperature. Serve with rye bread or plain crackers. This keeps well up to 2 weeks.

CROCKED BEER CHEESE

A great cheese spread to have on hand at all times. Hot and tangy!

Makes 3 cups

1½ pounds Cheddar cheese,
    grated
2 tablespoons
    Worcestershire sauce
2 cloves garlic, minced
1 to 2 teaspoons Tabasco
    sauce

¼ teaspoon salt
¼ teaspoon freshly ground
    black pepper
1 12-ounce can beer, allowed
    to go flat

Place all ingredients in the container of a blender or food processor and blend until a coarse purée. Place in a crock and chill for several hours or overnight before serving. Serve with crackers. This will keep for several weeks in the refrigerator.

LIPTAUER CHEESE

This lovely and delicious hors d'oeuvre idea was donated by Kurt Herbert Adler, Director of the San Francisco Opera. It gives each guest the choice of his own seasonings. Another way of serving it is to mix all the seasonings together with cheese and serve on bread.

Serves 8

8 ounces cream cheese
8 ounces creamed cottage
    cheese
Paprika
Onion, minced
Caraway seeds
Caviar

Capers
Chives, minced
Dry mustard
Parsley, chopped
Freshly ground coarse black
    pepper

Blend well the cream cheese and cottage cheese, place in the center of a platter, and surround with mounds of paprika, onion, caraway seeds, caviar, capers, chives, mustard, parsley, and pepper. Serve with thin slices of rye or black bread.

STUFFED GOUDA CHEESE

So attractive, and just right for that small group.

Serves 4

1 small Gouda cheese
2 to 3 tablespoons sherry

With a sharp knife, cut ¼ inch off the top of the cheese and remove the top circle of wax. Scoop out the inside cheese leaving ½ inch on the bottom and sides. Place the scooped-out cheese in the container of a blender or food processor and add the sherry. Blend until light and fluffy. Pile the cheese back into the Gouda shell, mounding it with a spatula. Serve with crackers.

COCKTAIL SAUCE À LA RITZ

Makes approximately 1 cup

3 tablespoons chili sauce
½ teaspoon Worcestershire
   sauce
2 medium-size ripe tomatoes,
   peeled, seeded, and
   chopped

1 teaspoon chopped chives
1 teaspoon chopped parsley
½ cup sour cream

Combine all ingredients and mix well. Allow to stand in the refrigerator for at least 1 hour before serving.

CURRY ALMOND SPREAD

Makes approximately 2 cups

16 ounces cream cheese,
   softened
1 cup chopped chutney

2 teaspoons curry powder
½ teaspoon dry mustard
¾ cup sliced almonds

Combine the cheese, ½ cup of the chutney, curry powder, and mustard. Blend well and place in a small bowl lined with plastic wrap. Refrigerate for at least 2 hours. Unmold on a serving platter and pour remaining chutney over the cheese. Top with almonds. Grated coconut and/or sliced green onions may be substituted for or combined with almonds. Serve with crackers.

SMOKED SALMON SPREAD

Serves 6 to 8

½ pound smoked salmon
1 medium onion, finely
   minced
1 tablespoon capers
2 teaspoons chopped fresh
   dill, or 1 teaspoon dried
   dill

½ cup sour cream
½ cup mayonnaise
Freshly ground black pepper
Chopped parsley

Chop the salmon and mix with the minced onion, capers, dill, sour cream, and mayonnaise. Blend well and spoon into a serving bowl. Top with pepper and chopped parsley. Cover and chill. Serve with thin slices of rye or pumpernickel.

SALMON BALL

Serves 10 to 12

1 16-ounce can salmon,
    drained and flaked
8 ounces cream cheese,
    softened
1 tablespoon fresh lemon
    juice

2 teaspoons chopped onion
2 teaspoons chopped fresh
    parsley
1 teaspoon prepared
    horseradish
½ cup chopped pecans

In a blender or food processor combine all ingredients and form into a ball. Chill and serve with crackers.

SHRIMP SALAD SPREAD

Makes about 1½ cups

1 pound shrimp, cooked,
    shelled, finely chopped
2 stalks celery, finely minced
3 green onions, finely diced
2 ounces canned pimientos,
    finely diced

2 tablespoons chopped
    parsley
2 tablespoons mayonnaise

Mix all ingredients with a spoon, blending well. Chill for several hours to allow the flavors to blend. Serve on cucumber slices, zucchini slices, rye bread, or as a filling for raw mushrooms caps.

CAVIAR MOLD

Serves 10 to 12

1 small onion, finely
   chopped
6 ounces cream cheese
⅓ cup sour cream
½ teaspoon salt
¼ teaspoon freshly ground
   pepper

6 tablespoons melted butter
4 ounces caviar
Lemon slices
Sprigs of parsley

Line a 1-cup-size bowl or mold with plastic wrap. In a blender or food processor mix the onion, cream cheese, sour cream, salt, and pepper until blended. Beat in melted butter, pour into the mold, and chill until firm. Unmold and top with caviar. Decorate the base of the mold with lemon slices and sprigs of parsley. Serve with crackers.

CRAB MEAT DIP

Serves 30

24 ounces cream cheese,
   softened
½ cup mayonnaise
¼ cup dry white wine
2 tablespoons Dijon mustard
1½ teaspoons powdered
   sugar

½ teaspoon onion juice
2 cloves garlic, pressed
1 pound flaked crab meat
½ cup toasted slivered
   almonds
¼ cup minced fresh parsley

Thoroughly combine cheese, mayonnaise, wine, mustard, sugar, onion juice, and garlic. Fold in crab and heat. Transfer to a warm chafing dish and sprinkle with almonds and parsley. Serve with crackers. May also be served cold.

TUNA PÂTÉ

Makes about 2 cups

1 7-ounce can tuna,
    undrained
3 tablespoons cognac
¼ teaspoon pepper
¼ teaspoon dillweed

8 ounces cream cheese
2 eggs, hard-cooked
3 tablespoons chopped
    pistachios

Place the tuna, cognac, pepper, and dill in a blender or food processor. Blend until smooth. Add the cream cheese and the eggs, and whip until smooth. Fold in the pistachios, place in a small serving bowl, and chill. Serve with crackers.

GUACAMOLE

Makes approximately 2 cups

3 large ripe avocados,
    mashed
3 ounces cream cheese,
    softened
1 medium onion, chopped
1 medium tomato, peeled
    and chopped

2 ounces green chilies,
    chopped
1 tablespoon olive oil
1 teaspoon red wine vinegar
½ teaspoon salt
Freshly ground pepper to
    taste

Mix all ingredients until creamy. If you are making this in advance, place it in a bowl with an avocado pit to prevent discoloring. Serve with corn chips or tortilla chips.

ORIENTAL DIP

Equally good as a salad dressing.

Makes about 2 cups

1 cup mayonnaise
1 cup sour cream
1 tablespoon soy sauce
2 tablespoons chopped water
   chestnuts

2 tablespoons chopped
   crystallized ginger, well
   rinsed and dried
1 tablespoon chopped fresh
   coriander (cilantro)

Combine all ingredients and blend well. Chill for several hours and serve with an assortment of raw vegetables or crackers.

CHAPTER IV

SOUPS

Union Square

The heart of the downtown shopping district is a two-and-a-half-acre green park called Union Square. Amid splendid hotels, theaters and some of the city's most elegant shops, it provides a setting for sunny lunch-hour picnics, for lively entertainment by actors and musicians beginning their reach for stardom, for display of crafts by local artisans, and it is a favorite resting spot for the weary shopper and the ever-present pigeon.

This urban oasis was given to the city in 1850 by Mayor John W. Geary. As the city was expanding beyond its original confines, building at a frantic pace, he saw the need to preserve open space. His generosity and foresight provided a common area in which the townspeople could meet. It was the pro-union meetings held there during the Civil War that gave the square its name.

During the dark days that followed the earthquake and fire of 1906, the square provided a place of refuge and a soup kitchen was established within its perimeter. It was soup that nourished a determined and united citizenry, regrouping for reconstruction. Soup kitchens also appeared in Golden Gate Park, and street kitchens fed families until the dangers in their homes had passed.

Today restaurants featuring soups are flourishing—one just across the street from Union Square. The once humble soup has achieved a newly regained prominence and its virtues of versatility, economy, nutrition, and taste are once again extolled.

You may prefer soups to start or soup for an entire meal; hot or cold, thick or clear, elegant or left over. But there's one thing that's certain—there's a soup for every occasion—even an earthquake.

CURRIED FRESH PEA SOUP

Serves 6

1 cup shelled fresh peas
1 medium onion, sliced
1 small carrot, sliced
1 clove garlic
1 stalk celery with leaves,
    sliced

1 medium potato, peeled and
    sliced
1 teaspoon salt
1 teaspoon curry powder
2 cups chicken stock
1 cup milk

Place all ingredients except 1 cup of the chicken stock and the milk in a heavy saucepan and bring to a boil. Reduce heat and simmer, covered, for 15 minutes, stirring occasionally. Remove from heat, pour into a blender or food processor, and purée. Add remaining chicken stock and milk. Mix well. Either reheat or served chilled with a dollop of whipped cream if desired.

CHILLED YELLOW SQUASH SOUP

Serves 8

1½ pounds yellow
    crookneck squash
2 tablespoons butter
1 medium onion, sliced
¼ lemon, sliced and seeds
    removed

¼ cup flour
6 cups chicken stock
1 cup heavy cream
1 teaspoon salt
¼ teaspoon white pepper

Wash and trim squash. Slice, reserving 8 paper-thin slices for garnish. In a large saucepan, melt butter and gently sauté onion and lemon. Sprinkle with flour and cook slowly until flour is absorbed. Add chicken stock gradually, then sliced squash, salt, and pepper. Simmer for 1 hour. Purée in blender or food processor, then stir in cream with a wire whisk. Add seasonings and chill until serving time. Garnish with reserved squash slices.

AVGOLEMONO SOUP

Serves 8

12 cups chicken stock
6 tablespoons fresh lemon
    juice
Grated rind of 1 lemon
12 egg yolks, lightly beaten

Salt to taste
White pepper to taste
1 cup cooked rice
Lemon slices

Heat the chicken stock until very hot but not boiling. Add the lemon juice and rind. Add a little of the hot stock to the egg yolks, then gradually stir the yolks into the stock. Reduce the heat immediately, add salt, pepper, and rice, and serve. Garnish with lemon slices.

CRAB SOUP

Serves 4

1 tablespoon butter
1 tablespoon all-purpose
    white flour
2 hard-cooked eggs, whites
    and yolks separated
1 10¾-ounce can condensed
    cream of celery soup
1 cup light cream

1 cup milk
1 tablespoon chopped fresh
    parsley
1 clove garlic, minced
½ pound flaked crab meat
1 tablespoon grated lemon
    rind
2 tablespoons dry sherry

In top of a double boiler, melt butter and blend in flour. Press the egg yolks through a coarse sieve and add to the butter and flour. Blend in the soup, cream, milk, parsley, and garlic. Cook, stirring constantly, until mixture is smooth and very hot. Add crab and heat gently. Just before serving press the egg whites through a coarse sieve and add them along with the lemon rind and sherry. Reheat but do not boil.

ARTICHOKE SOUP

Serves 8

8 medium artichokes,
   washed and trimmed
1 quart water
2 cups chicken stock

1 bunch scallions, chopped
1 teaspoon lemon juice
2 cups light cream
Salt and pepper to taste

In a large kettle, place the artichokes, water, chicken stock, and scallions. Bring to a boil and cook, covered, for 45 minutes. Drain and cool artichokes, reserving cooking liquid. Scrape off the tender parts from bottoms of leaves and remove hearts. Purée scrapings in a blender or food processor, adding cooking stock and lemon juice. When cool, add cream and seasonings.

ARTICHOKE CRAB MEAT BISQUE

Serves 4

2 large artichokes, trimmed
   and quartered
Water just to cover
2 teaspoons fresh lemon juice
1 teaspoon olive oil
1½ cups rich chicken stock
½ cup heavy cream
1 egg yolk
2 tablespoons all-purpose
   white flour

¼ teaspoon salt
½ cup finely chopped carrot
2 tablespoons sliced green
   onions
2 tablespoons water or as
   needed
¾ pound flaked crab meat
2 teaspoons lemon juice
Salt and white pepper to
   taste

Cook artichokes in the water, lemon juice, and oil for 15 to 20 minutes or until tender. Discard choke and scrape pulp from the leaves. Place pulp in a blender with artichoke hearts, chicken stock, cream, egg yolk, flour, and salt. Purée and set aside. Steam carrots and onions in 2 tablespoons water, covered, until tender. Add artichoke purée, cook, and stir until mixture is thickened and bubbly, do not boil. Stir in crab meat and lemon juice. Reheat and adjust seasoning.

COLD CREAM OF ARTICHOKE SOUP

Serves 4

1 10-ounce can artichoke
   hearts, water-packed
1¼ cups chicken stock
1 teaspoon salt

¼ teaspoon powdered
   oregano
2 tablespoons lemon juice
1 cup half-and-half

Drain artichoke hearts and purée in a blender with chicken stock, seasonings, and lemon juice. Transfer to a saucepan and heat slowly. Cool. Add half-and-half and mix well. Chill thoroughly and serve in chilled bowls with one of the following garnishes: hard-cooked egg slices, minced parsley or chives, a dollop of sour cream, sliced lemon or lime, watercress, or a dollop of whipped cream.

BULA BULA SOUP

Serves 4

1 10-ounce package frozen
   spinach, cooked and
   well drained
8 ounces clam juice
8 ounces minced clams with
   juice
8 ounces chicken stock

1½ cups half-and-half
2 tablespoons fresh lemon
   juice
1 tablespoon Worcestershire
   sauce
Pepper to taste
Chilled sour cream

In a blender or food processor purée spinach, clam juice, clams and juice, and chicken stock. Transfer to saucepan and add half-and-half, lemon juice, Worcestershire sauce, and pepper. Heat but do not boil. Adjust seasonings and ladle into individual heatproof bowls. Top each bowl with 2 teaspoons sour cream and broil for 2 minutes.

CARROT SOUP

Serves 4 to 6

8 ounces butter
8 cups thinly sliced carrots
1 cup chopped onion
6 cups chicken stock
1 cup milk
½ cup dry vermouth

Salt
Freshly ground black pepper
A pinch of mace
Fresh parsley, finely
    chopped for garnish

Melt butter in a heavy saucepan and sauté carrots over low heat for 5 minutes. Add onion and saute for 3 minutes more. Stir in stock and milk and simmer for 35 to 40 minutes. Add vermouth and seasonings and purée entire mixture in a blender or food processor. Return to the saucepan and reheat slowly before serving. Garnish each serving with chopped parsley.

CELERY ROOT SOUP

People who like celery root will love this soup—and there is no cream in the recipe, so even though it comes out thick and smooth, it is lower in calories than a cream soup.

Serves 6

1 quart chicken stock
2 medium-size celery roots
Salt
Freshly ground black pepper

Cayenne pepper
1 tablespoon freshly
    chopped parsley

Bring the chicken stock to a boil over medium heat. Pare the celery roots, coarsely dice, and place in the boiling stock. Cook until soft, about 15 minutes. Place the soup in a blender or food processor and purée. Season with salt and pepper and a pinch of cayenne. Serve hot, garnished with a sprinkling of parsley.

COLD PEA SOUP WITH MINT

Serves 4

1 10-ounce package frozen
    tiny peas
1 medium onion, thinly
    sliced
1 cup water
1 tablespoon minced fresh
    mint

3 cups chicken stock
2 tablespoons flour
½ cup heavy cream
Salt and freshly ground
    pepper to taste
Sour cream
Mint sprigs

Cook peas and onion in 1 cup water until very tender. Add minced mint and purée in a blender or food processor until smooth. Set aside. In a saucepan, blend ½ cup of the stock with the flour until smooth. Add the rest of the stock and cook, stirring, until thickened. Add puréed pea mixture and bring to a boil. Then add cream, salt, and pepper. Chill thoroughly. To serve: Ladle soup into chilled serving bowls, garnishing with a dollop of sour cream and a sprig of mint on each serving.

COLD TOMATO SOUP

Serves 10 to 12

12 large fresh tomatoes,
    peeled and seeded
3 medium onions, chopped
1 celery heart, chopped
1 tablespoon salt
Freshly ground pepper to
    taste

½ teaspoon dried basil
8 tablespoons sweet butter
1 pint sour cream
Fresh basil or fresh dill for
    garnish

Sauté tomatoes, onions, celery, salt, pepper, and basil in butter until soft (about 30 minutes). Put into a blender or food processor and blend. Chill in the refrigerator. Add sour cream and blend. Serve with a dollop of sour cream and sprinkle with fresh basil or fresh dill.

COLD PEACH SOUP

Very good soup—great for a summer picnic first course, maybe with a sprig of mint to decorate each cup. It's a lovely way to use beautiful California peaches without the added calories of cream. The juice extractor of a food processor is perfect for this recipe.

Serves 4

4 ripe peaches
2 cups dry white wine
1 cup water
3 tablespoons sugar

¼ teaspoon cinnamon
¼ teaspoon curry
3 whole cloves
Orange slices

Plunge peaches in boiling water for 1 minute. Remove skins and pits. Purée in a blender or food processor and transfer purée to an enameled saucepan. Add wine, water, sugar, cinnamon, curry, and cloves. Bring to a boil and simmer, stirring, for 10 minutes. Remove cloves and let soup cool. Chill for at least 4 hours and serve in chilled bowls, garnished with thin slices of orange.

CREAMED CORN AND CRAB SOUP

Serves 4

3 cups chicken stock
1 17-ounce can creamed
    corn
1 teaspoon cornstarch mixed
    with 1 tablespoon water

½ pound flaked crab meat
1 green onion, chopped

Bring chicken stock to a boil. Add corn and bring to a second boil. Stir in cornstarch. Cook and stir until thickened and clear (may be made ahead to this point). Add crab meat and serve immediately. Garnish with chopped green onion.

EGGPLANT SOUP

Serves 8

½ cup Great Northern
  white beans or navy
  beans
4 cups water
2 cups mixed chopped
  onions and white of
  leeks
3 tablespoons corn oil
2 bay leaves
1½ teaspoons salt
½ teaspoon grated black
  pepper or peppercorns,
  lightly crushed
½ teaspoon crumbled dried
  sage
½ teaspoon crumbled dried
  thyme
½ pound Polish sausage,
  sliced

1 1-pound eggplant, peeled,
  diced, and tossed with 4
  teaspoons salt
Olive oil for sautéeing
1 pound ripe tomatoes,
  peeled, seeded, and
  chopped
3 cloves garlic, minced
4 cups chicken stock, or as
  needed
Chopped fresh parsley
  and/or chives
Crumbled basil, oregano, or
  crushed fennel seed
½ cup freshly grated
  Parmesan cheese

Preheat oven to 350 degrees. Combine beans and water and bring to
rapid boil for 2 minutes, cover, remove from heat, and let stand for 1
hour. Sauté onions and leeks slowly in corn oil, raise heat, and brown
lightly. Add to the beans along with seasonings and herbs. Bring to simmer, cover with a tilted lid, and simmer for 1½ hours or until beans are
just tender. Bake sausage slices at 350 degrees for 20 minutes. Drain and
set aside. Place salted eggplant in a colander and drain for 20 minutes,
reserving liquid. Sauté eggplant in olive oil until lightly browned. Add
tomatoes, garlic, stock, and reserved eggplant liquid. Simmer, covered,
for 15 minutes, then combine with beans. Add sausage and cook slowly,
uncovered, for 15 minutes. Add more herbs if necessary and adjust with
salt and pepper. Serve with Parmesan cheese on the side.

FRENCH TOMATO SOUP

Serves 8 to 10

5 large carrots, grated
5 small onions, sliced
5 tablespoons butter
¼ cup raw long grain white
    rice
1 quart canned tomatoes,
    puréed

½ teaspoon soda
1 quart hot milk
½ cup warm light cream
Salt and freshly ground
    pepper to taste

In a large kettle, butter-steam carrots and onions, covered, for 15 minutes (without browning) or until tender. Steam rice and add to vegetables with tomatoes and soda. Add milk and cream. Reheat without boiling and season with salt and pepper.

GUMBO

This classic gumbo is rich in texture and flavor. It can be made with chicken, crab, or shrimp or any combination of these.

FOR CHICKEN GUMBO: 2 quarts chicken stock
FOR CRAB, SHRIMP OR COMINATION GUMBO: 2 quarts fish stock

Serves 8 to 10

¼ teaspoon thyme
1 bay leaf
4 cloves
1 teaspoon tomato paste
⅛ teaspoon cayenne
3 pounds fresh okra or 6
    packages frozen, sliced
    crosswise
3 tablespoons oil
3 cups chopped onion
1½ cups chopped celery
½ cup chopped green
    pepper

3 cloves garlic, minced
1 cup diced ham
1 1-pound can stewed
    tomatoes
2 tablespoons brown sugar
½ teaspoon dried basil
Salt and freshly ground
    pepper to taste
Tabasco sauce to taste
1 teaspoon Worcestershire
    sauce
1 pound cooked shrimp or
    crab or diced chicken

In a large kettle or Dutch oven, combine the stock, thyme, bay leaf, cloves, tomato paste, and cayenne. Bring to boil, then simmer. Meanwhile, in a skillet, heat oil and sauté sliced okra slowly for 30 minutes. Add chopped onion, celery, green pepper, and garlic, and sauté for another 20 minutes. Stir in the diced ham and continue cooking for 5 minutes. Then add stewed tomatoes, sugar, and basil. Simmer, partially covered, very slowly for 1 hour. Season with salt, pepper, Tabasco, and Worcestershire. Add shrimp, crab, or chicken and reheat. Serve in shallow bowls accompanied by hot rice.

OXTAIL SOUP

Serves 6

3 pounds oxtails, cut up
5 tablespoons all-purpose white flour
3 tablespoons rendered beef fat
2 carrots, diced
1 turnip, diced
1 large onion, diced
2 celery stalks, diced
6 tablespoons butter
2½ quarts beef stock

½ teaspoon salt
2 sprigs fresh oregano (or ½ teaspoon dried)
6 fresh basil leaves (or ½ teaspoon dried)
6 parsley sprigs
12 black peppercorns
2 tablespoons catsup
2 tablespoons fresh lemon juice
3 tablespoons dry sherry

Wash oxtail pieces and cut off excess fat. Place in a large saucepan, cover with water, bring to a rapid boil, then drain. Rinse out the saucepan. Rinse the oxtails, dry them, and dust with 3 tablespoons of the flour. In the saucepan brown on all sides in hot beef fat. Sauté vegetables in 3 tablespoons of the butter until golden. Add to the saucepan with beef stock, salt, herbs, and peppercorns. Bring to a boil, skim off any scum that rises to surface, and cover. Lower heat and simmer for 3 hours or until oxtails are very tender. Cool in liquid and remove meat from bones. Set meat aside. Drain liquid and chill until fat hardens, discard fat. Melt remaining butter until browned, sprinkle with 2 tablespoons flour, and cook and stir for 2 minutes. Pour in strained liquid and add reserved meat, catsup, lemon juice, and sherry. Reheat, adjust seasonings, and add sherry just before serving.

HEARTY CLAM CHOWDER

Serves 6

4 slices bacon, coarsely
    chopped
3 green onions, chopped
5 medium potatoes, peeled
    and cut into ½-inch
    cubes
2 tablespoons chopped green
    pepper
1 stalk celery, sliced

1 clove garlic, minced
2 cups water
1 teaspoon salt
½ teaspoon white pepper
1 teaspoon Worcestershire
    sauce
4 drops Tabasco sauce
2 cups raw clams with juice
2 cups half-and-half

Sauté bacon until crisp in a large kettle. Add onions, potatoes, green pepper, celery, and garlic. Add 2 cups water and season with salt, white pepper, Worcestershire, and Tabasco. Cover kettle and simmer for 15 minutes, or until potatoes are tender. In a separate pan, heat the clams in their juice for 3 minutes, or until tender. Add clams and juice to kettle, pour in half-and-half, and heat, stirring, until piping hot. Do not boil.

FRESH VEGETABLE SOUP

Serves 6

2 tablespoons butter
1 onion, diced
1 small bunch leeks (white
    part only), washed
    carefully and sliced
1 potato, peeled and diced

1 carrot, sliced
2 stalks celery, sliced
2 cups chicken stock
Salt to taste
Heavy cream
Chopped parsley for garnish

Melt butter in a deep pot or Dutch oven and sauté onion and leeks until golden. Add other vegetables and chicken stock. Season with salt and simmer, partially covered, until vegetables are tender, about 25 minutes. Remove soup to a blender or food processor and purée until smooth. Return soup to pot at medium heat, thicken with cream if desired, and garnish with parsley.

LENTIL SOUP

Serves 6 to 8

¼ pound bacon, diced
2 medium onions, sliced
2 medium carrots, diced
1 pound lentils, washed
3 quarts water
1 cup diced celery and some
   leaves
2 to 3 teaspoons salt

½ teaspoon pepper
½ teaspoon crumbled dried
   thyme
2 bay leaves
1 large potato
1 hambone or 2 ham hocks
2 tablespoons fresh lemon
   juice

Sauté bacon until limp. Add onions and carrots and sauté until onions are transparent and lightly browned. Add lentils, water, celery, seasonings, and spices. Grate potato into the mixture with medium grater and add hambone or ham hocks. Bring to a gentle boil, cover, lower heat, and simmer for 2½ to 3 hours, adding more liquid if needed. Stir occasionally to prevent sticking. Discard bay leaves. Remove hambone or hocks and cut meat into bite-size pieces. Return to soup. Reheat and add lemon juice. Adjust seasonings.

MISSION GAZPACHO

Serves 12

3 pounds ripe tomatoes
2 medium cucumbers
1 medium onion
¼ green pepper (more if
   you like)
1 clove garlic
2 cups tomato juice
3 tablespoons tarragon
   vinegar
Salt and freshly ground
   pepper to taste

Tabasco sauce to taste
½ teaspoon dried basil
½ teaspoon dried chervil
½ teaspoon dried tarragon
3 tablespoons chopped
   parsley
1 tablespoon chopped chives
3 tablespoons lemon juice
1 teaspoon paprika
½ cup olive oil

Peel and dice tomatoes without losing any juice. Peel and dice the cucumbers, onion, and green pepper. Rub a large bowl with garlic clove and add all ingredients. Stir and chill.

OYSTER BISQUE

Serves 6

1 green onion, finely
    shredded
3 tablespoons butter
2 tablespoons flour
¼ teaspoon onion salt
¼ teaspoon celery salt
¼ teaspoon nutmeg
Salt and cayenne pepper to
    taste

2 cups milk
2 cups half-and-half
1 9-ounce bottle Olympia
    oysters
2 tablespoons chopped
    parsley

Cook the onion gently for a few minutes in butter, add flour, seasonings, then the milk and the half-and-half. In a separate saucepan bring the oysters to a boil in their liquid and cook for a minute or two until their edges curl. Put them through a blender and add to the first mixture. Add parsley, correct seasonings, and set aside until serving time. Then heat gently (do not boil). Chives may be used as a garnish.

ONION SOUP GRATINÉ

Serves 6 to 8

8 large yellow onions, thinly
    sliced
4 tablespoons butter
1 tablespoon olive oil
1 teaspoon salt
1 teaspoon sugar
¼ cup sifted all-purpose
    white flour
4 cups chicken stock
4 cups beef stock

¼ cup dry Sauterne (or dry
    white wine)
1½ tablespoons brandy
Salt and freshly ground
    pepper to taste
6 to 8 well-toasted bread
    slices
Sliced Gruyère or
    Emmenthaler cheese

In a covered saucepan, slowly cook onions in butter and oil for 30 minutes, stirring occasionally. Remove lid. Add salt and sugar and continue cooking, stirring often, for 1 to 1½ hours until onions are golden. Stir in flour and cook, stirring, for 5 minutes. In a separate saucepan, bring chicken stock and beef stock to a boil. Add onion mixture and Sauterne. Bring back to a gentle boil, cover, and simmer for 45 minutes. Just before serving, add brandy, salt, and pepper. Fill individual soup crocks nearly to the top and place a bread slice on top. Arrange 3 to 4 slices of cheese on bread, covering top of bowl completely. Broil until cheese is melted, brown, and crusty.

PARSLEY SOUP

Serves 4 to 6

1 cup chopped onions
2 tablespoons butter
1 pound new white potatoes, scrubbed but not peeled
4 cups rich chicken stock
3 cups tightly packed chopped fresh parsley and some tender stems
1 tablespoon soy sauce

½ tablespoon fresh lemon juice
½ cup half-and-half
Salt and white pepper to taste
Garnish with minced fresh parsley and with paprika

In a medium-size saucepan sauté onions in butter until transparent and lightly golden. Slice potatoes and add to onions with stock. Cover, bring to boil, and cook over medium heat for 5 minutes. Add parsley, bring to a second boil, and cook until potatoes and parsley are soft. Purée in a blender and add soy sauce, lemon juice, half-and-half, and seasonings. Reheat without boiling and adjust seasonings with soy, lemon juice, salt, and white pepper. Serve in a crystal bowl with garnish.

POTAGE BELGIQUE

Serves 10 to 12

4 tablespoons butter
5 large leeks, washed
    carefully and thinly
    sliced
½ pound mushrooms, thinly
    sliced
4 cups chicken stock

Salt and freshly ground
    pepper to taste
4 medium potatoes, peeled
    and diced
1 cup light cream
Chopped fresh chives for
    garnish

In a large saucepan, melt butter and sauté sliced leeks and mushrooms for about 5 minutes, stirring constantly. Add chicken stock, salt, and pepper, and bring to a boil. Add potatoes and simmer, partially covered, for 30 minutes. Blend until smooth in a blender or food processor, adding cream. Garnish with chives and serve hot or cold. To reheat, stir over low heat or in top of double boiler, not allowing soup to boil.

PUMPKIN SOUP

Serves 6 to 8

4 tablespoons butter
4 green onions and tops,
    chopped
1 small onion, minced
2 tablespoons all-purpose
    white flour
4 cups chicken stock

3 cups pumpkin purée
½ teaspoon salt
½ teaspoon mace
¼ teaspoon white pepper
¾ cup half-and-half
Croutons

Melt 3 tablespoons of the butter until foamy, add onions and sauté until limp. Sprinkle with flour, cook and stir for 3 minutes, then gradually add chicken stock. Cook and stir until smooth and thickened. Add pumpkin purée, seasonings, and half-and-half. Reheat without boiling and adjust seasonings to taste. Stir in remaining 1 tablespoon butter until just melted. Serve immediately, topped with croutons.

SENEGALESE SOUP

Serves 6

2 medium onions, minced
2 large celery stalks, finely
  chopped
2 apples, cored, peeled, and
  chopped
2 tablespoons butter
2 tablespoons curry powder
¼ cup all-purpose white
  flour

4 cups chicken stock
Cayenne and salt to taste
¾ cup finely chopped
  cooked white meat
  chicken
2 cups chilled half-and-half
Garnish with slices of
  avocado and lime

Sauté onions, celery, and apples in butter until tender, do not brown. Add curry powder, cook and stir for 2 minutes. Blend in flour, cook and stir for 2 minutes. Gradually add chicken stock, cook and stir until smooth and thickened. Season with cayenne and salt. Add chicken and cool. Refrigerate until thoroughly chilled. Stir in half-and-half and adjust seasonings. Serve in chilled bowls with avocado and lime garnish.

SHELLFISH CHOWDER

Serves 4

¼ pound raw shrimp,
  shelled and deveined
1 cup light cream
½ cup peeled and diced
  potatoes
½ teaspoon salt
8 mussels or cherrystone
  clams, well scrubbed
¼ cup minced slab bacon or
  salt pork
¼ cup minced onion

¼ cup minced celery
⅛ teaspoon thyme
1 tablespoon butter
2 cups milk
½ pound scallops (halved or
  quartered if large)
Salt, white pepper, and
  cayenne to taste
Minced fresh parsley for
  garnish

Soak shrimp in cream for 30 minutes. Cook potatoes, covered, in a little water with the salt for 5 minutes. Drain and set aside. Steam mussels or clams until shells open. Drain and set aside. In a large saucepan, cook bacon or salt pork, onion, celery, and thyme in butter, covered, over low heat until just softened. Add milk and reserved potatoes and simmer for 10 minutes. Add shrimp and soaking cream, mussels or clams, and scallops. Bring to a gentle boil, lower heat, and simmer for 5 minutes or until shrimp and scallops are just cooked. Season to taste and transfer to a serving bowl or individual soup bowls and sprinkle with minced parsley.

SHRIMP GAZPACHO

Serves 8

2 28-ounce cans whole
    tomatoes, chopped
1 8-ounce can tomato sauce
2 cloves garlic, minced
1 medium red onion, finely
    chopped
1 green pepper, finely
    chopped
1 4-ounce can chopped
    green chilies
2 tablespoons
    Worcestershire sauce
1 teaspoon seasoned salt

2 teaspoons oregano
1 tablespoon unflavored
    gelatin
1 beef bouillon cube
½ cup boiling water
¾ pound small shrimp,
    cooked, shelled,
    deveined
½ cup sliced green olives
    with pimiento
1 cucumber, peeled, seeded,
    and diced
Croutons

Mix together the tomatoes, tomato sauce, garlic, onion, green chilies, Worcestershire, seasoned salt, and oregano. Simmer for 10 minutes and chill overnight. About 1 hour before serving, dissolve the gelatin and bouillon cube in the boiling water. Stir into the chilled mixture. Add the shrimp, green olives, and cucumber. Refrigerate until serving time. Garnish with croutons.

SOUPE AUX CHOUX

Serves 8

¼ pound slab bacon, diced
2 tablespoons butter
1 large head of cabbage,
  coarsely chopped
2 medium onions, chopped
3 cloves garlic, pressed or
  finely minced
  (optional)
2 tablespoons all-purpose
  white flour
6 to 8 cups rich chicken
  stock

½ teaspoon cinnamon
¼ teaspoon nutmeg
Freshly ground pepper to
  taste
1 cup heavy cream
2 egg yolks
8 thin slices French bread,
  browned in butter and
  olive oil

Brown bacon in butter. Add cabbage, onions, and garlic and cook for 2 to 3 minutes. Sprinkle with flour and stir well. Gradually add stock and seasonings. Stirring, bring to a boil, lower heat, cover, and simmer for 20 to 30 minutes. Just before serving, beat cream and egg yolks together, whisk in 1 cup hot soup and return to the rest of the soup. Reheat without boiling. Adjust seasonings and ladle over fried bread in large soup bowls.

SUMMER BERRY SOUP

Serves 4

1 cup strawberries
1 cup raspberries
⅓ cup sugar
½ cup sour cream

½ cup heavy cream
1½ cups water
½ cup light red wine

Place berries and sugar in a blender and purée. Pour into a pitcher and stir in creams until well blended. Add water and wine and chill.

WATERCRESS SOUP

Serves 4 to 6

2 bunches watercress
½ cup chopped onion
2 tablespoons chopped
    celery and tender leaves
2 tablespoons butter
1 teaspoon sugar
3 tablespoons all-purpose
    white flour

⅛ teaspoon salt
⅛ teaspoon white pepper
3 cups chicken stock
1 cup heavy cream
2 tablespoons dry sherry
Croutons

Wash watercress, discard tough stems and set remainder aside. In a large saucepan, sauté onion and celery in butter until onion is transparent. Stir in sugar, flour, salt, and pepper. Cook and stir for 2 minutes and gradually blend in chicken stock. Cook and stir until thickened. Add watercress and simmer for 5 minutes, stirring occasionally. Cool slightly and purée in a blender or food processor a little at a time, until mixture is a solid green color with only a few specks of dark green. Return to saucepan and add cream, blending well. Heat without boiling. Adjust seasonings and add sherry to taste. Serve immediately with croutons.

ZUCCHINI SOUP

A light, fresh, colorful soup that is just as good cold.

Serves 8

6 small zucchini, trimmed
    and cubed or shredded
Salt
2 medium onions, finely
    minced
1 clove garlic, minced
1 tablespoon oil
2 tablespoons sweet butter

5 cups chicken stock
2 tablespoons fresh
    herbs—combination of
    oregano, basil, parsley,
    chives
2 tablespoons lemon juice
Salt and freshly ground
    pepper to taste

Place cubed or shredded zucchini in a colander, sprinkle with salt, and allow to drain for about 30 minutes. In a large soup pot or dutch oven sauté onions and garlic in oil and melted butter until the onions are golden. Dry zucchini on paper towels and add to onions and cook over low heat for about 5 minutes. Add chicken stock and simmer for 15 minutes. Purée soup in a blender or food processor. Return to pot and season with herbs, lemon juice, and salt and pepper. Reheat and serve.

ZUCCHINI AND CHEESE SOUP

Serves 6

6 small zucchini
1 teaspoon salt
4 tablespoons unsalted butter
1 medium onion, finely
    chopped
½ clove garlic, finely
    minced
¼ teaspoon rosemary,
    crushed
⅛ teaspoon ground
    cardamom
Salt and freshly ground
    pepper to taste

1 quart chicken stock
1 tablespoon lemon juice
½ cup dry white wine
¾ cup grated Emmenthaler
    cheese
¼ cup dry Madeira wine
½ cup freshly grated
    Parmesan cheese
½ cup chopped raw
    zucchini for garnish

Scrub zucchini, trim off ends, but do not peel. Slice thinly, sprinkle with salt, and let stand for a few minutes to allow water to drain off. Pat dry with paper towels. Melt butter over low heat in a 3-quart saucepan. And onion and garlic and cook, stirring, until limp but not brown, about 5 minutes. Add zucchini slices and cook, stirring for another 5 minutes. Add seasonings, chicken stock, lemon juice, and white wine. Simmer over low heat, stirring occasionally, for about 20 minutes. Remove from heat and purée in a blender or food processor. Return soup to pot, add grated Emmenthaler cheese and Madeira. Simmer for another 5 minutes or until bubbling hot and cheese is melted. Garnish with chopped raw zucchini.

WINTER SAUSAGE SOUP

Serves 8

2 to 3 pounds Polish or
    Italian sausage,
    parboiled and sliced
1 medium onion, chopped
1 cup sliced carrots
1 28-ounce can whole
    tomatoes
1 cup chopped celery
3 potatoes, peeled and cubed
½ cup green egg noodles,
    cooked

½ cup white egg noodles,
    cooked
7 to 8 cups rich beef stock
1 clove garlic (optional)
1 teaspoon brown sugar
Salt and freshly ground
    pepper to taste
3 cups shredded cabbage
Garnish with 1 tablespoon
    freshly grated Parmesan
    cheese per serving

In a large soup pot brown sausage. Drain off all fat. Add remaining soup
ingredients except cabbage, being careful with salt and pepper because
sausage varies in seasonings. Bring to a boil, lower heat, cover, and simmer for 1 hour. Add cabbage and cook for 15 minutes. Adjust seasonings and serve with Parmesan cheese.

YOGURT SOUP

*Sounds awful, but you'll have to taste it to believe that it is fabulous.
Pretty to look at. Great for hot weather luncheon or first course.*

Serves 4 to 6

¼ cup white raisins,
    plumped in 1 cup cold
    water
3 cups plain yogurt
¼ cup skim milk
1 hard-cooked egg, chopped
¼ cup finely minced seeded
    cucumber

2 tablespoons finely chopped
    green onion
6 ice cubes
Garnish with 1 tablespoon
    chopped parsley and 1
    teaspoon dillweed

Combine first 7 ingredients well and refrigerate. Serve in chilled bowls
with garnish of parsley and dillweed.

CHAPTER V

SALADS & DRESSINGS

South of Market

Two of the most fashionable, sociably elite residential areas during the 1850s were located south of Market Street—an area later referred to as "south of the slot" because of the cable car tracks that ran the length of Market Street.

Rincon Hill (now the area under one of the approaches to the Bay Bridge) and South Park, an elliptical park surrounded by stately homes (now a warehouse district) were the most desirable neighborhoods for the town's leading citizenry. The climate was far superior to the fog-shrouded hills farther north, and, although estates of astounding dimension were established down the peninsula, Rincon Hill and South Park would remain the finest areas within the city until Nob Hill was developed in the 1870s.

Nearby on the corner of Market and Montgomery, the intersection of the two most important commercial streets of the day, was the site of the Palace Hotel—the epitome of grand and sophisticated living. Built by banker William C. Ralston, it covered two and a half acres, had elaborately luxurious rooms, and took five years to complete. The cuisine at the Palace was one of its major attractions, and by the end of the century it had become renowned for fine dining.

The first chefs of the Palace brought enormous creativity to their art. Delighting in the new and wondrous foods available in San Francisco, they offered cold artichokes as a salad—a gastronomic adventure for that day; mixed the local avocado with citrus for another combination that was novel in that time; and created the creamy tarragon dressing known as Green Goddess. The Palace cuisine flourishes to this day, offering such delectables as the famous Palace Court salad.

Salads are almost a way of life for Californians, with every imaginable ingredient at our fingertips and a growing preference for lighter meals. Salad before, salad after, salad with, salad instead of, hot or cold, vegetable or fruit, meat or seafood . . .

Ah, those salad days!

LAYERED VEGETABLE SALAD

*This looks beautiful, and the dressing adds so few calories that it's per-
fect for dieters. It keeps well, can be made the night before, and travels
like a trouper . . . and is therefore very popular on picnics. The
amounts can be adjusted to suit any crowd, and leftovers are delicious
between two slices of French bread.*

Serves 8

SALAD

1 head Boston lettuce
1 1-pound can beets, sliced
    and drained
1 cucumber, thinly sliced
1 large Bermuda onion,
    thinly sliced and crisped
    in cold water

2 large tomatoes, peeled and
    thinly sliced
Cottage cheese topping
    (given below)
3 tablespoons chopped fresh
    chives

COTTAGE CHEESE TOPPING

1 pint cottage cheese
2 tablespoons mayonnaise
1 teaspoon salt
½ teaspoon white pepper

1 tablespoon grated onion
Combine all ingredients and
    mix well.

Choose a clear glass straight-sided salad bowl. Chop lettuce and line
bottom of the bowl. Dot with 3 tablespoons cottage cheese topping.
Next place a layer of beets, then cucumber slices and onions rings. Layer
sliced tomatoes over all and cover with cottage cheese topping. Sprinkle
with chopped chives.

CUCUMBER SALAD BOATS

Serves 6

6 medium cucumbers, peeled
Salt and pepper
1½ cups crab meat
1½ cups cooked and shelled
    small shrimp

3 tablespoons chopped
    parsley
6 eggs, hard-cooked

Cut off the top third of each cucumber *lengthwise* and carefully scoop out seeds of the larger part. Cut off a very thin slice from the bottom for balance. Sprinkle the insides with salt and pepper. Toss together the crab and shrimp and fill the cucumber boats. Sprinkle with chopped parsley, garnish the platter with hard-cooked eggs. Pass Louis Dressing (see Index) separately to spoon over boats.

BENGAL SALAD WITH CHUTNEY DRESSING

This has an exotic effect with readily available ingredients.

Serves 4

2 cups diced cooked chicken
1 cup chopped celery
½ cup chopped cucumber
1 orange, peeled and sliced
1 apple, unpeeled, chopped
1 large banana, sliced

½ cup chopped peanuts
4 green onions, chopped
Watercress
Chutney Dressing (recipe
  given below)

Toss the first 8 ingredients together lightly and refrigerate for 1 hour. When ready to serve, place salad on a bed of watercress and spoon on Chutney Dressing.

Chutney Dressing

Makes approximately 1 cup

½ cup sour cream
3 tablespoons chopped
  chutney
1 teaspoon grated orange
  rind

1 teaspoon lemon juice
¼ teaspoon curry powder
Salt and freshly ground
  pepper to taste

Combine all ingredients and mix well.

PARTY SALAD

Serves 10

10 ounces fresh spinach
Salt and freshly ground
    pepper to taste
6 hard-cooked eggs, finely
    chopped
½ pound boiled ham, cut in
    julienne strips
1 small head iceberg lettuce,
    shredded
1 10-ounce package frozen
    tiny peas, thawed and
    patted dry

1 red onion, thinly sliced and
    separated into rings
1 cup sour cream
1 pint mayonnaise
½ pound Gruyère cheese,
    cut in julienne strips
½ pound bacon, crisply
    cooked and crumbled

Trim and discard tough spinach stems, rinse leaves well, pat dry, and break into bite-size pieces. Arrange spinach in the bottom of a large salad bowl. Sprinkle with salt and pepper. Add the eggs, ham, and lettuce in layers. Sprinkle with more salt and pepper and scatter peas over all. Then arrange the onion rings on the top. Combine sour cream and mayonnaise well and spread over salad. Scatter cheese strips over salad, cover the bowl tightly, and refrigerate overnight. Just before serving, sprinkle with bacon. Do not toss.

ASPARAGUS VINAIGRETTE

A classic treatment for our marvelous California asparagus. Marinate ahead to increase tartness.

Serves 8

48 fresh small asparagus
    spears
Red leaf or any loose-leaf
    lettuce

8 strips pimiento

Trim asparagus into pieces about 6 inches long. Scrape each spear with a vegetable peeler. Lay asparagus in a large skillet, cover with boiling salted water, and cook until tender-crisp (about 5 to 7 minutes). Drain and chill. Arrange asparagus in 8 separate bunches, spoke fashion, on a lettuce-covered round platter, and "tie" each bunch with a pimiento strip. Cover arranged asparagus and return to refrigerator. Just before serving, pour the desired amount of Spicy Vinaigrette Dressing (see Index) over all.

PALACE COURT SALAD

This original San Francisco tempter comes from the Garden Court of the Palace Hotel.

Serves 6

1 pound fresh crab meat or
  cooked and shelled
  small shrimp
2 cups diced celery
1 tablespoon minced onion
½ to 1 cup mayonnaise
2 large tomatoes, sliced
  thickly

6 large cooked artichoke
  bottoms
1 head iceberg lettuce,
  shredded
3 hard-cooked eggs, finely
  chopped

In a bowl combine the crab or shrimp, celery, and onion. Add just enough mayonnaise to bind the ingredients together. Set aside. On each plate place a thick slice of tomato, put an artichoke bottom on it, then the crab or shrimp mixture. Circle each mound with some shredded lettuce and garnish with chopped egg. Serve with Louis Dressing or Green Goddess Dressing (see Index for both) on the side.

BEAN SPROUT SALAD

This salad is hearty enough to be a main course if the seafood is included. It's a very refreshing addition to any meal.

Serves 8

1 pound bean sprouts,
    washed and drained
1 cup celery, thinly sliced
2 tablespoons finely minced
    green onions

1 cup slivered almonds,
    toasted
½ cup sliced water chestnuts
1 pound crab meat or shrimp
    (optional)

Combine bean sprouts with celery, onions, almonds, and water chestnuts. Add crab or shrimp if desired. Carefully toss with Cantonese Dressing (see Index) and serve on chilled salad plates.

BORSCHT JELLY SALAD

A good, spicy salad mold to beautify a buffet.

Serves 8

2 cans beef consommé
10½ ounces beet juice
2 3-ounce packages lemon
    gelatin
3 tablespoons cider vinegar
3 tablespoons lemon juice
2 tablespoons grated onion
2 tablespoons prepared
    horseradish

2 teaspoons salt
Freshly ground pepper to
    taste
1½ cups julienne beets,
    drained and chopped
2 cups finely shredded
    cabbage (optional)
Greek olives for garnish

Combine beef consommé and beet juice. Heat to boiling and pour over lemon gelatin. Stir until dissolved. Add cider vinegar and lemon juice. Chill until it begins to thicken and add onion, horseradish, salt, pepper, beets and cabbage if desired. Pour into an 8-cup ring mold and chill overnight. Unmold, garnish with Greek olives, and serve with Sour Cream Dressing (see Index).

CALIFORNIA BEEF SALAD

This is a perfect way to use leftover roast beef on a hot day. A good, hearty salad.

Serves 6

¼ cup red wine vinegar
¼ cup water
2 tablespoons lemon juice
2 tablespoons sugar
¼ teaspoon dillweed
½ teaspoon salt
Freshly ground pepper to
    taste

3 cups (about 12 ounces)
    cold roast beef cut in
    strips
1 small onion, thinly sliced
1 head romaine lettuce
1 cup sour cream
Artichoke hearts
Tomato wedges

Simmer the first 7 ingredients for 15 minutes. Cool. Combine with beef and onion, and chill several hours or overnight. Drain, saving the marinade. Break up lettuce and place in a large bowl. Top with beef and onion. Combine sour cream with reserved marinade. Toss with lettuce and beef. Garnish with artichoke hearts and tomato wedges.

CELERIAC RÉMOULADE

Serves 4

4 medium celery roots
2 cups cold water
⅔ cup mayonnaise
1 tablespoon Dijon mustard
1 teaspoon salt

½ teaspoon white pepper
2 tablespoons chopped
    parsley
Chopped parsley for garnish

Peel celery roots and cut into matchstick-size pieces. Place in a saucepan. Add 2 cups cold water and bring to a rolling boil. Cook for 3 minutes. Drain celery root in a colander and rinse with cold water. Dry thoroughly and place in a salad bowl. Combine mayonnaise, mustard, salt, pepper, and 2 tablespoons parsley. Stir into celery root and toss with fork to mix. Chill before serving. Serve garnished with chopped parsley.

BROWN DERBY SALAD

All the ingredients of this terrific salad complement each other, and you can really clean out the refrigerator with it. It is perfect to serve to a large group at a buffet, or with a simple steak dinner with French bread, good wine, and dessert. Be sure to show the salad before tossing with the dressing, since half of its appeal is the attractive way the colors and textures are arranged on top.

Serves 6

½ head Boston lettuce, shredded
2 chicken breasts, cooked, chilled, and diced
2 medium tomatoes, diced
3 hard-cooked eggs, chopped
6 slices bacon, cooked and crumbled

3 ounces Roquefort cheese, crumbled
2 medium avocados, halved and cut in wedges
1 small stalk French endive (optional)
1 tablespoon snipped chives

Place shredded lettuce in a large salad bowl. Over lettuce, arrange a row each of chicken, tomatoes, eggs, bacon, and cheese. Surround with avocado and endive. Sprinkle with chives. Toss at the table with Brown Derby Dressing (see Index).

CELERY VICTOR

Serves 6 to 8

3 bunches celery hearts
2 cups chicken stock
4 parsley sprigs
1 bay leaf
½ cup chopped fresh celery leaves
6 tablespoons red wine vinegar

1 tablespoon Dijon mustard
1 cup olive oil
1 teaspoon salt
½ teaspoon pepper
Pimiento strips
Anchovy fillets, drained and patted dry

Cut celery hearts in half lengthwise, and trim to approximately 6 inches long. Place in a skillet with chicken stock, parsley, bay leaf, and celery leaves. Bring to boil, lower heat, and simmer for 10 minutes until barely tender. Drain. Whisk the vinegar and mustard together, and gradually beat in the oil, salt, and pepper. Pour over celery and marinate for 24 hours, turning occasionally. Garnish with pimiento and anchovies. Serve as a side dish or salad.

COLD RICE SALAD

This salad is beautiful on a summer buffet. It keeps well, serves a lot of people, and is really refreshing.

Serves 12 to 16

4 cups chicken stock
2 cups uncooked long grain
    white rice
3 6-ounce jars oil-marinated
    artichoke hearts
5 green onions, chopped
1 4-ounce jar
    pimiento-stuffed olives,
    sliced (optional)

1 large green pepper, diced
3 large celery stalks, diced
¼ cup chopped fresh
    parsley
Reserved artichoke marinade
1 teaspoon curry powder
2 cups mayonnaise
Salt and freshly ground
    pepper to taste

Bring stock to boil, stir in rice, and return to boil. Lower heat, cover, and simmer for 20 minutes or until liquid is absorbed and rice is tender. Cool. Drain artichokes, reserving marinade, and chop. Add to rice with the onions, olives, green pepper, celery, and parsley. Combine reserved marinade with the curry, mayonnaise, salt, and pepper. Toss with rice and mix thoroughly. Refrigerate until ready to serve.

CENTRAL VALLEY SALAD

Very appealing to the eye as well as the palate—a very pretty addition to any table.

Serves 6

1 large head romaine lettuce
¼ pound black grapes,
  halved and seeded
2 small oranges, peeled,
  sectioned, and seeded

1 small red onion, sliced
1 avocado, peeled and sliced

Tear lettuce into large pieces. Toss with grapes, oranges, onion, and avocado. Just before serving, toss salad with Lemon Mustard Dressing (see Index).

CHICKEN SALAD HAWAIIAN

Serves 8

3 pounds unboned chicken
  breasts
Salt and freshly ground
  pepper
1 cup mayonnaise
½ cup sour cream
¼ cup chutney
1 tablespoon powdered
  ginger
1 tablespoon curry powder
½ teaspoon salt
1 cup thinly sliced celery

¼ cup thinly sliced green
  onions
4 small pineapples, green
  tops intact
2 ripe avocados
2 ripe papayas
Watercress sprigs
Condiments: chopped pea-
  nuts, chopped hard-
  cooked eggs, cooked
  chopped bacon

Sprinkle chicken breasts with salt and pepper. Steam until tender. Cool, bone, and cut into cubes. In a large bowl, combine mayonnaise, sour cream, chutney, ginger, curry and salt. Fold in chicken, celery, and onions. Chill for 2 hours and adjust seasonings. Cut pineapples, including the green tops, in half lengthwise and carefully cut out fruit, leaving shells approximately ½ inch thick. Cut some of the fruit into small slices and reserve for garnish. Just before serving, peel and dice avocados and papayas, fold into chicken mixture. Mound into the pineapple shells and garnish with reserved pineapple slices and watercress. Pass condiments in small bowls.

COLD SALMON MOUSSE WITH CUCUMBER SAUCE

Serves 6

2 cups flaked cold cooked
    salmon
3 tablespoons fresh lemon
    juice
3 tablespoons mayonnaise
¾ teaspoon salt
⅛ teaspoon cayenne

1 envelope unflavored
    gelatin
½ cup cold water
½ cup heavy cream,
    whipped
Cucumber Sauce (given
    below)

Combine salmon with lemon juice, mayonnaise, salt, and cayenne. Soften gelatin in ½ cup cold water and dissolve over low heat. Cool slightly and combine with salmon mixture. Fold in whipped cream, adjust seasonings, and pour into oiled small molds or a 1-quart mold. Chill. Combine cucumber sauce ingredients (below) and chill. Unmold mousse and serve garnished with cucumber sauce as a luncheon or first course.

Cucumber Sauce

1 cup sour cream
½ cup seeded and chopped
    cucumber, thoroughly
    drained

2 teaspoons chopped chives
¾ teaspoon dillweed
Salt and freshly ground
    pepper to taste

Combine ingredients and chill.

CRAB SALAD

Serves 4

¾ cup mayonnaise
¼ teaspoon garlic salt
Juice of ½ lime
3 teaspoons Dijon mustard
1 teaspoon Worcestershire
   sauce
½ teaspoon dried tarragon
   leaves

8 dashes Angostura bitters
1 tablespoon brandy
Lettuce leaves for garnish
1 pound fresh crab meat,
   chilled

Mix all ingredients except lettuce leaves and crab meat. Chill. Garnish individual salad plates with lettuce leaves. Gently fold crab meat into sauce mixture and arrange on top of lettuce.

ENSALADA DE COLIFLOR

Serves 4 to 6

1 whole large cauliflower,
   cleaned and trimmed,
   left whole
2 large ripe avocados,
   mashed
½ teaspoon lemon juice
½ small onion, minced
2 canned whole green
   chilies, seeded and
   chopped

Salt and freshly ground
   pepper to taste
½ small head of lettuce,
   shredded
Parmesan cheese, grated
Pimiento for garnish

Cook whole cauliflower in boiling salted water to cover until done but still firm. Refresh in cold water, drain thoroughly, and chill. Mix together avocados, lemon juice, onion, chilies, salt, and pepper. To assemble: Place shredded lettuce on a serving platter. Place whole cauliflower in center and cover with avocado mixture. Sprinkle with Parmesan cheese. Decorate with strips of pimiento.

HEARTS OF PALM SALAD

Serves 4

1 can hearts of palm
Spinach leaves, trimmed,
    washed, and well dried
6 tablespoons salad oil
3 tablespoons fresh lemon
    juice
½ teaspoon salt
½ teaspoon sugar
¼ teaspoon paprika

½ teaspoon aromatic bitters
1 tablespoon finely minced
    celery
2 tablespoons finely minced
    pimiento-stuffed green
    olives
2 tablespoons finely minced
    scallions (with tops)
Pimiento for garnish

Arrange hearts of palm, sliced lengthwise, on spinach leaves. Combine
the remaining ingredients except the garnish and pour over the salad.
Garnish with pimiento.

KOREAN SALAD

A wonderful variation on the usual spinach salad.

Serves 6

1 pound fresh spinach
3 hard-cooked eggs, diced
6 to 8 slices crisp cooked
    bacon, crumbled

2 cups fresh bean sprouts
1 8-ounce can water
    chestnuts, sliced

DRESSING
1 cup oil
⅔ cup sugar
Salt to taste
1 medium onion, grated

¼ cup vinegar
⅓ cup catsup
1 tablespoon Worcestershire
    sauce

Trim and discard tough spinach stems, rinse leaves well, pat dry, and
break into bite-size pieces in a salad bowl. Add remaining salad ingredients. Mix dressing ingredients together. Toss salad with dressing.

CURRIED SPINACH SALAD

The diced chicken or turkey can be added for a more substantial lunch-eon dish. Otherwise, the salad stands alone to accompany roast meats or a casserole.

Serves 4

2 pounds fresh spinach
2 Red Delicious apples,
    unpeeled
⅔ cup dry-roasted Spanish
    peanuts
½ cup seedless raisins

⅓ cup thinly sliced green
    onions
2 tablespoons toasted sesame
    seeds
1 cup diced cooked chicken
    or turkey (optional)

DRESSING
½ cup white vinegar
⅔ cup salad oil
1 tablespoon finely chopped
    chutney

1 teaspoon curry powder
1 teaspoon salt
1 teaspoon dry mustard
¼ teaspoon Tabasco sauce

Trim and discard tough spinach stems, rinse leaves well, pat dry, and break into bite-size pieces. Wrap in toweling and chill. Core and dice apples into a serving bowl and add remaining salad ingredients. Arrange over a bed of spinach and top with diced chicken or turkey. Combine dressing ingredients and stir well. Pour over salad just before serving.

GREEN BEAN SALAD PROVENÇAL

Serves 4 to 6

1¼ pounds fresh green
    beans
1 fennel bulb, thinly sliced
4 ripe tomatoes, peeled,
    seeded, and quartered

1 cup pitted small black
    olives
Minced fresh chervil to taste

GARLIC DRESSING

2 cloves garlic, minced
6 to 8 fresh basil leaves,
    minced
¼ cup olive oil
3 tablespoons wine vinegar
Salt and freshly ground
    pepper to taste

12 anchovy fillets, drained
3 hard-cooked eggs, sliced
1½ tablespoons minced
    fresh basil

Cut beans into thin julienne strips and steam until barely tender. Rinse in cold water, drain, and arrange with fennel, tomatoes, olives, and chervil in a salad bowl. Combine dressing ingredients and pour over vegetables. Toss well. Refrigerate for 2 to 3 hours. Garnish with anchovies and egg slices and sprinkle with basil.

FROSTED CANTALOUPE SALAD

This could also be made with a casaba or honeydew melon.

8 ounces cream cheese,
    softened
2 tablespoons milk
1 large cantaloupe
6 cups mixed fresh fruits
    (for example: bananas,
    apples, peaches, grapes,
    strawberries), cut into
    bite-size pieces

¾ cup toasted flaked
    coconut
Mint leaves for garnish

Beat cream cheese and milk until smooth and fluffy. Set aside. Remove the rind from the melon and cut a little from one end so the melon will stand up. Slice off 2 inches from other end. Scoop out seeds. Fill the melon with 1 cup of fruit. Frost the ouside of the melon with cheese mixture. Press coconut lightly into cheese frosting and refrigerate. When ready to serve, place the melon on a serving platter and garnish with mint leaves. At the table, cut melon into 6 wedges and place each on a salad plate with some of the fruit inside melon. Top with remaining fruit and serve with Sesame Dressing (see Index).

GUACAMOLE SALAD RING

Fill the center of this colorful ring mold with sliced tomatoes and avocados. Serve French Vinaigrette Salad Dressing with it (see Index).

Serves 14 to 16

3 envelopes unflavored
   gelatin
¾ cup cold water
2¼ cups hot water
½ cup plus 2 tablespoons
   fresh lime juice
2 cloves garlic, pressed
½ cup minced green onion
1 tablespoon salt

5 cups mashed avocado (7 to
   8 avocados)
1 cup sour cream
Tabasco sauce to taste
2 tablespoons seeded and
   chopped green chilies
½ cup chopped and
   well-drained fresh
   tomatoes

Soften gelatin in cold water and then dissolve in hot water. Cool slightly and mix with remaining ingredients. Pour into a 2-quart ring mold that has been oiled with olive oil. Cover and chill until firm. May be made a day ahead.

PERSIMMON SALAD

Serves 4

4 large ripe persimmons
Lettuce
1 cup diced fresh pears
¾ cup seedless grapes
1 cup diced fresh pineapple
4 teaspoons chopped pine
   nuts

4 teaspoons finely chopped
   walnuts
1 cup mayonnaise thinned
   with a little fresh
   pineapple juice and
   fresh lemon juice

Cut persimmons into quarters, almost to the stem end, and spread apart. Place on a bed of lettuce. Combine pears, grapes, and pineapple and mound within persimmons. Sprinkle each one with 1 teaspoon pine nuts and 1 teaspoon walnuts. Serve with mayonnaise.

MARINATED CUCUMBERS

Serves 6

3 large cucumbers
Salt
¾ cup cider vinegar

¼ cup sugar
¼ cup chopped parsley
4 green onions, chopped

SAUCE
1 cup sour cream
1 tablespoon sugar
1 teaspoon dry mustard

2 tablespoons cider vinegar
1 teaspoon salt

Peel cucumbers, cut in half lengthwise, and seed. Slice very thin. Sprinkle lightly with salt and let stand for 1 hour. Drain. Combine ¾ cup cider vinegar, sugar, parsley, and green onions. Marinate cucumbers in this for 2 to 3 hours. Drain. Combine sauce ingredients. Toss cucumbers carefully with sauce.

MEXICAN CHEF'S SALAD

Almost as good and not nearly as fattening as a taco.

Serves 4 to 6

1 head of lettuce
1 large onion, chopped
4 large ripe tomatoes, peeled and chopped
4 ounces Cheddar cheese, freshly grated
1 8-ounce bag tortilla chips, crushed

1 pound ground beef
1 15-ounce can red kidney beans
1 cup Thousand Island dressing mixed with Tabasco sauce to taste
1 ripe avocado for garnish

Tear lettuce into bite-size pieces. Add cheese and toss. Place in a large bowl along with onion and tomatoes. Add the tortilla chips. Brown the ground beef well. Add kidney beans and heat thoroughly. Combine hot meat and bean mixture with cold salad and toss with Thousand Island dressing. Garnish with avocado slices.

MOLDED CUCUMBER MOUSSE

A tart, refreshing salad.

Serves 6

1 3-ounce package lime
    gelatin
1⅓ cups boiling water
3 tablespoons fresh lemon
    juice
½ teaspoon salt
1 cup cottage cheese
½ cup mayonnaise

1 tablespoon freshly grated
    onion juice
1 cucumber, peeled, seeded,
    and chopped
1 cup slivered almonds
1 teaspoon prepared
    horseradish

Stir gelatin into the boiling water, lemon juice, and salt, refrigerate until slightly set. Whip and add cottage cheese, mayonnaise, onion juice, cucumber, almonds, and horseradish. Pour into an 8-inch ring mold and refrigerate until set. Serve with mayonnaise to which a little pineapple juice has been added.

MUSHROOM TOMATO SALAD

Serves 6

1 pound fresh mushrooms,
    caps and stems sliced
Boiling water to cover
½ cup tarragon wine
    vinegar
½ cup water
½ cup olive oil
1 bay leaf

3 cloves garlic, bruised
6 whole black peppercorns
Salt to taste
Butter lettuce leaves for
    garnish
3 large tomatoes, sliced
1 avocado, sliced
Chopped fresh parsley

Add mushrooms to boiling water and simmer for 1 to 2 minutes. Drain and place in a jar with vinegar, ½ cup water, olive oil, bay leaf, garlic, peppercorns, and salt. Refrigerate overnight. Arrange lettuce and tomatoes on salad plates. Drain mushrooms and arrange on top. Garnish with avocado. Serve with Brown Derby Dressing (see Index) and sprinkle with parsley.

ZUCCHINI SALAD

Serves 6

1 cup mayonnaise
½ cup sour cream
½ cup chopped parsley
3 green onions with tops,
    chopped
3 tablespoons white wine
    vinegar
½ teaspoon minced fresh
    tarragon
1 teaspoon Worcestershire
    sauce
½ teaspoon dry mustard

¼ teaspoon freshly ground
    black pepper
2 cloves garlic
1 tablespoon fresh lemon
    juice
2 tablespoons chopped
    chives
8 medium zucchini, thinly
    sliced on the diagonal
Lettuce leaves
Cherry tomatoes for garnish

Place all ingredients except zucchini and cherry tomatoes in a blender or food processor and blend thoroughly. Toss with zucchini on lettuce leaves and garnish with cherry tomatoes.

SEMI-CAESAR SALAD

A super Caesar salad for people who abhor anchovies.

Serves 6

1 head romaine lettuce, the
    leaves broken into large
    pieces
2 heads Bibb lettuce, broken
    into large pieces
1 egg
1 teaspoon garlic salt
3 tablespoons sour cream

½ teaspoon freshly ground
    pepper
3 tablespoons oil
1 teaspoon wine vinegar
½ cup croutons
½ cup freshly grated
    Parmesan cheese

Place the lettuces in a large bowl. In a separate bowl combine egg, garlic salt, sour cream, pepper oil, and vinegar for the dressing. Mix well. Just before serving add croutons and cheese to lettuce and toss with dressing.

MOLDED SALMON SALAD

Serves 6

½ envelope unflavored
  gelatin
2 tablespoons cold water
2 eggs, separated
1 teaspoon salt
1 teaspoon Dijon mustard
Cayenne to taste
1½ tablespoons butter,
  melted

¾ cup milk
2 tablespoons white wine
  vinegar
1 16-ounce can salmon,
  flaked
3 tablespoons capers
Lettuce leaves
Cucumber slices for garnish

Soften gelatin in 2 tablespoon cold water. Slightly beat egg yolks and mix with salt, mustard, and cayenne. Add melted butter, milk, and vinegar and cook in the top of a double boiler, stirring constantly, until mixture thickens. Add softened gelatin and cook, stirring, until gelatin is disolved. Set aside and cool. Beat egg whites until stiff and fold into sauce mixture. Then fold in salmon and capers. Pour into a lightly oiled mold and refrigerate until firm. To serve: Unmold onto a bed of lettuce leaves and surround with cucumber slices.

SHRIMP SALAD

Very good contrasting of flavors and textures. The amounts do not have to be exact, so the cook can cut down on onions or adjust any ingredient to suit his or her own taste. A good luncheon dish.

Serves 6

1 pound small shrimp,
  cooked and shelled
3 hard-cooked eggs, chopped
1 cup chopped celery
¾ cup chopped green
  onions

Mayonnaise
1 tablespoon fresh lemon
  juice
1 3-ounce can chow mein
  noodles
Avocado slices for garnish

Combine shrimp, eggs, celery, green onions, and just enough mayonnaise to bind. Add lemon juice and carefully stir in chow mein noodles. Place on serving plates and garnish with avocado slices.

SEAFOOD MOLD

Serves 12

1 10½-ounce can condensed
tomato soup
1½ cups V-8 juice
8 ounces cream cheese
2 envelopes unflavored
gelatin
½ cup water
¾ cup minced green pepper
¾ cup minced celery
¼ cup minced onions

¼ cup chopped green
onions and tops
1 cup mayonnaise
1 tablespoon fresh lemon
juice
2 avocados, chopped
1 pound flaked crab meat or
cooked shrimp, shelled,
deveined, and coarsely
chopped

Heat soup and juice with cream cheese, stirring until cheese is melted. Soften gelatin in ½ cup water and then dissolve in hot soup mixture. Stir in green pepper, celery, onions, and green onions. Chill until slightly thickened. Fold in mayonnaise, lemon juice, avocados, and crab or shrimp. Pour into a 3-quart mold that has been rinsed in cold water. Chill until set. Unmold on a chilled serving platter and serve as a luncheon or buffet salad.

SEAFOOD SALAD

Serves 4

1 small onion, minced
3 hard-cooked eggs, chopped
1 cup cooked, shelled,
deveined small shrimp
1 cup crab meat
½ cup chopped celery
1 cup mayonnaise

2 cups cooked rice, chilled
3 tablespoons Lemon
Mustard Dressing (see
Index)
Lettuce leaves
Sliced almonds

Combine the onion, eggs, shrimp, crab meat, celery, and mayonnaise and chill for several hours. Toss the rice with the dressing and set aside. To serve: Place a mound of rice on lettuce leaf, make a center, and fill it with seafood mixture. Garnish with sliced almonds.

SPINACH AND MUSHROOM SALAD

A classic combination of flavors with the added interest of mushrooms and tarragon.

Serves 6 to 8

1 clove garlic
1½ pounds fresh spinach
½ pound mushrooms, sliced
6 slices crisp cooked bacon,
    crumbled
3 hard-cooked eggs, finely
    chopped

Croutons made of 4 to 6
    slices French bread,
    buttered, cubed, and
    baked

Rub a wooden salad bowl with garlic. Trim and discard tough spinach stems, rinse leaves well, pat dry, and break into bite-size pieces. Place spinach, mushrooms, bacon, eggs, and croutons in the bowl. Toss with Tarragon Dressing (see Index).

SWEET AND SOUR ZUCCHINI

A sweet-sour salad that must be done ahead—grand for picnics.

Serves 6 to 8

½ package onion soup mix
½ cup wine vinegar
¾ cup sugar
1 teaspoon salt
1 teaspoon freshly ground
    pepper
⅓ cup vegetable oil

⅔ cup cider vinegar
½ cup chopped green
    pepper
½ cup chopped celery
7 small zucchini, thinly
    sliced

Soak onion soup mix in wine vinegar. Combine sugar, salt, pepper, oil, vinegar, green pepper, and celery. Add soup mixture and zucchini. Stirring occasionally, chill for 4 to 6 hours. Just before serving, drain and serve as a salad.

TABBOULEH

This salad is not only delicious but very colorful and easy. It is a snap to make with a food processor, and it keeps and travels well. On an elegant picnic, it can be served in lettuce leaves thus eliminating forks, plates, and mess.

Serves 6 to 8

1 cup fine bulgur (cracked wheat)
1 pound tomatoes, peeled, seeded, and chopped
2 cups chopped green onions
3 cups chopped parsley

¼ cup chopped fresh mint
½ cup olive oil
⅓ cup fresh lemon juice
1¼ teaspoons salt
½ teaspoon freshly ground pepper

Rinse the wheat, cover with boiling water, and let stand for 30 minutes. Drain thoroughly and squeeze dry in a piece of cheesecloth or a clean dish towel. Set aside. Combine the tomatoes, green onions, parsley, and mint. Beat together oil, lemon juice, salt, and pepper; gently fold into tomato mixture. Mix in wheat until well blended.

TONNATO TOMATO

This flavorful rendition of that good old standby, tuna salad, is great as a first course and perfect also as a luncheon surprise.

Serves 6

6 medium tomatoes hollowed out and drained
2 7-ounce cans tuna, drained
2 anchovy fillets, mashed
1 teaspoon Dijon mustard
1 tablespoon raisins
2 tablespoons mayonnaise or yogurt

Salt and freshly ground pepper to taste
Lettuce
2 hard-cooked eggs, forced through a sieve
Parsley, finely minced
Lemon wedges

Prepare tomatoes for filling, invert, and set aside to drain. In a mixing bowl, combine the tuna, anchovies, mustard, raisins, mayonnaise or yogurt, salt, and pepper until well blended. Fill tomato shells, place each on a bed of lettuce on a separate salad plate, and garnish with sieved egg, parsley, and a lemon wedge.

VERMICELLI SALAD

A nice and easy luncheon dish that can be done ahead. Substituting chopped ham for the shrimp would make it a good picnic item.

Serves 12

5 hard-cooked eggs, chopped
5 stalks celery, finely
   chopped
6 gherkin pickles, finely
   chopped
¼ cup chopped onions
1½ cups mayonnaise
¼ cup juice from pickles
Salt and seasoned salt to taste

12 ounces vermicelli,
   broken, cooked, and
   well drained
1 pound raw shrimp,
   cooked, shelled,
   deveined, coarsely
   chopped
Paprika
Chopped parsley

Combine eggs, celery, pickles, onions, mayonnaise, pickle juice, and salts. Add vermicelli, toss, and chill overnight. Just before serving add shrimp, and toss. Garnish with paprika and chopped parsley.

TARRAGON DRESSING

½ cup olive oil
½ cup salad oil
½ cup white tarragon
   vinegar
½ teaspoon dried tarragon

1 teaspoon sugar
½ teaspoon Dijon mustard
Salt and freshly ground
   black pepper to taste

Combine all ingredients and set aside for at least 24 hours.

CANTONESE DRESSING

1 cup mayonnaise
¼ cup soy sauce
2 teaspoons curry powder

2 teaspoons powdered ginger
2 teaspoons fresh lemon juice

Several hours before serving, mix together all ingredients and refrigerate.

LOUIS DRESSING

2 cups mayonnaise
½ cup heavy cream,
    whipped
½ cup chili sauce
¼ cup chopped green
    onions

Salt and freshly ground
    pepper to taste
1 tablespoon lemon juice

Combine all ingredients in a jar and shake well to mix thoroughly. Let stand for at least 1 hour to allow the flavors to blend. Can be stored in the refrigerator for several days.

SESAME DRESSING

2 teaspoons powdered sugar
½ teaspoon paprika
½ teaspoon dry mustard
½ teaspoon salt
½ cup currant jelly, melted

¼ cup fresh lemon juice
1 tablespoon cider vinegar
1 cup salad oil
1 tablespoon toasted sesame
    seeds

Combine sugar, paprika, mustard, and salt. Stir in jelly, lemon juice, and vinegar. Gradually beat in oil. Add sesame seeds, stir well, and refrigerate.

SOUR CREAM DRESSING

Makes approximately 2 cups

1 pint sour cream
Juice of 1 lemon
2 teaspoons dillweed

Combine ingredients and mix well.

PINK VELVET DRESSING

Makes 2 cups

2 tablespoons Dijon mustard
3 tablespoons red wine
    vinegar
1¼ cups olive oil
1 egg white
¼ cup chopped parsley

1 tablespoon fresh lemon
    juice
2 tablespoons dry red wine
Salt and freshly ground
    pepper to taste

Combine mustard and vinegar in a blender. Turn on blender at low speed and gradually add ¼ cup of the oil. Add egg white and continue mixing. Gradually add remaining oil while blending. Remove from blender and add parsley, lemon juice, red wine, and seasonings.

POPPY-SEED DRESSING

Makes approximately 2 cups

½ cup sugar
1 teaspoon dry mustard
1 teaspoon salt
½ cup olive oil

½ cup vegetable oil
⅓ cup vinegar
¼ cup grated onion
1½ teaspoon poppy seeds

With a rotary beater or wire whisk, beat together the sugar, mustard, salt, olive oil, vegetable oil, and vinegar. Add onion and poppy seeds. Store in a tightly closed jar. Will keep in the refrigerator for several weeks.

FRENCH VINAIGRETTE SALAD DRESSING

This salad dressing is incomparable. It does magic things to a simple head of lettuce and miracles to any cold vegetable. It goes a long way and keeps for ages, since it gives such a creamy coating to the greens.

Makes approximately 2 cups

2 teaspoons salt
1 teaspoon white pepper
½ teaspoon cracked black
    pepper
¼ teaspoon sugar
½ teaspoon dry mustard
Juice of ½ lemon

1 clove garlic, pressed
5 tablespoons tarragon
    vinegar
½ cup vegetable oil
2 tablespoons olive oil
1 egg, lightly beaten
½ cup light cream

Combine all ingredients in the order given in a jar with a tightly fitting lid. Shake vigorously to blend, and store in the refrigerator. Will keep for several weeks.

SPICY VINAIGRETTE DRESSING

Makes approximately 2 cups

½ cup red wine vinegar
¾ teaspoon salt
¼ teaspoon freshly ground
    black pepper
1½ cups olive oil
1 teaspoon capers

1 teaspoon of each, finely
    chopped: chives, green
    olive, green onions,
    parsley
1 egg, hard-cooked

Combine ingredients and mix well.

GREEN GODDESS DRESSING

Makes approximately 2 cups

1¾ cups mayonnaise
¼ cup sour cream
6 to 8 anchovy fillets, mashed
3 tablespoons minced fresh tarragon leaves

2 tablespoons minced fresh chives
1 tablespoon chopped fresh parsley
¼ cup tarragon vinegar
1 clove garlic, minced

Combine all ingredients in a jar and shake well to mix thoroughly. Let stand for at least 1 hour to allow the flavors to blend. Can be stored in the refrigerator for several days.

LEMON MUSTARD DRESSING

Makes approximately 1½ cups

1 cup olive oil
¼ cup lemon juice
½ teaspoon salt
1 teaspoon Worcestershire sauce

1½ teaspoons Dijon mustard
1½ teaspoons honey
¼ teaspoon white pepper

Combine all ingredients in a jar and shake vigorously until well blended. Tightly covered, it will keep in the refrigerator for up to 2 weeks.

FRENCH DRESSING

Makes 1 cup

¾ cup salad oil
¼ cup white wine vinegar
Salt and freshly ground pepper to taste

Combine ingredients and stir vigorously.

ANCHOVY SALAD DRESSING

Makes 1 quart

1 celery stalk, chopped
½ medium onion, chopped
3 to 4 cloves garlic, bruised
1 2-ounce can flat anchovies,
    drained (amount may
    be increased to taste)
1 teaspoon freshly ground
    black pepper

½ teaspoon sugar
2 tablespoons Dijon mustard
1 tablespoon fresh lemon
    juice
3 eggs
1½ to 2 cups salad oil

Purée celery, onion, garlic, anchovies, pepper, sugar, mustard, and lemon juice in a blender or food processor until smooth. Blend in eggs one at a time. Add oil, a little at a time, blending after each addition, until dressing consistency is reached. Serve on seafood or plain salad greens.

AVOCADO SALAD DRESSING

Substitute this for your regular dressing for a new and different taste.

Makes approximately 3 cups

2 ripe avocados
Juice of 1 lemon
1 tablespoon mayonnaise
1 teaspoon grated onion

Salt and freshly ground
    pepper to taste
¾ cup salad oil
¼ cup white wine vinegar

Mash avocados until smooth with a silver fork. Add the lemon juice, mayonnaise, onion, and salt and pepper to taste. Mix thoroughly. In a separate bowl, blend salad oil with white wine vinegar. Stir this into the avocado mixture. Serve over peeled and sliced tomatoes or toss with a green or seafood salad.

SAVORY SALAD DRESSING

This dressing is especially good on a salad of avocado slices and mandarin oranges.

Makes approximately 2 cups

⅓ cup sugar
1 teaspoon salt
½ teaspoon dry mustard
⅓ cup cider vinegar

1 cup olive oil
¼ cup grated onion
1 tablespoon celery seed
½ teaspoon summer savory

Combine all ingredients in a jar and shake vigorously until blended. Tightly covered, it will keep in the refrigerator for up to 2 weeks.

BLUE CHEESE DRESSING

Serves 6

¼ pound Danish or Oregon
   blue cheese
6 tablespoons heavy cream
1 teaspoon fresh lemon juice
3 tablespoons mayonnaise
2 tablespoons olive oil
Mashed garlic to taste
   (optional)

½ teaspoon Worcestershire
   sauce
Tabasco sauce to taste
Salt and freshly ground
   pepper to taste

Combine blue cheese, cream, and lemon juice in the small bowl of a mixer. Let stand for 5 minutes. Beat until well blended. Add mayonnaise and blend well. Gradually beat in olive oil. Add garlic and season to taste with Worcestershire, Tabasco, salt, and pepper. Add more lemon juice if desired. Serve on romaine lettuce.

CARAWAY SALAD DRESSING

Excellent on greens with avocado and fruit.

Makes approximately 1½ cups

3 tablespoons brown sugar
3 green onions, finely
    chopped
¼ teaspoon celery salt
¼ teaspoon salt

1 teaspoon caraway seeds
1 teaspoon paprika
⅓ cup tarragon wine vinegar
¾ cup oil, ½ olive and ½
    salad

Mash first 6 ingredients with a mortar and pestle. When paste consistency is reached, add vinegar and stir. Put in a blender and blend at low speed for 1 to 2 minutes. Then gradually blend in oil. Store in refrigerator for 24 hours to allow flavors to blend. Serve with an avocado or fruit salad.

CREAMY BASIL SALAD DRESSING

A traditional San Francisco recipe—basil being a regional favorite.

Makes approximately 2½ cups

¼ cup fresh basil leaves,
    firmly packed
1 cup mayonnaise
½ cup sour cream
½ cup chopped parsley
3 green onions with tops,
    chopped
3 tablespoons vinegar
⅛ teaspoon dried tarragon

1 teaspoon Worcestershire
    sauce
½ teaspoon dry mustard
¼ teaspoon freshly ground
    black pepper
1 clove garlic
2 tablespoons chopped
    chives

Combine all ingredients in a blender and blend until smooth.

BROWN DERBY DRESSING

Makes approximately 2 cups

½ cup red wine vinegar
1 tablespoon lemon juice
1½ teaspoons pepper
1 teaspoon salt
½ teaspoon sugar

½ teaspoon dry mustard
1½ teaspoons
    Worcestershire sauce
1 clove garlic, minced
1½ cups salad oil

Combine ingredients and mix well.

OLD-FASHIONED BOILED SALAD DRESSING

A very good, versatile dressing.

Makes approximately 1 cup

½ cup sugar
1 teaspoon salt
1 teaspoon dry mustard
1 tablespoon flour

½ cup milk
1 egg, beaten
½ cup cider vinegar
½ cup sour cream

In a saucepan, combine the sugar, salt, mustard, and flour. Add the milk and beaten egg. In a separate pan, heat the vinegar and gradually add to the mixture. Cook over low heat until dressing has thickened. Cool slightly and mix with sour cream.

CHAPTER VI

EGGS & CHEESE

Cow Hollow

Cow Hollow is a picturesque residential neighborhood on the northern tip of the San Francisco Peninsula, dating back to the earliest days of Spanish settlement. It has seen bleak days as sand hills and tule marshes; bustling days of hog ranches, slaughterhouses and dairies, hence its name; bucolic days of gardens and nurseries interspersed among houses great and small; and the more recent thriving days of development as a desirable residential area through which Union Street, once the Presidio Road, cuts a fine swath. Union Street is a recent phenomenon of transformation from Victorian dwellings to thriving restaurants, antique shops, boutiques, and all manner of diversion.

Reminiscent of the days when cows and farms dotted its landscape, many a restaurant features untold varieties of omelettes and quiches, eggs Benedict for the leisurely weekend brunch, and fizzes silver and golden, none of which could exist without cream and eggs. Cheese specialty shops sell fine California wines as a complement to the wheels of Monterey Jack, Brie, and Camembert made in nearby counties. And somewhere in Cow Hollow someone is tasting, for the first time, a dish called Hangtown Fry—eggs scrambled with oysters and bacon. It is a culinary remnant of the gold rush days when a condemned man's requested last meal gave him extra time to live, since eggs, selling for $1.50 each, were so difficult to find in the mining camps.

Just as it was a long way from a milking shed in Cow Hollow to a hangman's noose in the Sierra foothills, so we offer here a wide and wonderful spectrum of the versatile egg and cheese.

BAKED EGGS IN MUSHROOM SAUCE

This is great for brunch, and it is delicious piled on toasted English muffins for a luncheon main course.

Serves 6 to 8

1 pound mushrooms, sliced
4 tablespoons butter
3 tablespoons flour
1 beef or chicken bouillon
    cube, dissolved in 1
    tablespoon hot water
1 tablespoon grated onion
2 cups heavy cream

Salt and freshly ground
    pepper to taste
1 tablespoon chopped
    parsley
1 egg yolk, slightly beaten
6 to 8 eggs
Grated Parmesan cheese for
    garnish

Preheat oven to 350 degrees. Sauté mushrooms in butter for 5 minutes. Remove mushrooms from skillet. Stir flour, dissolved bouillon cube, and onion into remaining liquid. Cook, stirring, until mixture is thickened. Then slowly stir in cream. Add mushrooms, salt, pepper, and parsley. Add 1 teaspoon of this sauce to the egg yolk, stir, then beat egg yolk into mushroom sauce. Cook a little longer. Cover the bottom of a buttered large baking dish with the sauce to a depth of 1 inch. Carefully drop eggs, one at a time, into sauce so that the eggs will be partly covered. Sprinkle with cheese. Bake for about 15 minutes or until eggs are set.

EGG MIMOSA

Serves 4

4 hard-cooked eggs
4 ounces small shrimp,
    cooked, shelled,
    coarsely chopped

¾ cup homemade
    mayonnaise
Watercress sprigs for garnish

Halve the eggs lengthwise. Remove yolks and pass them through a ¼-inch sieve. Set aside 1 tablespoon of the yolks. Mix remaining yolk with shrimp and 2 tablespoons of the mayonnaise, or enough to bind. Spoon mixture into the cavities of the egg whites. Thin remaining mayonnaise with a little water and completely coat stuffed eggs. Sprinkle reserved yolks over tops of eggs and garnish with watercress sprigs.

FLUFFY OMELET WITH CRAB NEWBURG SAUCE

Serves 6

3 tablespoons butter
¼ cup flour
¼ teaspoon dry mustard
⅛ teaspoon freshly ground
    pepper

1 cup milk
4 eggs, separated
½ teaspoon salt

Preheat oven to 325 degrees. Butter a 12 by 7 by 2-inch baking dish. Melt 3 tablespoons butter in a saucepan. Blend in flour, mustard, and pepper. Add milk gradually, stirring constantly until sauce is thickened. Cool slightly. Beat egg yolks until thick. Add sauce to egg yolks. Beat egg whites and ½ teaspoon salt until stiff peaks form. Gently fold into sauce. Pour mixture into the prepared baking dish and bake for 20 minutes, or until knife inserted in center comes out clean. Serve in baking dish immediately with Crab Newburg Sauce.

Crab Newburg Sauce

¼ cup butter
2 tablespoons chopped
    onions
1½ cups sliced mushrooms
¼ cup flour
½ teaspoon salt
½ teaspoon paprika
Freshly ground pepper to
    taste

1½ cups milk
1 teaspoon Worcestershire
    sauce
2 egg yolks, slightly beaten
2 tablespoons dry white
    wine
¾ pound crab meat

Melt butter in a skillet and gently cook onions and mushrooms until soft. Add flour, salt, paprika, and pepper. Gradually add milk and Worcestershire sauce and cook, stirring constantly, over medium heat until thick and bubbly. Remove from heat and cool slightly. Stir in beaten egg yolks. Add white wine and crab meat. Keep warm in the top of a double boiler until serving time.

HUEVOS RANCHEROS

Serves 6

2 medium onions, finely
chopped
1 tablespoon oil
¼ cup red chili sauce
1 tablespoon green chili
sauce
1 8-ounce can tomato sauce
½ teaspoon dried oregano,
crumbled

3 large ripe tomatoes, peeled,
seeded, and chopped
1 to 2 teaspoon chopped
fresh coriander
(cilantro)
6 tortillas
Oil as needed
6 fried eggs, sunny side up
12 slices avocado

Sauté onions in 1 tablespoon oil until transparent. Add red and green chili sauces, tomato sauce, and oregano, bring to a boil. Lower heat and simmer, uncovered, for 15 minutes, stirring occasionally. Add chopped tomatoes and coriander. Heat thoroughly and keep warm. Fry tortillas on both sides in hot oil and dip in sauce, coating both sides. Place on individual serving dishes and top with a fried egg. Spoon remaining sauce evenly over eggs and top with avocado slices. Pass extra green chili sauce.

HANGTOWN FRY

Serves 6

½ pound bacon, cut into
large pieces
2 tablespoons butter
12 medium oysters
Flour for dredging
1 egg, lightly beaten, for
dipping

1 cup bread crumbs
6 eggs, lightly beaten
Salt and freshly ground
pepper to taste

Fry the bacon in a large skillet until crisp. Remove and drain. Pour the bacon fat from the skillet and add the butter. Dip each oyster in flour, egg, and bread crumbs and fry over medium heat until golden brown. Add the eggs and cook until set, stirring very carefully to cook eggs through. Add the bacon on top, heat, and serve immediately.

CHILES RELLENOS

A great Sunday supper dish, it is quick and easy. Also a good accompaniment to almost any meat dish.

Serves 6

2 7-ounce cans green chilies, seeded
½ pound Cheddar cheese, grated
½ pound Monterey Jack cheese, grated

2 cups evaporated milk
4 eggs
⅓ cup flour
1 teaspoon salt

Preheat oven to 350 degrees. In an 8 by 12-inch baking dish, layer green chilies, Cheddar cheese, and Monterey Jack cheese. Put the evaporated milk, eggs, flour, and salt in a blender, blend thoroughly, and pour over the chilies and cheeses. Bake for 45 minutes.

GREEN CHILI FRITTATA

Serves 8 as a luncheon dish,
12 as hors d'oeuvre

½ cup all-purpose white flour
1 teaspoon baking powder
10 eggs, lightly beaten
¼ pound butter or margarine, melted and slightly cooled

2 cups small curd cottage cheese
1 pound Monterey Jack cheese, grated
3 4-ounce cans diced green chilies
Salt to taste

Preheat oven to 350 degrees. Butter a 9 by 13-inch shallow baking dish. Mix flour and baking powder. Add eggs and butter, blending well. Blend in remaining ingredients. Put mixture in the prepared baking dish and bake for 35 to 45 minutes, or until set. Cut into squares and serve very hot.

MEXICAN RAREBIT

Good on English muffins for brunch or for Sunday supper wtih a green salad.

Serves 4 to 6

3 tablespoons chopped green
   pepper
1 tablespoon butter
½ cup canned tomatoes,
   drained and chopped
1 8-ounce can whole-kernel
   corn
2 tablespoons diced canned
   green chilies

¼ teaspoon salt
1 pound sharp Cheddar or
   Monterey Jack cheese,
   or a combination of
   both
¼ cup bread crumbs
1 egg, lightly beaten
Sliced pimiento
Minced parsley

In the top of a double boiler, sauté green pepper in butter until tender. Place over hot water and add tomatoes, corn, chilies, salt, and cheese. Stir until well blended and cheese is melted. Blend in crumbs and egg. Cook and stir until mixture is thickened. Put in a chafing dish, garnish with sliced pimiento and minced parsley, and serve over toast.

ONION CHEESE PIE

Good Sunday supper or luncheon main course.

Serves 6 to 8

1 cup milk, scalded
3 cups sliced onions
2 tablespoons oil
3 eggs, beaten
1 cup grated sharp Cheddar
   cheese

¼ teaspoon oregano
½ teaspoon salt
1 9-inch piecrust, partially
   baked (see Index)

Preheat oven to 350 degrees. Cool scalded milk to lukewarm. Sauté sliced onions in oil until transparent. Blend onions with milk and add eggs, cheese, oregano, and salt. Mix thoroughly and spoon into the pie shell. Bake for 25 minutes or until a knife inserted in the center comes out clean.

ZUCCHINI-TOMATO PIE

Serves 12

2 9-inch pieshells, partially
  baked
½ large onion, sliced
3 tablespoons olive oil
1 pound zucchini, thinly
  sliced
2 cloves garlic, minced
1 14½-ounce can tomatoes
1 8-ounce can tomato sauce
½ teaspoon dried oregano,
  crumbled

½ teaspoon dried basil,
  crumbled
Salt and freshly ground
  pepper to taste
2 cups ricotta cheese
3 eggs, beaten
½ cup milk
8 ounces mozzarella cheese,
  shredded
½ cup freshly grated
  Parmesan cheese

Preheat oven to 375 degrees. Sauté onion in oil until transparent. Add zucchini and sauté for approximately 5 minutes, or until tender but crisp. Remove from pan and set aside. Add garlic, tomatoes, tomato sauce, and seasonings to pan. Cook over medium-high heat, stirring occasionally, until reduced to 2 cups. Set aside. Beat ricotta with eggs and milk and set aside. Spoon zucchini mixture into the bottom of each pie shell. Pour ¼ cup tomato mixture over each and top with ricotta mixture. Bake for 40 minutes. Spread remaining tomato mixture over pies and top with mozzarella and Parmesan. Bake for 7 to 8 minutes longer.

CALIFORNIA DELI QUICHE

Serves 8

1 9-inch piecrust, partially
    baked (see Index)
1 egg white, lightly beaten
¾ pound liverwurst
¼ cup chopped onions
2 cloves garlic, finely minced
¼ cup dry bread crumbs
¼ teaspoon nutmeg

2 eggs, lightly beaten
1 cup heavy cream
¼ teaspoon salt
¼ teaspoon cinnamon
¼ cup grated Parmesan
    cheese
2 tablespoons sherry

Preheat oven to 375 degrees. Brush the bottom and sides of the pie shell
with the egg white. Set aside. In a bowl, combine the liverwurst,
onions, garlic, bread crumbs, and nutmeg. Spread this mixture evenly
on the bottom of the pie shell. Set aside. In a bowl beat the eggs with
the cream, salt, cinnamon, cheese, and sherry. Pour this mixture into the
pie shell and bake for 30 to 40 minutes or until the center is slightly
firm. Cool before cutting.

ITALIAN SPINACH QUICHE

Serves 6

1 10-inch piecrust, partially
    baked (see Index)
¼ pound Italian sausage,
    crumbled and browned
1 10-ounce package frozen
    spinach, thawed and
    well drained
¼ pound mushrooms, sliced
2 cups ricotta cheese
½ cup shredded or grated
    Gruyère cheese
¼ cup freshly grated
    Parmesan cheese

¼ cup chopped onions
1 to 2 teaspoons Dijon
    mustard
½ teaspoon powdered
    oregano
1 egg, lightly beaten
Salt and freshly ground
    pepper to taste
1½ cups homemade tomato
    sauce (optional)

Preheat oven to 375 degrees. Spread sausage evenly on pie shell. Combine spinach, mushrooms, cheeses, onions, mustard, oregano and egg. Add salt and pepper. Spread evenly over sausage. Bake for 25 to 30 minutes or until set. Serve with warm tomato sauce if desired.

MAMA'S QUICHE

The classic quiche from Mama Sanchez's restaurant. It adapts to any filling.

Serves 6

1 egg
4 teaspoons all-purpose
    white flour
½ cup mayonnaise
½ cup milk
8 ounces Gruyère cheese,
    grated

8 ounces flaked fresh crab
    meat
1 tablespoon finely chopped
    green onion
1 prebaked 9-inch piecrust
    shell (see Index)

Preheat oven to 350 degrees. Beat egg with a wire whisk, blend in flour, and beat in mayonnaise. Add milk and blend well. Fold in cheese, crab, and onion. Fill pie shell and bake for 45 minutes or until toothpick inserted in center comes out clean.

VARIATIONS

Substitute cooked, chopped shrimp for half the crab and mix in 1 cup of frozen chopped spinach, thawed and well drained.

Substitute 12 pieces of bacon, cooked crisp and crumbled, for the crab.

Substitute 10 ounces Monterey Jack cheese for the Gruyère and add 1 4-ounce can diced green chili peppers.

ZUCCHINI QUICHE

Serves 6 to 8

1 prebaked 9-inch piecrust
  shell (see Index) with
  high fluted sides
⅔ cup freshly grated
  Gruyère cheese
2 eggs, lightly beaten
1 cup heavy cream

Salt and freshly ground
  pepper to taste
¼ teaspoon freshly grated
  nutmeg
1 pound zucchini, coarsely
  grated and thoroughly
  drained

Preheat oven to 350 degrees. On the bottom of the pie shell sprinkle half the cheese. Beat eggs, cream, and seasonings together, then add zucchini. Pour into the pie shell and sprinkle with remaining cheese. Bake for 30 minutes or until a toothpick inserted in center of custard comes out clean.

CHEESE SOUFFLÉ

Serves 3 to 4

Grated Parmesan cheese
2 tablespoons butter
2 tablespoons all-purpose
  white flour
¾ cup milk
Salt and cayenne to taste
4 egg yolks

1 cup grated cheese
  (Appenzeller, Gruyère,
  Camembert, or Brie)
Tabasco sauce
Dry mustard
5 egg whites

Heat oven to 400 degrees. Butter a 1-quart soufflé dish and dust with grated Parmesan cheese. Melt butter until foamy. Sprinkle with flour, cook, stirring, for 2 to 3 minutes. Gradually add milk and stir until sauce is smooth and thickened. Add salt and cayenne, lower heat, and beat in egg yolks one at a time. Add cheese, stir until melted, and season to taste with a little Tabasco and with dry mustard. Remove from heat and cool. Beat egg whites until stiff peaks form. Stir a large spoonful into soufflé base and then fold in remaining egg whites. Pour mixture into the prepared soufflé dish. Lower oven heat to 375 degrees and bake for 30 minutes.

CRAB SOUFFLÉ

Delicious, light, and elegant. Serve it for Sunday lunch with a green salad. It would be just as appropriate as a first course for a formal dinner. Considering that it uses only ¾ cup crab meat, it is not as expensive as it may seem, and it would easily serve 6 as a first course or 4 as a main luncheon dish.

Serves 4 to 6

Grated Parmesan cheese
2 tablespoons minced shallots
    or scallions
3 tablespoons butter
3 tablespoons flour
1 cup scalded milk
½ teaspoon salt
⅛ teaspoon freshly ground
    pepper

4 egg yolks
½ cup grated Swiss cheese
¾ cup flaked fresh crab
    meat
5 egg whites
Pinch of cream of tartar
⅛ teaspoon salt
Grated Parmesan cheese

Preheat oven to 400 degrees. Butter a 6-cup soufflé dish and dust with grated Parmesan cheese. Cook shallots in butter for several minutes. Stir in flour and cook for 2 minutes. Remove from heat. Gradually blend in milk, salt, and pepper. Cook, stirring, until thick and smooth. Remove from heat and cool slightly. Beat in egg yolks, one at a time. Add Swiss cheese and cook, stirring, until blended. Fold in crab meat. Cool. Beat egg whites until frothy. Add cream of tartar and ⅛ teaspoon salt. Beat until stiff peaks form. Gently fold into soufflé base. Pour the mixture into the prepared soufflé dish and sprinkle the top with grated Parmesan cheese. Place on the middle rack of the oven and immediately lower heat to 375 degrees. Bake for 30 to 35 minutes.

BREAKFAST SOUFFLÉ

Nice and easy brunch dish that can be prepared ahead and refrigerated. Perfect for a holiday—Christmas morning or New Year's Day.

Serves 8

8 slices bacon, diced
4 tablespoons butter
2 3-ounce packages chipped
    beef, coarsely shredded
½ pound fresh mushrooms,
    sliced and lightly
    sautéed in butter

½ cup all-purpose flour
¼ teaspoon pepper
1 quart milk
12 eggs, lightly beaten
¼ teaspoon salt
¾ cup milk or half-and-half
4 tablespoons butter, melted

Preheat oven to 350 degrees. Butter a 9-inch soufflé dish. Cook bacon and discard fat from skillet. Remove skillet from heat and add butter, chipped beef, and ¾ of the mushrooms. Mix well and sprinkle with flour and pepper. Gradually stir in milk, cook, stirring, until mixture is thickened and smooth. Cover and set aside. Combine eggs, salt, and ¾ cup milk. Cook in butter until softly scrambled; do not overcook or eggs will be dry. In the prepared soufflé dish, layer eggs and sauce twice, ending with sauce. Garnish with remaining mushrooms and bake for 15 to 20 minutes.

MEXICAN CORN BREAD SOUFFLÉ

Serves 6 to 8

1 cup creamed corn
2 eggs, beaten
⅓ cup corn oil
¾ cup milk
1 cup cornmeal
½ teaspoon salt

½ teaspoon baking soda
1 4-ounce can green chilies,
    seeded and diced
1½ cups grated sharp
    Cheddar cheese

Preheat oven to 375 degrees. Combine corn, eggs, oil, and milk. Mix cornmeal, salt, and soda together and add to milk mixture, blending well. Pour half the batter into a 1-quart casserole, spread the chilies on top, and sprinkle with half the cheese. Pour remaining batter over and sprinkle with remaining cheese. Bake for 40 to 45 minutes.

CHEESE PUDDING

Since it must be done the day before, this is a convenient brunch or luncheon main course. Add any meat or seafood to make it heartier.

Serves 6 to 8

16 slices day-old white bread
1 pound sharp Cheddar
   cheese, grated
6 eggs
3 cups milk
1 teaspoon salt

1 teaspoon dry mustard
¼ teaspoon paprika
½ teaspoon Worcestershire
   sauce
¼ pound butter, melted

Butter a 2-quart casserole or soufflé dish. Remove crusts from bread and cut into ½-inch cubes. Divide cheese and bread each into 3 portions. Layer the casserole with ⅓ of the bread, then ⅓ of cheese, then repeat twice. Beat eggs with milk, and add all seasonings. Slowly pour this mixture over bread and cheese, and then pour melted butter over top. Cover casserole and refrigerate *overnight*. Remove from refrigerator 45 minutes before baking. Preheat oven to 350 degrees. Place in a pan of water and bake, uncovered, for 1 hour and 15 minutes. Pudding should puff like a soufflé and brown on top.

FONDUE SANDWICHES

This is an easy and delicious family supper dish. It also is a good dish with a green salad served for a luncheon meeting.

Serves 6

¼ cup butter, softened
1 tablespoon Dijon mustard
12 ½-inch-thick slices of
good quality bread
Very sharp Cheddar cheese,
in slices ¼-inch thick
4 eggs
2½ cups milk

1 tablespoon chopped fresh
chives
1 tablespoon chopped fresh
parsley
2 tablespoons chopped fresh
basil
¼ teaspoon salt
⅛ teaspoon white pepper

Combine butter with mustard and spread on bread slices. Make sandwiches using the slices of Cheddar cheese. Trim crusts and fit the 6 sandwiches into a large baking dish. Beat eggs into milk, and add chives, parsley, basil, salt, and pepper. Pour over sandwiches, and let stand for 2 hours or overnight in the refrigerator. Preheat oven to 350 degrees. Bake, uncovered, for 1 hour.

RYE CHEESE SANDWICH

These are delicious made on small pieces of bread as hors d'oeuvres or on large slices of bread as an accompaniment to soup and hearty salad for a luncheon. Try them in any shape.

Serves 4 as a luncheon dish, 8 as hors d'oeuvres

1 cup grated Cheddar cheese
2 tablespoons minced green
onions
1 small can chopped black
olives

½ cup mayonnaise
1 teaspoon Dijon mustard
2 teaspoons curry powder or
to taste
Rye bread, thinly sliced

Combine first 6 ingredients. Leave rye bread slices whole for a luncheon dish or cut them into rounds for hors d'oeuvres. Toast on one side. Turn over immediately after removing from toasting pan. Cover untoasted sides with spread and broil until bubbly.

CHAPTER VII

PASTA & RICE

North Beach

North Beach is so named because in San Francisco's infancy an inlet and broad beach actually existed between Russian Hill and Telegraph Hill. The original beach was obliterated by landfill a great many years ago, but the name remains.

Although the boundaries of this colorful neighborhood, often referred to as Little Italy, overlap those of Chinatown and the two hills that border it, North Beach landmarks are among the city's most distinctive. Recognized the world over is Coit Tower, standing silent sentry over the Bay atop Telegraph Hill. It was erected as a memorial to the city's volunteer firemen through the bequest of Lillie Coit, who was "mascot" to Engine Company Number 5. This hill has always been prominent in the life of the city and was originally a look-out point for arriving ships. Down in the heart of the neighborhood the twin spires of Sts. Peter and Paul Church rise protectively over Washington Square—a place for sun, quiet reflection, or perhaps a little bocce ball.

With signs of its colorful past still evident in the coffeehouses and bookstores, the bawdy night spots and tempting delicatessens, North Beach is sought out by tourists and locals alike for its many fine Italian restaurants where a wide variety of regional specialties are available from *fettuccine al pesto* to *risotto milanese* to *cannelloni alla napoletana*. San Franciscans are drawn to this neighborhood seeking fresh pasta and inspiration for their kitchens. Salamis, hanging in delicatessen windows, and the smell of espresso coffee drifting past cafe curtains are indelible and delectable reminders of the Italian influence on San Francisco's cuisine.

SUPERB SPAGHETTI SAUCE

Makes approximately 6 cups

1 pound ground beef
4 cloves garlic, minced
2 tablespoons olive oil
2 large carrots, coarsely
    chopped
3 medium onions, coarsely
    chopped
10 cups tomato juice or
    mixed vegetable juice
6 tablespoons tomato paste

2 1-pound cans whole
    tomatoes
4 tablespoons chopped
    parsley
1½ teaspoons oregano
1½ teaspoons dried basil
2 bay leaves
2 tablespoons butter
1 teaspoon chili powder

Sauté the ground beef and garlic in the olive oil in a skillet until brown. Remove to a large heavy kettle. Sauté the carrots and onions in the same skillet, adding a little more olive oil if necessary, over very low heat for 30 minutes. Add the vegetables to the kettle. Then add all the remaining ingredients and cook very slowly over low heat for 6 hours, stirring occasionally.

ARTICHOKE SAUCE FOR PASTA

This is good over spaghetti and is pretty as a side dish. Equally lovely as a sauce over veal chops. To purée or not to purée is up to the cook.

Serves 6

2 tablespoons vegetable oil
1 small onion, finely
    chopped
1 clove garlic, minced
1 package frozen artichoke
    hearts, thawed and
    chopped
3 medium tomatoes, peeled
    and chopped

1 tablespoon chopped fresh
    parsley
1 teaspoon sweet basil
Salt and freshly ground
    pepper to taste
Parmesan cheese, freshly
    grated

Heat oil in a heavy skillet and cook onion and garlic until transparent. Add artichoke hearts, tomatoes, parsley, basil, salt, and pepper. Cook slowly, stirring occasionally, for about 1 hour or until thickened. Serve over pasta or brown rice. Sprinkle with Parmesan cheese.

COUNTRY GARDEN PASTA SAUCE

Makes approximately 2 quarts

2 cups chopped onions
½ to ¾ cup butter
2 green peppers, seeded and
 chopped
3 large celery stalks,
 chopped
2 cloves garlic, minced
½ pound fresh mushrooms,
 sliced
2 medium zucchini, chopped
12 large fresh tomatoes,
 peeled and chopped, or
 2 28-ounce cans whole
 tomatoes, chopped and
 not drained

1 12-ounce can tomato paste
1 tablespoon chopped fresh
 basil, or 1 teaspoon
 dried basil
½ teaspoon thyme
1 tablespoon chopped fresh
 oregano, or 1 teaspoon
 dried oregano
1 bay leaf
2 teaspoons salt or to taste
Freshly ground pepper to
 taste

Sauté onions in 4 tablespoons of the butter for 2 minutes. Add peppers, celery, and garlic, and cook until onions are translucent. Place in a 4- to 6-quart heavy skillet. Add 2 tablespoons of butter to the skillet and add the mushrooms. Sauté over medium high heat for 2 to 3 minutes until they have absorbed the butter. Add to the onion mixture. Put the remaining butter into the skillet and add the zucchini. Brown for several minutes and add to the onion mixture. Add the tomatoes, tomato paste, herbs, salt, and pepper. Simmer for 45 minutes to 1 hour. Adjust seasonings. Do not boil.

PESTO SAUCE

Makes about 2 cups

2 cups fresh basil leaves,
  firmly packed (about 4
  bunches of basil)
1 tablespoon minced garlic
  or to taste (about 3
  cloves)
½ cup pine nuts

1 cup parsley (optional)
½ cup freshly grated
  Parmesan cheese
½ teaspoon salt
½ teaspoon pepper
½ to 1 cup olive oil

Purée all ingredients in a blender or food processor. If a food processor is used, as little oil as possible should be used, no more than ½ cup. Put sauce in jars, pour a light film of oil on top, and cover with lids. Leave a small space between the top of the oil and the lids if the jars are to be frozen. Refrigerate up to 2 months, or freeze up to 1 year. Serve with lightly buttered, freshly cooked pasta; or spread on broiled meats or chicken; or add to soups for extra flavor; or use as a seasoning for salad dressing or combine a little with mayonnaise for a vegetable dip; or serve over steamed fresh vegetables or new potatoes.

FETTUCCINE AL PESTO

Serves 8 to 10

1 cup chopped parsley,
  firmly packed
½ cup olive oil
½ cup cream
¼ pound butter, soft
3 or 4 cloves garlic, mashed
1 teaspoon or more salt
½ teaspoon freshly ground
  pepper

1 cup freshly grated
  Parmesan cheese
1 cup chopped fresh basil
  leaves, firmly packed
½ cup pine nuts or chopped
  walnuts
2 tablespoons boiling water
2 pounds fettuccine, cooked

Place all ingredients except fettuccine in a saucepan, adding the water last, and simmer for 10 minutes, stirring frequently. Keep sauce warm. Cook the fettuccine according to directions on the package, drain. Toss the sauce lightly with fettuccine and serve immediately.

WALNUT PESTO

Makes approximately 2 cups

½ cup shelled walnuts
¼ cup pine nuts
3 tablespoons olive oil
½ cup ricotta cheese

Dash of nutmeg
Salt and freshly ground
    pepper to taste
½ cup heavy cream

In a wooden bowl or food processor mash walnuts and pine nuts until they have a grainy consistency. Add all remaining ingredients except cream and mix thoroughly. (Sauce may be prepared ahead of time to this point.) Add cream just before serving. Serve over fettuccine, ravioli, or cappelletti.

FISHERMAN'S SPAGHETTI

Serves 4

4 tablespoons butter
½ cup finely chopped
    onions
8 mushrooms, sliced
½ pound flaked crab meat
¼ pound small shrimp
1 teaspoon dried oregano
2 tablespoons brandy
½ cup white wine
1 cup light cream

Salt and freshly ground
    pepper to taste
Dash of Angostura bitters
1 pound spaghetti, cooked
2 egg yolks
½ cup freshly grated
    Romano cheese
¼ cup freshly grated
    Parmesan cheese
Dash of nutmeg

Melt butter in a skillet and add onions, sauté until soft. Add mushrooms and sauté for several minutes longer. Stir in the crab and shrimp. Add the oregano, brandy, and wine. Reduce heat and slowly add cream, salt and pepper, and bitters. (May be prepared ahead to this point.) Cook spaghetti according to directions on the package, drain well, keep hot. Just before serving, beat the egg yolks with a small amount of the sauce, and add this to the skillet. Reheat if necessary but do not allow the sauce to boil. Add a dash of nutmeg. Serve over hot spaghetti.

CALAMARI SAUCE FOR PASTA

Serves 10 to 12

2 medium onions, chopped
5 tablespoons olive oil
2 cloves garlic, crushed
3 cups white wine
1 cup canned plum tomatoes,
    puréed with the juice
½ cup chopped fresh
    parsley

1 teaspoon oregano
Salt and freshly ground
    pepper to taste
4 pounds small calamari,
    cleaned and sliced
    crosswise into rings
1 pound mushrooms, sliced

In a heavy skillet sauté onions in olive oil until golden. Add the garlic and wine and boil for 3 minutes to let the alcohol evaporate. Add tomato purée, parsley, oregano, salt, and pepper. Add calamari, cover, and cook over medium heat for about 45 minutes, stirring frequently. Add the mushrooms about 5 minutes before serving. Serve over freshly cooked pasta.

SPAGHETTI CARBONARA

Good late evening or after-theater supper.

Serves 2

½ pound vermicelli
½ pound fresh mushrooms,
    sliced
¼ cup olive oil
2 tablespoons butter
1 cup diced Canadian bacon

1 cup diced ham steak
6 tablespoons freshly grated
    Parmesan cheese
2 eggs, well beaten
Additional grated Parmesan
    cheese

Cook spaghetti according to directions on the package, drain well, and keep hot. Sauté mushrooms in oil and butter until starting to turn golden. Add Canadian bacon and ham. Heat but do not brown. Remove from heat and stir in cheese and eggs. Combine quickly with hot spaghetti and serve immediately with extra Parmesan cheese.

MANICOTTI WITH TOMATO SAUCE

Serves 4

STUFFING

½ pound ground beef
1 clove garlic, minced
¼ cup olive oil
1 cup ricotta cheese
4 ounces mozzarella cheese,
    grated

1 egg, lightly beaten
½ teaspoon salt
½ teaspoon dried oregano,
    crumbled

Brown beef and garlic in olive oil. Drain off any fat and place the beef and garlic in a bowl. Stir in ricotta and mozzarella cheeses, beaten egg, salt, and oregano. Set aside. Prepare the tomato sauce:

TOMATO SAUCE

½ cup chopped onions
½ cup chopped green
    pepper
2 cloves garlic, minced
½ cup olive oil
1 2-pound can whole
    tomatoes
1 cup tomato purée

1 teaspoon salt
1 teaspoon sugar
½ teaspoon dried oregano,
    crumbled
½ teaspoon dried basil,
    crumbled
½ pound mushrooms, sliced

Sauté onions, green pepper, and garlic in olive oil until onions are transparent. Add remaining ingredients, mix well, and simmer for at least 1 hour, the longer the better. Adjust seasonings.

8 manicotti
Freshly grated Parmesan cheese

Preheat oven to 350 degrees. Cook manicotti in boiling salted water for 8 to 10 minutes or until *al dente* (cooked through but still firm). Drain them and allow to cool. Fill them with stuffing and place in a buttered shallow baking dish. Cover with sauce. Sprinkle generously with Parmesan cheese, cover with foil, and bake for 15 minutes. Remove foil and bake for another 10 minutes until heated through and bubbly.

CANNELLONI

Making your own pasta is fun, but it does require experience or a pasta machine to roll it out evenly. Cannelloni can be bought in many markets and cooked according to directions on the package, then stuffed.

Serves 6

PASTA
1½ cups flour
2 eggs
Olive oil

Mix the flour with the eggs and a little olive oil. Roll out to the number 3 setting on the pasta machine and cut into rectangles 3 by 4 inches with a sharp knife. Allow pasta to firm up for a few minutes and then cook each piece in boiling salted water until *al dente* (cooked through but still firm). Plunge the pasta into cold water to stop the cooking. Drain thoroughly and dry on paper towels. Use immediately or stack in the refrigerator or freezer.

FILLING

2 10-ounce packages frozen
    spinach, thawed, or 2
    pounds fresh spinach
2 tablespoons finely chopped
    onions
4 tablespoons butter
4 tablespoons chopped
    prosciutto or mortadella

1 cup ricotta cheese
1 cup freshly grated
    Parmesan cheese
¼ teaspoon freshly grated
    nutmeg
1 egg yolk

Bring a large pot of salted water to a boil and plunge in the spinach. Cook for 5 minutes. Drain, squeeze lightly to remove moisture, and chop. In a large skillet, sauté the onions in the butter for 5 minutes. Add the chopped prosciutto and the spinach. Sauté for 2 or 3 minutes more. Put the skillet contents in a mixing bowl and add the cheeses, nutmeg, and egg yolk. Mix thoroughly.

BÉCHAMEL SAUCE
6 tablespoons butter
5 tablespoons flour
2½ to 3 cups light cream

Melt the butter in a heavy saucepan. Stir in the flour gradually and cook for 2 minutes without browning the flour. Add 2½ to 3 cups light cream and cook until the sauce has a consistency of very thick cream.

TOMATO SAUCE

| 1 2-pound can peeled tomatoes, chopped | ½ teaspoon freshly ground pepper |
| ½ teaspoon salt | ½ teaspoon sugar |

Place all ingredients in a heavy saucepan and simmer gently for about 1 hour. Put through a sieve or food mill to remove the seeds.

FINAL PREPARATION

Preheat oven to 350 degrees. Butter a rectangular baking dish. Lay a pasta strip flat and spread a tablespoon of filling on it, covering the whole strip except a ½-inch border. Roll the strip up on its narrow side and place it in the baking dish, seam side down. Proceed until you have made 12 cannelloni. Dot with butter, cover with foil, and bake for 15 minutes. Let the cannelloni rest for 10 minutes before serving. To serve: place 2 cannelloni on each plate. Spoon some béchamel sauce over the cannelloni and place 2 tablespoons of tomato sauce on top of the béchamel. Serve immediately.

PASTA WITH YOGURT SAUCE

Serves 4

8 ounces green noodles
2 8-ounce cartons plain
   yogurt at room
   temperature
1 cup small curd cottage
   cheese at room
   temperature
½ cup coarsely chopped
   green onion

½ to 1 clove garlic, minced
2 tablespoons fresh dillweed
1 teaspoon salt
1 tablespoon minced fresh
   oregano, or 1 teaspoon
   dried
2 tablespoons butter

Cook noodles according to directions on package, drain, and keep hot. Combine yogurt, cottage cheese, onion, garlic, and seasonings. Purée in a blender or food processor. Heat slightly. Toss noodles with butter and then with yogurt-cheese mixture. Serve immediately.

GREEN NOODLE CASSEROLE

Serves 4

1 8-ounce package green or
   spinach noodles
1 pound shelled and
   deveined cooked
   shrimp, or crab meat, or
   diced cooked chicken
1 bunch green onions,
   chopped

¼ cup diced green pepper
¾ cup mayonnaise
¾ cup sour cream
¼ teaspoon Worcestershire
   sauce
1 cup grated sharp Cheddar
   cheese

Preheat oven to 350 degrees. Butter a 2-quart casserole and set aside. Cook noodles in salted boiling water until just barely *al dente* (cooked through but still firm). Drain thoroughly and place in the bottom of the prepared casserole. Place shrimp, onions, and green pepper on top. Combine mayonnaise, sour cream, and Worcestershire sauce. Pour over shrimp and noodles, and sprinkle top with grated cheese. Bake for 30 minutes.

MIXED NOODLES

Excellent contrast of textures in this casserole.

Serves 6 to 8

1 8-ounce package fine
   noodles
5 tablespoons sweet butter
¼ cup light cream
¼ cup grated Swiss cheese

Salt to taste
Freshly cracked black
   pepper to taste
1 cup uncooked fine noodles

Cook the 8-ounce package of noodles in boiling salted water according to package directions. Drain but do not wash. Place in a warm serving dish and add 2 tablespoons of the butter, the light cream, grated cheese, and seasonings. Keep in a warm oven. Fry the remaining uncooked noodles in 3 tablespoons butter until lightly browned. Toss with hot cooked noodles and serve immediately.

NOODLES BASILICO

Colorful noodles to go with any main dish of chicken, beef, lamb.

Serves 6

1 12-ounce package egg
   noodles
1 8-ounce package cream
   cheese
1 small can chopped black
   olives, drained
¼ cup butter

1½ teaspoons dried basil
   (basilico) or ½ cup
   loosely packed chopped
   fresh basil
Salt and freshly ground
   pepper to taste

Preheat oven to 325 degrees. Cook noodles according to directions on the package. Drain and keep hot. Soften cream cheese and stir in olives. Stir cream cheese mixture into hot noodles, continuing to stir until cheese has completely melted. Melt butter, add basil, salt, and pepper. Stir into noodles. Place in a 2-quart casserole and bake for 20 to 30 minutes.

SOUBRETTE

Serves 6

8 ounces lasagne noodles
¼ cup chopped onions
2 tablespoons butter
1 10-ounce package frozen
    chopped spinach
1 pound Monterey Jack
    cheese, grated

3 cups small curd cottage
    cheese
2 eggs, beaten
Butter as needed
⅓ cup grated Cheddar
    cheese
Paprika

Preheat oven to 350 degrees. Cook noodles according to directions on package and set aside. Sauté onions in butter until transparent. Set aside. Cook spinach until thawed, then drain and squeeze dry. Add onions and set aside. Combine Monterey Jack cheese, cottage cheese, and eggs. Divide cheese mixture into 2 equal parts and place in 2 bowls. Add spinach mixture to one bowl, blending well. Arrange a layer of noodles in a well-buttered shallow baking dish. Cover with the cheese-spinach mixture and dot with butter. Place another layer of noodles on top and cover with the plain cheese mixture. Sprinkle with Cheddar cheese and sprinkle with a little paprika. Bake for 30 minutes or until bubbly and cooked through.

NOODLE LOAF

Serves 5 to 6

1 6-ounce package of
    noodles
1 cup fine bread crumbs
2 eggs, beaten
1 teaspoon salt
2 tablespoons chopped green
    pepper
⅔ cup grated Cheddar
    cheese

1 1-pound can tomatoes
¼ cup butter, melted
1½ teaspoons prepared
    mustard
⅛ teaspoon white pepper
Mushroom Sauce (given
    below)

Preheat oven to 350 degrees. Cook noodles in boiling salted water according to package directions. Drain. In a large bowl combine bread crumbs, eggs, salt, green pepper, cheese, tomatoes, butter, mustard, and white pepper. Gently stir in the noodles, then transfer to a buttered 1½-quart loaf pan or ring mold. Bake for 35 minutes. Unmold onto a warm platter and serve with Mushroom Sauce.

Mushroom Sauce

½ pound mushrooms, sliced   1 cup milk
3 tablespoons butter   Salt to taste
2 tablespoons flour

Sauté mushrooms until soft in 1 tablespoon of the butter. Set aside. Melt the remaining butter in a saucepan. Add flour and gradually stir in milk. Continue stirring until sauce is thick and smooth. Add mushrooms, season with salt, and serve over noodle loaf.

BRAZILIAN RICE

The orange peel and nuts really add to this dish. It is a good accompaniment to any meat or poultry main course.

Serves 10

3 cups water   1 teaspoon brown sugar
2 cups raw brown rice   1 teaspoon very finely grated
1 teaspoon salt   fresh orange rind
3 tablespoons butter   1 cup sliced Brazil nuts
1 teaspoon chili powder   1 small can chopped black
⅛ teaspoon garlic powder   olives, drained

Boil the water. Add rice, salt, butter, chili powder, garlic powder, brown sugar, and *finely* grated orange rind. Stir briefly, cover, lower heat, and cook for 30 to 40 minutes or until moisture is absorbed and rice is tender. Stir in nuts and black olives. Cover and let stand for several minutes over very low heat.

SPICED RICE

This is colorful and tasty and the perfect accompaniment for a leg of lamb, roast ham or pork. Good rice goes with everything, and this is no exception.

Serves 6

1 cup uncooked rice
2 cups boiling salted water
1 1-inch piece of fresh
    ginger, peeled
¼ cup seedless raisins
¼ cup currants
2 ounces dried apricots,
    chopped

Freshly ground pepper to
    taste
½ teaspoon ground nutmeg
2 teaspoons minced shallots
1 tablespoon lemon juice
½ teaspoon coriander
1 tablespoon olive oil
½ cup toasted pine nuts

Cook rice with peeled ginger, in boiling salted water, until done, about 25 minutes. While rice is cooking, soak the raisins, currants, and chopped apricots in hot water to cover, then drain when plump. When rice is ready, remove ginger and place rice in a warm serving casserole. To the rice in the casserole, add pepper, nutmeg, shallots, lemon juice, coriander, and olive oil. Gently fold in the plumped raisins, currants, and apricots. Keep warm until ready to serve. Just before serving, sprinkle with pine nuts.

GRANADA RICE

Serves 4 to 6

4 tablespoons butter or
    margarine
⅓ cup chopped blanched
    filberts
⅓ cup finely chopped onions
1 cup raw white rice
2 cups chicken or veal stock

1½ cups grated Gruyère
    cheese
¼ cup chopped
    pimiento-stuffed green
    olives
Whole pimiento-stuffed
    green olives

Melt 2 tablespoons of the butter in a heavy saucepan. Add filberts and sauté until lightly browned. Remove filberts with a slotted spoon and set aside. Add remaining butter, chopped onions, and rice to saucepan. Sauté, stirring occasionally, until rice is opaque and starting to turn golden. Add stock, stir, and bring to a boil. Cover tightly, reduce heat to low, and cook for 12 to 15 minutes or until liquid is absorbed and rice is tender. Just before serving, mix in reserved filberts, cheese, and chopped olives. Garnish with whole stuffed olives and serve with baked chicken or roast game hens.

FRIED RICE

Serves 6

4 cups cooked long grain
    white rice, cold
2 tablespoons corn oil or
    peanut oil
Chicken stock if needed
2 tablespoons soy sauce
½ teaspoon salt
½ teaspoon sugar
1 teaspoon dry sherry

2 eggs, beaten
1 cup diced barbecued pork
1 cup frozen peas, thawed
2 to 3 dried Chinese
    mushrooms, soaked to
    soften and diced
¼ cup minced green onions
    or chopped Chinese
    parsley

Stir the rice gently with a 2-pronged fork to separate the grains. Heat oil, add rice, and stir gently to heat through, adding up to 3 tablespoons chicken stock if rice seems too dry. Add soy sauce, salt, sugar, and sherry, mixing well. Make a well in center and add eggs. Cook until eggs begin to set, and then blend into rice. Toss in pork, peas, and mushrooms. Heat through, garnish with green onions or Chinese parsley, and serve.

BROWN RICE STUFFING

An unusual and tasty stuffing for any poultry. The reserved juice from the raisins makes a delicious basting sauce.

Makes approximately 6 cups

1½ cups golden raisins
¾ cup cognac or Bourbon
½ pound butter
1 small onion, chopped

½ teaspoon salt
4½ cups cooked brown rice
¾ cup pine nuts

Plump raisins in cognac or Bourbon. Drain and reserve juices. Sauté raisins briefly in butter, add onion, and sauté until onion is transparent. Remove from heat, add salt, and combine with rice and pine nuts.

SPINACH-WILD RICE CASSEROLE

Serves 6

1 package mixed white and
    wild rice
1 10-ounce can beef stock
2 10-ounce packages frozen
    chopped spinach
8 ounces cream cheese,
    softened

Salt to taste
1 pound mushrooms, thinly
    sliced
2 to 3 tablespoons butter

Preheat oven to 350 degrees. Butter a 2-quart casserole. Set aside. Cook rice as directed on package, substituting the beef stock for an equivalent amount of water. Cook spinach, covered, until tender; drain well and combine with cream cheese. Add salt. Sauté mushrooms in butter until just golden. In the prepared casserole, layer half the rice, half the spinach, and half the mushrooms. Repeat layers. Cover and bake for 40 minutes.

CHILI RICE CASSEROLE

Serves 6

3 cups cooked long grain
    white rice
Salt and freshly ground
    pepper to taste
3 cups sour cream
1 teaspoon salt

1 7-ounce can diced green
    chilies
¾ pound Monterey Jack
    cheese, cut in strips
½ cup grated Cheddar
    cheese

Preheat oven to 350 degrees. Butter a 1½-quart casserole. Season rice with salt and pepper. Combine sour cream, salt, and chilies. In the prepared casserole, place a layer of rice, cover with a layer of the sour cream mixture, and top with strips of Monterey Jack cheese. Repeat, making 2 or 3 layers and ending with rice on top. Bake for 40 to 45 minutes or until heated through. Sprinkle with grated Cheddar cheese and return to oven until cheese is melted.

CONFETTI RICE

A colorful and good rice casserole.

Serves 6

½ cup chopped onions
½ cup diced green pepper
6 tablespoons butter
10 medium-size mushrooms,
    sliced
3 cups cooked rice
½ teaspoon salt

¼ teaspoon pepper
½ teaspoon *fines herbes*
2 tablespoons finely chopped
    fresh parsley
2 tablespoons chopped
    pimiento

Preheat oven to 350 degrees. Lightly butter a 1½-quart baking dish. Sauté onions and green pepper in butter until almost tender. Add mushrooms and cook until mushrooms are just tender. Combine with remaining ingredients, adjust seasonings, and put in prepared baking dish. Cover and bake for 30 minutes or until heated through.

LEMON DILL RICE

A very tasty and different rice dish. For added flavor and color, garnish top with grated lemon rind and minced parsley.

Serves 6 to 8

1 large onion, minced
2 cups long grain white rice
3 tablespoons butter
4 cups water

2 tablespoons salt
2 tablespoons dill seed
¼ cup fresh lemon juice or
   to taste

Preheat oven to 325 degrees. Brown onion and rice in butter in a heavy skillet. Add water, seasonings, and lemon juice. Bring to a boil, then transfer to a 3-quart casserole. Bake for 1 hour.

BARLEY AND PINE NUT CASSEROLE

A very good and interesting substitute for rice. The whole family will love it.

Serves 6

1 cup pearl barley
¼ to ½ cup pine nuts (or
   almonds)
3 tablespoons butter
1 medium onion, chopped
½ cup minced parsley
¼ cup minced chives (or
   green onions)

¼ teaspoon salt
¼ teaspoon freshly ground
   pepper
3 cups chicken or beef stock,
   heated to boiling
Chopped parsley for garnish

Preheat oven to 375 degrees. Rinse and drain barley. Toast pine nuts in 1 tablespoon of the butter in a skillet. Remove nuts with a slotted spoon and set aside. Add remaining 2 tablespoons of butter to the skillet, and add onion and barley, stirring until barley is toasted. Stir in nuts, parsley, chives, salt, and pepper. Spoon into a 1½-quart casserole. Pour hot stock over casserole, and mix well. Bake, uncovered, for 1 hour and 15 minutes. Garnish with chopped parsley.

RICE SOUFFLÉ

A surprising way to serve rice, and a delicate accompaniment to roast beef.

Serves 6

4 tablespoons butter
3 tablespoons all-purpose
  white flour
1 cup milk
1 teaspoon salt
¼ teaspoon Worcestershire
  sauce

⅛ teaspoon white pepper
1 cup cooked rice
4 eggs, separated
2 tablespoons freshly grated
  Parmesan cheese

Preheat oven to 350 degrees. In a heavy 2-quart saucepan melt the butter until bubbly, sprinkle with flour, and cook and stir for 3 minutes. Gradually add milk, stirring constantly until smooth and thickened. Remove from heat, and add seasonings, rice, and beaten egg yolks. Beat egg whites until stiff. Fold 2 tablespoons into rice mixture to lighten it, then fold in the remaining egg whites. Put mixture in a 2-quart casserole or soufflé dish and sprinkle with Parmesan cheese. Bake for approximately 45 minutes or until toothpick inserted in center comes out clean.

GRITS SOUFFLÉ

Delicious with ham steak, roast chicken, or roast anything. No one ever knows it is grits, and it is infallible.

Serves 6

¾ cup instant grits
¾ cup milk
¾ cup water
½ teaspoon salt

½ cup butter
6 ounces Cheddar cheese,
  grated
3 eggs, lightly beaten

Preheat oven to 350 degrees. Place the grits, milk, water, and salt in the top of a double boiler. Cook, stirring occasionally, until moisture is absorbed. Place butter and grated cheese in a 1-quart soufflé dish and add cooked grits, blending until cheese and butter are melted. Cool slightly, and beat in eggs. Bake for 30 to 40 minutes or until the top is slightly browned.

CHAPTER VIII

VEGETABLES

Mission District

It is a city within a city; home to most of the Spanish-speaking citizens of San Francisco, although not theirs exclusively by any means; rich with history, fraught with traditions and famous for San Francisco's oldest building, Mission Dolores, which gives the neighborhood its name. This church with whitewashed adobe walls four feet thick, glorious in its simplicity, was almost completely rebuilt in 1782, replacing the original, which was erected in 1776 to honor St. Francis of Assisi. The adjacent cemetery contains a veritable history of early San Francisco.

Of all the city's neighborhoods, the Mission boasts the best weather, and historically it has been the funnel through which produce has flowed into the city. It was the Mission that supplied food for the early Presidio, as anything planted there flourished in the warm sunshine. Because of California's ideal climate, artichokes grow year round in fields near Monterey Bay. Avocados, first brought to the San Francisco Bay Area by Spanish missionaries from Mexico, abound; onions and garlic are grown where days are warm and fog is cool. Pumpkins and squash, carrots and broccoli, lettuce and tomatoes, and herbs of every description sprout colorfully.

Stroll through the bustling Farmers' Market in the Mission District and you can see this bounteous supply, a lavish display of nature's harvest.

ARTICHOKES JAMBON

Serves 8 to 10

2 dozen fresh small
   artichokes
Juice and rind of 2 lemons
2 eggs, beaten
1½ cups fine bread crumbs
Olive oil and butter as
   needed
¼ cup olive oil
2 tablespoons all-purpose
   flour

2 cups water
½ cup dry white wine
1 chicken bouillon cube
Salt and freshly ground
   pepper to taste
Thin strips of cooked ham
   for garnish

Preheat oven to 400 degrees. Trim artichokes down to tender hearts. Cook in boiling salted water, to which lemon juice and rind have been added, until just tender. Halve lengthwise and remove any chokes. Dip halves in beaten egg and coat with bread crumbs. Brown lightly in oil-butter mixture and arrange in shallow baking dish. Heat ¼ cup olive oil, stir in flour, gradually add 2 cups water, wine, and bouillon cube. Cook and stir until bouillon cube is dissolved and sauce thickened. Season with salt and pepper. Pour sauce over artichokes and garnish with strips of ham. Bake for 15 minutes.

ARTICHOKE MEDLEY

Serves 6 to 8

1 10-ounce package frozen
   artichoke bottoms
1 cup diagonally sliced
   celery
4 tablespoons butter
½ pound mushrooms, sliced

2½ tablespoons chopped
   fresh chives
½ cup sliced water chestnuts
   or toasted slivered
   almonds (optional)
Salt to taste

Cook artichoke bottoms in salted water until just tender. Drain, slice each in half and set aside. Sauté celery in butter until just tender. Add mushrooms and cook and stir until mushrooms are just tender. Blend in reserved artichokes, chives, and optional water chestnuts or almonds. Season with salt. Heat thoroughly but do not overcook. Serve immediately.

ARTICHOKE RING

This is really delicious and lovely and is a very impressive vegetable course for dinner. When it is unmolded on the platter, its center can be filled with parsley or any vegetable.

Serves 6

¼ pound prosciutto, sliced
2 10-ounce packages frozen
artichoke hearts,
thawed and drained
1 to 1½ tablespoons butter
1 medium onion, finely
chopped
1 clove garlic, chopped

4 eggs
1 cup heavy cream
½ cup freshly grated
Parmesan cheese
Salt and freshly ground
pepper to taste
¼ teaspoon nutmeg

Preheat oven to 350 degrees. Oil a 4-cup ring mold and line with prosciutto slices. Leave 2 to 3 inches of prosciutto hanging over the edges of the mold for enclosing later. Chop artichokes finely in a blender or food processor. In a skillet melt butter and sauté onion and garlic until soft. Set aside. In a large bowl beat eggs lightly and add cream, cheese, onion-garlic mixture and seasonings. Stir in artichokes and pour mixture carefully into the prosciutto-lined mold. Cover top with overhanging prosciutto. Place in a pan of hot water in the oven and bake for 25 to 30 minutes or until a knife inserted in the center comes out clean.

ASPARAGUS WRAPPED IN PROSCIUTTO

An easy, attractive first course.

Serves 6

24 to 36 fresh asparagus
    stalks, trimmed
6 slices prosciutto
½ cup freshly grated
    Parmesan cheese

½ cup melted butter
Freshly ground pepper to
    taste

Preheat oven to 350 degrees. Steam asparagus for 5 minutes or until just tender. Wrap 4 to 6 stalks in a slice of prosciutto, and repeat to make a total of 6 bundles. Place them in a buttered shallow baking dish and sprinkle evenly with cheese. Drizzle butter over all and sprinkle with pepper. Bake for 8 to 10 minutes or until bundles are heated through and cheese is melted. If making them ahead, cover and chill. Bring to room temperature before baking.

STIR-FRIED ASPARAGUS

Serves 6

1½ pounds asparagus
½ cup chicken stock
1 teaspoon salt
2 tablespoons soy sauce

1 teaspoon sugar
1 tablespoon peanut oil
1 tablespoon cornstarch
    (optional)

After trimming the asparagus, cut them on the diagonal in sections about 1 inch long. Parboil in boiling water for 2 to 4 minutes. Cool under cold water and drain well. In a skillet or wok combine chicken stock, salt, soy sauce, sugar and peanut oil. Stir-fry the asparagus in this mixture for 1 minute, adding cornstarch for thickening if desired.

HERBED GREEN BEANS

Serves 4

1 pound fresh green beans
4 tablespoons butter
½ cup minced onion
½ clove garlic, minced
¼ cup minced celery
½ cup minced parsley

1 teaspoon fresh rosemary or
  ¼ teaspoon dried
  rosemary
¼ teaspoon dried basil
¾ teaspoon salt

Trim ends from beans, then cut them diagonally into 2-inch pieces. Cook in 2 inches of boiling water in a covered pan for 15 to 20 minutes or until tender. Drain and keep warm. In the meantime, in a skillet melt butter and sauté onion, garlic, and celery and cook for about 5 minutes. Add parsley, rosemary, basil, and salt, cover, and simmer for 10 minutes. Just before serving, toss the green beans with the herb-flavored butter.

CURRIED KIDNEY BEANS

Serves 12

¼ pound butter
2 medium onions, chopped
2 green peppers, chopped
2 tart apples, chopped
2 teaspoons curry powder or
  to taste
2 28-ounce cans tomatoes
4 15-ounce cans kidney
  beans, drained

2 cups brown sugar
2 tablespoons white vinegar
Salt and freshly ground
  pepper to taste
Freshly grated Parmesan
  cheese

Preheat oven to 350 degrees. Melt butter and sauté onions, peppers, apples, and curry powder until tender. Place tomatoes in a colander and squeeze until all liquid is removed (reserve liquid for other uses). Combine drained tomatoes with onion mixture, kidney beans, brown sugar, vinegar, salt, and pepper in a casserole. Bake for 30 minutes. Sprinkle with Parmesan cheese before serving. Especially good with baked ham.

BLACK BEANS JOSÉ MANUEL

Serves 8 to 10

1 pound black beans, rinsed
2 large onions, coarsely
   chopped
3 large green peppers,
   coarsely chopped
1 cup olive oil
1 6-ounce can tomato paste
2 cloves garlic, minced

1 tablespoon salt
½ teaspoon freshly ground
   pepper
1 teaspoon powdered,
   crumbled, or dried
   oregano
1 teaspoon sugar
2 tablespoons white vinegar

Soak beans in water to cover overnight. In same water bring to boil, lower heat, and cook beans slowly until tender, adding more water if needed. Drain and reserve liquid. Set aside. Sauté onions and green peppers in olive oil until tender. Cool slightly and purée in a blender. Combine with tomato paste, garlic, salt, pepper, and oregano. Cook while stirring for 5 minutes. Add beans and cook for 10 minutes more, adding reserved liquid to thin to slightly syrupy consistency. Blend in sugar and vinegar and adjust seasonings. Cool and refrigerate. Best made 3 days ahead. Reheat gently, adjusting seasonings, and serve with pork or beef roast.

BEETS WITH PARSLEY BUTTER

A beautiful and nutritious accompaniment to any main course.

Serves 6

6 medium-size fresh beets,
   about 1¼ pounds,
   green tops removed
2 tablespoons butter
½ teaspoon crumbled dried
   basil leaves, or 2
   tablespoons minced
   fresh basil

½ teaspoon salt
Freshly ground pepper to
   taste
1½ tablespoons chopped
   parsley

Cook beets in boiling water until tender, about 25 to 35 minutes. Drain, cool slightly, slip off skins, and trim off tops. Cut into ¼-inch-thick slices and place in a saucepan. Add butter, basil, salt, and pepper, and cook until heated thoroughly. Turn into a warm serving dish and sprinkle with chopped parsley.

SICILIAN BROCCOLI

Serves 4 to 6

1 bunch broccoli
4 tablespoons butter
2 cloves garlic, minced
¼ to ½ cup sliced, pittted
    large black olives

Freshly grated Parmesan
    cheese
Lemon wedges

Divide broccoli into flowerets and steam until cooked but still crisp. Place in a warm serving dish. In a small pan melt butter, sauté garlic in it for a few minutes, and add sliced olives. Pour butter mixture over broccoli, sprinkle Parmesan cheese on top, and serve with lemon wedges.

BROCCOLI SAUTÉ À LA NIÇOISE

Festive and different. All components can be cooked ahead and just tossed together to heat through in a heavy skillet or wok just before serving. Green beans may be substituted for the broccoli.

Serves 4 to 6

1½ to 2 pounds broccoli
3 strips bacon
½ cup bread crumbs
3 tablespoons oil

½ cup minced onion
1 clove garlic, minced
Salt and freshly ground
    pepper to taste

Trim broccoli but leave some stem. Place it in a wire basket and plunge it into boiling salted water. Cook until just tender, drain and set aside. Dice bacon and sauté until crisp. Drain and set aside. In the same skillet, sauté bread crumbs in bacon drippings until browned. Remove and set aside. Put 3 tablespoons oil in the skillet and add onion and garlic, sauté until translucent. (May be made ahead to this point.) Add broccoli to the skillet with onion and garlic, gently tossing until heated through. Add bread crumbs and bacon, adjust seasonings, mix lightly, and serve immediately.

BROCCOLI PURÉE

The beauty of this recipe is its marvelous versatility. You may substitute almost any fresh or frozen vegetable for the broccoli. Serve it in hollowed-out tomatoes, on baked winter squash, large mushroom caps, or artichoke bottoms.

Serves 6 to 8

1 large bunch fresh broccoli
3 tablespoons butter
3 tablespoons flour
Salt and freshly ground
    pepper to taste

¼ teaspoon nutmeg
4 tablespoons melted butter
4 tablespoons sour cream

Trim broccoli and cook until just tender. Drain and set aside. In a heavy 1-quart saucepan make a roux by melting 3 tablespoons butter in a saucepan and, when foaming begins to subside, stirring in 3 tablespoons flour, and cooking for a few minutes to lightly brown the flour. Remove from heat. In a blender or food processor purée the cooked broccoli and stir into the roux. Add salt, pepper, nutmeg, melted butter and sour cream, and mix well.

BRUSSELS SPROUTS MILANESE

Serves 6

4 cups Brussels sprouts,
    trimmed and bottoms
    scored
1 stalk celery with leaves,
    coarsely chopped
Salt and freshly ground
    pepper to taste

6 tablespoons butter, melted
½ cup freshly grated
    Gruyère cheese
¼ cup freshly grated
    Parmesan cheese

Preheat oven to 350 degrees. Steam sprouts and celery until just tender. Set aside. Sprinkle a well-buttered shallow baking dish with salt and pepper and coat bottom of dish with 4 tablespoons of the melted butter. Heat in the oven for 5 minutes. Reset oven to 425 degrees. Combine cheeses. Layer sprouts and celery with cheeses in the baking dish, ending with a layer of cheese. Drizzle remaining 2 tablespoons butter over all and bake for 10 minutes or until cheese topping is melted and vegetables are warmed.

CAULIFLOWER WITH PURÉE OF PEAS

A colorful, beautiful way to serve cauliflower. Place it in the center of a large platter and surround it with sautéed cherry tomatoes.

Serves 8

2 10-ounce packages frozen
    tiny peas
2 small carrots, halved
    lengthwise
2 green onions, trimmed
1 tablespoon sugar
½ teaspoon dried thyme,
    crumbled

Salt and freshly ground
    pepper to taste
6 to 7 tablespoons butter
½ cup light cream
1 large cauliflower

Cook peas with carrots, onions, and seasonings in a small amount of water for 2 minutes or until tender. Discard carrots and onions. Purée in a food processor or food mill the peas, their pan juices, butter, and cream. Adjust seasonings and keep warm in the oven or the top of a double boiler. Steam whole cauliflower until just tender. Carefully place on a heated serving dish and pour purée of peas over.

BAKED CAULIFLOWER PURÉE

This looks like mashed potatoes but is a delightful surprise. It is creamy, smooth, very tasty, and attractive. It can be made ahead, then reheated slowly in the oven.

Serves 8

1 large cauliflower, separated
    into flowerets
1 medium onion, chopped
½ cup buttermilk

Salt and freshly ground
    pepper to taste
3 tablespoons butter
Chopped parsley for garnish

Preheat oven to 350 degrees. Place cauliflower flowerets in a saucepan with water to cover. Add onion and cook cauliflower for about 15 minutes or until tender. Place mixture in a blender or food processor and purée until smooth, slowly adding buttermilk. Season with salt, pepper, and butter and then purée for a few seconds more to melt butter. Place cauliflower purée in a buttered 1-quart soufflé dish and place in the oven until heated through. Garnish with chopped parsley.

CAULIFLOWER WITH CAPER SAUCE

The caper sauce makes plain cauliflower exotic and special. For best results, serve immediately.

Serves 6

1 whole large cauliflower
1 tablespoon cornstarch
1 tablespoon water
3 tablespoons butter
3 tablespoons fresh lemon
    juice

1 tablespoon grated onion
Salt to taste
⅛ teaspoon freshly ground
    pepper
1 teaspoon turmeric
2 tablespoons capers

Place cauliflower in a heavy saucepan in 1 inch of boiling salted water. Cover and cook until tender, about 20 minutes. Remove cauliflower to a warm serving dish and keep warm. Reserve 1 cup of cooking liquid. Soften cornstarch in 1 tablespoon water. Blend cornstarch into reserved cooking liquid, stirring constantly. Add butter, lemon juice, onion, salt, pepper, and turmeric. Cook, stirring, until sauce thickens. Remove from heat, stir in capers, and pour over cauliflower.

CHESTNUT PUFF

Serves 6

1 medium carrot, coarsely
    shredded
2 medium onions, chopped
2 tablespoons butter
½ teaspoon salt
1 15½-ounce can chestnut
    purée

3 tablespoons port wine
4 egg yolks
2 ounces sliced almonds
4 egg whites

Preheat oven to 350 degrees. In a skillet sauté shredded carrot with onions in butter until onions are transparent. Place onion and carrot mixture in a bowl and add salt, chestnut purée, port, and egg yolks. Beat with an electric mixer until well blended. Stir half of the almonds into mixture. Beat egg whites until stiff but not dry, and fold into purée mixture. Pour into a well-buttered soufflé dish or shallow baking dish. Sprinkle top with remaining almonds. Bake for 40 minutes or until puffed and brown.

FRIED PEPPERED CABBAGE

Serves 6

1 medium-size head white
  cabbage
¼ cup butter

Salt and freshly ground
  pepper to taste
3 tablespoons sour cream

Wash cabbage, remove core, and coarsely chop. Melt butter in a large skillet or wok over high heat. Add cabbage and sauté, stirring constantly, for about 2 minutes, just until cabbage is tender-crisp. It should not wilt or cook through. Season with salt and a very generous amount of pepper. Stir in sour cream. Serve immediately.

SCHROEDER'S GERMAN RED CABBAGE

Serves 6

1 4-pound red cabbage
2 cups boiling chicken or
  veal stock
4 tablespoons butter
2 tablespoons cider vinegar
2 tart apples, peeled and
  coarsely grated

2 whole cloves
1 tablespoon sugar
½ stick cinnamon
Salt and freshly ground
  pepper to taste
½ cup red wine

Remove wilted leaves, if any, from cabbage. Cut head in half and remove core. Shred cabbage finely, place in a large saucepan, pour boiling stock over it, add butter, and cook for 30 minutes over low heat. Add vinegar, apples, cloves, sugar, cinnamon, salt, and pepper and cook for another 30 minutes, stirring frequently. Ten minutes before serving, add red wine and simmer until ready to serve.

SCHROEDER'S POTATO PANCAKES

This classic recipe and the one preceeding both come from San Francisco's renowned German restaurant.

Serves 6

3 pounds potatoes
4 eggs, lightly beaten
1¼ cups all-purpose flour
½ tablespoon salt
Freshly ground pepper to
taste

½ teaspoon grated onion
1 large tart apple, peeled and
grated
Lard for frying

Peel potatoes, wash, and let stand in a bowl of water to crisp. Just before cooking drain and grate coarsely, then drain again. Place in a large bowl and mix in eggs, flour, salt, pepper, onion, and apple. Heat lard until very hot in an 8-inch heavy iron skillet. Spoon about one-fourth of the potato mixture into the skillet. This recipe will make 3 to 4 8-inch pancakes. Brown on one side, turn and brown on other side. Drain and keep warm in oven until ready to serve. Pancakes should be crisp, so do not cover.

SHREDDED CARROTS

Serves 6 to 8

6 cups finely shredded
carrots
2 cups finely sliced green
onions
Chicken stock for simmering
(approximately 1 cup)
4 tablespoons butter

¾ teaspoon dried fennel
2 tablespoons
orange-flavored liqueur
Chopped parsley for garnish
2 tablespoons grated orange
rind for garnish

Over low heat, stirring occasionally, simmer carrots and onions in stock to cover for 2 to 4 minutes or until liquid has cooked away completely. Add butter and fennel and mix well. Just before serving, stir in orange-flavored liqueur and sprinkle with chopped parsley and grated orange rind.

CARROT RING

This is a lovely party dish, a feast for the eyes.

Serves 8

8 large carrots, sliced, or
enough to make 4 cups
of purée
1½ tablespoons butter
1½ tablespoons flour
1½ cups milk
3 eggs, separated

2 tablespoons finely grated
onion
½ teaspoon salt
White pepper to taste
¼ teaspoon nutmeg
1 tablespoon sugar
½ cup slivered almonds
Fresh parsley for garnish

Preheat oven to 350 degrees. Place carrots in enough boiling salted water to cover, and cook for 15 minutes or until barely tender. Drain and put carrots in a blender or food processor or through a food mill. Set aside. Over medium heat, melt butter and stir in flour, cooking for 1 to 2 minutes. Gradually add milk and stir until sauce is thickened. Let cool for a minute and add egg yolks, one at a time, stirring thoroughly. Add puréed carrots, onion, salt, pepper, nutmeg, and sugar. Beat egg whites until stiff peaks form, and gently fold into carrot mixture. Then fold in almonds. Pour into a buttered 8-cup ring mold and place in a pan of hot water, with the water reaching a height of 1 inch up the side of the mold. Bake for 45 minutes. Unmold on a warm serving platter.

CARROTS IN VERMOUTH A LA SHEARING

This proves that George Shearing's fingers are just as deft in the kitchen as at the piano.

Serves 6

2 pounds carrots, sliced ¼
inch thick
3 medium stalks celery with
leaves, finely diced

1 small onion, finely minced
⅓ cup sugar
2 tablespoons butter
¾ cup dry vermouth

Place all ingredients in a saucepan and cook over low heat for about 20 to 25 minutes or just barely tender.

BUTTER-GLAZED CARROTS

Serves 4

1 pound or 1 medium-size
    bunch carrots
4 tablespoons butter
Salt and freshly ground
    pepper to taste

2 tablespoons dry sherry
Finely minced parsley for
    garnish

Scrub or peel carrots, trim, and cut into halves lengthwise. Place in a vegetable steamer and steam until barely tender. Melt butter in a skillet, and when butter begins to brown add carrots, salt, and pepper, and stir constantly until carrots are completely coated and heated through. Remove to a warm serving dish. Add sherry to the skillet, stirring to mix in all the remaining butter, and pour over carrots. Sprinkle with minced parsley. Serve immediately.

EGGPLANT PARMIGIANA

Serves 8

1 large eggplant
2 eggs, beaten
½ teaspoon oregano
¼ teaspoon dried basil
Salt and freshly ground
    pepper to taste
¼ teaspoon garlic salt
1 cup fine dried bread
    crumbs, or as needed

Olive oil for browning
3 cups tomato sauce
½ pound fresh mushrooms,
    sliced and sautéed in 1
    tablespoon butter
12 ounces mozzarella cheese,
    thinly sliced
2 ounces Parmesan cheese,
    freshly grated

Preheat oven to 325 degrees. Peel eggplant if desired and slice ¼ inch thick. Dip into egg, which has been beaten with oregano, basil, salt, pepper, and garlic salt, then into bread crumbs. Brown quickly in olive oil, turning once. In a shallow baking dish arrange eggplant and cover with half of the tomato sauce, mushrooms, mozzarella slices, and Parmesan. Repeat with other half of each. Bake for 45 minutes or until heated through and bubbly.

EGGPLANT CANNELLONI

Serves 6

FILLING

1¼ cups shredded
   mozzarella cheese
½ cup ricotta cheese
½ cup freshly grated
   Parmesan cheese
½ cup chopped mortadella

2 eggs, slightly beaten
1½ tablespoons chopped
   parsley
⅛ teaspoon freshly ground
   pepper

EGGPLANT

¼ cup all-purpose white
   flour
1 egg
⅔ cup milk

1 tablespoon salad oil
2 large eggplants
1 cup corn oil
Flour as needed

BAKING

2 cups tomato sauce
½ cup freshly grated Parmesan cheese
Parsley sprigs for garnish

Preheat oven to 375 degrees. To make the filling, combine in a bowl mozzarella, ricotta, and Parmesan cheeses, the mortadella, eggs, chopped parsley, and pepper. Mix well to blend. Set aside. To prepare the eggplant, make a batter of the flour, egg, milk, and salad oil. Set aside. Peel eggplants and trim off pointed ends to obtain a more uniform shape. Cut each eggplant lengthwise into 6 equally thick slices. In a large skillet heat corn oil. Dust eggplant slices in flour, shake off any excess, and dip in batter. Then fry slices in hot oil for about 5 minutes or until lightly browned, using a spatula to slightly flatten the eggplant slices as they cook. Remove and drain on paper towels. Repeat until all slices are cooked, adding more oil as needed.

Spoon filling across center of each eggplant slice and fold ends over to close. Arrange, seam side down, in a shallow casserole. Spoon tomato sauce over eggplant and bake for 15 to 20 minutes or until heated through. To serve, sprinkle with Parmesan cheese and garnish with sprigs of parsley.

EGGPLANT WITH CLAMS IN CASSEROLE

This casserole may be served as a entree or as a rich vegetable accompaniment to cold chicken or turkey and especially lamb.

Serves 4

1 8-ounce can minced clams
2 cloves garlic
1 large eggplant, peeled and
    coarsely chopped
2 tablespoons minced parsley

4 tablespoons minced chives
¼ teaspoon salt
Cayenne to taste
½ to 1 cup bread crumbs

Preheat oven to 300 degrees. Drain clams, reserving juice. Place clam juice in a large saucepan, add garlic and heat, then remove and discard garlic. Add chopped eggplant to juice and cook until tender, about 10 minutes. Add parsley and chives and cook for another 2 minutes. Drain eggplant, discard juice, and mix eggplant with clams, add seasonings, and transfer to a buttered baking dish. Sprinkle top with bread crumbs. Bake for about 10 minutes or until heated through.

TIMBALLO DI MELANZANE

A good, rich vegetable dish for a roast chicken.

Serves 6

1 eggplant
All-purpose white flour
Olive oil as needed
¼ cup finely minced onion
¼ cup finely chopped green
    pepper
Salt and freshly ground
    pepper to taste
Fresh parsley, minced
Fresh thyme, minced

2 large ripe tomatoes, peeled
    and sliced
8 ounces mozzarella cheese,
    sliced
1 cup heavy cream
½ cup light cream
3 eggs, lightly beaten
2 egg yolks
Salt, freshly ground pepper,
    and nutmeg to taste

Preheat oven to 375 degrees. Peel and cut eggplant into round slices ¼-inch thick. Dredge slices in flour seasoned with salt and pepper and sauté in hot oil until browned and softened. Sauté onion and green pepper in oil until tender, set aside. Place a layer of eggplant slices in a large flat pie dish and sprinkle with some salt, pepper, parsley, and thyme. Cover with a layer of tomato slices and sprinkle with salt, pepper, parsley, onion, and green pepper. Cover with cheese slices and repeat layers. Beat the heavy cream, light cream, eggs, and egg yolks. Season with salt, pepper, and nutmeg. Pour over eggplant layers and bake for 20 to 25 minutes until toothpick inserted in center comes out clean and cheese topping is lightly browned.

GLAZED FENNEL

Serves 4

2 pounds bulb fennel
¼ cup olive oil
1 whole garlic bud, separated
    into cloves, unpeeled

Salt to taste
½ cup water
Freshly ground black pepper
    to taste

Remove tough outer stalks from fennel bulbs and split each bulb in half. In a large skillet with a lid place olive oil, fennel in a single layer, and garlic cloves. Sprinkle with salt and cook over medium heat for about 30 minutes or until lightly browned, turning fennel occasionally. Add ½ cup water and bring to a boil, reduce heat, and simmer, tightly covered, for about 1 hour. The fennel will be soft but will hold its shape, and the liquid will be reduced to a syrupy caramelized consistency. With a slotted spoon, carefully remove all garlic cloves. Place fennel on a warm serving dish and pour pan juices over it, and season with pepper.

LIMA BEAN PURÉE

This purée is lovely with a pork roast. It is also versatile enough to be used in sautéed mushroom caps or baked tomatoes.

Serves 6 to 8

2 10-ounce packages frozen
    lima beans
1 tablespoon butter

⅓ cup light cream
Salt and freshly ground
    pepper to taste

Cook lima beans as directed on the package. Drain and reserve cooking liquid. Purée beans in blender or food processor, adding butter, cream, and enough of the reserved cooking liquid to make a smooth consistency. Add salt and pepper. Keep warm until ready to serve. To serve with a pork roast, spread lima bean purée around the edge of a serving platter, place the roast in the center.

BAKED MUSHROOMS

Serves 4 to 6

⅓ cup olive oil
2 tablespoons wine vinegar
1 medium onion, grated
½ to 1 clove garlic, minced
2 tablespoons chopped fresh
    parsley
⅛ teaspoon dried basil
1 teaspoon salt
¼ teaspoon pepper

1½ pounds fresh
    mushrooms, sliced
4 tablespoons butter, or as
    needed
½ cup coarse, homemade
    bread crumbs
1 tablespoon freshly grated
    Parmesan cheese

Combine oil, vinegar, onion, garlic, herbs, salt, and pepper. Add mushrooms and, basting frequently, marinate for 3 hours. Drain and sauté in butter over high heat for 1 minute. Reduce heat to low and cook for 10 minutes, stirring frequently. Transfer to a buttered baking dish and sprinkle bread crumbs and cheese over mushrooms. Broil until top is browned. Serve as a first course or vegetable accompaniment to meat or fowl.

CHAMPIGNONS DE CANNE À L'ESCARGOT

A very rich and elegant way to serve mushrooms as either a first course or as an accompaniment to a simple roast. From Escargot restaurant in Carmel.

2 pounds small whole button
    mushrooms
4 shallots, finely minced
½ cup butter
Salt and freshly ground
    pepper to taste
4 ounces cognac
3 cloves garlic
1 tablespoon chopped
    parsley
1 teaspoon rosemary
1 teaspoon thyme

1 teaspoon basil
½ teaspoon turmeric
½ teaspoon powdered
    cumin
½ teaspoon powdered
    coriander
½ teaspoon powdered
    ginger
½ teaspoon black pepper
3 cups heavy cream
Cayenne pepper to taste
Parsley sprigs for garnish

Sauté mushrooms and shallots in butter for 2 minutes. Season with salt and pepper and pour cognac over, stirring until heated. Ignite and stir until flame dies. Set aside. In a blender or food processor mix the garlic, herbs, and spices, blending for a few seconds, then add cream until thoroughly mixed. Add cayenne. Add cream mixture to mushrooms, cooking until thickened. Serve in small ramekins garnished with parsley.

MUSHROOM ROLL

Serves 6 to 8

1½ pounds fresh mushrooms
6 eggs, separated
¼ pound butter, melted
Salt and freshly ground
    pepper to taste
2 tablespoons fresh lemon
    juice

4 to 5 whole mushroom caps,
    cleaned, peeled and
    decoratively trimmed
1 tablespoon butter
Chopped parsley, for garnish
2 cups Hollandaise Sauce
    (see Index)

Preheat oven to 350 degrees. Butter a jelly-roll pan (10½ by 15 inches) and line with buttered baking parchment. Finely chop mushrooms and squeeze all moisture out, a handful at a time, using the corner of a dish towel. Beat egg yolks until fluffy, then add mushrooms, melted butter, salt, pepper, and lemon juice. Beat egg whites until they hold soft peaks, then gently fold into the mushroom mixture. Pour into the prepared pan and smooth with a rubber spatula. Bake for 15 minutes. Cool, then carefully turn out onto another sheet of parchment paper. Peel off top paper, then roll up like a jelly roll, and place on a serving dish. Sauté mushroom caps in 1 tablespoon butter over high heat for 2 minutes, season with salt and pepper. Arrange on top of mushroom roll. Sprinkle with chopped parsley and pass hollandaise sauce separately.

ONIONS AMANDINE

Serves 6

2 dozen small white onions
¼ pound butter
½ cup sliced almonds
1 tablespoon dark brown
    sugar

1 clove garlic, minced
½ teaspoon salt
¼ teaspoon freshly ground
    pepper
¼ cup white wine

Preheat oven to 350 degrees. Peel onions by cooking in boiling water for a minute or so until the skin slips off easily. Set aside. In a heavy skillet, melt butter and stir in almonds and sugar. Add garlic, stir for a minute or so, and add salt, pepper, and wine. Add onions to butter mixture and stir until onions are well coated. Cover pan and bake for 30 to 40 minutes, shaking pan every 15 minutes to prevent sticking.

STUFFED ONIONS

Serves 8

8 onions of uniform size (at least 3 inches in diameter)
Boiling salted water

STUFFING

V-shaped cores of onions
    (see preparation below)
¼ pound butter
½ pound mushrooms, sliced
1 medium tomato, peeled
    and chopped
½ cup reserved onion water
1 cup dry white wine
½ cup brown rice
½ cup freshly grated
    Parmesan cheese
¼ cup heavy cream
    (optional)

2 tablespoons basil or 1
    tablespoon tarragon
¼ teaspoon sage
¼ teaspoon oregano
¼ cup chopped fresh
    parsley
2 tablespoons bread crumbs
Salt and freshly ground
    pepper to taste
Dry white wine as needed

Preheat oven to 350 degrees. Cut top and bottom off onions and peel. Place bottom ends down and with sharp knife cut a cone-shaped core from top part of onions. Being careful to leave a ½-inch bottom in the shell, dig out centers of onions and reserve. Place onion shells in boiling salted water, and when water returns to boil, simmer, uncovered, for 10 minutes or until just tender. Do not overcook, as onions must hold their shape. Remove and let drain upside down. Reserve liquid. Chop the reserved onion cores. Melt butter and sauté the cores and mushrooms for 10 minutes. Add tomato, reserved onion water, 1 cup white wine, and rice. Cover and simmer for 45 minutes or until rice is tender and most of liquid has been absorbed. Add cheese, cream, herbs, bread crumbs, salt, and pepper, adjusting seasonings to taste. Stuff onion shells, place in a shallow baking dish to hold onions close together, and pour in white wine to a depth of about ¾ of an inch. Bake for 20 minutes or until heated through.

SPANAKOPITA

A most attractive dish—delicious and excellent with lamb. This freezes very well. Tasty and different.

Serves 8

½ pound feta cheese
4 ounces cream cheese
2 eggs
2 tablespoons dried parsley
1 teaspoon nutmeg
4 ounces Monterey Jack
  cheese
1 10-ounce package frozen
  chopped spinach,
  thawed and squeezed
  dry

1 medium onion, chopped
2 tablespoons butter
½ pound phyllo pastry
  (about 30 sheets or
  layers)
12 tablespoons butter,
  melted

Preheat oven to 350 degrees. Blend feta cheese, cream cheese, eggs, parsley, nutmeg, and Monterey Jack cheese, a little at a time, in a blender or food processor. Combine with spinach. Sauté onion in the 2 tablespoons butter until transparent. Add to spinach mixture. Cut the phyllo sheets to fit a 9 by 12-inch baking dish. Butter the dish and place 12 layers of phyllo in it, brushing each with melted butter. Spread cheese-spinach mixture over phyllo layers and top with 10 to 15 more phyllo sheets, buttering each as you layer. To make cutting easier, place the dish in the freezer for approximately 20 minutes. Cut into squares or diamonds and bake for 45 minutes or until brown and crisp. May be made ahead and reheated. It may also be frozen unbaked; thaw and bake as directed.

SPINACH TIMBALE

Serves 6 to 8

½ cup chopped onion
5 tablespoons butter
1 cup fine bread crumbs
½ cup grated Gruyère
   cheese
½ teaspoon salt
½ teaspoon freshly grated
   nutmeg

Cayenne pepper to taste
5 eggs
1 cup milk
3 cups cooked chopped
   spinach, well drained
2 cups Hollandaise Sauce or
   Mushroom Sauce (see
   Index for both sauces)

Preheat oven to 350 degrees. Sauté onion in 1 tablespoon of the butter until soft and translucent but not browned. Combine with ⅔ cup of the bread crumbs, the cheese, salt, nutmeg, and cayenne. One at a time, beat in eggs. Heat milk and remaining 4 tablespoons butter until butter is melted. Gradually add to egg mixture. Fold in spinach and pour into a buttered 1½-quart mold. Sprinkle with remaining bread crumbs, place mold in a pan of water and bake for 35 to 40 minutes or until a tooth-pick inserted in center comes out clean. Remove from oven and water bath and let stand for 5 minutes. Unmold on heated platter and serve with hollandaise sauce or mushroom sauce.

HERBED SPINACH BAKE

A good and easy vegetable casserole to accompany almost any main dish—especially roast chicken. It can be prepared ahead, refrigerated, then baked until puffy and golden.

Serves 6

10-ounce package frozen
   chopped spinach,
   thawed and squeezed
   dry
1 cup cooked rice
2 eggs, slightly beaten
⅓ cup milk

1 teaspoon salt
2 tablespoons chopped onion
1 cup grated Cheddar cheese
2 tablespoons butter, melted
½ teaspoon Worcestershire
   sauce
¼ teaspoon rosemary

Preheat oven to 350 degrees. Combine all ingredients in a mixing bowl, blending thoroughly. Pour into a buttered 9 by 9-inch baking dish and bake for 20 to 25 minutes or until a knife inserted in the center comes out clean.

ACORN SQUASH WITH APPLESAUCE

Delicious and colorful. The applesauce and squash go very well together and look lovely surrounding a standing rib roast or large pork roast.

Serves 4

2 acorn squash	¼ cup brown sugar
2 teaspoons lemon juice	3 tablespoons chopped
¼ cup seedless raisins	walnuts
1½ cups applesauce	Butter

Preheat oven to 400 degrees. Scrub and halve acorn squash, then remove seeds. Place, cut side up, in a baking dish. Mix together the lemon juice, raisins, applesauce, brown sugar, and chopped walnuts. Spoon mixture into the cavities of the squash and dot with butter. Pour ½ inch of hot water into the bottom of the baking dish, cover, and bake for 30 minutes. Remove cover and bake for 30 minutes more.

CROOKNECK SQUASH

This is excellent as a stuffing for parboiled zucchini shells.

Serves 4 to 6

1 pound yellow crookneck squash, unpeeled and cut up	3 to 4 tablespoons freshly grated Parmesan cheese
2 to 3 tablespoons butter	Salt and freshly ground pepper to taste
¼ cup heavy cream	1 egg, slightly beaten

Cook squash in salted water until soft. Drain, mash well, and place in the top of a double boiler set over hot water. Stir in butter, cream, cheese, salt, and pepper. Heat and gradually beat in egg. Cook and stir over hot, not boiling, water until thickened. Serve immediately.

CHERRY TOMATOES IN CREAM

Serves 4

1 pint cherry tomatoes
2 tablespoons butter
¼ teaspoon salt
2 tablespoons brown sugar

¼ cup heavy cream
Chopped fresh parsley for
  garnish

In a large skillet, sauté tomatoes in butter, with salt and sugar, for 2 to 3 minutes, stirring constantly. Remove tomatoes to a serving dish. Add cream to pan juices, stir, and pour over tomatoes. Garnish with chopped parsley and serve immediately.

HERBED SCALLOPED TOMATOES

Serves 8 to 10

7 pounds ripe tomatoes,
  peeled, seeded, and
  chopped
2½ cups herb-seasoned
  stuffing
1 small onion, chopped
2 tablespoons sugar
1 teaspoon salt

¼ teaspoon freshly ground
  pepper
½ teaspoon nutmeg
½ teaspoon powdered
  oregano
¼ teaspoon powdered
  rosemary
4 to 6 tablespoons butter

Preheat oven to 375 degrees. Drain tomatoes well. Toss with 2 cups of the stuffing, onion, sugar, salt, pepper, nutmeg, oregano, and rosemary. Place in a buttered 3-quart casserole. Sprinkle with the remaining ½ cup stuffing and dot with butter. Bake for 45 minutes,

SHERRIED BROILED TOMATOES

These tomatoes are beautiful and delicious surrounding a roast beef or platter of lamb chops. Tomatoes go well with almost anything, and this recipe is especially good.

Serves 8

4 large tomatoes, ripe but
    firm
¼ cup dry sherry
½ teaspoon salt
¼ teaspoon pepper

1 teaspoon dried oregano
8 tablespoons mayonnaise
¼ cup grated Parmesan
    cheese

Preheat oven to 300 degrees. Cut tomatoes in half, place in a shallow baking dish, cut side up, and prick with a fork. Sprinkle with sherry, allowing it to be absorbed into pulp. Sprinkle with salt, pepper, and oregano. Place in the oven for about 5 minutes. Remove from the oven and turn heat to broil. Top tomato halves with mayonnaise, then dust with Parmesan cheese. Broil until lightly browned. Serve immediately.

FRIED GREEN TOMATOES

Supermarkets usually have green tomatoes in the back, where they are kept to ripen.

Serves 6

½ cup flour
Salt and freshly ground
    pepper to taste
4 medium green tomatoes

4 tablespoons bacon fat or oil
    (do not substitute
    butter)

Season flour on a plate with salt and pepper. Cut tomatoes in thick slices and dredge in flour mixture. Heat bacon fat in a heavy skillet and fry tomato slices, turning to brown both sides.

TOMATOES STUFFED WITH BACON AND CHEESE

Serves 4

4 large beefsteak tomatoes
8 slices bacon
1 medium onion, chopped
4 tablespoons minced parsley
1 tablespoon chopped fresh
  basil, or 1 teaspoon
  dried basil

Salt and freshly ground
  pepper to taste
4 ounces Monterey Jack
  cheese, freshly grated
Chopped parsley for garnish

Preheat oven to 350 degrees. Slice top off each tomato. Remove pulp from them and reserve. Stand tomato shells upside down to drain. Fry bacon until crisp, drain, reserving 2 tablespoons bacon drippings, then crumble. Sauté onion and tomato centers in reserved bacon drippings and reduce most of liquid. Remove from heat, add parsley, basil, salt, pepper, crumbled bacon, and cheese. Fill tomato shells with mixture and place in a baking dish. Bake, uncovered, for 20 to 30 minutes. Do not overcook or tomatoes will fall apart. Sprinkle with chopped parsley before serving.

TOMATOES STUFFED WITH MUSHROOMS

Serves 4

4 medium tomatoes, ripe but
  firm
Salt and freshly ground
  pepper
¼ teaspoon sugar
6 green onions, thinly sliced
3 tablespoons butter
¾ pound mushrooms, thinly
  sliced

1½ tablespoons fresh lemon
  juice
2 tablespoons dry sherry
1 teaspoon paprika
¾ cup light cream
3 tablespoons freshly grated
  Parmesan cheese
3 tablespoons freshly grated
  Gruyère cheese

Preheat oven to 400 degrees. Cut tops off tomatoes, scoop out the pulp, reserving liquid. Chop pulp and set aside. Sprinkle insides of tomato shells lightly with salt, pepper, and sugar. Stand tomatoes upside down to drain for 30 minutes. Sauté green onions in butter until softened. Add mushrooms and sauté until golden. Stir in reserved tomato pulp, lemon juice, sherry, paprika, and salt to taste. Continue cooking for 2 minutes. Turn heat to high and add cream. Cook, stirring, until liquid is reduced and thickened. Place tomato shells in a buttered shallow baking dish or 4 buttered ramekins. Fill with mushroom mixture and top each with Parmesan and Gruyère. Bake for 10 minutes. Place under the broiler to brown. Serve immediately.

TOMATOES WITH SOUBISE SAUCE

Serves 6 to 8

6 to 8 large tomatoes
2 teaspoons salt
½ teaspoon freshly ground
 pepper
4 tablespoons butter
3 medium onions, thinly
 sliced
6 tablespoons raw rice
2 tablespoons flour

½ cup light cream
1 tablespoon fresh lemon
 juice
¼ cup chicken stock
2 egg yolks
¼ cup chopped parsley
¼ cup freshly grated
 Parmesan cheese

Preheat oven to 350 degrees. Slice tomatoes ½ inch thick. Sprinkle with 1 teaspoon salt and the pepper and place on a large shallow baking dish.

SOUBISE SAUCE

In a saucepan melt 2 tablespoons butter, stir in remaining 1 teaspoon salt, onions, and rice. Cover and cook over medium heat for 30 minutes or until rice is soft. Purée in a blender. In another saucepan melt the remaining 2 tablespoons butter, stir in flour, and whisk in cream, lemon juice, and chicken stock. Remove from heat. Beat egg yolks. Stir in egg yolks, onion-rice purée, and parsley, and taste for seasoning. Put 1 tablespoon soubise sauce and 1 teaspoon Parmesan on each tomato slice. Bake for about 10 minutes or until bubbly.

ZUCCHINI CASSEROLE

Serves 6 to 8

3 pounds zucchini
4 eggs, beaten
½ cup milk
1 4-ounce can diced green
    chilies
¼ cup chopped parsley

1 pound Monterey Jack
    cheese, cubed
1 teaspoon salt
2 teaspoons baking powder
1 cup bread crumbs
2 tablespoons butter

Preheat oven to 350 degrees. Cube zucchini and steam until just barely tender. Combine eggs, milk, chilies, parsley, cheese, salt, and baking powder. Toss in zucchini and mix well. Transfer mixture to a buttered casserole that has been dusted with half the bread crumbs, then sprinkle the top with remaining bread crumbs and dot with butter. Bake for 45 minutes or until cooked through and lightly browned.

ZUCCHINI FLAN

Zucchini is available almost year round in many parts of the country. Try this flan for a different way to enjoy it.

Serves 6

1 pint ricotta cheese
2 egg yolks
½ teaspoon salt
1 teaspoon dried marjoram,
    crumbled
½ teaspoon dried thyme,
    crumbled
¼ teaspoon dried tarragon,
    crumbled

2 tablespoons butter
1½ pounds zucchini, sliced
1 small onion, cut in thin
    wedges
1 clove garlic, minced
2 tablespoons butter, melted
½ cup freshly grated
    Parmesan cheese

Preheat oven to 400 degrees. In a mixing bowl combine ricotta cheese, egg yolks, salt, marjoram, thyme, and tarragon. Set aside. Melt 2 table-spoons butter in a skillet and sauté zucchini, onion, and garlic, stirring, until zucchini is just tender-crisp. Butter a 2-quart shallow casserole and put in it half the zucchini mixture. Spread ricotta cheese mixture over it, and top with remaining zucchini. Sprinkle with Parmesan cheese, pour melted butter over, and bake, uncovered, for 20 minutes or until heated through and lightly browned.

TIAN DE ZUCCHINI

An unusual zucchini and rice casserole with cheese.

Serves 8

2 to 2½ pounds zucchini
Salt as needed
½ cup long-grain rice
3 cups boiling salted water
½ cup minced onion
2 tablespoons olive oil
2 cloves garlic, finely minced
2 tablespoons all-purpose
    white flour

Milk and reserved zucchini
    juices to make 2½ cups
⅔ cup freshly grated
    Parmesan cheese
Salt and freshly ground
    pepper to taste

Preheat oven to 425 degrees. Grate zucchini coarsely and sprinkle with salt. Let stand for 30 minutes and then squeeze out all moisture, reserving juice. Set aside. Pour rice into the 3 cups of boiling water and boil for 5 minutes. Drain and set aside. Slowly sauté onion in olive oil until lightly browned. Add garlic and zucchini; toss and sauté for 5 minutes. Sprinkle with flour, sauté and stir for 3 minutes more, then gradually add milk and zucchini juice. Cook and stir until thickened. Add rice and all but 2 tablespoons of the cheese. Adjust seasonings with salt and pepper and transfer to a buttered 2-quart shallow baking dish. Sprinkle with reserved cheese and bake for 30 minutes.

ZUCCHINI MOUSSE AU GRATIN

Serves 4 to 6

6 medium zucchini (about
 1½ pounds)
3 tablespoons butter
4 green onions, chopped
¼ cup chopped parsley
1 tablespoon fresh dill, or 1
 teaspoon dried

1 teaspoon salt
⅛ teaspoon freshly ground
 pepper
⅔ cup sour cream
3 to 4 tablespoons freshly
 grated Parmesan cheese

Preheat oven to 375 degrees. Grate zucchini and let stand in a colander for 20 minutes to drain. In a skillet melt butter and sauté onions until soft and transparent. Stir in parsley, dill, salt, pepper, and sour cream. Add the drained zucchini, then pour into a 1-quart casserole, sprinkle cheese on top, and bake for 30 minutes.

ZUCCHINI PUFFS

These, made small and bite size, are perfect for cocktails. Cooking larger portions creates a different and delicious side dish to any roast of meat or fowl. The batter can be prepared ahead, then brought out to make fritters at the last minute.

Makes approximately 3 dozen appetizers

2 cups flour
1 teaspoon baking powder
1 egg
2 tablespoons olive oil
1¼ cups milk
½ teaspoon salt
¼ teaspoon pepper
1 cup grated Cheddar cheese
3 medium zucchini, grated
 and drained in a
 colander

2 cloves garlic, crushed
2 tablespoons finely chopped
 onion
1 tablespoon minced parsley
Oil for frying
Salt to taste

Sift together the flour and baking powder. Set aside. In a large bowl combine the egg, olive oil, ½ cup of the milk, salt, and pepper. Beat to a smooth paste and gradually add sifted flour mixture (consistency will be very stiff). Add grated cheese and remaining milk to make a smooth but stiff batter. Blend in grated zucchini, garlic, onion, and parsley. Heat oil to the deep-fry stage and drop in batter by spoonfuls. Fry until golden. Remove with a slotted spoon and drain on paper towels. Keep warm until all are cooked. Lightly salt to taste and serve immediately.

POTATOES GRATIN DAUPHINOIS

Serves 6

4 cups very thinly sliced
    potatoes
1 teaspoon salt
¼ teaspoon freshly ground
    pepper
⅛ teaspoon freshly grated
    nutmeg
1 clove garlic, very finely
    minced

1¼ cups grated Gruyère or
    Emmenthaler cheese
4 tablespoons butter
2 eggs, lightly beaten
1 cup heavy cream
2 tablespoons freshly grated
    Parmesan cheese

Preheat oven to 375 degrees. In a large bowl, toss to coat thoroughly the potatoes with ½ teaspoon of the salt, ⅛ teaspoon of the pepper, the nutmeg, and garlic. Place ⅓ of the seasoned potatoes in the bottom of a well-buttered shallow baking dish, sprinkle with ⅓ of the Gruyère cheese and dot with ⅓ of the butter. Repeat twice. In a small bowl, beat eggs, cream, and remaining salt and pepper. Pour evenly over potato layers and sprinkle with Parmesan cheese. Bake, covered, for 35 minutes. Remove cover and bake for another 10 minutes or until potatoes are softened and top is golden brown and bubbly.

MAYFIELD CLUB POTATOES

These are very rich and also very good. The beauty is the slow cooking, so they take no last-minute preparation. Be sure not to add the salt and pepper while they cook or the cream will curdle.

Serves 6

4 large new potatoes
4 cups heavy cream
¼ pound sweet butter

Peel potatoes and grate through a medium grater. Immediately place in the top of a double boiler and pour heavy cream over them. Place butter on top. Cover and cook over boiling water for 30 minutes. Stir potatoes, cover again, and cook over simmering water for 3 hours, occasionally checking the water level in the bottom pan. When cooked, potatoes should be golden and creamy in color. Turn into warm serving dish and pass salt and pepper separately.

SAUTÉED POTATOES

Plain and perfect with any main course. For variety, use a melon baller to make round shapes and sprinkle with a little Parmesan cheese just before serving.

Serves 4 to 6

6 medium potatoes
2 tablespoons oil
4 tablespoons butter
Salt and freshly ground
    pepper to taste

Chopped fresh parsley for
    garnish

Peel potatoes and cut into uniform pieces about 1½ inches long, similar to French fries. Place in a bowl of salted cold water to crisp until ready to cook. Just before cooking, drain and dry thoroughly on paper towels. Heat oil and butter in a large skillet, and cook potatoes without crowding. Shake and turn until potatoes are glazed and brown, about 20 minutes. Sprinkle with salt and pepper, reduce heat to low, cover pan tightly, and steam for 15 minutes. Shake pan occasionally to prevent sticking. Before serving sprinkle with freshly chopped parsley.

SWEET POTATO CASSEROLE

Serves 8

6 large sweet potatoes
¼ pound butter, softened
½ cup light cream
½ cup Madeira wine
½ teaspoon cinnamon
½ teaspoon salt

½ teaspoon nutmeg
1 tablespoon freshly grated
   orange rind
Butter as needed
Chopped pecans or walnuts
   (optional)

Preheat oven to 375 degrees. Bake sweet potatoes for 40 minutes or until tender. Reset oven to 350 degrees. Mash sweet potatoes, adding butter, cream, and Madeira. Add cinnamon, salt, nutmeg, and orange rind, adjust seasonings, and place in a buttered baking dish. Dot with butter, sprinkle with optional pecans or walnuts, and bake for 25 minutes.

TORTA DE PLÁTANOS

An interesting and different vegetable dish. Plantains are cousins to the Banana and are found in most Mexican markets.

Serves 6

2 large plátanos, or plantains
4 tablespoons butter
3 eggs, beaten

1 cup mild grated Cheddar
   cheese

Preheat oven to 350 degrees. Peel plátanos and cut into small pieces. Melt butter in a heavy skillet and brown plátanos. Transfer to a buttered baking dish. Pour over beaten eggs, then cover with grated cheese. Bake for 30 minutes.

GRATIN DE POTIRON D'ARPAJON

This is a very rich squash or pumpkin casserole from Arpajon, France, quite unusual and easy for entertaining a large group.

Serves 12

3 tablespoons butter
½ cup diced onion
½ cup diced celery
¼ cup diced carrots
3 tablespoons butter
2 pounds pumpkin or winter
    squash, coarsely
    chopped
2 cloves garlic, mashed
1 bay leaf
⅛ teaspoon thyme
½ teaspoon salt

2½ cups cooked white beans
    (1 cup dried beans,
    soaked overnight,
    cooked in water to
    cover for 1 hour)
2 eggs, slightly beaten
½ cup heavy cream
Salt and freshly ground
    pepper to taste
3 tablespoons butter
2 ounces Swiss cheese, grated

Preheat oven to 350 degrees. In a large ovenproof serving dish with a lid, melt butter and add onions, celery, and carrots. Cook, covered, on top of stove until tender, about 10 minutes. Stir in pumpkin or squash, garlic, bay leaf, thyme, and salt. Bring to a simmer, cover with waxed paper and lid, and bake for 30 to 40 minutes. Remove from the oven and discard bay leaf. Reset oven to 425 degrees. Add beans to squash mixture and purée in a blender or food processor. Return mixture to the ovenproof serving dish and stir in beaten eggs and cream. Season with salt and pepper, dot with 3 tablespoons butter, and sprinkle with cheese. Heat in 425 degree oven for 25 to 30 minutes or until hot.

VEGETABLE SOUFFLÉ

Serves 8

3 tablespoons flour
3 tablespoons butter
1 cup milk
12 ounces cooked corn or
   broccoli or spinach or
   artichokes
3 eggs

½ cup mayonnaise
4 to 5 green onions and tops,
   minced
Salt and freshly ground
   pepper to taste
Curry powder to taste
   (optional)

Preheat oven to 350 degrees. To make the white sauce: In a saucepan, melt butter until foamy, sprinkle with flour, and cook and stir for 3 minutes. Gradually add milk, cook and stir until thickened. In a blender or food processor purée vegetable, eggs, mayonnaise, green onions, seasonings, and white sauce. Pour into an unbuttered 1-quart soufflé dish and bake for 1 hour.

SAUTÉED JULIENNE VEGETABLES

The beauty of this recipe is that it not only is colorful and lovely to look at, but is the hostess's dream. All can be cooked ahead, refreshed under cold water, and set aside. Just before serving, toss in heated butter and serve.

Serves 6

1 large bunch fresh broccoli
3 large carrots, peeled
2 medium potatoes, peeled
4 tablespoons butter

Salt and freshly ground
   pepper to taste
2 tablespoons finely chopped
   fresh parsley

Trim broccoli stems and reserve flowerets for another use. Slice broccoli stems, carrots, and potatoes into julienne and steam separately until just barely tender. Refresh in cold water and drain. May be made ahead to this point. Melt butter until foamy and toss vegetables into butter to coat well. Season with salt and pepper and cook and stir for 3 to 4 minutes to heat through. Sprinkle with parsley.

VEGETABLE FRITTATA

This dish can be made ahead of time, refrigerated, and baked later—a nice idea for a buffet or for roast chicken, and the amounts can be adjusted to suit any crowd.

Serves 8

3 large zucchini, sliced
1 unpeeled eggplant, sliced
½ pound mushrooms, sliced
2 tablespoons olive oil
2 cloves garlic, minced
⅓ cup green onions and
    tops, chopped
3 eggs

1 teaspoon Italian seasoning
1 teaspoon salt
½ teaspoon freshly ground
    pepper
2 cups grated Monterey Jack
    cheese
½ cup freshly grated
    Parmesan cheese

Preheat oven to 350 degrees. Using the slicing blade on a food processor, or a very sharp knife, thinly slice the zucchini, eggplant, and mushrooms. Heat the olive oil in a large skillet and sauté garlic until limp, then add chopped onions and prepared vegetables. Sauté, turning and stirring, for about 7 minutes. Meanwhile, beat eggs until frothy, adding seasonings. Combine the vegetables with the beaten eggs. Place in a baking dish, cover with Monterey Jack cheese and then Parmesan cheese. Bake for 40 minutes.

GHIVECIU Vegetable Casserole

This is the Romanian name for a superb vegetable casserole that is very similar to the Bulgarian ghivetch. Almost any vegetable may be used, with the exception of beets and spinach. Feel free to substitute or leave out one or two. Notice that no liquid is used. It reheats well and is a delicious leftover served at room temperature. Fine for picnics.

Serves 12

1 cup olive oil
4 cloves garlic, minced
¼ cup minced fresh parsley
1 teaspoon crumbled bay
    leaves
1 tablespoon thyme
2 teaspoons marjoram
2½ tablespoons salt
¼ to ½ teaspoon crushed
    dried red pepper flakes
1 eggplant, unpeeled and
    cubed
3 zucchini, sliced ½ inch
    thick
3 red and/or green peppers,
    cut in 1-inch cubes
3 large onions, sliced

1 cup sliced celery
2 cups shredded cabbage
1 cup 2-inch cut green beans
1 cup sliced carrots
2 potatoes, peeled and sliced
1 celery root, peeled and
    thinly sliced
1 acorn squash, peeled,
    seeded, and cubed
1 small cauliflower, broken
    into small flowerets
3 medium ripe tomatoes,
    peeled, seeded, and
    sliced
¼ pound seedless grapes
½ cup fresh peas (or
    frozen, defrosted)

Preheat oven to 350 degrees. Beat together olive oil, garlic, herbs, 2 tablespoons of the salt, and red pepper flakes. Prepare vegetables except tomatoes and peas. Lightly oil a large heavy 7- to 8-quart pot or casserole. Sprinkling each layer with oil mixture, layer the eggplant, zucchini, peppers, onions, celery, cabbage, beans, carrots, potatoes, celery root, squash and cauliflower. Cover tightly and bake for 1½ hours. Place tomatoes, grapes, and peas on top, sprinkle with remaining salt, and cover. Continue baking for 15 minutes longer.

CAPONATA

excellent

Caponata *is an interesting variation of ratatouille. It keeps beautifully, travels well, and is best served at room temperature or only slightly warm.*

Serves 10 to 12

1 cup olive oil

1 1½-pound eggplant, peeled and cut into 1-inch cubes

use a combo of red, yellow & (2 altogether) 3 large green peppers, cut into 1-inch pieces

2 large onions, diced

2 cloves garlic, minced

1 28-ounce can solid pack tomatoes, undrained

⅓ cup red wine vinegar

2 tablespoons sugar

2 tablespoons capers, *rinsed*

2 tablespoons tomato paste

2 teaspoons salt

½ cup chopped fresh parsley

½ cup pimiento-stuffed green olives, rinsed and thickly sliced

½ teaspoon freshly ground pepper

2 teaspoons crumbled dried basil

½ cup pine nuts, sautéed in olive oil.

In a large, heavy saucepan combine 1 cup olive oil, eggplant, green peppers, onions, garlic, and tomatoes, and cook for about 20 to 30 minutes or until just tender. Add wine vinegar, sugar, capers, tomato paste, salt, parsley, green olives, pepper, and basil. Cover and simmer for 15 minutes. Add pine nuts and serve warm, not hot, at room temperature, or cold. May be refrigerated for up to 3 weeks.

CHINESE VEGETABLES AND CASHEW NUTS

Any fresh vegetables can be substituted for those listed. Do not over-cook, since the texture should be slightly crunchy.

Serves 8 to 10

2 tablespoons rendered pork
    fat or corn oil or peanut
    oil
1 cup diagonally cut celery
1 cup coarsely chopped red
    onion
1 cup coarsely chopped
    water chestnuts
1 cup frozen peas, thawed,
    or fresh peas cooked
    until crunchy

1 teaspoon garlic salt
1 teaspoon sugar
1 tablespoon soy sauce
½ cup chicken stock
1 cup salted cashew nuts
1 teaspoon cornstarch
    dissolved in 1
    tablespoon water

In a wok or heavy skillet heat fat or oil. Stir-fry celery and onion for 15 seconds. Add water chestnuts, peas, garlic salt, sugar, soy sauce, and chicken stock. Cook and stir until heated through. Add nuts and blend in cornstarch mixture. Cook and stir until thickened and transparent. Serve immediately.

HOLLANDAISE SAUCE

All three methods are good, but No. 2 seems to be the least time-consuming and the one that offers the most control. The secret to good hollandaise is to keep it warm but not hot until ready to serve.

Method No. 1

Makes approximately 2 cups

8 egg yolks
8 tablespoons butter
1 tablespoon fresh lemon
  juice

Salt to taste
Dash white pepper
Dash cayenne pepper

In a saucepan beat egg yolks until creamy. Place over very low heat or in the top of a double boiler over simmering water, and, stirring constantly, add 1 tablespoon of butter at a time. Gradually add all but 1 tablespoon. Add lemon juice, remove from heat, and stir in the last tablespoon of butter to prevent further cooking. Season to taste.

Method No. 2

Makes approximately 1 cup

8 tablespoons butter
3 egg yolks
2 tablespoons fresh lemon
  juice

Salt and cayenne pepper to
  taste

Place butter, egg yolks, and lemon juice in a small saucepan and set aside until mixture reaches room temperature. With a small whisk, stir constantly over very low heat until sauce is thickened. Season to taste.

Method No. 3

Makes approximately 1 cup

6 tablespoons butter
3 egg yolks
2 tablespoons fresh lemon
  juice

Salt and freshly ground
  pepper to taste

Melt butter until foamy. Place remaining ingredients in a blender and turn on high. While blending, slowly add melted butter in a steady stream,

'HEAD-OF-TIME HOLLANDAISE SAUCE

Makes approximately 1 cup

8 tablespoons butter
3 egg yolks
2 tablespoons heavy cream
2 tablespoons fresh lemon
    juice

Salt and cayenne pepper to
    taste

Several hours before serving, put ingredients into a saucepan, stir lightly just to mix, and allow to stand at room temperature until 3 minutes before serving. Cook, stirring constantly, over medium heat until thickened. Serve immediately.

MUSHROOM SAUCE

Makes approximately 2 cups

½ pound fresh mushrooms,
    quartered
½ cup chopped onion
2 tablespoons butter
1 tablespoon flour

1 cup light cream
½ teaspoon salt
¼ teaspoon freshly ground
    pepper
½ cup sour cream

Sauté the mushrooms and onion in butter until tender. Stir in flour. Add cream, salt, and pepper and stir until thickened and bubbly. Remove sauce from heat and stir in sour cream. Serve over any fresh vegetable.

LEMON CREAM SAUCE

This sauce is superb over green beans, broccoli, or fresh asparagus. A nice departure from hollandaise.

Makes 1½ cups

4 tablespoons butter
¾ cup heavy cream
1 egg
¼ teaspoon salt
¼ teaspoon freshly ground
  pepper

2 tablespoons freshly grated
  Parmesan cheese
¼ teaspoon nutmeg
3 to 4 tablespoons fresh
  lemon juice

In a saucepan melt butter and add all but 2 tablespoons of the cream. Cook over low heat for 5 minutes. In a bowl, beat together egg, salt, pepper, and remaining 2 tablespoons cream. Add cheese and nutmeg. While beating constantly with a wire whisk, slowly add lemon juice. Stir this mixture into butter-cream mixture and cook over medium heat, stirring, until well thickened. Mixture should coat the back of a spoon. Pour over vegetables that have been cooked until just tender-crisp.

SAUCE MALTAISE

Makes approximately 1 cup

8 tablespoons butter
3 egg yolks
2 tablespoons fresh orange
  juice

Salt and freshly ground
  pepper to taste

Melt butter until foamy. Blend egg yolks, orange juice, salt, and pepper in a blender while slowly pouring, in a steady stream, the melted butter into the mixture. Adjust seasonings and serve immediately or keep warm until ready to serve in a bowl of lukewarm water.

MUSTARD SAUCE

Delicious on hot steamed broccoli, asparagus spears or green beans.

Makes 2 cups

¾ cup mayonnaise
3 tablespoons fresh lemon
    juice
1½ tablespoons Dijon
    mustard

½ cup heavy cream,
    whipped

Mix together the mayonnaise, lemon juice, and mustard. Fold in the whipped cream.

CHAPTER IX

FISH

Fisherman's Wharf

The sound of early morning foghorns; fishermen hawking their day's catch beside steaming caldrons on the sidewalks; old men, backs to the wind, bending low over their nets; sea gulls following the wake of fishing boats, returning in the early afternoon from the sea; and the bustle of twentieth-century commerce—all are part of the quaint but contemporary neighborhood called Fisherman's Wharf.

In keeping with nautical tradition, every year the fishing fleet is blessed. A colorful parade, beginning at Sts. Peter & Paul Church in North Beach, proceeds to Fisherman's Wharf, where an Old World ceremony honors the patron saint of fishermen, Santa Maria del Lume, and focuses civic attention on our historic ties to the sea. Extracted from the generous waters around us is a vast array of fish and crustaceans such as petrale sole, the finest of the Pacific soles; delicately flavored sand dabs; red snapper; the plentiful squid; tiny bay shrimp and abalone, whose scarcity only whets the appetite; trout from lake and stream; Dungeness crab, amazingly on the increase; Delta crayfish; salmon, swimming through the Golden Gate on their way to spawn upstream; even shark, a new and abundant taste. All these and more are ready to be added to the kettle to yield rich *cioppino*, to be filleted and complemented with a sauce or to sizzle in a buttery pan with lemon the solitary garnish. Barbecued or baked, poached or pan-fried, these delectable delicacies from the wharf add greatly to the repertoire of good food and have been a mainstay of San Francisco cuisine since its beginning.

CALAMARI CALABRESE

*Scoma's Restaurant developed this especially delicious rendition of an Italian seafood classic. The sauce may be made ahead and the squid (*calamari*) added at the last minute.*

Serves 6 to 8

TOMATO SAUCE
1 large onion, chopped
1 clove garlic, mashed
3 tablespoons olive oil
2 1-pound cans whole
    tomatoes

1 tablespoon tomato paste
2 whole bay leaves
½ teaspoon oregano
¼ teaspoon sage

CREAM SAUCE
3 tablespoons butter
3 tablespoons flour
1 cup milk

½ cup white wine
Salt and freshly ground
    pepper to taste

VEGETABLES AND SQUID
1 large onion, coarsely
    chopped
2 cloves garlic, minced
½ pound fresh mushrooms,
    sliced

1 teaspoon red pepper flakes,
    crushed
3 pounds squid
Flour
Olive oil

To make the tomato sauce, sauté the onion and garlic in the olive oil for 5 to 6 minutes. Add the other ingredients and cook, stirring occasionally, for about 30 minutes or until the sauce thickens slightly. Set aside to cool. To prepare the cream sauce: melt the butter over low heat until it bubbles, then gradually stir in the flour, and cook, stirring, for 3 to 5 minutes. Slowly stir in the milk and continue to stir until the sauce is very thick and smooth. Add the wine and seasonings. Set aside. In a skillet, sauté all the vegetables together for 5 minutes. Set aside. In a large pan, combine the tomato sauce, cream sauce, and vegetables. Clean the squid by removing the ink sack, eyes, and cuttlebone. Cut squid into bite-size pieces, rinse, and drain thoroughly. Dredge the squid lightly in flour and fry in the oil over high heat until well browned. Remove from skillet and drain thoroughly. Add the squid to the sauce, reheat slightly, and serve.

CLAM AND SPINACH SHELLS

Serves 4

3 tablespoons butter
1 scallion with some green
    top, finely chopped
2 7½-ounce cans minced
    clams
½ cup dry white wine
1 10-ounce package frozen
    chopped spinach,
    thawed and drained
2 tablespoons cornstarch

¼ cup heavy cream
¼ teaspoon salt
Freshly ground pepper to
    taste
⅛ teaspoon nutmeg
2 tablespoons grated
    Parmesan cheese
2 tablespoons grated Swiss
    cheese
4 lemon slices

Preheat oven to 400 degrees. Melt 2 tablespoons butter in a skillet and gently sauté scallion until soft. Drain clams, reserving juice, and add clams to skillet, stirring until well coated. Add wine and cook until liquid is reduced by half. In a separate skillet, melt remaining tablespoon of butter and heat drained spinach, stirring, until just heated through. In a small saucepan combine cornstarch, clam juice, and cream, cook and stir until thickened. Season with salt, pepper, and nutmeg. Mix together the spinach and clam mixtures, add thickened cornstarch sauce, and spoon into four buttered scallop shells. Combine grated cheeses and sprinkle over tops. Bake for 15 minutes. Garnish with lemon slices.

FRESH CRAB MEAT AND MUSHROOMS

Serves 6

1 medium onion, chopped
½ pound fresh mushrooms,
    thinly sliced
4 tablespoons butter
¼ cup all-purpose flour
1½ cups light cream
1 pound flaked fresh crab
    meat

Juice of ½ lemon
½ teaspoon paprika
Salt and white pepper to
    taste
Bread crumbs

Preheat oven to 375 degrees. Sauté onion and mushrooms in butter until soft. Sprinkle with flour and cook and stir for 3 minutes. Gradually add cream and cook and stir until well blended and thickened. Fold in crab meat. Add lemon juice and adjust seasonings with paprika, salt, and pepper to taste. Fill 6 scallop shells or ramekins with mixture, sprinkle liberally with bread crumbs, and bake for 10 minutes or until bubbly and golden brown.

DEVILED DUNGENESS CRAB

Very good first course, since it can all be prepared ahead and refrigerated. Elegant and easy.

Serves 4

6 to 8 tablespoons butter
2 tablespoons all-purpose
    flour
1 cup light cream
½ teaspoon Worcestershire
    sauce
½ teaspoon grated onion

¾ pound fresh Dungeness
    crab or any locally
    available fresh crab
½ cup bread crumbs
4 lemon slices
½ teaspoon paprika

Preheat oven to 425 degrees. Melt 2 tablespoons butter in a saucepan until foamy. Add flour and cook for 3 minutes. Slowly add light cream, Worcestershire sauce, and onion, stirring until thoroughly blended and thickened. Remove from heat and stir in crab meat until well mixed. Spoon mixture into 4 scallop shells and refrigerate until well chilled. Remove filled shells from refrigerator and top with bread crumbs, dots of remaining butter, lemon slices, and paprika. Bake for 15 minutes or until bread crumbs are browned and crab mixture is bubbly. Serve immediately.

CRAB ALASKA

Serves 12

4 tablespoons butter
⅓ cup all-purpose flour
¼ cup mayonnaise
1 small can sliced mushrooms
 or 1 cup sliced fresh
 mushrooms sautéed in
 butter
Mushroom juices and light
 cream to make 2 cups
6 eggs, separated
¼ cup dry sherry
½ teaspoon Worcestershire
 sauce

¾ teaspoon salt
¼ teaspoon freshly ground
 white pepper
⅛ teaspoon cayenne pepper
2 cups flaked crab meat
12 thin slices white bread,
 trimmed and buttered
 on one side
½ teaspoon salt
½ teaspoon cream of tartar
1 cup freshly grated
 Parmesan cheese

Melt butter in a large, heavy saucepan until foamy. And flour, blend, and cook for 3 minutes. Stir in mayonnaise. Drain mushrooms, reserving juice, and set aside. Blend mushroom juice-cream mixture into flour mixture. Cook and stir until well blended and thickened. Remove from heat. Beat egg yolks and sherry until creamy, and gradually stir in half the cream sauce. Add this mixture to remaining cream sauce, return to heat, and stir, without allowing to boil, for 3 minutes. Add Worcestershire sauce, salt, pepper, cayenne, mushrooms, and crab. Cut buttered bread slices in half. Place 12 half-slices 2 inches apart on a large cookie sheet and spread with half of the crab mixture. Cover with the other halves of buttered bread and spread with remaining crab, making a two-decker open-face sandwich. Chill thoroughly. Preheat oven to 375 degrees. Beat egg whites and ½ teaspoon salt until foamy. Add cream of tartar and beat until stiff but not dry. Spread on top and sides of each sandwich, sealing completely. Sprinkle with Parmesan cheese and bake for 15 to 20 minutes until golden brown.

CRAB TOMATO SANDWICHES

Serves 6

TOPPING

3 ounces cream cheese,
 softened

½ cup shredded crab meat

1 teaspoon lemon juice

1 egg, lightly beaten

6 slices sandwich bread,
 crusts removed

3 tablespoons mayonnaise

2 tablespoons minced parsley

2 tablespoons grated
 Parmesan cheese

Dash of cayenne pepper

2 large tomatoes, ripe but
 firm

Preheat oven to broil. Combine topping ingredients and blend carefully. Toast one side of the bread slices. Cut tomatoes into thick slices and place on untoasted side of bread slices. Spread with topping mixture and broil about 5 inches from heat until puffed and browned.

CRAB CAKES

Lovely luncheon dish with the freshest crab and a crisp green salad.

Serves 4

3 slices white bread, crusts
 removed

1 pound flaked crab meat

1 tablespoon chopped fresh
 parsley

⅛ teaspoon Worcestershire
 sauce

1 cup mayonnaise

Salt and freshly ground
 pepper to taste

Paprika

Butter as needed

Crumble bread and combine with crab. Add parsley and Worcestershire sauce and bind with mayonnaise. Add salt and pepper and form into 8 1-inch-thick cakes. Sprinkle lightly with paprika and chill at least 1 hour. Carefully sauté in butter until heated through and golden brown, turning once.

CRAB CREPES WITH OYSTER SAUCE

Serves 6

1½ pounds flaked crab meat
½ teaspoon summer savory
Salt and freshly ground
    pepper to taste

12 crepes (see Index)
Oyster Sauce (see Index)

Preheat oven to 350 degrees. Divide crab into 12 portions and place on crepes. Sprinkle with savory, salt, and pepper. Roll crepes and arrange in a buttered shallow ovenproof serving dish, rolled edge down. Pour Oyster Sauce over crepes and bake, covered, for 20 minutes or until heated through.

RED PEPPERS STUFFED WITH SHRIMP

Serves 4 to 6

2 large or 3 medium sweet
    red peppers
3 tablespoons butter
¼ cup chopped onion
¼ cup all-purpose flour
1 cup sour cream at room
    temperature
1 teaspoon fresh lemon juice
1 teaspoon Dijon mustard
2 tablespoons chopped fresh
    parsley

1 8-ounce can water
    chestnuts, drained and
    thinly sliced
2 cups cooked tiny shrimp
Salt and freshly ground
    pepper to taste
½ cup shredded Monterey
    Jack cheese

Preheat oven to 350 degrees. Halve peppers lengthwise and remove seeds and membrane. Blanch for 4 minutes in boiling water, drain, and set aside. Melt butter and sauté onion until soft. Sprinkle with flour and cook until bubbly. Remove from heat and blend in sour cream. Cook and stir over low heat until thickened. Add lemon juice, mustard, parsley, water chestnuts, and shrimp. Season with salt and pepper. Spoon into pepper shells and sprinkle tops with cheese. Bake for 30 minutes or until heated through and cheese is bubbly.

GARIDES ME FETA

You will shout, "Eureka" when you try this Greek rendition of shrimp in a tomato sauce with feta cheese.

Serves 4

½ cup minced onion
1½ tablespoons butter
1½ tablespoons oil
½ cup dry white wine
4 ripe medium tomatoes,
    peeled, seeded, and
    chopped
1 small clove garlic, minced
1 teaspoon salt

¼ teaspoon freshly ground
    pepper
¾ teaspoon oregano
4 ounces feta cheese,
    crumbled
1 pound raw large shrimp,
    shelled and deveined
¼ cup chopped fresh
    parsley

In a heavy skillet, sauté onion in butter and oil until soft. Add wine, tomatoes, garlic, salt, pepper, and oregano. Bring to boil, lower heat to medium, and simmer until sauce is slightly thickened. Stir in cheese and simmer for 10 to 15 minutes. Adjust seasonings. Just before serving, add shrimp to hot sauce and cook for 5 minutes or until shrimp are just tender. Do not overcook. Garnish with parsley and serve immediately in large bowls with crusty French bread.

SHRIMP AND MUSHROOMS IN SOUR CREAM

A lovely luncheon dish or first course.

Serves 4

½ pound tiny shrimp
¾ cup sour cream
1 tablespoon prepared
    horseradish
2 teaspoons cognac

¼ pound fresh mushrooms,
    cut in strips
Lettuce leaves
Fresh parsley, finely
    chopped

Combine shrimp and sour cream, add horseradish, cognac, and mushrooms, and mix gently but well. Place lettuce on individual serving dishes, mound with shrimp mixture, and sprinkle with parsley.

SHRIMP CURRY

Serves 4

3 green onions, chopped
1 clove garlic, minced
4 tablespoons butter
3 tablespoons all-purpose
    flour
2 tablespoons curry powder
½ teaspoon powdered
    ginger

1 cup chicken stock
1 cup light cream
2 tablespoons fresh lemon
    juice
1 pound cooked tiny shrimp

CONDIMENTS
Sliced bananas
Chopped chives
Chutney

Chopped peanuts
Coconut
Chopped egg

Sauté onions and garlic in butter until soft. Sprinkle with flour, curry powder, and ginger. Stir and cook for 3 minutes. Gradually add chicken stock, then cream. Cook and stir until well blended and thickened. Add lemon juice and shrimp. Adjust seasonings. Serve over rice with condiments.

SCAMPI ALLA LIVORNESE

This well-known favorite from the Blue Fox Restaurant is easy to prepare and always a hit.

Serves 6

12 jumbo shrimp or scampi
1 cup milk
4½ to 5 tablespoons
    all-purpose flour
Salt and freshly ground
    pepper to taste
Oil, enough to fill skillet to
    1-inch depth

2 cups dry white wine
1 tablespoon minced shallots
½ teaspoon minced garlic
2 teaspoons fresh lemon juice
½ cup butter at room
    temperature
Chopped fresh parsley

Shell and devein shrimp, making a long cut down the backs to spread open or butterfly. Soak in milk, to cover for about 15 minutes. Drain, dry on paper towels, and lightly dredge with 3 tablespoons of flour, salt, and pepper. Heat oil in a skillet and fry the shrimp, a few at a time, for about 2 minutes or until lightly browned. Drain on paper towels and keep warm. Set aside. Combine wine, shallots, and garlic in a large shallow pan and bring to a boil. Reduce liquid to 1 cup. Add shrimp and boil at high heat for 1 minute. Remove from heat and sprinkle with remaining flour, stirring until blended. Return to heat, add lemon juice and butter, and cook just until butter is melted. Sprinkle with chopped parsley. Serve as a first course.

SHRIMP IN BLACK BEAN SAUCE

Serves 6

1 tablespoon dry sherry
2 tablespoons minced fresh
    ginger
1 tablespoon soy sauce
¼ teaspoon freshly ground
    white pepper
1 pound raw shrimp, shelled
    and deveined
¼ cup peanut or corn oil
1 cup diced onions

1 10-ounce package frozen
    tiny peas, thawed
1 small green pepper, diced
2 cloves garlic, minced
2 tablespoons Chinese
    fermented black beans,
    rinsed and mashed
2 teaspoons cornstarch
    dissolved in ¼ cup
    water

Combine sherry, ginger, soy sauce and white pepper. Pour over shrimp and let marinate, for 15 minutes, drain. Heat 2 tablespoons of the oil in a heavy skillet or wok and stir-fry onions, peas, and green pepper for 2 minutes; remove with slotted spoon and set aside. Add remaining oil to skillet or wok and stir-fry garlic and black beans in it for 10 seconds. Add drained shrimp and stir-fry until shrimp turn pink. Return vegetables to skillet or wok and whisk in cornstarch mixture. Stir well and cook until sauce thickens.

SZECHUAN SHRIMP

Serves 6 to 8

2 tablespoons peanut oil
1 pound extra-large raw
    shrimp, shelled and
    deveined
¼ cup minced green onion
2 tablespoons minced fresh
    ginger
3 cloves garlic, finely minced

2 tablespoons dry sherry
2 tablespoons soy sauce
2 teaspoons sugar
½ teaspoon salt
2 to 3 tablespoons catsup
2 tablespoons chili sauce
1 teaspoon red pepper flakes

Heat oil in a wok or large, heavy skillet. Add shrimp, green onion, ginger, and garlic. Stir-fry until shrimp are pink. Add sherry, soy sauce, sugar, and salt. Stir well and blend in catsup, chili sauce, and red pepper flakes. Serve with piping-hot rice.

SHRIMP AND SCALLOP BROCHETTE

Serves 6

½ cup oil
¼ cup dry vermouth
¼ cup soy sauce
½ teaspoon powdered
    ginger

1 clove garlic, crushed
2 pounds raw large shrimp,
    shelled and deveined
1 pound raw scallops

Combine oil, vermouth, soy sauce, ginger, and garlic to make a marinade. Marinate shrimp and scallops for 30 minutes. Thread onto bamboo skewers that have been soaked in water. Broil, turning frequently and basting with marinade, for 5 minutes or until just cooked.

delic!

EASY AND ELEGANT SCALLOPS

Surprisingly good and very attractive to serve. A perfect Sunday lunch.

Serves 6

1 cup dry vermouth
½ cup water
½ teaspoon salt
4 peppercorns
1 bay leaf
2 sprigs parsley
2 pounds scallops
10 tablespoons butter
1 onion, sliced
½ pound mushrooms, sliced
3 medium tomatoes, peeled,
    seeded, and chopped

4 tablespoons all-purpose
    flour
1 cup reserved court
    bouillon (given below)
2 tablespoons light cream
Bread crumbs
Paprika
Chopped fresh parsley for
    garnish

Preheat oven to 400 degrees. In a large saucepan combine and bring to boil the vermouth, water, salt, peppercorns, bay leaf, and parsley. Simmer for 10 to 15 minutes to make a court bouillon. Add scallops and poach for 2 minutes. Remove scallops and set aside. Strain court bouillon and reserve. Cut scallops into pieces and place in a large mixing bowl. Melt 4 tablespoons butter in a skillet and sauté onion, mushrooms, and tomatoes for about 10 minutes until soft. Remove from heat and add to scallops. Melt 4 tablespoons butter in a saucepan until foamy, add the 4 tablespoons flour, and cook for 3 minutes. Slowly add 1 cup reserved court bouillon and cook, stirring constantly, until well blended and thickened. Blend cream into sauce. Add to scallop mixture in bowl and mix thoroughly. Place in scallop shells, sprinkle with bread crumbs, and dot with remaining butter. Bake for 10 minutes. Dust with paprika and garnish with chopped parsley.

SCALLOPS PROVENÇALE

Serves 6 to 8

1½ pounds scallops
2 tablespoons fresh lemon
    juice
4 tablespoons butter
1 to 2 cloves garlic, crushed
2 shallots, minced
3 medium ripe tomatoes,
    peeled, seeded, and
    chopped

½ cup dry white wine
¼ teaspoon salt
¼ teaspoon white pepper
Fresh parsley, finely
    chopped

Marinate scallops in lemon juice for 15 minutes. Drain, pat dry, and halve or quarter if large. In a large skillet, melt butter until foamy and quickly sauté scallops for 2 minutes, turning once to brown on 2 sides. Do not crowd in skillet or scallops will cook too slowly and will stew rather than brown. Remove scallops with slotted spoon and set aside. To skillet add garlic, shallots, tomatoes, wine, salt, and pepper. Cook uncovered, stirring occasionally, for 15 minutes. Return scallops to skillet, cover, and cook gently for 5 to 6 minutes, shaking pan frequently to prevent sticking. Adjust seasonings and spoon into heated scallop shells or serving dish. Sprinkle with parsley and serve immediately.

TOMALES BAY OYSTERS

Serves 6

8 tablespoons butter,
    softened
2 teaspoons onion juice
¼ teaspoon seasoned salt
⅛ teaspoon cayenne pepper
¼ cup seasoned bread
    crumbs
½ pound fresh spinach,
    washed and stems
    removed

Rock salt
6 individual ovenproof
    dishes
12 oyster shells or 6 scallop
    shells
12 large oysters

Combine the softened butter with onion juice, salt, pepper, and bread crumbs, and mix until well blended. Set aside. Cook the spinach in boiling water, drain very thoroughly, and chop coarsely. Place some rock salt in each ovenproof dish. Place two oyster shells on the salt and in each shell put a tablespoon of spinach, an oyster, then a teaspoon of the butter mixture. If you use scallop shells, use 1 per serving with 2 oysters and twice the amount of spinach and butter mixture per shell. Place under a preheated broiler until the butter melts and the oysters are slightly brown around the edges. Serve immediately.

BROILED SALMON STEAKS WITH MUSTARD SAUCE

Beautiful to look at, good to eat.

Serves 4

4 salmon steaks, 1 inch thick
¼ cup dry white wine
¼ cup milk

Salt and freshly ground
   pepper to taste

MUSTARD SAUCE
1 cup sour cream at room
   temperature
½ cup finely chopped
   scallions with some
   green tops
1½ tablespoons Dijon
   mustard
1 tablespoon chopped fresh
   parsley

½ teaspoon powdered
   thyme
½ teaspoon powdered
   marjoram
Salt and freshly ground
   pepper to taste

Marinate salmon steaks in wine and milk for 2 hours.

To make the mustard sauce: combine sour cream, scallions, mustard, parsley, thyme, marjoram, salt, and pepper. Set aside. Drain salmon and place in a shallow baking dish lined with foil. Sprinkle lightly with salt and pepper. Broil 6 inches below heat for 7 minutes. Turn the salmon steaks and spread each evenly with sauce. Return to broiler for 5 minutes or until fish flakes easily with a fork. Do not overcook.

BROILED MARINATED SALMON

This is just the simple yet elegant kind of recipe that appeals to any hostess. The marinade is good and the salmon moist and delicious. Very versatile with any accompanying dishes.

Serves 4

½ cup dry vermouth
½ cup salad oil
2 tablespoons fresh lemon
    juice
¾ teaspoon salt
⅛ teaspoon freshly ground
    pepper

½ teaspoon thyme
½ teaspoon marjoram
¼ teaspoon sage
1 tablespoon minced fresh
    parsley
4 salmon steaks

Combine vermouth, oil, lemon juice, salt, pepper, thyme, marjoram, sage, and parsley. Mrainate salmon steaks for 2 to 3 hours in this mixture. Place steaks on greased broiler rack or grill and cook, basting frequently with marinade, for 7 to 8 minutes on each side or until salmon flakes easily with fork.

SALMON LOAF SUPREME WITH CUCUMBER SAUCE

Serves 4

1 pound poached fresh
    salmon, flaked, or
    canned equivalent
½ cup grated mild Cheddar
    cheese
1 egg, beaten
1 tablespoon finely chopped
    green pepper

¾ cup milk
½ cup cracker crumbs
½ tablespoon butter, melted
½ tablespoon fresh lemon
    juice
½ teaspoon salt
Cucumber Sauce (see Index)

Preheat oven to 350 degrees. Blend all ingredients. Place in a buttered 1½-quart loaf pan, sprinkle top with a few additional cracker crumbs, and bake for 45 to 60 minutes. Serve with cucumber sauce.

POACHED SALMON MOUSSELINE

Serves 4

4 salmon steaks
1 cup dry white wine
2 tablespoons flour
2 tablespoons butter, melted
2 egg yolks at room
    temperature
Juice of ½ lemon

¼ pound butter at room
    temperature
Salt and freshly ground
    white pepper to taste
½ cup heavy cream,
    whipped
4 lemon slices

Poach salmon steaks in wine for approximately 8 minutes or until they flake easily with a fork, reserve wine. Remove salmon to a serving platter and keep warm. Add flour and melted butter to wine and stir with a whisk until thickened. Set aside. Place egg yolks, lemon juice, and butter in a small, heavy saucepan and stir constantly over very low heat until thickened. Season with salt and pepper. Add egg yolk mixture to wine sauce, stirring until just heated. Fold whipped cream into sauce and pour over salmon steaks. Garnish with lemon slices.

SALMON STEAKS WITH CAPER SAUCE

Serves 6

2 tablespoons butter
¾ cup finely sliced carrots
½ cup finely sliced celery
¼ cup finely sliced shallots
4 to 5 sprigs fresh parsley,
    chopped
¾ teaspoon fennel seed

CAPER SAUCE
3 egg yolks, lightly beaten
Salt and freshly ground
    pepper to taste

½ teaspoon thyme
Salt and freshly ground
    pepper to taste
6 salmon steaks
1 cup dry white wine
½ cup fish stock or clam
    stock

2 tablespoons capers
Chopped parsley for garnish

Preheat oven to 350 degrees. In a large skillet, melt butter and sauté the carrots, celery, shallots, parsley, fennel seed, and thyme for 2 to 3 minutes, stirring constantly. Cover the skillet and cook gently over medium heat for 10 minutes. Spread the vegetables in the bottom of a large heatproof dish. Season salmon steaks with salt and pepper and arrange them on the vegetables. Cover with white wine and stock and bring liquid to simmer over low heat. Cover the dish tightly with foil and bake the salmon for 15 to 20 minutes or until fish flakes easily. Reserve braising stock. Transfer salmon to a heated serving platter and keep warm while making sauce.

To make the caper sauce: Strain the braising stock into a saucepan and, over low heat, slowly beat in the egg yolks, using a wire whisk and stirring constantly until thickened and smooth. Do not let sauce boil. Add salt and pepper, fold in capers, and spoon sauce over salmon steaks. Garnish with chopped parsley.

BAKED SALMON WITH SOUR CREAM SAUCE

Serves 10

1 6- to 7-pound whole
    salmon
4 slices bacon
2 lemons, sliced
2 large onions, chopped
4 tablespoons butter
1 cup dry sherry
2 cups Béchamel Sauce (see
    Index)

1 cup sour cream at room
    temperature
2 tablespoons salmon juice
    (from baking)
1 tablespoon fresh lemon
    juice
Fresh parsley for garnish
Lemon wedges for garnish

Preheat oven to 350 degrees. Cover salmon with bacon and lemon slices. Wrap in heavy duty foil and bake for 1 hour and 15 minutes or until salmon flakes easily with a fork. Do not overcook. To make sauce: sauté onions in butter until soft. Add sherry and cook until liquid is absorbed. Add béchamel sauce and gently reheat. Just before serving add sour cream, salmon juice, and lemon juice, and adjust seasonings. Spoon over salmon and garnish with parsley and lemon.

GRAVLAX

Gravlax is a sublime way to treat salmon. It makes any picnic "gourmet," and any leftovers just lightly broiled are good for brunch. There is no need to waste a bite.

Serves 8 to 10

1 whole salmon, 4 to 5 pounds, split, with large bones, head, and tail removed

2 teaspoons freshly ground white pepper

4 tablespoons salt

2 tablespoons sugar

Fresh dillweed

Crush together the white pepper, salt, and sugar. Rub half the mixture into the cut sides of both halves of the salmon. On a large piece of aluminum foil, sprinkle a liberal amount of dillweed and place half of salmon, skin side down, on foil. Add more dillweed and seasonings to cut side. Place second half of salmon, skin side up, on top of first piece. Sprinkle with remaining seasoning mixture and fold up foil to tightly enclose salmon. Place on a large platter and weight down with bricks. Refrigerate for approximately 48 hours, turning foil package every 12 hours to distribute marinade evenly. Before serving, scrape off dill and seasonings, slice thinly on the bias, and serve with Mustard Dill Sauce (see Index).

SPICED POACHED SALMON

Serves 6 to 8

FISH

2 quarts water

1 bottle dry white wine

2 medium onions stuck with 2 whole cloves each

1 stalk celery, sliced

2 carrots, sliced

1 bay leaf

½ teaspoon thyme

½ teaspoon salt

3- to 4-pound whole salmon

PICKLING LIQUID
1 quart rice vinegar
½ cup pickling spices
½ cup sugar

In a fish poacher or pan that will comfortably hold the fish, place the 2 quarts water, wine, onions, celery, carrots, bay leaf, thyme, and salt, and simmer for 1 hour to make a court bouillon. Add the fish on a poaching rack or wrapped in a double thickness of cheesecloth, leaving long ends of cloth for easy removal of fish. (Measure the fish at its thickest point, then poach for 10 minutes per inch. For example, a 3-inch-thick fish should be poached for 30 minutes.) When fish is cooked, remove from stock and set aside to cool. Stock can be strained and frozen for another use. Carefully remove the skin from the salmon and place fish in a deep dish. Pour over pickling liquid and chill for 24 to 48 hours. Drain and serve garnished with watercress.

BAKED RED SNAPPER

Serves 4

1 whole red snapper,
    approximately 1 to 1½
    pounds
1 teaspoon rosemary
Salt and freshly ground
    pepper to taste

4 tablespoons butter
½ lemon, chopped and
    seeded
Fresh parsley, finely
    chopped

Have the fish cleaned and scaled, leaving on the head and tail. Preheat oven to 325 degrees. Sprinkle cavity and outside of fish generously with rosemary, salt, and pepper. Place in a buttered baking dish and dot with remaining butter. Bake for 25 minutes or until fish flakes easily with a fork. Just before serving, sprinkle with chopped lemon and parsley.

STEAMED SEA BASS

Serves 6

1 sea bass, about 2 pounds
1 tablespoon dry sherry
3 tablespoons peanut oil
2 tablespoons finely
shredded fresh ginger

2 scallions, finely shredded
3 tablespoons soy sauce
1 teaspoon sugar
Fresh coriander (cilantro),
chopped

Have the fish cleaned and scaled, but leave on the head and tail. Rinse it in cold water and pat dry. Place it on a shallow dish or foil and sprinkle it with sherry. Let sit for 10 minutes. Put the fish on the rack of a steamer, making certain that the water level is below the rack. Cover and steam for 15 minutes. Just before the fish is ready, heat a wok for 30 seconds over high heat. Add the oil and swirl around. Add ginger and stir-fry for 1 minute, then add scallions, soy sauce, and sugar. Stir mixture for a few seconds. Remove the fish to a serving platter and pour the sauce over it. Garnish with the fresh coriander and serve immediately.

HALIBUT WITH SHRIMP SAUCE

Serves 6

¼ pound fresh mushrooms,
sliced
9 tablespoons butter
2 medium ripe tomatoes,
peeled, seeded, and
chopped

1 clove garlic, minced
Salt and freshly ground
pepper to taste
6 medium halibut steaks
Shrimp Sauce (see Index)

Preheat oven to 400 degrees. Sauté mushrooms in 3 tablespoons melted butter until just soft. Stir in tomatoes and garlic. Heat through and season with salt and pepper. Place halibut steaks close together in a shallow baking dish. Spoon sauce over them and bake, uncovered, for 20 to 30 minutes or until fish flakes easily with a fork. Transfer halibut steaks to a deep heatproof platter and spoon cooked vegetables over them. Pour shrimp sauce over all and sprinkle with remaining Parmesan cheese called for in sauce recipe. Broil until bubbly.

CEVICHE

This is a great recipe for entertaining, since it can be done so far ahead and the marinade "cooks" the fish. It is also perfect for picnics or outdoor parties, because it travels so well. Just drain it and serve.

Serves 10

2 pounds boneless firm white fish fillets, such as red snapper or flounder
½ pound scallops
1½ cups fresh lime (or lemon) juice
1½ teaspoons salt
1 bunch scallions with some green tops, minced
1 large red onion, minced
2 large ripe tomatoes, peeled and chopped
2 bay leaves, crumbled

1½ teaspoons chili powder
1 teaspoon dried oregano or 1 tablespoon minced fresh oregano
⅓ cup whole small stuffed olives
1 cup dry white wine
½ cup safflower oil
¼ to ½ cup green chilies, diced (optional)
½ pound small shrimp, cooked, shelled

Cut fish and scallops into bite-size pieces and gently toss them in lime (or lemon) juice and salt. Cover and refrigerate, stirring occasionally, for 4 hours or until seafood is translucent. Drain and add scallions, onion, tomatoes, bay leaves, chili powder, oregano, olives, wine, oil, peppers, and shrimp. Mix well and refrigerate for several hours. Just before serving, drain, adjust seasonings. Serve as a first course, hors d'oeuvre, or salad.

BAKED FISH WITH ALMOND STUFFING

This excellent stuffing makes an ordinary fish a special dish, and it can easily be prepared hours ahead.

Serves 6

¼ cup chopped onion
2 tablespoons butter
3 cups soft bread crumbs
½ cup chopped celery
½ cup chopped green pepper
½ cup chopped and toasted almonds
3 eggs, lightly beaten

2 tablespoons chopped fresh parsley
1 teaspoon dried tarragon
8 tablespoons butter
Salt and freshly ground pepper to taste
1 5- to 6-pound whole bass or red snapper, cleaned and washed

Preheat oven to 400 degrees. Sauté onion in 2 tablespoons butter until soft. Add bread crumbs, celery, green pepper, almonds, eggs, parsley, and tarragon and mix well. Stuff cavity of fish with mixture and sew shut. Melt 8 tablespoons butter, line a large shallow baking dish with foil, and pour a little melted butter over the bottom. Place fish on the foil and sprinkle with salt and pepper. Bake for 1 hour and 15 minutes, basting frequently with remaining melted butter, or until fish flakes easily with a fork. Do not overcook.

POACHED FILLETS OF SOLE

Serves 8

½ pound fish skin and bones of white fish
½ cup water
¾ cup dry white wine
¼ teaspoon salt
4 peppercorns
1 teaspoon tarragon
8 fillets of sole, rolled

½ pound sweet butter at room temperature
4 egg yolks, lightly beaten
4 tablespoons heavy cream
½ teaspoon salt
¼ teaspoon cayenne pepper
Fresh parsley for garnish

Preheat oven to 350 degrees. Make a fish stock by combining fish skin and bones, water, wine, salt, peppercorns, and tarragon, and bring to a boil. Simmer for 15 minutes, partially covered, cool, and strain. Butter a shallow baking dish and place rolled fillets in it in a single layer. Pour fish stock over fillets and cover with a piece of buttered wax paper. Poach for 10 minutes. Carefully remove the fillets to a warm serving platter and keep warm. Strain the liquid into a heavy saucepan and boil until it has reduced to about 6 tablespoons. Set aside to cool. When cool, add sweet butter, egg yolks, cream, salt, and cayenne, stirring over a low heat until sauce thickens. Spoon sauce over fish fillets and garnish with parsley.

FILLET OF SOLE GRUYÈRE

This is so good and different. The whole dish can be put together ahead of time (a few hours), then popped in the hot oven to cook. It is surprisingly light, and the cheese gives just the right flavor.

Serves 4

3 tablespoons butter
1 medium onion, sliced
½ pound mushrooms, sliced
1 cup grated Gruyère cheese
4 fillets of sole

Salt and freshly ground
    pepper to taste
½ teaspoon paprika
4 sprigs fresh parsley

Preheat oven to 400 degrees. Melt butter in a heavy skillet and lightly sauté onion and mushrooms until soft, about 5 minutes. Butter a shallow baking dish and cover the bottom of the dish with half of the onion and mushroom mixture. Sprinkle with half of the cheese. Fold each fillet in half and arrange over the onion mixture, slightly overlapping. Top fillets with remaining onion and mushrooms, then remaining cheese. Season with salt, pepper, and paprika. Bake for 20 minutes, then brown quickly under the broiler until the cheese bubbles. Garnish with sprigs of parsley and serve immediately.

BOURRIDE

A French classic. This stew from Provence looks complicated but is really nothing more than fish poached in a savory stock. The fish is served on a platter and the stock is passed separately. For each serving, place a piece of toasted French bread in the bottom of a flat soup bowl. First pass the fish to go on top of the bread, then the thickened stock to be laddled over the fish. Last pass the reserved aioli sauce to go on top. Beware, however, that the strong garlic flavor may not appeal to everyone.

Serves 8 to 10

STOCK

3 to 4 tablespoons olive oil	2 cups dry white wine
1 cup sliced onions	2 bay leaves
1 cup sliced carrots	¼ teaspoon thyme
1 cup sliced leeks	¼ teaspoon fennel
2 medium tomatoes, peeled and chopped	2 large strips of dried orange peel
2 quarts fresh fish trimmings (bones, heads, etc.)	2 cloves garlic
	2 pinches powdered saffron
3 quarts water	1½ tablespoons salt

In a large kettle or casserole, heat the olive oil and gently cook the onions, carrots, and leeks until soft but not brown. Add tomatoes and cook for a few more minutes. Add remaining ingredients and bring to a boil, then simmer for about 40 minutes, skimming the surface occasionally. Strain and set aside.

AIOLI (an egg-yolk-enriched garlic mayonnaise)

⅓ cup stale bread crumbs	½ teaspoon salt
Few drops of white wine vinegar	6 egg yolks
	1½ cups olive oil
6 to 8 cloves garlic	White pepper to taste

Moisten bread crumbs with drops of wine vinegar and grind into a paste, using a mortar and pestle. Force garlic through a press and grind until smooth, using the mortar and pestle. Transfer the garlic mixture to a bowl. Add salt and 2 egg yolks and stir until mixture is sticky. Slowly add olive oil by drops, beating constantly, until sauce is thick and heavy like mayonnaise. Season with white pepper. Remove half of this sauce to a sauceboat and cover tightly. Set aside. Beat remaining 4 egg yolks into other half of sauce in the bowl and cover.

TO ASSEMBLE AND SERVE

4 pounds assorted white fish, cleaned, boned, and filleted

Salt and freshly ground white pepper to taste

Chopped fresh parsley

8 to 10 slices toasted French bread

Cut fish into 8 to 10 portions. Fifteen minutes before serving, bring strained stock to a rolling boil. Add fish, making sure that stock covers them, and boil gently for 8 to 10 minutes. Remove fish to a serving platter and keep warm. Very slowly, ladle a little of the hot stock into the bowl of aioli that contains the 4 egg yolks. Stir continuously and be very careful not to scramble the yolks. After about a cup of stock has been incorporated, pour the diluted aioli sauce into the stock. Simmer gently to thicken, and check seasonings. Ladle thickened stock into a serving bowl and garnish with parsley. Assemble each serving at the table according to directions in recipe note.

CABLE CAR TUNA CASSEROLE

Serves 6

6 ounces egg noodles, cooked *al dente* and drained

½ teaspoon thyme

¼ teaspoon salt

1 10½-ounce can cream of celery soup

½ cup milk

2 7-ounce cans solid white tuna, drained and flaked

1 cup coarsely chopped celery

⅓ cup coarsely chopped green pepper

⅓ cup sliced water chestnuts

⅓ cup chopped scallions with some green tops

½ cup mayonnaise

¾ cup grated sharp Cheddar cheese

¼ cup chopped toasted almonds

Preheat oven to 425 degrees. In a 2-quart casserole combine noodles, thyme, and salt. Set aside. Mix together the soup and milk in a saucepan and heat, stirring constantly, until smooth. Add tuna, celery, green pepper, water chestnuts, scallions, mayonnaise and all but 2 tablespoons of the cheese. Heat and stir until cheese is melted. Add cheese sauce to casserole and mix thoroughly. Sprinkle top with remaining grated cheese and almonds. Bake for about 20 minutes until bubbly and lightly browned.

PAN-FRIED FISH PARMESANA

Trader Vic's restaurant in San Francisco, a local tradition as well as a tourist favorite, suggested this tasty and unusual way to prepare fish.

Serves 6

1 tablespoon lemon juice
1 tablespoon
    Worcestershire
    sauce
2 pounds rock cod or
    red snapper fillets,
    cut into 6 pieces
Salt and freshly ground
    pepper to taste

½ cup flour
3 eggs, lightly beaten
1 cup grated Parmesan
    cheese
3 tablespoons butter
2 tablespoons vegetable
    oil

Preheat oven to 400 degrees. Combine lemon juice and Worcestershire sauce, and sprinkle on the fish pieces. Salt and pepper the fish, then dredge lightly in flour. Dip the fish in eggs, then coat generously with the grated cheese. In a heavy skillet, sauté the fish in a mixture of butter and oil over medium heat for 3 to 4 minutes to brown. Turn and brown the other side. Place the skillet in the oven for 4 to 5 minutes to heat through. Serve immediately.

SEAFOOD AU GRATIN

Serves 4

¼ pound scallops
8 teaspoons fresh lemon juice
¼ cup dry vermouth
⅛ teaspoon salt
⅛ teaspoon white pepper
½ cup sliced celery
½ cup chopped onion
½ cup chopped green
　pepper
½ cup sliced fresh
　mushrooms
4 tablespoons butter
3 tablespoons all-purpose
　flour
Milk and reserved scallop
　juices to make 1½ cups

1 teaspoon Worcestershire
　sauce
2 tablespoons fresh lemon
　juice
½ pound small shrimp,
　cooked
½ cup sliced and toasted
　almonds
Salt and freshly ground
　black pepper to taste
½ cup grated Gruyère
　cheese
½ cup seasoned bread
　crumbs

Preheat oven to 350 degrees. Halve or quarter scallops if large. Pat dry and marinate in 2 teaspoons lemon juice for 10 minutes. Place scallops and juices in saucepan with vermouth, salt, and white pepper. Bring to a boil, cover, lower heat, and simmer, shaking pan often to prevent sticking, for 2 minutes or until scallops are just tender. Do not overcook. Drain, reserving cooking juices, and set aside. Sauté celery, onion, green pepper, and mushrooms in butter until vegetables are soft. Sprinkle with flour and gradually blend in milk and reserved scallop juices. Cook and stir over medium heat until thickened. Add Worcestershire sauce, lemon juice, shrimp, scallops, and almonds. Adjust seasonings with salt and pepper. Spoon mixture into 4 scallop shells or ramekins. Combine cheese and bread crumbs and sprinkle over tops to cover evenly. Bake for approximately 20 minutes or until heated through and bubbly.

FISH STEW

This is a great family fish stew. All kinds of shellfish can be added. Use red snapper for the white fish, and you can add shrimp, crab, scallops, etc.

Serves 6

2 medium onions, minced
2 celery stalks, diced
1 small green pepper, diced
1 medium carrot, diced
4 cloves garlic, lightly
 bruised
3 tablespoons butter
2 tablespoons all-purpose
 flour
1 1-pound can whole
 tomatoes

1 teaspoon salt
⅛ teaspoon freshly ground
 pepper
Cayenne pepper to taste
2½ pounds rock cod, red
 snapper, or other firm
 white fish, cut into
 1½-inch cubes
6 cups hot cooked rice

Sauté onions, celery, green pepper, carrot, and garlic in butter over low heat for 15 minutes or until vegetables are soft. Discard garlic. Sprinkle cayenne. Cook and stir for 20 minutes until almost of sauce consistency. Add fish cubes and simmer for 10 to 15 minutes or until fish flakes easily. Do not overcook. Serve in individual bowls on a bed of hot rice.

CALIFORNIA CIOPPINO

Serves 8

2 freshly cooked whole
    crabs, approximately
    1½ to 2 pounds each
24 clams, well scrubbed
3 cups dry white wine
⅓ cup olive oil
1 medium onion, finely
    chopped
3 large cloves garlic, minced
1 medium green pepper,
    coarsely chopped
2 pounds fresh tomatoes,
    peeled, seeded, and
    chopped
3 ounces tomato paste

1 teaspoon freshly ground
    pepper
½ teaspoon dried oregano
½ teaspoon dried basil, or 1
    tablespoon finely
    chopped fresh basil
2 pounds fresh white fish
    such as sea bass, rock
    cod, halibut, ling cod,
    cut into large pieces
¾ pound scallops
¾ pound raw shrimp, peeled
    and deveined
Chopped fresh parsley

Remove the legs and claws from the crab and break the body in half, reserving as much of the soft, mustard-colored center ("crab butter") as possible. Set crab pieces aside and force the crab butter through a sieve into a small bowl. Set aside. Place the clams in a pan, add 1 cup of wine, and steam, covered, over medium heat for 4 to 6 minutes or until clams open. Remove clams, discarding any that do not open. Strain the stock through cheesecloth and reserve. In an 8-quart heatproof casserole or a kettle, heat the oil. Add the onion, garlic, and green pepper and sauté over medium heat, stirring occasionally, for approximately 5 minutes or until vegetables start to soften. Add tomatoes, tomato paste, remaining 2 cups of wine, pepper, herbs, and clam stock. Partially cover and simmer for 20 minutes. Add the fish, scallops, shrimp, crab, and crab butter. Simmer for approximately 5 minutes or until all seafood is cooked. Do not stir. Add the clams and heat for a scant 1 minute. Sprinkle with parsley and serve immediately from the cooking pot.

SEAFOOD AND ARTICHOKE CASSEROLE

Serves 6

½ pound fresh mushrooms,
  sliced
6 tablespoons butter
1½ pounds cooked shrimp
  (shelled and deveined)
  or crab meat (or
  combination)
8 to 10 cooked artichoke
  hearts, coarsely
  chopped

¼ cup all-purpose flour
1½ cups light cream
½ cup dry sherry
1 tablespoon Worcestershire
  sauce
Salt and freshly ground
  pepper to taste
¼ teaspoon paprika
½ cup freshly grated
  Parmesan cheese

Preheat oven to 350 degrees. Sauté mushrooms in 2 tablespoons of the butter until soft. Layer a 3-quart casserole with mushrooms, seafood, and artichoke hearts. Melt remaining butter until foamy, add flour, cook, and stir for 3 minutes. Gradually add cream, cook and stir until sauce is well blended and thickened. Add sherry, Worcestershire sauce, salt, pepper, and paprika. Pour over casserole ingredients and sprinkle with Parmesan. Bake for 30 to 40 minutes until bubbly hot and lightly browned.

CUCUMBER SAUCE

Makes 2½ cups

2 cups sour cream at room
  temperature
½ tablespoon finely
  chopped onion
1 large cucumber, peeled,
  seeded, and finely
  chopped

Salt and freshly ground
  pepper to taste
1½ tablespoons fresh lemon
  juice
Dried dill to taste

Blend sour cream, onion, cucumber, salt, pepper, and lemon juice. Add dill and adjust seasonings.

MUSTARD DILL SAUCE

Makes 1½ cups

2 tablespoons prepared
    mustard
2 tablespoons Dijon mustard
2 tablespoons sugar

2 tablespoons vinegar
½ cup dillweed
1 cup olive oil

Place mustards, sugar, vinegar, and dillweed in a blender, add olive oil slowly until mixture is thickened and well blended.

SAUCE VERTE

This versatile, elegant sauce is an absolute mainstay of any good kitchen.

Makes approximately 3½ cups

2 bunches watercress, stems
    removed
24 fresh spinach leaves,
    stems removed
2 cups mayonnaise
1 cup sour cream
2½ tablespoons fresh lemon
    juice

3 to 4 tablespoons fresh lime
    juice
1 teaspoon Worcestershire
    sauce
⅛ teaspoon garlic salt
Dash of nutmeg
¼ teaspoon salt
¼ teaspoon white pepper

Purée watercress, spinach, and mayonnaise in a blender or food processor. Transfer to a mixing bowl and stir in remaining ingredients. Chill and adjust seasonings. Serve with cold or hot fish, as a raw vegetable dip, or as a salad dressing.

OYSTER SAUCE

Makes 3½ cups

6 tablespoons butter
6 tablespoons all-purpose
    flour
2¼ cups milk
¾ cup light cream
½ teaspoon salt

½ teaspoon celery salt
6 ounces Olympia (very
    small) oysters and juice
Grated rind of 1 lemon
3 tablespoons fresh lemon
    juice

Melt butter until foamy, add flour, cook and stir for 3 minutes. Gradually add milk, cream, salt, and celery salt. Stir constantly until smooth and thickened. In a separate pan, bring oysters and their juice to a boil and add to sauce. Add lemon rind and juice. Adjust seasonings.

SHRIMP SAUCE

Makes 3½ cups

6 tablespoons butter
6 tablespoons all-purpose
    flour
1½ cups light cream
1 cup fish stock or clam
    stock
¼ cup dry vermouth

½ cup shredded Gruyère
    cheese
½ cup freshly grated
    Parmesan cheese
½ pound small shrimp,
    cooked, shelled

Melt 6 tablespoons butter until foamy. Sprinkle with flour, cook and stir for 3 minutes. Gradually add cream, stock, and vermouth. Cook and stir until well blended and thickened. Stir in Gruyère cheese and ¼ cup of Parmesan cheese (remaining ¼ cup of cheese is used after sauce has been poured over a prepared dish; for example, Halibut with Shrimp Sauce—see Index). Cook until cheeses are melted. Adjust seasonings. Add shrimp and keep warm.

CHAPTER X

POULTRY

Chinatown

Overtones of intrigue and traces of an opium-scented history threading through dim back alleys are still to be found in that quaint and gaudy tangle of lanterns and neon called Chinatown.

Located on the hillside between Nob Hill and the financial district is the largest Chinese settlement in the United States. At its heart is historic Portsmouth Square, the center of town during San Francisco's earliest days.

As the city grew and its townspeople prospered, they moved away from the foggy hillside to sunnier climes. The buildings left behind were then inhabited by the men and women who arrived from China to build the railroads, and they stayed on to create a community of their own. With them they brought four thousand years of civilization, transforming the hillside into a semblance of a Chinese city. Pagodas and balconies were added to façades, while native dress and customs, manners and attitudes added mysterious subtleties to the life of early San Francisco.

The growing community of Chinatown was sustained by a steady stream of immigrants from China. Traditions flourished as barriers subsided. And so, with time, it was more than silk, tea, and cheap labor that the Oriental presence provided. Gradually, artistic approaches to everyday things, especially in the art of food preparation and presentation, became incorporated into Western ways.

Szechuan, Mandarin, Cantonese, stir-fry, sweet and sour, *dim sum* all became an integral part of San Francisco's culinary language. East met West, resulting in new combinations, delightful to the eye as well as the palate. Chinese chicken salad with its biting coriander, pressed duck with its sweet and crunchy taste, and delectable clear stocks sizzling with rice or swirling with seaweed lead a long list of enticing and interesting new flavors—such splendid treasures from the Orient.

CHICKEN PAPRIKA

Serves 8 to 10

1 cup flour
2½ teaspoons paprika
¼ teaspoon cayenne pepper
¼ teaspoon powdered
    ginger
¼ teaspoon dried basil
⅛ teaspoon nutmeg
2 teaspoons salt
¼ teaspoon freshly ground
    pepper
10 to 12 chicken pieces,
    boned, skinned

¼ cup butter and/or oil (or
    as needed)
1 large clove garlic, finely
    minced
2½ cups chicken stock
2 cups sour cream at room
    temperature
2 tablespoons
    Worcestershire sauce
½ cup dry sherry
15 water chestnuts, drained
    and sliced

Preheat oven to 325 degrees. In a paper bag, combine flour, paprika, cayenne, ginger, basil, nutmeg, salt, and pepper. Shake chicken pieces, a few at a time, in flour mixture. Shake off excess flour and brown on all sides in butter and/or oil. Transfer to a shallow baking dish. Adding more butter if needed, sauté garlic for 2 minutes, then blend in chicken stock, sour cream, Worcestershire sauce, sherry, and water chestnuts. Heat, stirring constantly, without allowing to boil. Pour over chicken and bake uncovered, for 1 hour or until chicken is tender.

CHICKEN MARSALA

Serves 6

½ cup all-purpose flour
1 large frying chicken, cut in
    pieces
4 tablespoons olive oil
Salt and freshly ground
    pepper to taste
½ teaspoon rosemary

½ teaspoon dried basil
½ teaspoon oregano
2 cups dry Marsala wine
1 10-ounce jar red currant
    jelly
2 cups sour cream at room
    temperature

Preheat oven to 350 degrees. Place flour in a bag and lightly dust chicken pieces. Heat oil in a skillet and brown chicken. When brown, season with salt, pepper, rosemary, basil, and oregano. Pour 1 cup of the Marsala over chicken and simmer, uncovered, for 10 minutes. Transfer chicken and sauce to a casserole and adding remaining Marsala. Bake uncovered for 45 minutes or until tender. In a separate pan, melt jelly and blend in sour cream. When ready to serve chicken, remove it from the casserole, blend sour cream sauce with sauce in casserole. Serve with Noodles Basilico (see index). Put remaining sauce in a bowl and pass separately to serve over the noodles.

POULARDE BASQUAISE

Serves 4

4 medium whole white
   onions, peeled
2 tablespoons butter
2 tablespoons bacon
   drippings
1 frying chicken, quartered
Salt and freshly ground
   pepper to taste
½ pound fresh mushrooms,
   quartered
½ small eggplant, peeled and
   cut into fingers

2 medium tomatoes, peeled
   and quartered
1 small green pepper, cut
   into strips
1 clove garlic, mashed
¼ teaspoon thyme
1 bay leaf
½ teaspoon dried basil
¼ cup white wine

Preheat oven to 350 degrees. Sauté white onions in butter and bacon drippings until lightly browned. Remove from skillet and set aside. In same skillet, brown chicken pieces, season with salt and pepper, then transfer to a deep earthenware casserole. To the skillet add mushrooms, eggplant, tomatoes, green pepper, onions, garlic, and herbs. Sauté together for 3 minutes while gradually adding wine. Season with more salt and pepper. Arrange sautéed vegetables around and over chicken in the casserole. Cover and bake for 45 minutes.

JEAN VARDA CHICKEN A LA BEACH

This is Scott Beach's version of a North Beach favorite from the beat-nik era of the 1950s. Delicious for an informal dinner accompanied with good conversation and salad.

Serves 4

1 large frying chicken, cut
    up
2 tablespoons butter, melted
1 teaspoon salt
½ teaspoon freshly ground
    pepper

½ teaspoon garlic powder
2½ cups rich chicken stock
4 tablespoons butter

Preheat oven to 350 degrees. Place chicken pieces in one layer in a shallow roasting pan, and brush generously with melted butter. Sprinkle with seasonings, add chicken stock, and bake, covered, for 1½ hours. Just before serving, add 4 tablespoons butter to stock and stir until melted. Serve in the roasting pan or a heatproof serving dish with pieces of French bread to dip in the sauce.

NORMANDY CHICKEN

Serves 8

3 tablespoons butter
2 tablespoons oil
4 tart green apples, peeled,
    cored, sliced, and
    sprinkled with lemon
    juice
½ teaspoon cinnamon
2 teaspoons sugar
¼ teaspoon ground ginger
¼ teaspoon thyme
¼ teaspoon ground cloves

8 whole chicken breasts,
    boned
1 cup white wine
¾ cup apple juice
1 tablespoon cornstarch
1 cup heavy cream
Salt and freshly ground
    pepper to taste
2 tablespoons calvados or
    apple brandy

Preheat oven to 350 degrees. Melt butter and oil in a skillet and sauté apples with cinnamon, sugar, ginger, thyme and cloves for about 5 minutes, or until limp, stirring occasionally. Place apples in the bottom of a baking dish and set aside. Brown chicken breasts in the skillet in remaining butter, adding more if necessary, and place on top of apples. Pour in wine and apple juice, cover the baking dish with foil, and bake for 30 minutes. With a bulb baster remove juices from the baking pan to a small saucepan and reduce to 1 cup. Dissolve cornstarch in 2 tablespoons of the cream, blend into rest of cream, and then add to juices. Cook, stirring until thickened, but do not allow to boil. Season to taste with salt and pepper. Add brandy to sauce and pass sauce separately with chicken and apples.

BONED STUFFED CHICKEN

Serves 4 to 6

4 whole chicken breasts,
   boned and skinned
1 large chicken, boned and
   butterflied

¼ cup cognac
½ cup Madeira wine

FORCEMEAT
Chicken cubes in marinade
¼ cup ham or smoked
   tongue, chopped
4 shallots
1 tablespoon green
   peppercorns

½ teaspoon salt
½ teaspoon freshly grated
   nutmeg
2 egg whites
5 tablespoons heavy cream
1 tablespoon cognac

Preheat oven to 375 degrees. Have the butcher bone and butterfly the whole chicken. Cube chicken breasts and marinate in cognac and Madeira for 15 minutes. Remove chicken and reserve marinade. Lay the butterflied chicken flat, skin side down, on a piece of wax paper. Pound gently with the flat side of a broad knife or meat cleaver to flatten. Be careful not to break the skin. Brush the inside of the chicken with a little of the cognac and Madeira marinade. Finely chop all forcemeat ingredients together in a food processor or pass through a meat grinder, and mix well. Spread forcemeat over inside of butterflied chicken, gently roll up, skin side out, and tie at various intervals. Place in a roasting pan, brush with a little marinade, and bake for 1 hour basting often with marinade. To serve: allow to rest for about 15 minutes before carving, or serve cold.

BARBECUED CHICKEN

Serves 6 to 8

2 frying chickens, cut up

MARINADE

1½ cups dry red wine
½ cup soy sauce
½ cup salad oil
2 cloves garlic, sliced

2 teaspoons powdered ginger
½ teaspoon crumbled dried
    oregano

Combine ingredients for marinade and pour over chicken pieces. Cover and refrigerate overnight, turning pieces occasionally. Barbecue chicken pieces, basting occasionally with reserved marinade.

POULET MADEIRA

Serves 6

6 whole large chicken
    breasts, skinned, boned,
    and split
1 4-ounce can pâté de
    Strasbourg

3 tablespoons butter
Pastry (recipe below)
½ pound fresh mushrooms,
    sliced and sautéed

PASTRY

6 ounces cream cheese
¾ cup butter
1½ cups flour

Glaze made of 1 egg yolk
    and 1 tablespoon water

MADEIRA SAUCE

2 cups beef stock
½ cup red wine
2 large sprigs fresh parsley
1 medium onion, coarsely
    chopped
1 large carrot, sliced

1 bay leaf
½ cup Madeira wine
2 tablespoons flour
3 tablespoons soft butter
Salt and freshly ground
    pepper to taste

Preheat oven to 425 degrees. Cut a pocket in the side of each chicken breast and fill it with 1 to 1½ teaspoons pâté. Sauté the breasts in the 3 tablespoons butter for about 3 minutes on each side or until they are golden brown. Set aside. To make the pastry, mix the cream cheese, butter, and flour, and roll pastry out into a rectangle approximately 18 by 12 inches. Cut it into 6 pieces approximately 6 inches square. Place a chicken breast in the center of each pastry square, top with 1 to 2 table-spoons mushrooms, fold the pastry over the top, and seal. Brush the top with the egg-water glaze. Prick each chicken breast with a fork and bake, uncovered, for 30 to 35 minutes on an ungreased cookie sheet. Meanwhile, prepare the Madeira sauce by placing the beef stock, red wine, parsley, onion, carrot, and bay leaf in a 2-quart saucepan. Bring to a boil, reduce heat, and simmer rapidly for 20 to 25 minutes or until the liquid is reduced to 1½ cups. Strain the reduced stock into a 1-quart saucepan, pressing as much juice as possible from the vegetables, and add the Madeira. In a separate bowl, mix together the flour and butter. Over low heat, stir this mixture into the Madeira stock, add salt and pepper, and continue stirring until thickened. Pour over chicken breasts and serve.

BAKED HERB CHICKEN

Serves 6

1 cup commercial herb
    stuffing, crushed
⅓ cup freshly grated
    Parmesan cheese
¼ cup finely chopped fresh
    parsley

1 clove garlic, minced
1 3-pound frying chicken,
    cut up
¼ pound butter, melted

Preheat oven to 350 degrees. Combine stuffing, cheese, parsley, and gar-lic. Set aside. Dip chicken pieces in melted butter and then in stuffing, coating thoroughly. Place chicken pieces, not touching, on a cookie sheet or shallow baking pan, skin side up. Bake, uncovered, for 45 min-utes to 1 hour, turning oven down if chicken browns too quickly. Chicken may be baked ahead and served at room temperature.

ENCHILADAS VERDES

Serves 6

6 whole chicken breasts,
  skinned and boned
4 tablespoons butter
7 ounces green chilies
2 to 3 canned hot peppers,
  seeded (optional)
2 10-ounce cans tomatillos
  verdes, drained and
  liquid reserved
  (Mexican green
  tomatoes, available in
  specialty stores)

4 to 5 sprigs fresh coriander
  (cilantro)
2 cups heavy cream
2 eggs, lightly beaten
1 teaspoon salt
2 8-ounce packages cream
  cheese, softened
6 green onions, chopped
Oil for frying tortillas
12 corn tortillas
1 pint sour cream

Preheat oven to 325 degrees. Sauté the chicken breasts in the butter until tender, cool slightly, and shred meat by hand to make approximately 6 cups. Set aside. In a blender purée chilies, hot peppers, tomatillos, and coriander, adding liquid from tomatillos if purée is thicker than heavy cream. Add cream, eggs, and salt, adjust seasonings, and transfer to a saucepan. Cover and warm over very low heat. Combine cream cheese mixture, chicken, and green onions, and set aside. Heat oil in a heavy skillet and fry the tortillas one at a time for just a moment. Drain on paper towels. Spread 1 tablespoon of warm sauce on each tortilla, then 5 tablespoons of the chicken mixture. Roll and place, seam side down, in a buttered large shallow baking dish. Pour remaining sauce over stuffed tortillas and bake, uncovered, for 30 minutes. Serve immediately and pass sour cream on side.

CHINESE CHICKEN SALAD

Some of the ingredients in this recipe are unusual and can be found only in Oriental or specialty food stores. It's well worth the search.

Serves 4

2½ tablespoons hoisin sauce
1 tablespoon soy sauce
1 tablespoon dry sherry
4 whole large chicken
    breasts, skin intact
Peanut oil for browning
½ teaspoon Oriental sesame
    oil
¼ cup finely chopped
    peanuts

¼ cup toasted sesame seeds
½ cup finely chopped green
    onions
¼ pound rice stick noodles,
    deep fried as directed
    on package
1 head iceberg lettuce,
    shredded
Fresh coriander sprigs for
    garnish

Combine 1 tablespoon of the hoisin sauce with soy sauce and sherry. Marinate chicken breasts in mixture for 30 minutes. Brown marinated breasts in peanut oil, cover, and cook for 15 minutes or until chicken is tender. Skin should remain crisp. Cool chicken meat, then shred it. Cut skin in julienne. Combine with remaining hoisin sauce, sesame oil, 2 tablespoons of the peanuts, 2 tablespoons of the sesame seeds, and green onions. Toss mixture lightly with ⅔ of the fried rice stick noodles. Place shredded lettuce on a serving platter, mound chicken mixture on top, and sprinkle with remaining fried rice stick noodles, peanuts, and sesame seeds. Garnish with coriander sprigs.

POULET À LA MOUTARDE

Serves 10 to 12

6 whole chicken breasts,
halved, boned, and
skinned
6 tablespoons butter
4 tablespoons Dijon mustard
1 teaspoon salt
1 teaspoon freshly ground
pepper

3 tablespoons all-purpose
flour
1 cup milk
Salt and freshly ground
white pepper to taste
Rind of 1 lemon, minced
2 cups light cream

Preheat oven to 400 degrees. Gently pound chicken breasts between sheets of wax paper to flatten. Roll flattened breasts and place seam side down in a buttered shallow casserole. Combine 4 tablespoons butter, 2 tablespoons mustard, the salt and pepper. Mix well to make a paste and spread over rolled breasts. Bake, uncovered, for 30 minutes. Ten minutes before breasts are done, place remaining 2 tablespoons butter and the flour in a blender. Heat milk and add to flour mixture. Cover and start blending at low speed. Turn to high and blend for 30 seconds. Add salt and white pepper and set aside. In a small saucepan, cover the lemon rind with water, bring to a boil, and simmer for 10 minutes. Drain and set rind aside. Remove chicken to a heated serving platter and keep warm. To the liquid in the casserole, add remaining 2 tablespoons mustard, stirring well. Blend in white sauce, and then slowly add cream, stirring briskly. Adjust seasonings, add reserved lemon rind, and pour sauce over chicken.

POULET AU POIVE VERT

This is an elegant and lovely dish, but the peppercorns may seem too strong for some tastes. If so, capers may be substituted. The sauce is heavenly and the whole thing is easy to do. A nice party dish.

Serves 6 to 8

8 tablespoons butter
3 tablespoons green
    peppercorns
4 whole chicken breasts,
    halved, skinned, and
    boned
3 tablespoons cognac
1 cup chicken stock

2 tablespoons minced shallots
2 tablespoons all-purpose
    flour
½ cup dry white wine
¾ cup heavy cream
3 egg yolks
Salt and freshly ground
    pepper to taste

Preheat oven to 350 degrees. Make a paste of 2 tablespoons butter and 1 tablespoon green peppercorns. Flatten breasts gently with a rolling pin and make a slit on the thick side to form a small pocket. Brush breasts with 1 tablespoon of the cognac and place about 1 teaspoon of the paste in the pocket of each. In a large skillet, heat 4 tablespoons of the butter and slowly brown the breasts on each side. When all are done, remove to a serving platter and keep warm. Drain off all but 1 tablespoon of the butter from the skillet and add remaining cognac to deglaze the pan. Stir and warm cognac, then ignite to burn off alcohol. Add pan glaze to chicken stock and set aside. Melt remaining 2 tablespoons butter in the skillet, add shallots, and cook briefly. Sprinkle with flour, cooking and stirring, for about 3 minutes. Slowly add chicken stock and wine, cook and stir until sauce is smooth and thickened. In a small bowl, beat together the heavy cream and egg yolks. Add a tablespoon or two of the warm sauce, then slowly pour it into the skillet. Add remaining 2 tablespoons peppercorns and correct seasonings. Pour sauce over warm chicken and reheat all in the oven for 10 minutes.

STUFFED CHICKEN BREASTS

Serves 6

6 whole chicken breasts,
    halved, skinned, and
    boned
½ cup fresh lemon juice
8 ounces cream cheese

⅓ cup chopped green onions
½ teaspoon dried tarragon
½ teaspoon salt
12 slices bacon

Preheat oven to 350 degrees. Pound chicken breasts carefully between pieces of wax paper to flatten. Dip in lemon juice. Combine cream cheese, onions, tarragon, and salt. Place approximately 2 tablespoons of this mixture on each piece of chicken. Roll like a jelly roll and wrap with a slice of bacon. Secure with toothpicks or skewers. Place in a buttered shallow baking dish and bake, uncovered, for 30 to 40 minutes.

VINTAGE CHICKEN

Serves 10 to 12

1 pound fresh mushrooms,
    sliced
1 cup chopped green onions
4 tablespoons butter
¾ cup all-purpose flour
4 teaspoons garlic salt
Freshly ground pepper to
    taste

1 tablespoon rosemary
6 whole chicken breasts,
    halved, boned, and
    skinned
2¼ cups dry white wine

Sauté mushrooms and green onions in 2 tablespoons of the butter until soft. Set aside. Combine flour, garlic salt, pepper, and rosemary. Dust chicken breasts lightly with flour mixture. Melt remaining 2 tablespoons of butter in a large skillet and brown chicken breasts on both sides. Set aside and keep warm as they are cooked. Add white wine, mushrooms, and green onions to the skillet, cook, and stir to deglaze. Return chicken breasts to skillet. Cover and cook for another 15 minutes.

CHICKEN AVOCADO CASSEROLE

Serves 6 to 8

4 whole chicken breasts, split
   in half
6 tablespoons butter
4 tablespoons all-purpose
   flour
1 cup light cream
1 cup chicken stock
Salt and freshly ground
   pepper to taste

½ cup freshly grated
   Parmesan cheese
2 dashes Tabasco sauce
½ teaspoon rosemary
½ teaspoon dried basil
¼ pound mushrooms, sliced
½ cup chopped toasted
   almonds
1 to 2 avocados

Preheat oven to 350 degrees. Steam the chicken breasts until tender. Cool and bone. Melt 4 tablespoons of the butter until foamy, stir in flour, and cook for 3 minutes. Slowly add the cream and chicken stock, stirring until smooth and thickened. Season with the salt, pepper, Parmesan, Tabasco, and herbs. Set aside. Sauté mushrooms in remaining 2 tablespoons butter. Place the chicken in a 2-quart casserole and top with mushrooms. Sprinkle with salt and pepper. Pour sauce over and bake, uncovered, for 25 minutes. Remove from oven. Sprinkle with almonds. Return to oven for 10 minutes. Peel and slice avocados lengthwise. Place over casserole before serving.

CHICKEN BREASTS IN CHAMPAGNE

Serves 6

4 whole chicken breasts,
   boned and skinned
⅓ cup all-purpose flour
1 teaspoon salt
⅛ teaspoon freshly ground
   white pepper

4 tablespoons butter
2 tablespoons olive oil
1½ cups champagne
1 cup heavy cream
Sautéed mushrooms
   (optional)

Flatten the chicken breasts with palm of hand. Combine the flour, salt, and pepper and dust breasts on both sides. Sauté, full side down, in butter and oil for 5 minutes, shaking the pan to prevent sticking. Turn the chicken and add champagne. Cook for another 15 minutes until the chicken is done and champagne is reduced by half. Remove the chicken to a heated serving platter and keep warm. Add the cream to the pan juices and cook until thickened. Add sautéed mushrooms if desired. Pour sauce over the chicken and serve.

CHICKEN CURRY

Serves 6

1 4- to 5-pound stewing chicken, cut up
1 large onion, quartered
4 whole cloves
1 large carrot, diced
3 celery stalks with leaves, coarsely chopped
2 tablespoons chopped parsley
8 peppercorns
1 bay leaf
1½ teaspoons salt
Dry white wine as needed
¼ pound butter
1 clove garlic, minced
1 green apple, pared and chopped
2 medium onions, sliced

1 medium tomato, peeled, seeded, and chopped
6 tablespoons all-purpose flour
2 tablespoons curry powder
½ teaspoon ground cardamom
½ teaspoon ground ginger
½ teaspoon freshly ground pepper
Grated rind and juice of 1 lime
¼ cup seedless raisins
½ cup grated unsweetened coconut
½ cup light cream
2 tablespoons chopped chutney

CONDIMENTS
Chopped hard-cooked eggs
Chopped peanuts
Grated orange rind
Quartered limes
Chutney

Minced green onions
Heated raisins
Crisp, freshly cooked bacon, crumbled
Chopped banana

Place chicken in a large pot and cover with water. Stick a clove into each onion quarter and add to pot with carrot, celery, parsley, peppercorns, bay leaf, and 1 teaspoon salt. Bring to a gentle boil and simmer for 2½ hours or until chicken is tender. Cool in stock. Remove chicken, skin and bone meat, and cut into bite-size pieces. Strain stock and add enough white wine to make 4 cups. Set aside. Melt butter in a large skillet and add garlic. When hot, add apple, sliced onions, and tomato. Cover and simmer for 8 to 10 minutes or until tender. Combine flour, curry, cardamom, ginger, remaining ½ teaspoon salt, and pepper. Stir into vegetables, mixing well. Cook and stir for 3 minutes until well blended. Slowly add reserved chicken stock and wine, grated lime rind, juice, and raisins. Simmer, uncovered, stirring occasionally, for 30 minutes. Add chicken, coconut, cream, and chutney. Heat over low heat for 15 minutes. At this point mixture may be cooled and refrigerated for reheating next day. Serve with rice and 6 or more condiments.

CHICKEN BREASTS
IN SOUR CREAM-ALMOND SAUCE

Serves 4 to 6

4 to 6 whole chicken breasts, halved, boned, and skinned
3 tablespoons butter
2 tablespoons chopped onion
1 clove garlic, minced
1 tablespoon tomato paste
2 tablespoons all-purpose flour
1½ cups chicken stock
3 tablespoons dry sherry

2 tablespoons shredded almonds
½ teaspoon minced fresh tarragon
Salt and freshly ground pepper to taste
¾ cup sour cream at room temperature
½ cup grated Gruyère cheese

Sauté the chicken on both sides in butter, remove from the skillet. Add the onion and garlic, cook and stir for 2 to 3 minutes. Add tomato paste and flour to skillet, stir until blended and smooth. Gradually add the chicken stock and sherry, cook and stir until smooth and slightly thickened. Return the chicken to the skillet. Add the almonds, tarragon, salt, and pepper. Cover and simmer over low heat for 30 minutes or until tender. Arrange the chicken in a shallow baking dish. Stir the sour cream into sauce and pour over chicken. Sprinkle with grated cheese and brown under broiler. Serve with rice or noodles.

CHICKEN INDIENNE

Serves 4

1 2½ to 3-pound frying chicken, cut in pieces
3 tablespoons fresh lemon juice
3 tablespoons all-purpose flour
1 teaspoon salt
⅛ teaspoon freshly ground pepper
3 tablespoons oil
1 tablespoon butter
1 large onion, chopped

2 to 3 tablespoons curry powder
½ cup water
½ cup heavy cream
1 teaspoon chicken-flavored stock base
2 tablespoons chopped candied ginger
1 papaya, peeled and cut into wedges
8 lime wedges

Sprinkle chicken with lemon juice and let stand for 30 minutes. Pat dry. Mix flour, salt, and pepper and dredge chicken pieces to coat evenly. In a heavy skillet with a tight lid, heat oil and butter. Sauté chicken, sprinkling with any leftover flour mixture, until browned on both sides. Remove from skillet and set aside. Add onion and sauté until golden. Add curry powder, cook and stir for 2 minutes. Gradually beat in water and cream, cook and stir until thickened. Add chicken stock base and ginger, stir, and return chicken to the skillet. Cover and simmer, turning chicken once, for 40 minutes or until chicken is tender. Transfer to a heated serving platter and surround with papaya and lime wedges.

PLUM BLOSSOM CHICKEN

Serves 6

6 large whole chicken breasts, halved, or 2 frying chickens, cut in pieces
2 tablespoons butter

1 teaspoon curry powder
½ cup plum jam
¼ cup cream sherry
1 lemon, thinly sliced

In heavy skillet, brown chicken pieces in butter. Stir curry into pan juices. Blend plum jam and sherry and pour over chicken. Cover each piece with 1 or 2 slices lemon, cover skillet, and simmer for 35 to 40 minutes. Remove chicken to heated serving platter and keep warm. Boil pan juices to reduce slightly, spoon over chicken, and serve.

PARCHMENT CHICKEN

Makes 15 to 20

2 whole chicken breasts
½ cup chopped green onion
½ cup chopped Chinese parsley

Foil or baking parchment for wrapping
2 to 3 cups peanut oil for deep frying

MARINADE NO. 1
2 tablespoons beef bouillon powder
2 tablespoons Worcestershire sauce

2 tablespoons dry sherry or Bourbon
1½ tablespoons soy sauce
2 tablespoons sesame oil

MARINADE NO. 2
2 tablespoons light soy sauce
2 tablespoons dry sherry

1 tablespoon hoisin sauce
1 tablespoon cornstarch

MARINADE NO. 3
½ cup hoisin sauce
1 tablespoon dry sherry
2 tablespoons corn or peanut oil

1 tablespoon cornstarch
1 teaspoon salt
Freshly ground pepper to taste

Bone chicken breasts and cut into 1-inch cubes. Skin may be discarded or cut into thin strips and combined with chicken. Marinate for 30 minutes in one of the marinades. Cut foil or parchment into 3-inch squares. Place 2 pieces of chicken in the center, top with some green onion and Chinese parsley, and fold envelope-style to close. Fry, with seams down, a few at a time in deep oil for 5 minutes. Drain thoroughly and keep warm in a 200-degree oven until all pieces are deep-fried.

CHICKEN LIVERS BAKED WITH RICE

Serves 4

All-purpose flour for
  dredging
½ pound chicken livers,
  each cut into 2 or 3
  pieces
Salt and freshly ground
  pepper

3 tablespoons butter
3 tablespoons minced onion
1 cup raw long grain rice
2 cups chicken stock
1 teaspoon freshly minced
  parsley
½ teaspoon dried basil

Preheat oven to 350 degrees. Place a small amount of flour in a paper
bag. Sprinkle chicken livers with salt and pepper and shake them in
flour to coat. Sauté chicken livers in melted butter until brown, then
transfer to a 6-cup casserole. In butter remaining in skillet, sauté onion
and raw rice until golden. Add a little more butter if necessary. Add
chicken stock, stir well and deglaze the skillet. Add parsley and basil
and pour over chicken livers. Cover casserole tightly and bake for 30
minutes or until rice is tender and all liquid has been absorbed. Stir with
a *fork* before serving to release steam.

CHICKEN LIVERS NORMANDE

Serves 2

3 thick slices bacon, diced
3 tablespoons butter
1 tart green apple, peeled
  and thinly sliced
¾ pound whole chicken
  livers
3 tablespoons all-purpose
  flour

1 tablespoon olive oil
2 tablespoons dry Marsala
2 green onions, including
  green tops, chopped
Salt and freshly ground
  pepper to taste

Fry bacon pieces in a skillet until crisp. Drain on a paper towel and
pour out all but ½ tablespoon bacon grease. Add 1 tablespoon of the

butter to the skillet and sauté apple slices until soft. Set aside. Lightly dredge chicken livers in the flour. Melt remaining 2 tablespoons butter with olive oil in skillet, sauté chicken livers for about 5 minutes. Add Marsala, apples, bacon, green onions, and seasonings, cook for a few more minutes to blend flavors.

CHICKEN SALTIMBOCCA

Serves 10 to 12

6 whole chicken breasts, halved, skinned, and boned
12 slices prosciutto
12 slices Gruyère cheese
¼ cup all-purpose flour
2 eggs, lightly beaten
1 cup fine dry bread crumbs
2 tablespoons freshly grated Parmesan cheese

¼ teaspoon garlic salt
¼ teaspoon dried tarragon
4 tablespoons butter
1 cup chicken stock
1 cup dry sherry
1 tablespoon cornstarch, dissolved in 1 tablespooon cold water

Preheat oven to 350 degrees. Place each half chicken breast between sheets of wax paper and pound lightly to flatten. Place on each flattened breast a slice of prosciutto and a thin slice of Gruyère cheese. Roll up lengthwise and close with toothpicks. Dip chicken rolls in flour, shaking off excess, and then dip in beaten egg. Roll in bread crumbs seasoned with Parmesan cheese, garlic salt, and tarragon. Brown chicken rolls in butter on all sides, transfer to a baking dish and pour over chicken stock mixed with sherry. Bake, uncovered, for 30 to 40 minutes. Remove chicken rolls and keep warm. Drain juices into a saucepan and bring to a boil. Blend in cornstarch mixture, stirring constantly until thickened. Spoon over chicken and serve.

CHICKEN STROGANOFF

Serves 6

2 large whole chicken
 breasts, boned and
 skinned
2 tablespoons all-purpose
 flour
½ teaspoon salt
¼ teaspoon freshly ground
 pepper
4 teaspoons butter
4 teaspoons minced shallots
 thinly sliced

¾ pound fresh mushrooms,
½ cup dry white wine
1 tablespoon paprika
2 cups sour cream at room
 temperature
1½ teaspoons
 Worcestershire sauce
½ teaspoon beef bouillon
 powder

Slice chicken into julienne strips about 3 inches by ¼ inch. Combine flour, salt, and pepper in a bag. Add chicken and shake to coat. In a skillet sauté chicken in butter over medium-high heat just until golden and tender. Remove to a serving dish and keep warm. Add shallots, mushrooms, and wine to the skillet. Cook, stirring, until liquid disappears. Reduce heat to low. Stir in paprika, sour cream, Worcestershire, and beef bouillon powder. Season to taste with salt and pepper. Heat sauce and pour over chicken.

FLOWER DRUM SONG CHICKEN

Serves 4 to 6

4 whole chicken breasts,
 boned, skinned, and cut
 in 1-inch cubes
1 tablespoon cornstarch
1 tablespoon dry sherry
1 tablespoon soy sauce
2 tablespoons peanut oil
¼ pound fresh mushrooms,
 coarsely chopped

1 green pepper, coarsely
 chopped into 1-inch
 pieces
1 heaping tablespoon hoisin
 sauce
Salt to taste
⅓ cup cashews

Sprinkle chicken pieces with cornstarch and toss until thoroughly coated. Add sherry and soy sauce and marinate for at least ½ hour. Heat oil until faintly smoking. Add chicken and sauté quickly until barely done. Add mushrooms and green pepper, and sauté for approximately 45 seconds. Add hoisin sauce, salt, and cashews, and toss until thoroughly mixed. Serve immediately.

CHICKEN WITH WALNUTS

Serves 4

2 whole chicken breasts, approximately ¾ pound each	1 cup walnut halves
	3 slices fresh ginger root
	3 cloves garlic, bruised
1 tablespoon lightly beaten egg white	10 to 15 small dried whole chili peppers
1 tablespoon cornstarch	½ cup frozen peas, thawed
½ teaspoon sugar	1 tablespoon soy sauce
¼ teaspoon salt	1 tablespoon dry white wine
1 cup peanut oil	

Skin and bone chicken breasts and cut into ½-inch cubes. Combine egg white, cornstarch, sugar, and salt. Toss the chicken in the mixture and coat well, then refrigerate until ready to cook. (May be refrigerated for several hours.) Heat peanut oil in a heavy skillet or wok until it is almost smoking. Stir chicken, then turn all at once into hot oil. Stir-fry for 30 to 60 seconds or until chicken pieces are cooked. Quickly remove chicken with a slotted spoon and set aside. Reheat oil and carefully sauté the walnuts for 15 seconds or until just slightly colored. They burn easily, so do not overcook. Quickly remove walnuts with a slotted spoon and set aside. Add ginger, garlic, and chili peppers to the hot oil. Cook and stir for 30 to 60 seconds until lightly browned. Discard the ginger, garlic, and peppers but retain the oil. Add the cooked chicken, peas, soy sauce, and wine. Toss well until chicken and peas are heated. Place on a serving dish and arrange walnuts on the side. Serve immediately.

CHICKEN LO MEIN

Serves 6

2 whole chicken breasts, skinned, boned, and cut into bite-size pieces
1 tablespoon Bourbon
2 tablespoons light soy sauce
1 teaspoon sugar
8 to 10 cups water
2 teaspoons salt
4 tablespoons peanut oil
½ pound uncooked egg noodles
1 teaspoon Oriental sesame oil
⅓ cup light soy sauce
4 dried Oriental mushrooms, soaked, sliced, and squeezed dry

1 cup diagonally sliced celery
½ pound bean sprouts, chopped
½ pound snow peas, sliced diagonally
⅓ cup julienne barbecued pork
1 green onion, including some green top, chopped
Chinese parsley sprigs
¼ cup oyster sauce (optional) (see Index for recipe)

Marinate chicken pieces in a mixture of Bourbon, 2 tablespoons light soy sauce, and sugar for at least ½ hour. Bring 8 to 10 cups water to a boil with 2 teaspoons salt and 1 tablespoon of the peanut oil. Add noodles, keeping water at a hard boil and stirring to prevent sticking, until just *al dente* (cooked through but still firm). Drain and rise under cold water. Drain and spread on a flat serving platter. Combine 1 tablespoon peanut oil, 1 teaspoon sesame oil, and ⅓ cup soy sauce. Toss noodles with mixture and set aside. Heat 2 tablespoons peanut oil in a wok or heavy skillet and stir-fry chicken for 3 minutes or until just done. Remove and, adding more oil if necessary, stir-fry mushrooms and celery for ½ minute. Add bean sprouts and stir-fry until slightly tender. Add reserved noodles, chicken, and snow peas. Cook and stir until just heated through. Garnish with pork strips, green onion, and Chinese parsley sprigs. If desired, pour oyster sauce over all.

CHICKEN WITH WILD RICE

A perfect casserole for a potluck supper, a new neighbor, or a holiday buffet. One cup of wild rice goes a long way to make this luxuriously different.

Serves 6

3 whole chicken breasts,
  halved, skinned
3 cups chicken stock
1 cup uncooked wild rice
3 tablespoons butter
3 tablespoons all-purpose
  flour
1 cup heavy cream

2 tablespoons Madeira or
  sweet sherry
1 cup canned water
  chestnuts, drained and
  thinly sliced
½ cup freshly grated
  Parmesan cheese

Preheat oven to 325 degrees. Poach chicken breasts in stock until tender. Remove and cool, reserve stock. Bone chicken and cut into large pieces. Rinse the wild rice and cook as directed (use additional chicken stock if desired). Melt butter until foamy, add flour, and cook and stir for 3 minutes. Gradually add 2 cups reserved chicken stock. Cook and stir until thickened. Cool to room temperature and blend in cream and Madeira or sherry. Combine cooked rice and water chestnuts. In a buttered casserole, layer chicken breasts and rice mixture, making 2 layers. Pour sauce over and sprinkle with cheese. Bake, uncovered, for 15 minutes. Cover and bake for 15 minutes more.

CHILAQUILA CON POLLO

When in a Latin mood, prepare this layered casserole for the freezer. A Spanish "fiesta" could win you bravos after a neighborhood cocktail party. The sauce here is unforgettable—but follow directions explicitly, and have plenty of cold beer on hand.

Serves 6 to 8

2 pounds chicken breasts or thighs
1 medium onion, cut up
1 medium carrot, thickly sliced
1 celery stalk, thickly sliced
1 bay leaf
Salt and freshly ground pepper to taste
1 7-ounce can green chilies, seeded (if a hotter flavor is desired, do not seed chilies)
12 to 16 ounces tomatillos (Mexican green tomatoes available in specialty stores)

1 medium onion, cut in chunks
2 cloves garlic, peeled
¼ cup firmly packed fresh coriander
3 tablespoons lard
1 cup rich chicken stock
12 corn tortillas, cut in strips
Lard as needed for frying
1 to 1½ pounds Monterey Jack cheese, grated
Avocado slices

Poach chicken with onion, carrot, celery, bay leaf, salt, and pepper in water to cover until tender. When cool enough to handle, bone chicken and cut into bite-size pieces. Set aside. Purée, in a blender or food processor, the chilies, tomatillos, onion, garlic, and coriander. Melt 3 tablespoons lard in a heavy skillet and add purée. Cook and stir for about 5 minutes and gradually stir in chicken stock. Heat and adjust seasonings with salt and pepper. Quickly fry tortilla pieces in hot lard until just crisp but not brown. Drain on paper towels. In a buttered 8 by 12-inch shallow baking dish, layer tortillas, chicken, cheese, and sauce. Repeat until ingredients are used, reserving enough cheese to sprinkle on top of last layer. Cover and refrigerate for 8 hours or overnight. Bake, uncovered, in a preheated 350-degree oven for 45 minutes or until heated through and cheese is melted. Garnish with avocado slices and serve with Salsa Cruda (recipe follows).

Salsa Cruda

Makes 3 cups

4 ripe medium tomatoes,
    peeled and chopped
4 4-ounce cans green chilies,
    seeded and chopped
1 small onion, minced

¼ cup chopped fresh
    coriander (cilantro)
    leaves
Salt to taste
Sugar to taste

Two hours before serving, mix tomatoes, chilies, onion, coriander, salt, and sugar. (Add extra chilies if desired.) Serve with Chilaquila con Pollo.

ORANGE LEMON CHICKEN

Serves 8

2 3-pound frying chickens,
    cut in pieces
¼ pound butter
2 tablespoons oil
1 teaspoon freshly grated
    lemon rind
1 teaspoon freshly grated
    orange rind
¾ cup fresh orange juice
¼ cup fresh lemon juice

½ teaspoon dried tarragon
1 cup heavy cream
¼ cup Madeira wine
¼ cup dry white wine
Salt and freshly ground
    pepper to taste
2 tablespoons cornstarch
¼ cup freshly grated
    Parmesan cheese
¼ teaspoon paprika

Preheat oven to 350 degrees. Sauté the chicken pieces in butter and oil until golden and almost cooked through. Transfer chicken to a shallow baking dish and set aside. To the butter in the skillet, add the orange and lemon rind, ½ cup of the orange juice, the ¼ cup lemon juice, and tarragon. Cook and stir over low heat, and with a whisk gradually beat in cream. Beat in wines and season with salt and pepper. Dissolve cornstarch in remaining ¼ cup orange juice and stir into sauce. Cook and stir just until thickened. Pour over chicken, sprinkle with cheese and paprika, and bake for 30 minutes. Just before serving brown under the broiler.

CHINESE CHICKEN LIVERS

Serves 4

2 tablespoons soy sauce
2 tablespoons water
1 tablespoon cornstarch
3 slices bacon
1 pound chicken livers, each
    cut into 3 pieces

4 green onions, chopped
1 medium green pepper,
    chopped

Mix together the soy sauce, water, and cornstarch. Set aside. Fry bacon crisp, drain, and crumble. Brown chicken livers and green onions in bacon fat. Near end of browning, add green pepper and soy mixture. Stir to blend. Serve immediately over hot rice.

MEXICAN CREPES

Serves 6

¼ pound plus 4 tablespoons
    butter
2 cups sliced fresh
    mushrooms
1 cup chopped green onions,
    with some tops
1½ pounds cooked chicken
    or turkey, cut into
    bite-size pieces
¼ cup dry white wine
1 cup condensed milk
¾ cup fresh milk

6 tablespoons all-purpose
    flour
1½ teaspoons salt
¼ cup minced fresh parsley
½ cup slivered and toasted
    almonds
1 4-ounce can green chilies,
    chopped
12 crepes (see Index)
1 cup grated Monterey Jack
    cheese
12 avocado slices

Preheat oven to 350 degrees. Melt butter and sauté mushrooms and onions until soft. Add chicken or turkey and simmer gently for 10 minutes. Meanwhile in a blender mix wine, condensed milk, fresh milk, flour, and salt. Transfer to a saucepan and cook over medium heat, stirring constantly, until thickened. Combine with chicken or turkey mixture and add parsley, almonds, and chilies. Place 1 to 2 tablespoons of filling on each crepe and roll. Arrange in a buttered shallow ovenproof serving dish rolled edge down. Top with cheese. Bake, covered, for 15 minutes. Remove cover and add avocado. Return to oven for 2 to 3 minutes.

PAELLA

Serves 10

¼ cup olive oil
4 pounds frying chicken
    pieces
¼ cup all-purpose flour
1 teaspoon salt
⅛ teaspoon freshly ground
    pepper
¼ cup water
1 teaspoon oregano
2 cups chopped onion
2 cloves garlic, minced
3 tablespoons butter
2 cups uncooked long grain
    white rice
¼ teaspoon powdered
    saffron

4 cups chicken stock
½ pound chorizo sausage,
    sliced
1 package frozen artichoke
    hearts, thawed
2 cups peas
1 28-ounce can tomatoes,
    drained and coarsely
    chopped
1 pound raw shrimp, shelled
    and deveined
1 7-ounce can pimientos, cut
    in strips
24 cherrystone clams

Preheat oven to 350 degrees. Heat olive oil in a large skillet with a cover. Dust chicken pieces with flour, salt, and pepper and brown well in oil. Add ¼ cup water and oregano. Cover and cook for 30 minutes over low heat. Remove chicken and set aside. Add chopped onion and garlic to skillet and sauté, stirring, for 5 minutes. Set aside. In a saucepan melt butter. Add rice and saffron. Stir over low heat for 5 minutes. Add chicken stock, cover, and cook for 15 to 20 minutes. Stir rice into skillet with onions. In a separate skillet, brown chorizo sausage lightly. Set aside. In a 4-quart shallow casserole or pan, mix the artichoke hearts and peas with the rice, then lightly toss in the tomatoes, chorizo, and shrimp. Arrange the chicken pieces on top and garnish with pimiento. Bake, uncovered, for 30 minutes. Meanwhile, steam the clams in a separate container, discarding any that do not open, and place on top of casserole for last 3 to 5 minutes of baking.

PACIFIC AVENUE CASSEROLE

Serves 6

1 3-pound frying chicken,
    cut up
Salt, freshly ground pepper,
    and paprika
4 tablespoons butter
¼ pound fresh mushrooms,
    sliced

2 tablespoons all-purpose
    flour
1 cup chicken stock
3 tablespoons sherry
¼ teaspoon rosemary
1 16-ounce can artichoke
    hearts, drained

Preheat oven to 375 degrees. Sprinkle the chicken pieces with salt, pepper, and paprika. Melt butter in a heavy skillet and brown chicken pieces on both sides. Remove to a casserole with a cover. Add the mushrooms to pan drippings and gently sauté. Add the flour to mushrooms and gradually stir in chicken stock and sherry. Season with rosemary, and deglaze the skillet. Arrange the artichoke hearts among the chicken pieces, pour sauce over chicken, cover, and bake for 40 minutes or until chicken is tender.

CHICKEN AND HAM CREPES

Serves 6

1 medium onion, chopped
⅓ pound fresh mushrooms,
    chopped
4 tablespoons butter
¼ cup all-purpose flour
2 cups milk
½ teaspoon salt
Freshly ground white
    pepper to taste

2 cups medium white sauce
    (recipe given below)
2 cups diced cooked chicken
1 cup diced cooked ham
12 crepes (see Index)
2 tablespoons dry white
    wine
¼ cup freshly grated
    Parmesan cheese

Preheat oven to 325 degrees. Sauté onion and mushrooms in butter until soft. Add flour, stir well, and cook for 3 minutes, gradually adding milk. Stir until thickened. Add salt, pepper, chicken, and ham. Put 3 to

4 tablespoons of filling on each crepe, and roll. Arrange in a buttered shallow ovenproof serving dish, rolled edge down. Combine white sauce and wine, heat, and add cheese. Stir to melt cheese, pour over crepes, and bake for 20 minutes until heated through and bubbly.

Makes 2 cups

MEDIUM WHITE SAUCE

5 tablespoons butter
5 tablespoons flour
2 cups milk

½ teaspoon salt
¼ teaspoon white pepper

Melt butter in a saucepan over low heat and blend in flour. Gradually add milk, stirring constantly. Heat and stir until sauce is thickened. Add seasonings and remove from heat.

CREPES

Crepes may be made in advance, stacked with waxed paper between every 3 or 4, and refrigerated or frozen. Return crepes to room temperature before trying to separate. Handy to have around for desserts, hors d'oeuvres, first courses, or luncheons.

Makes about 24 crepes

4 eggs
2 cups milk
6 tablespoons butter, melted

½ teaspoon salt
1 cup sifted all-purpose
    flour

Combine ingredients in a blender and blend until smooth. Chill thoroughly before making crepes. Heat a 6- or 7-inch crepe pan and brush lightly with butter or oil. Ladle in about 2 tablespoons batter and quickly tilt pan to spread batter evenly; pour out any excess. Cook until lightly browned, about 1 minute, then turn and cook until browned on the other side.

BASTILA

Serves 10 to 12

2 whole chicken breasts,
skinned and boned
3 cups chicken stock
1 cup finely chopped onions
1 cup butter, softened
7 tablespoons olive oil
1 tablespoon finely chopped
fresh coriander
2 tablespoons finely chopped
parsley
1 teaspoon ground ginger
½ teaspoon cumin
¼ teaspoon cayenne pepper

¼ teaspoon turmeric
⅛ teaspoon saffron threads
4 teaspoons cinnamon
6 eggs, plus 2 egg yolks
2 tablespoons sugar
1½ cups coarsely chopped
and toasted almonds
10 sheets phyllo pastry
3 tablespoons powdered
sugar
12 whole almonds, toasted
and reserved for garnish

Preheat oven to 375 degrees. Poach chicken breasts in stock for 30 minutes or until tender. Reserve stock. Cool chicken and coarsely chop. Set aside.

In a heavy skillet, sauté the onion in 4 tablespoons of the butter and 4 tablespoons of oil until golden. Stir in coriander, parsley, ginger, cumin, cayenne, turmeric, saffron, and ¾ teaspoon cinnamon. Add the reserved stock, mix well, and bring to a boil. Simmer for 15 minutes. Add the chicken and cook for another 10 minutes. Pour 1½ cups of the liquid from the skillet into a bowl. Reduce remaining liquid in the skillet to about ¼ cup. Remove the chicken mixture to a bowl and set aside.

In a separate bowl, beat together the 6 eggs and 2 yolks. Return the 1½ cups of the liquid to the skillet, add the beaten eggs, stirring over moderate heat until the mixture forms soft creamy curds. Remove from heat and set aside.

In a small bowl, combine the sugar, 1¼ teaspoons cinnamon, and the chopped almonds.

Melt remaining 12 tablespoons butter with remaining 3 tablespoons olive oil. Lightly brush a 10-inch round baking dish or 10-inch iron skillet with the butter-oil mixture. Working quickly, overlap 6 sheets of phyllo pastry in a circle in the baking dish. Fold 2 sheets of phyllo in half separately. Place them, one on top of the other, in the center of the circle. Brush the phyllo with butter, then sprinkle the almond mixture over the pastry. Spread with half of the egg mixture, top with the chicken mixture, then cover with remaining egg mixture. Coat all exposed edges of phyllo with butter and fold a few over the filling. Add remaining 2 sheets of phyllo, folded in half separately, and brush with butter. Bring up all the edges of phyllo to enclose the chicken filling and brush the entire surface with butter. Bake for 30 to 40 minutes.

To serve, invert onto a serving plate. Combine powdered sugar and remaining 2 teaspoons cinnamon. Sprinkle the mixture on top. Draw a diamond pattern across the top, and center each diamond with a whole toasted almond. Cut in wedges.

HOT TURKEY SANDWICHES

Serves 8

8 slices sourdough French bread, toasted
1 large Bermuda onion, thinly sliced
8 slices turkey to cover toast (approximately 1 pound)
Salt and freshly ground pepper to taste
3 to 4 ripe tomatoes, sliced
8 medium slices Monterey Jack cheese to cover toast (approximately ½ pound)

4 tablespoons butter
¼ cup all-purpose flour
3 cups milk
2 cups grated Gruyère cheese
1 teaspoon salt
¼ teaspoon freshly ground white pepper
⅛ teaspoon paprika

Preheat oven to 325 degrees. Place toast in one layer in a buttered shallow baking dish. Layer with slices of onion and turkey. Sprinkle with salt and pepper. Add slices of tomato and cheese. Bake for 10 minutes. In a saucepan melt butter until foamy, sprinkle with flour, cook and stir for 3 minutes. Slowly add milk and cook and stir until smooth and thickened. Stir in cheese until melted, add seasonings, and spoon sauce generously over each sandwich. Bake for 10 minutes until sauce is hot and bubbly and cheese topping is browned.

BREAST OF TURKEY ARTICHOKE

Serves 8 to 10

3 packages frozen artichoke
    hearts
½ cup butter
½ pound mushrooms,
    quartered
6 to 8 cups cooked turkey
    breast, in large cubes
½ cup flour
3 cups rich chicken stock
4 cups grated Cheddar
    cheese

⅛ teaspoon thyme
Dash nutmeg
¼ teaspoon Worcestershire
    sauce
Dash Tabasco sauce
Salt and freshly ground
    pepper to taste
½ cup bread crumbs

Preheat oven to 350 degrees. Cook artichokes according to package directions, drain, and place in an 11 by 13-inch baking dish. In a skillet melt butter and gently sauté mushrooms until soft. Remove mushrooms and add to baking dish. Add cubed turkey. To butter in the skillet, add flour, stir and cook for 3 minutes until well blended. Add chicken stock, stir and cook until thickened. Add 3 cups of the cheese and stir until melted and blended. Add thyme, nutmeg, Worcestershire, Tabasco, salt, and pepper. Pour sauce over turkey mixture in baking dish and sprinkle top with bread crumbs. Cover with remaining cup of grated cheese and bake, uncovered, for 30 minutes until bubbling hot and browned.

TURKEY AND SAUSAGE CASSEROLE

Serves 8 to 10

½ pound bulk pork sausage
1 cup chopped celery
1 cup chopped onion
1 tart green apple, peeled,
    cored, and chopped
3 cups chicken stock
1 cup uncooked rice

4 ounces egg noodles,
    cooked al dente
4 cups cubed cooked turkey
½ cup sliced blanched
    almonds
French-fried onion rings for
    garnish

Preheat oven to 350 degrees. Sauté sausage, celery, and onion until meat is browned. Add apple, chicken stock, rice, noodles, turkey, and almonds. Transfer to a 3-quart casserole, cover, and bake for 1 hour. Top with French-friend onion rings, return to oven, and bake, uncovered, for 5 minutes longer.

TURKEY AND HAM CASSEROLE

Serves 6

½ cup chopped onion
7 tablespoons butter
3 tablespoons all-purpose
  flour
½ teaspoon salt
¼ teaspoon freshly ground
  pepper
1 4-ounce can sliced
  mushrooms and liquid
1 cup light cream

4 tablespoons dry sherry
2 cups cubed cooked turkey
1 cup cubed cooked ham
5 ounces canned water
  chestnuts, drained and
  sliced
½ cup coarsely grated Swiss
  cheese
1½ cups soft bread crumbs

Preheat oven to 400 degrees. In a heavy 2-quart saucepan, sauté chopped onion in 4 tablespoons of the butter until onion is soft. Blend in flour, salt, and pepper. Add mushrooms and liquid, light cream, and sherry. Cook and stir until thickened. Add turkey, ham, and water chestnuts. Transfer to a shallow 2-quart baking dish or casserole. Top with cheese. Melt remaining 3 tablespoons butter, mix with bread crumbs, and sprinkle around the edge of the casserole. Bake for 25 to 30 minutes until bubbly hot and light brown.

ROCK CORNISH GAME HENS WITH WILD RICE STUFFING

Serves 8

STUFFING

1 cup uncooked wild rice	4 tablespoons butter, melted
7 cups water	1 medium onion, chopped
1 teaspoon salt	½ pound mushrooms, sliced
1 cup uncooked white rice	⅓ cup slivered almonds

Wash wild rice and drain. Bring 7 cups water to a boil, add salt and wild rice gradually. Lower heat, cover pan, and simmer for 15 minutes. Add white rice, bring back to a boil, then lower heat and continue to simmer for 30 minutes or until all liquid is absorbed. Add melted butter, onion, and mushrooms. Cook for 5 minutes, then stir in almonds.

ROCK CORNISH GAME HENS

8 Rock Cornish game hens	½ cup Bourbon
1½ cups butter, melted	½ cup red currant jelly,
1½ teaspoons salt	melted
¼ teaspoon pepper	

Preheat oven to 425 degrees. Stuff hens with wild rice stuffing, truss them, and place in a shallow baking dish. Pour ½ cup of the melted butter over the hens and sprinkle with salt and pepper. Roast for 20 minutes. Add Bourbon and melted jelly to remaining butter. Reduce heat to 350 degrees and roast for another 30 minutes, basting often with Bourbon mixture.

"FOUR AND TWENTY GAME BIRDS BAKED IN A PIE"

Serves 8

Pinch of salt
⅓ cup shortening
1 cup flour, sifted
2 tablespoons ice water
4 to 6 tablespoons butter
12 quail (or other small
    game birds) split in half
16 small white onions, peeled
2 cups rich chicken stock
Grated rind and juice of 1
    lemon
½ cup dry Marsala wine
1 tablespoon chopped fresh
    parsley

2 celery stalks, chopped
1 large carrot, diced
¼ teaspoon thyme
½ teaspoon savory
2 tablespoons cornstarch
    mixed with ¼ cup cold
    water
12 small new potatoes,
    unpeeled, halved
1 cup fresh peas
1 egg, beaten

Preheat oven to 375 degrees. Select a large, deep baking dish and set aside. Put salt, shortening, and flour together. Cut shortening into flour with a pastry blender until it has the consistency of oatmeal. Sprinkle with ice water and mix gently with a fork to blend. Divide dough in half. Roll half of dough to size of baking dish you have selected. Line dish with pastry, cover, and refrigerate until filling is ready. Melt butter in a heavy skillet and sauté birds for 10 minutes. Remove them and place in pastry-lined baking dish. Add onions, stock, lemon rind and juice, Marsala, parsley, celery, carrot, thyme, and savory to remaining juices in skillet. Simmer, covered, until vegetables are tender. Remove them with a slotted spoon and add to birds. To the remaining gravy, add cornstarch, stir to blend, and cook until slightly thickened. Correct seasonings and pour gravy over birds. Cook potatoes in boiling water until just tender. Add to baking dish, then sprinkle in peas. Roll out remaining dough and cover baking dish with a top crust. Trim, leaving a ½-inch overhang. Turn under, press firmly to edge of dish, and make a scalloped edge. Brush pie with beaten egg. With a knife cut several slits in a pattern for steam vents. Bake for 30 minutes or until pastry is golden.

SPANISH GROUSE

Serves 4

2 grouse
Salt and freshly ground
    pepper
2 tablespoons butter
¼ teaspoon paprika

1 pound canned pear halves
    and juice
1 cup heavy cream
½ cup dry white wine

Preheat oven to 350 degrees. Split grouse into halves and rub with salt and pepper. Melt butter in a heavy skillet and sauté grouse halves until golden. Transfer to a shallow baking dish. Bake, uncovered, for 15 to 20 minutes or until tender. Meanwhile, to the juices in the skillet, add paprika, pear juice, cream, and wine. Stir and simmer until well mixed and hot. Adjust seasonings. Arrange pear halves around grouse, pour sauce over all, and brown for a few minutes under the broiler.

ROAST WILD GOOSE FRANCISCO

Serves 6

2 medium carrots, grated
⅔ cup minced stuffed green
    olives
2 cups chopped onion
1 clove garlic, minced
2 tablespoons chopped fresh
    parsley
2 tablespoons chopped fresh
    celery leaves
6 whole cloves
1 teaspoon thyme
1 teaspoon sage
¼ cup olive oil
2 tablespoons fresh lemon
    juice

3 cups water
1 cup dry sherry
¼ cup good brandy
Salt and freshly ground
    pepper to taste
1 large wild goose
2 cups peeled and diced
    apples
½ pound butter
¼ cup seedless raisins
4 tablespoons brown sugar
2 cups coarse bread crumbs

Combine carrots, olives, 1 cup of the chopped onion, garlic, parsley, celery leaves, cloves, thyme, sage, oil, lemon juice, water, sherry, brandy, salt, and pepper to make a marinade. Marinate goose from 8 to 12 hours, making sure that there is plenty of the marinade and vegetables in the cavity. Turn and baste the goose frequently. Pour marinade into a saucepan and cook until reduced by half.

Preheat oven to 325 degrees. To prepare stuffing, sauté the remaining chopped onion and apples in ¼ pound of the butter until onions become soft. Add raisins, brown sugar, remaining butter, and salt. Heat until butter melts. Add bread crumbs and toss mixture until crumbs absorb butter. Stuff cavity and neck of goose. Truss and roast for 25 to 30 minutes per pound. Thirty minutes before goose has finished cooking, add hot marinade sauce to the pan and baste frequently.

DUCKLING AUX CERISES

Serves 8

2 5-pound domestic
    ducklings
2½ cups pitted black
    cherries with juice
4 tablespoons butter
½ cup finely chopped
    onions

¾ cup dry Marsala wine
1½ cups chicken stock
1 bay leaf
3 tablespoons cornstarch
1 teaspoon salt
⅛ teaspoon freshly ground
    pepper

Preheat oven to 500 degrees, then reduce to 350 degrees. Rinse, pat dry, and quarter ducks. Brown quarters in butter in a skillet. Place pieces on a rack in a shallow pan and roast, uncovered, at 350 degrees for 90 minutes. Pour off all but 2 tablespoons fat from the skillet in which duck was browned. Sauté onions in skillet for 5 minutes or until soft. Add Marsala, stock, and bay leaf. Drain cherries and mix ¾ cup cherry juice with cornstarch, salt, and pepper. Stir into sauce in the skillet and simmer until thickened. Add cherries and simmer for 5 minutes. Put duck on a warmed platter and cover with some sauce. Serve the rest of the sauce in a bowl.

ROAST DUCKLING WITH GREEN PEPPERCORN AND KUMQUAT SAUCE

A very special recipe from Fournou's Ovens in the Stanford Court Hotel.

Serves 6

DUCKLINGS

3 ducklings, 4 to 5 pounds each

1 medium onion, coarsely chopped

2 stalks celery, cut in 1-inch slices

6 medium carrots, peeled and sliced

Salt and pepper to taste

Preheat oven to 425 degrees. Divide onion, celery, and carrots into thirds and stuff each duck cavity with vegetables. Truss ducks and sprinkle with salt and pepper. Roast ducks on a rack for 45 minutes.

KUMQUAT SAUCE

1 quart fresh kumquats

¼ cup vinegar

1 cup sugar

1 cup fresh orange juice

¼ cup fresh lemon juice

½ teaspoon crushed black peppercorns

1 bay leaf

1 small sprig thyme, or ¼ teaspoon dried

1 small leek, thinly sliced

2 cups Brown Sauce (see Index)

½ cup tomato paste

1 ounce Cointreau or Grand Marnier

3 ounces green peppercorns

Peel half of the kumquats, removing all pulp from peels. Reserve pulp. Cut peels in fine julienne, cover with boiling water for 1 minute. Drain and reserve. In a saucepan over medium heat, cook vinegar and sugar until they begin to caramelize. Add orange and lemon juices and the reserved pulp from the peeled kumquats. Cook until liquid reduces about one fourth. Add kumquat peel julienne, crushed black peppercorns, bay leaf, thyme, and leek. Simmer until golden brown. Then add brown sauce and tomato paste. Simmer, stirring occasionally, for 1 hour.

TO SERVE

Drain all juices and fat from roast ducks. Halve them and arrange on a warm platter. Arrange stuffing vegetables around halved ducks. Strain sauce through a fine sieve, add the Cointreau and green peppercorns, and set aside. Keep warm. Thinly slice remaining kumquats and garnish duck platter. Warm again if necessary. Pass sauce separately.

CALIFORNIA WILD DUCK STEW

Serves 8 to 10

¼ pound fresh mushrooms, sliced
4 large tomatoes, peeled, seeded, and quartered
3 tablespoons butter
1 large carrot, diced
1 medium green pepper, diced
1 medium onion, sliced
1 cup chopped celery and leaves
1 clove garlic, peeled and quartered
1 cup pitted ripe olives
1 tablespoon tomato paste
¼ cup olive oil

2 cups dry red wine
1 tablespoon Worcestershire sauce
⅛ teaspoon cinnamon
⅛ teaspoon ground cloves
⅛ teaspoon allspice
⅛ teaspoon mace
⅛ teaspoon thyme
1 bay leaf, crushed
1 teaspoon salt
¼ teaspoon freshly ground pepper
4 wild ducks, plucked, drawn, and cut in serving pieces
20 small new potatoes

Sauté mushrooms and tomatoes in 3 tablespoons butter for 3 minutes. Combine with carrot, green pepper, onion, celery, garlic, olives, tomato paste, olive oil, wine, Worcestershire, cinnamon, cloves, allspice, mace, thyme, bay leaf, salt, and pepper to make a marinade. Add duck pieces and marinate overnight or for at least 10 hours. Simmer duck in marinade 1½ to 2 hours or until tender. Boil potatoes in salted water for approximately 15 minutes or until tender, and add to stew just before serving.

WILD DUCK IN WINE SAUCE

Serves 2

2 wild ducks
4 tablespoons butter
Salt and freshly ground
    pepper
6 ounces cream cheese
½ cup dry Marsala wine
½ teaspoon cinnamon
½ cup currant jelly

2 tablespoons prepared
    horseradish
Grated rind of 1 lemon
1 tablespoon fresh lemon
    juice
Parsley for garnish
1 orange, thinly sliced, for
    garnish

Preheat oven to 500 degrees. Rub ducks with butter, sprinkle generously with salt and pepper. Place half of cream cheese in the cavity of each bird. Truss and place in a roasting pan. Roast for 20 to 25 minutes or until skin is nicely browned. Meanwhile, mix Marsala, cinnamon, currant jelly, horseradish, lemon rind and juice in a saucepan. Simmer for 15 minutes, stirring occasionally. Remove ducks to heated serving platter, discard cream cheese, and pour sauce over. Garnish with parsley and orange slices.

CUMBERLAND SAUCE

Makes approximately ½ cup

3 tablespoons plus 1 teaspoon
    red currant jelly
1 tablespoon sherry
1 tablespoon Madeira
2 tablespoons fresh orange
    juice
1 tablespoon fresh lemon
    juice

½ teaspoon dry mustard
½ teaspoon paprika
½ teaspoon ground ginger
1½ teaspoons freshly grated
    orange rind

Heat jelly until it melts, blend in wines, juices, and seasonings. Serve at room temperature with roast wild duck or goose.

SEVILLA SAUCE

A rich orange sauce that is excellent with boned poached chicken breasts, duck or Rock Cornish game hens. Would make a lovely Christmas gift, spooned into a decorative jar.

Makes approximately 2½ cups

⅓ cup julienne of orange rind
1¼ cups white wine
½ teaspoon ground ginger
½ teaspoon ground allspice
½ teaspoon ground nutmeg
1 tablespoon brown sugar
½ cup granulated sugar

1 tablespoon vinegar
1 cup fresh orange juice
2 tablespoons fresh lemon juice
Grated rind of 1 orange
¼ cup Grand Marnier
2 tablespoons currant jelly
2 teaspoons cornstarch

Remove the rind (not the peel) from an orange with a potato peeler. Cut into very thin julienne slivers with a sharp knife. Combine 1 cup of the wine, ginger, allspice, nutmeg, and brown sugar in a saucepan. Simmer the orange rind in this liquid for 20 minutes, uncovered. Drain and set orange rind aside. Caramelize the granulated sugar and vinegar in a heavy saucepan over medium heat. Add ¾ cup of the orange juice, lemon juice, orange rind, Grand Marnier, and remaining wine. Stir and cook for 5 minutes. Add jelly. Dissolve cornstarch in remaining ¼ cup of orange juice and add to sauce, stirring until thickened. Add the julienne of orange rind.

HUNTER'S SAUCE FOR WILD DUCK

Makes 2 cups

1 cup red currant jelly
1 teaspoon dry mustard
½ teaspoon Worcestershire sauce

Juice of 2 lemons
1 tablespoon prepared horseradish sauce
1 cup dry red wine

Combine ingredients in a small, heavy saucepan and bring to a boil. Simmer slowly until slightly thickened.

PURPLE PLUM SAUCE

A superb sauce or basting liquid for quail, pheasant, or Rock Cornish game hens.

Makes approximately 2 cups

1 pound canned purple
    plums, pitted
¼ cup butter
3 tablespoons finely chopped
    onion
¼ cup fresh lemon juice

¼ cup brown sugar
2 tablespoons chili sauce
1 teaspoon Worcestershire
    sauce
½ teaspoon ground ginger

Drain plums and reserve juice. Purée plums in a blender. Melt butter in a small saucepan. Add onion and sauté until golden. Stir in remaining ingredients. Add puréed plums and reserved plum juice. Simmer for about 30 minutes or until thickened.

GOURMET STUFFING FOR POULTRY

Makes approximately 10 cups

1½ cups chopped onion
1 cup chopped celery, leaves
    included
¾ cup butter
½ pound ground pork
    sausage meat
½ cup coarsely chopped
    mushrooms
8 cups unseasoned coarse
    bread crumbs
1 tablespoon salt

½ teaspoon freshly ground
    pepper
1 teaspoon sage
½ teaspoon thyme
½ teaspoon rosemary
½ teaspoon nutmeg
1 cup white wine or chicken
    stock
1 large egg, lightly beaten
½ cup chopped dried
    apricots

Sauté onion and celery in butter until tender. In a separate skillet, cook sausage and mushrooms. Pour off the fat and add to onion and celery. Combine this mixture with the bread crumbs and add all the seasonings. Moisten with the wine or chicken stock, add the egg and apricots and mix well. Stuff the poultry just before roasting.

CHAPTER XI

MEATS

Visitacion Valley

The southernmost reaches of San Francisco's city limits encompass a large area of gently rolling hills and bay frontage called Visitacion Valley. In days past, cattle grazed on the slopes of what is now McLaren Park, and in the valley livestock pens and barns sat amid plentiful truck gardens and small fruit-packing plants.

One cornerstone of California's early economy was the cattle industry—a source of hides and tallow as well as beef. In San Francisco, a spreading population forced farms and ranches to move south, away from the growth of residential neighborhoods to areas with greater open space. By 1870, the slaughterhouses that had once occupied a part of Cow Hollow were ordered removed for reasons of public health, to an area of Visitacion Valley near Islais Creek. It soon bore the nickname "butchertown" and remained known as such until junkyards and shipyards began to replace the slaughterhouses during World War II. Today a prominent reminder of this neighborhood's past is the Cow Palace, standing just across the county line, a gigantic structure that is home to the famous Grand National Livestock Exposition.

Meat of one sort or another has had a prominent place in the Western diet since the days of the fur trapper's campfire and the miner's stewpot. Varied ethnic approaches to technique and flavor-blending have been added along the way so that today there is a seemingly endless variety of meat dishes. Moussaka, veal piccata, beef with bok choy, butterflied leg of lamb, and even venison grace San Francisco tables now, all of them a part of the great American tradition—Meat.

STEAK AU POIVRE VERT

An elegant entree for entertaining. The green peppercorns give a distinctive flavor.

Serves 6

6 filet mignon steaks, about ⅓ pound each
6 slices dense white bread
2 cups heavy cream
½ cup rendered beef fat
2 beef bouillon cubes
1 tablespoon fresh lemon juice

½ teaspoon salt
3 tablespoons medium-dry sherry
½ cup brandy
4 tablespoons green peppercorns, rinsed and drained

Tie steaks into compact round shape and set aside. Cut bread into rounds to fit steaks and toast under broiler to evenly brown both sides. Place toasted bread on a serving platter and set aside. In a heavy saucepan over high heat cook cream, stirring occasionally, until reduced to approximately 1 cup. The cream should be thick. Set in refrigerator. In a skillet large enough to hold the filets in a single layer, heat rendered fat until smoky. Cook the steaks for 3 to 4 minutes per side and place on toast rounds. Keep warm. Pour off excess fat from the skillet and deglaze with brandy. Set aside. To the cream add bouillon cubes, lemon juice, salt, and sherry. Stirring constantly, bring to a boil. Remove from heat and add deglazing liquid along with the peppercorns. Reheat and pour a small amount over each steak. Serve remaining sauce in a gravy boat.

BEEF BOURGUIGNONNE

A classic dish—time-consuming but well worth the effort. Must be made in advance, so it is perfect for any hostess. This recipe is a beautiful blend of flavors. Serve with a good Burgundy and a brown rice casserole.

Serves 8

¼ pound salt pork, diced
¼ cup cognac
¼ cup chopped fresh
    parsley
⅛ teaspoon freshly ground
    pepper
½ cup flour
1½ teaspoons salt
½ teaspoon pepper
Dash cayenne pepper
3 pounds bottom round, cut
    in 1½-inch pieces

¼ pound butter
4 medium onions, chopped
2 cups beef stock or as
    needed
1½ cups Burgundy wine
½ teaspoon dried thyme
½ teaspoon dried marjoram
1 pound fresh mushrooms
16 small white onions, peeled
Chopped fresh parsley for
    garnish

Marinate salt pork in cognac, parsley, and ⅛ teaspoon pepper for 2 to 3 hours. Combine flour, salt, pepper, and cayenne. Dredge beef in seasoned flour. Melt half the butter in a heavy skillet and brown meat on all sides. Add chopped onions and brown. Transfer beef and onions to a 3-quart casserole with a tight-fitting lid. Drain salt pork, reserving marinade, and brown it in 1 teaspoon butter. Add to beef. Deglaze skillet with marinade and ¼ cup beef stock. Pour over meat. Add wine, thyme, marjoram, and enough stock to cover meat. Cover and bake in a preheated 375-degree oven for 2 hours. Sauté mushrooms in 2 tablespoons butter until just barely cooked. Add to meat. Parboil white onions for 3 minutes, drain well, and sauté in remaining butter to brown lightly. Add to meat, replace cover, and continue cooking for 1 more hour. Add more wine or stock if needed. Adjust seasonings and serve sprinkled with chopped fresh parsley.

BEEF STROGANOFF

Serves 6

1½ pounds sirloin steak
2 tablespoons fresh lemon
   juice
1 small onion, grated
4 tablespoons butter
2 tablespoons flour
½ teaspoon dried basil

⅛ teaspoon nutmeg
Salt and freshly ground
   pepper to taste
1 pint sour cream
1 tablespoon brandy
3 tablespoons chopped fresh
   chives

Slice meat very thinly in diagonal slices across the grain. Sprinkle with lemon juice and set aside. Sauté onion in butter, add meat and lemon juice, flour, and seasonings. Cook and stir for several minutes. The meat should remain pink. Stir in sour cream and brandy. Adjust seasonings and stir in chives. Serve immediately with hot rice.

MARINATED CHUCK ROAST

The marinade turns an economical cut of meat into a tender and tasty entree. The secret is the long marinating time—overnight is preferred.

Serves 8 to 10

4-pound chuck roast, approximately 1½ inches thick

MARINADE
1 medium onion, chopped
2 tablespoons salad oil
2 cloves garlic, mashed
¼ cup chopped fresh
   parsley
⅓ cup soy sauce
1 teaspoon powdered ginger

1 teaspoon allspice
1 teaspoon dried rosemary
3 tablespoons red wine
   vinegar
2 tablespoons brown sugar
1¼ cups beef broth

Sauté onion in oil until transparent. Stir in remaining marinade ingredients and bring to a boil. Remove from heat and cool. Place roast in a deep glass container. Pour marinade over roast and refrigerate for 6 hours or overnight, turning occasionally. Broil the roast over medium coals for 30 to 40 minutes.

FILET OF BEEF IN PHYLLO PASTRY WITH MADEIRA SAUCE

Easy and very elegant. The main cooking of the meat comes with the searing, so later it only warms while the pastry is baking. The phyllo pastry is buttery, flaky, golden brown, and delicious. This is also excellent made ahead and sliced and served cold for a buffet or an elegant picnic.

Serves 6

3-pound filet mignon, trimmed
Salt
2 tablespoons sweet butter
½ pound mushrooms, minced and thoroughly dried

2 shallots, minced
1 package phyllo pastry
½ cup melted butter
Madeira Sauce (see Index)

Preheat oven to 400 degrees. Rub filet with salt. In a heavy skillet sear the meat over high heat in sweet butter until brown on all sides to seal in the juices. Set aside. In the same pan, sauté mushrooms and shallots for 2 to 3 minutes or until soft. Set aside. Layer 12 pieces of phyllo pastry together, brushing each layer with melted butter. Spread about half of the mushroom mixture on the pastry and place the seared beef on top. Then place remaining mushrooms on top of filet and fold the phyllo dough around the filet. Prepare an additional 5 to 6 layers of phyllo pastry, each brushed with butter. Seal all the edges by overlapping them with this additional pastry and brush with butter. Place beef in a buttered baking pan and bake for about 40 to 45 minutes or until pastry is browned and flaky. Remove beef to a serving dish and serve with Madeira sauce.

GOLDEN GATE SWISS STEAK

Serves 4

⅓ cup all-purpose flour
2 teaspoons dry mustard
½ teaspoon salt
¼ teaspoon freshly ground
    pepper
1½ pounds round steak, 1
    inch thick

2 tablespoons vegetable oil
4 large tomatoes, peeled and
    chopped
3 large carrots, thinly sliced
2 tablespoons
    Worcestershire sauce
1 tablespoon brown sugar

Combine flour, mustard, salt, and pepper. Dredge the meat with this mixture, then work the flour into the meat with a meat pounder. Cut steak into 4 individual portions. In a heavy skillet or Dutch oven, heat oil and brown meat on both sides. Combine tomatoes, carrots, Worcestershire sauce, and brown sugar, and pour over meat. Cover and either bake in a preheated 350-degree oven or simmer on top of stove for approximately 1½ hours or until meat is tender.

GERMAN BEEF STEW

A cold winter's night delight. It is unusually flavorful and perfect with noodles, green beans, and a tossed salad.

Serves 4

1½ pounds beef stew meat,
    cut in 1-inch cubes
2 tablespoons vegetable oil
1 large tart green apple,
    peeled and shredded
1 medium carrot, shredded
½ medium onion, sliced
½ cup water
⅓ cup dry red wine

½ teaspoon anchovy paste
1 clove garlic, minced
2 beef bouillon cubes
1 small bay leaf
⅛ teaspoon dried thyme,
    crushed
4 teaspoons cornstarch
¼ cup cold water

Brown meat in oil. Add apple, carrot, onion, water, wine, anchovy paste, garlic, bouillon cubes, bay leaf, and thyme. Cover and cook over low heat for 2 hours or until beef is tender. Remove bay leaf. Combine cornstarch and the ¼ cup cold water, add to beef mixture. Cook and stir until thickened.

SPICED POT ROAST

Serves 10

2 cloves garlic
2 teaspoons seasoned salt or herb salt
1 5-pound boned rump of beef
3 tablespoons salad oil
3 medium onions, sliced
4 teaspoons chili powder
½ teaspoon ground cumin
½ teaspoon ground coriander

Additional seasoned salt or herb salt to taste
⅓ cup tomato paste
1 17-ounce can whole tomatoes
1 beef bouillon cube
2 cups cooked white rice
1 cup canned red kidney beans, heated
2 avocados, sliced, for garnish

Mash garlic with seasoned salt or herb salt. With sharp knife, cut small holes in meat and fill them with garlic mixture. Heat oil in a Dutch oven and brown meat on all sides. Add onions and sauté for several minutes. Add spices, seasonings, and tomato paste. Drain tomatoes reserving the juice, and set tomatoes aside. If necessary, add water to the juice to make 1¼ cups. Add bouillon cube to juice and heat to dissolve. Add this to meat, cover, and simmer for 2¼ hours or until almost tender. Add tomatoes and simmer for another 15 minutes or until meat is tender and tomatoes are heated through. Adjust seasonings. Toss rice with heated kidney beans. Transfer meat to heated platter, pour juices over, surround with rice and kidney bean mixture and garnish with avocado slices.

GLAZED CORNED BEEF

Serves 8 to 12

1 6- to 10-pound corned
    beef brisket
12 peppercorns, lightly
    crushed

2 bay leaves
1 large onion, studded with 6
    to 8 whole cloves
2 cloves garlic, bruised

GLAZE

¾ cup firmly packed dark
    brown sugar

1 tablespoon dry mustard
1 tablespoon cider vinegar

Place corned beef in a large pot with peppercorns, bay leaves, onion, garlic, and enough water to cover. Bring to a boil, skim off any scum that rises to the top, lower heat, and simmer, covered, for 2½ to 3 hours or until tender. Cool meat in the cooking water. Combine all the glaze ingredients. Transfer the corned beef to a roasting pan and coat with the glaze. Bake uncovered, basting occasionally, in a preheated 300-degree oven for 1 hour.

SMOKED BEEF BRISKET

Beef brisket, allowing ⅓
    pound per person
Freshly cracked black
    pepper

Salt to taste
4 tablespoons bacon fat

Preheat oven to 350 degrees. Cover the entire surface of the brisket with cracked pepper and salt. In a skillet, brown the brisket in the bacon fat. Bake the brisket for 30 minutes per pound. Remove from the oven and place well above a low charcoal fire for 1 hour to smoke the meat. Slice thinly to serve.

STUFFED FLANK STEAK

This is a most attractive way to serve a flank steak. Because the meat is butterflied, the stuffing doesn't spill out while it is cooking. The meat becomes firm and holds its shape nicely while being carved. It looks most appealing on the plate with the swirls of stuffing showing, and it is delicious besides. Good for a dinner party, since it requires long and slow braising, allowing the hostess to be with her guests.

Serves 6

3 medium onions, minced
4 tablespoons butter
6 tablespoons olive oil
2 cloves garlic, minced
1 4½-ounce can chopped
   ripe olives
½ cup chopped cooked ham
1 teaspoon thyme
1 teaspoon salt

1 teaspoon freshly ground
   pepper
2 egg yolks, beaten
2 tablespoons minced parsley
1 2½-pound flank steak,
   butterflied
1½ tablespoons butter
2 cups beef stock

Preheat oven to 300 degrees. Sauté onions in the butter and olive oil until limp. Add garlic, olives, ham, thyme, salt, and pepper. Remove from heat and stir in beaten egg yolks and parsley, blending well. Stuff this mixture into the cavity of the butterflied steak. Roll up steak carefully and tie with string at several intervals. Melt 1½ tablespoons butter in a Dutch oven or heatproof casserole and brown flank steak on all sides. Add beef stock and braise in a 300 degree oven, covered, for 2 hours. When done, lift meat from Dutch oven and place on a warm serving dish. Carefully cut and remove strings. Rapidly boil down liquid in the pot. Spoon boiled-down gravy over meat and carve.

KOREAN BARBECUED SHORT RIBS

Serves 4

4 pounds meaty beef short
   ribs

3 tablespoons sugar
¼ cup sesame oil

MARINADE
½ cup soy sauce
1 tablespoon cider vinegar
2 green onions and tops,
   minced
2 cloves garlic, minced
1 tablespoon finely minced
   ginger root

1 teaspoon dried red pepper
   flakes
¼ cup sesame seeds
1 tablespoon flour

Make deep cuts in the meat between the ribs so the meat will absorb the
marinade. Rub well with sugar and oil and let sit for 30 minutes. Combine ingredients, pour over ribs, and let stand for 1 hour. Bake or barbecue, turning and basting frequently with marinade, for 20 to 30 minutes or until meat is cooked.

SCHROEDER'S SAUERBRATEN

Serves 6

5 pounds top round or rump
   of beef in 1 piece
2 cups cider vinegar
4 cups water
1 large onion, sliced
3 tablespoons whole pickling
   spices

½ teaspoon salt
Rendered beef fat or
   shortening
5 tablespoons all-purpose
   flour
2 tablespoons sugar
½ cup red wine

Place meat in a deep glass container. Combine vinegar, water, onion,
spices, and salt. Pour over meat and marinate, turning frequently, for 2
to 3 days. Remove meat from marinade and brown well on both sides in

beef fat in a skillet. Transfer meat to a roasting pan and add 3 tablespoons of the flour to the skillet, stirring until browned. Stir in marinade and sugar, and cook for 3 minutes. Pour over meat, cover, and, basting often, bake in a preheated 350-degree oven for 2½ to 3 hours or until meat is almost done. One half hour before end of cooking time, add red wine. Transfer meat to a heated platter. Mix remaining flour with enough water to make a thin binder and thicken gravy. Adjust with salt and more vinegar if needed. Strain gravy into a gravy bowl. Note: Serve meat with Potato Pancakes and Red Cabbage.

BEEF WITH BOK CHOY

Serves 4

MARINADE

1 tablespoon soy sauce	1 pound bok choy
1 tablespoon peanut oil	(Chinese cabbage)
1 tablespoon sherry	2 tablespoons peanut oil
1 teaspoon brown sugar	1 tablespoon minced fresh
1 teaspoon cornstarch	ginger root
½ pound flank steak	

Mix together all marinade ingredients. Cut the beef in thin diagonal slices across the grain. This is easier to do if you partially freeze the meat first. Add beef to the marinade. Separate leaves from stems of the bok choy. Cut the stems and leaves diagonally into 2-inch pieces. In a wok or skillet heat 1 tablespoon of the oil until very hot. Add the ginger root and toss for a few seconds until light brown. Add beef, stir and toss vigorously for 2 to 3 minutes or until it is seared. Remove and set aside. Add remaining oil. Stir in white part of bok choy, cover, and cook for 30 seconds. Remove cover and stir until slightly soft, then add green part of bok choy and beef. Heat for 1 to 2 minutes, thoroughly. If necessary a little chicken stock may be added so the bok choy is lightly glazed. Usually there is enough moisture in the vegetable itself to do this. Serve immediately.

TERIYAKI FOR VENISON STEAKS

Serves 4

¼ cup soy sauce
¼ cup dry sherry
2 tablespoons peanut or corn
    oil
2 cloves garlic, mashed

2 teaspoons grated fresh
    ginger root
4 venison steaks,
    approximately ½
    pound each

Combine all ingredients and marinate venison steaks for 2 to 3 hours. Grill venison on charcoal, basting with marinade, for about 8 minutes per side. Do not overcook the meat or it will become tough.

WIENER SCHNITZEL

Serves 4

4 large veal chops, boned
2 eggs, beaten
2 tablespoons fresh lemon
    juice
1 cup bread crumbs
¼ cup freshly grated
    Parmesan cheese
1 tablespoon toasted wheat
    germ
½ teaspoon salt

¼ teaspoon white pepper
¼ teaspoon powdered
    thyme
¼ teaspoon onion powder
¼ teaspoon garlic powder
¼ teaspoon paprika
3 tablespoons butter or
    vegetable oil
4 lemon wedges
4 parsley sprigs

Pound veal with a meat pounder or edge of a heavy plate until very thin, being careful not to tear meat. Beat eggs with lemon juice. Set aside. Combine bread crumbs, cheese, wheat germ, and seasonings. Dip veal in egg and then in bread crumb mixture, coating evenly. Place meat on a cookie sheet in one layer and refrigerate, covered with wax paper, for at least 1 hour to help keep coating intact when cooking. Sauté slices until lightly browned on both sides, 7 to 10 minutes in all, in butter or oil. Serve immediately, garnished with lemon wedges and parsley.

THREE-WAY BEEF JERKY

Makes approximately 1½ pounds

2 pounds flank steak, bottom round, or any lean beefsteak or
     roast

SPICY MARINADE

½ cup Teriyaki sauce (see   ¼ teaspoon Tabasco sauce
     Teriyaki Sauce for   2 tablespoons sherry
     venison steaks in the   Dash garlic powder
     Index)   Salt and freshly ground
1 teaspoon olive oil   pepper to taste

SMOKY MARINADE

1½ tablespoon liquid smoke   ¼ teaspoon freshly ground
     sauce   pepper
1 cup water   ½ teaspoon garlic powder
2 teaspoons salt

ORIENTAL MARINADE

1 cup soy sauce   ½ cup brown sugar
1 cup Chinese oyster sauce   1 cup sugar

Trim all fat from meat and partially freeze to facilitate cutting. Cut into
very thin slices, cutting with the grain. Combine marinade ingredients
of your choice and stir in meat. Marinate overnight, stirring occasionally. Place cake racks on foil-covered cookie sheets or cover bottom
of oven with foil and use oven racks. Drape meat slices on racks and
roast for 8 to 10 hours or overnight at 175 degrees. Cool and store in an
airtight container.

VEAL CHOPS FONTINA

Serves 6

6 large veal loin chops, ¾
  inch thick
6 slices Italian fontina cheese
⅓ cup flour
½ teaspoon salt
½ teaspoon paprika
¼ teaspoon freshly ground
  pepper

¼ teaspoon thyme
1 egg, beaten
1 tablespoon lemon juice
½ cup fine bread crumbs
¼ cup butter
¼ cup veal or chicken stock

With a sharp knife, make a pocket in the side of each chop and place a slice of cheese inside. Close pocket securely with a toothpick. Mix together flour, salt, paprika, pepper, and thyme. Set aside. Beat egg with lemon juice. Dip chops in flour mixture, then in egg, then in bread crumbs. Place chops in one layer on a large plate and refrigerate, covered with wax paper, for at least 1 hour. Heat butter in a heavy skillet and, when foaming subsides, slowly brown chops on one side. Turn, cover, and brown on other side for about 30 minutes. Remove chops to a warm serving platter. Deglaze pan with stock, and pour over chops.

VEAL FRANCISCO

Serves 4

4 1½ inch-thick veal steaks
All-purpose flour for
  dredging
2 tablespoons olive oil
2 cloves garlic, mashed
¾ cup dry white wine
1 large bay leaf, crumbled
1 tablespoon
  Worcestershire sauce
¼ cup chopped fresh
  parsley

⅓ teaspoon dried thyme,
  crumbled
Grated rind of 1 lemon
4 thick slices lemon
1 cup sliced fresh
  mushrooms
Salt and freshly ground
  pepper to taste
1 cup sour cream
Paprika for garnish
Parsley sprigs for garnish

Dredge veal steaks lightly with flour. In a large skillet brown veal steaks on both sides in oil. Add garlic and brown lightly. Add wine and sprinkle each steak with some bay leaf, Worcestershire sauce, parsley, thyme, and lemon rind. Top each steak with a lemon slice, cover skillet, and simmer for 1 hour or until meat is tender. Add more wine if needed. Add mushrooms, and cook for 10 minutes until mushrooms are tender. Season with salt and pepper, remove from heat, and carefully stir in sour cream. Sprinkle with paprika and garnish with parsley sprigs.

VEAL AND WATER CHESTNUT CASSEROLE

Serves 6

2½ to 3 pounds boneless
    veal from leg, cut into
    cubes
8 tablespoons butter
1 large onion, grated
2 cloves garlic, minced
Salt and freshly ground
    pepper to taste
Dash cayenne pepper
1 pound mushrooms, cut
    into quarters
1½ cups beef stock

¼ teaspoon nutmeg
¼ teaspoon thyme
1 bay leaf
1 8-ounce can water
    chestnuts, drained and
    sliced
½ cup heavy cream
2 egg yolks, beaten
2 tablespoons fresh lemon
    juice
Chopped parsley for garnish

Preheat oven to 375 degrees. Brown veal in a skillet in 4 tablespoons of the butter on all sides. Add onion and garlic and cook for 3 minutes. Season with salt, pepper, and cayenne. Transfer to a 3-quart casserole and set aside. Sauté mushrooms in remaining butter over high heat, cooking quickly. Transfer mushrooms to casserole then deglaze skillet with ½ cup of the stock. Pour remaining stock in to skillet and add nutmeg, thyme, bay leaf, and water chestnuts. Pour this liquid over veal and mushrooms and mix well. Cover and bake for 1½ hours. Combine cream, egg yolks, and lemon juice. Add to casserole, stir and bake, uncovered, for 15 minutes. Sprinkle with chopped parsley.

VEAL KNOTS PICCATA

Serves 4

2 pounds veal scallops,
 pounded very thin
1 cup flour
½ teaspoon salt
¼ teaspoon white pepper
8 tablespoons butter
½ cup white wine

4 tablespoons fresh lemon
 juice
3 tablespoons capers, drained
2 egg yolks, beaten
4 tablespoons chopped fresh
 parsley

Cut the scallops in long strips approximately 1 inch wide. Combine the flour, salt, and pepper and roll the veal strips in it. Gently tie each strip into a knot and reseason with flour mixture if necessary. Melt the butter in a skillet and brown the knots on all sides. Add wine, lemon juice, and capers to the meat and simmer until tender, approximately 6 minutes. Remove meat from the skillet to a warm serving platter. Make a sauce by adding egg yolks to the skillet and blending quickly until thickened. Pour sauce over knots and sprinkle with parsley to garnish.

LAMB WITH MUSTARD GLAZE

The glaze on this lamb comes out golden and delicious. Be sure to use the pan juices as a sauce.

Serves 8

½ cup Dijon mustard
1 tablespoon soy sauce
1 clove garlic, minced
½-inch slice ginger root,
 minced

1 teaspoon crushed dried
 rosemary
¼ cup olive oil
1 6½-pound leg of lamb,
 boned

Preheat oven to 325 degrees. Combine mustard, soy sauce, garlic, ginger, and rosemary. Gradually whisk in olive oil. With a brush, coat lamb thickly and evenly with this mixture and let stand at room temperature for 2 to 3 hours. (If all the glaze isn't used, baste with remainder while lamb is roasting.) Place lamb on a rack in a roasting pan and roast for 1 hour and 45 minutes or until done to taste.

BUTTERFLIED LEG OF LAMB

The most economical and elegant way to serve a leg of lamb . . . no bone to carve around, no waste. Equally easy to do on the grill or in the oven.

1 leg of lamb (Allow ½ pound bone-in weight per person)

MARINADE
¾ cup vegetable oil
¼ cup red wine vinegar
½ cup chopped onion
2 cloves garlic, bruised
2 teaspoons Dijon mustard
2 teaspoons salt
½ teaspoon crumbled dried
  oregano

½ teaspoon crumbled dried
  basil
1 bay leaf, crushed
⅛ teaspoon freshly ground
  pepper

Have your butcher bone the leg of lamb and cut into butterfly shape. Keep bones and scraps for soup stock. Combine marinade ingredients in a plastic bag, add lamb, and place bag in a large bowl. Turning occasionally, marinate under refrigeration for 24 to 48 hours, the longer the better. Remove lamb from marinade and broil or barbecue, fat side up 4 inches from heat, for 10 minutes. Turn, baste with marinade, and broil for 10 minutes more. If using the oven, continue roasting in a 425-degree oven for 10 to 15 minutes, or until done to taste. If barbecuing, raise the grill slightly and continue basting and cooking until done to taste. Lamb should be crusty on outside and pink inside.

ROAST LAMB WITH SOUBISE SAUCE

Serves 8

1 6- to 7-pound leg of lamb,
  boned
2 cloves garlic, slivered
4 tablespoons coarse salt
3 tablespoons freshly
  cracked pepper
10 tablespoons butter
1 teaspoon salt
½ teaspoon freshly ground
  white pepper
3 medium onions, thinly
  sliced

6 tablespoons uncooked rice
2 tablespoons flour
½ cup light cream
1 tablespoon fresh lemon
  juice
¼ cup chicken stock
2 egg yolks, lightly beaten
¼ cup chopped parsley
¼ cup dry bread crumbs
¼ cup melted butter

Preheat oven to 350 degrees. Trim fat from lamb, roll and tie it. Make tiny pockets in the meat and insert garlic slivers. Rub with coarse salt and cracked pepper. Set on a rack and roast for 18 minutes per pound. When done, pour off fat and deglaze pan. While lamb is roasting, prepare the soubise sauce. In a saucepan melt 8 tablespoons of the butter, stir in salt, white pepper, onions, and rice. Cover and cook over medium heat for 30 minutes or until soft. Pureé in a blender. In another saucepan melt 2 tablespoons butter, stir in flour, and whisk in cream, lemon juice, and chicken stock. Remove from heat. Stir in egg yolks, pureé, and parsley. Adjust seasonings. Slice lamb into serving slices, spread some soubise sauce over each slice. Arrange slices, overlapping, on a platter and sprinkle with bread crumbs. Drizzle with melted butter. Reheat for 10 to 15 minutes at 400 degrees. This dish can be prepared ahead. Cool, cover with plastic wrap, and refrigerate. Bring to room temperature before reheating.

RACK OF LAMB PERSILLÉ

A simple yet elegant main course that goes beautifully with any pasta, rice, or potato dish.

Serves 6

3 slices bread, crusts
 removed
¼ cup chopped parsley
Salt and freshly ground
 pepper to taste

1 clove garlic, minced
2 6-rib racks of lamb
Olive oil
½ cup clarified butter
Parsley sprigs for garnish

Preheat oven to 500 degrees. Place 3 slices bread in a blender or food processor and make bread crumbs. Place in a small bowl with the chopped parsley, salt, pepper, garlic, and toss until blended. Set aside. Trim racks of lamb of all fat. With meat at room temperature, place racks in an oiled roasting pan, bone side up, and brush racks thoroughly with olive oil. Roast racks for 10 minutes, then turn them over and cover with bread crumb mixture, carefully spooning over the clarified butter. Continue to cook the racks for another 5 to 8 minutes, depending on desired rareness. Garnish platter with sprigs of parsley and serve immediately.

INDIVIDUAL LEGS OF LAMB

These are delicious and easy to do for entertaining, since they cook so long and so slowly. The onions come out soft and flavorful, and many vegetables will complement them.

Serves 4

4 lamb shanks
1 clove garlic
Salt and freshly ground
 pepper to taste
¼ teaspoon each of basil,
 oregano, rosemary, and
 thyme

½ teaspoon curry powder
1 bay leaf, crumbled
4 large onions, thinly sliced
2 tablespoons soy sauce
¼ cup dry white wine
¼ cup water

Preheat oven to 400 degrees. Rub lamb shanks with garlic, place in a roasting pan, and sprinkle with salt and pepper. Mix together the herbs and curry powder and bay leaf and sprinkle over shanks. Place sliced onions on top of lamb and pour soy sauce over meat. Roast, uncovered, for 15 minutes, then reduce heat to 300 and roast for 2 hours. Pour off fat, then add wine and water, cover, and roast for 1 hour more.

LAMB CHOPS WITH ZUCCHINI AND TOMATOES

This recipe is the kind that takes only a few moments to prepare, and the hostess can sit back and enjoy her guests. Tender, savory, and so pretty.

Serves 4

4 large lamb chops
2 tablespoons butter
2 medium onions, sliced
1 medium green pepper, seeded and finely chopped
1 pound zucchini, sliced

1 pound tomatoes, skinned and sliced
Salt and freshly ground pepper to taste
1 tablespoon chopped parsley
1 teaspoon sugar

Preheat oven to 350 degrees. Melt the butter in a skillet and brown the chops quickly, then transfer them to a 2-quart casserole. Add the onions and green pepper to the skillet and sauté gently over low heat for about 10 minutes, or until soft. Cook zucchini in boiling water for 3 to 4 minutes, then drain. Add zucchini and tomatoes to onion mixture, then spoon over chops. Cover casserole and bake for 1½ hours, stirring occasionally. No additional liquid is necessary. Place the lamb chops on a warm serving dish and drain the vegetables, reserving the liquid. Spoon the drained vegetables around the meat. Garnish with parsley. Season the reserved juices to taste and add the sugar. Serve separately to spoon over lamb chops.

AFRICAN LAMB CURRY

An unusual, flavorful buffet dish—particularly elegant with a rice ring. Serve with chutney, chopped hard-cooked eggs, and coconut. Cucumber, melon, and watercress salad is a refreshing accompaniment.

Serves 4

2 pounds lean lamb, cubed
4 tablespoons butter
¼ cup all-purpose flour
¼ teaspoon thyme
¼ teaspoon ground ginger
1½ tablespoons curry
    powder
1 cup chopped onion
2 cloves garlic, minced
4 to 5 ounces dried apples,
    chopped
2 to 3 cups beef stock

1 teaspoon freshly grated
    lemon rind
Salt and freshly ground
    pepper to taste
½ cup chopped walnuts
½ cup seedless raisins,
    plumped in Madeira
    wine to cover
½ cup unsweetened
    shredded coconut

Brown meat in butter in a skillet, sprinkle with flour, thyme, ginger, and curry. Stir well and add onion, garlic, and apples. Cook and stir for 3 minutes. Gradually add 2 cups of the stock, cook and stir until slightly thickened and smooth. Add lemon rind, salt, and pepper. Cover and simmer for 1 hour, adding more stock if needed, until meat is tender. Stir in walnuts, raisins, soaking liquid, and coconut. Simmer for 30 minutes to heat thoroughly.

LAMB CURRY KHORMA

This is a fancy version of basic lamb curry, using unusual spices.

Serves 8

4 pounds boneless lamb, well
    trimmed of fat
1½ tablespoons turmeric
½ cup olive oil
6 medium onions, thinly
    sliced
3 cloves garlic, minced
6 whole cardamom seeds
6 bay leaves
6 whole cloves
1 stick cinnamon
½ cup water
2 tablespoons cumin
1 teaspoon ground coriander
¼ teaspoon mace

¼ teaspoon nutmeg
1½ teaspoons dried dillweed
1 teaspoon cayenne pepper,
    or to taste
¼ teaspoon powdered
    ginger
Salt to taste
Beef stock or water if
    needed
1 tablespoon cornstarch
    dissolved in ¼ cup beef
    stock
Condiments (given in
    recipe)

Cut lamb in 1-inch cubes and roll in turmeric to coat thoroughly. In a large skillet heat the olive oil and lightly brown onions and garlic. In a small saucepan combine cardamom seeds, bay leaves, cloves, cinnamon, and ½ cup water. Bring to a boil and boil gently for 10 minutes. Strain the liquid and discard spices. Set liquid aside. Combine remaining spices and add to onion-garlic mixture. Cook and stir for 10 minutes. Add the meat and salt, stirring well to mix, then stir in reserved spice liquid. Bring to a gentle boil, cover, lower heat, and simmer for 1½ hours or until meat is tender, adding stock or water if needed. Add cornstarch, cook and stir until thickened. Adjust seasonings and serve with a choice of these condiments: chopped bacon, chopped peanuts, shredded coconut, sliced eggs, chutney, chopped green onions, lime wedges.

MOUSSAKA

Serves 8

2 large eggplants
1 cup all-purpose flour
1 cup olive oil
1 pound bulk sausage meat
2 cups chopped onion
2 pounds lean ground lamb
1 teaspoon salt
1 teaspoon crumbled dried
  oregano
2 cloves garlic, minced
1 cup tomato purée
¼ cup minced fresh parsley

Salt and freshly ground
  pepper to taste
1 cup red wine
12 to 14 fresh spinach leaves
½ pound fresh mushrooms,
  sliced
4 tablespoons butter
½ cup all-purpose flour
2 cups light cream
½ teaspoon salt
Nutmeg to taste
½ cup ricotta cheese

Preheat oven to 400 degrees. Peel and slice eggplants crosswise. Salt well and set in a single layer on paper towels. Set aside to bleed for 30 minutes. Pat dry. Place flour in a paper bag and shake a few eggplant slices at a time in it to coat. Heat oil in a large skillet and lightly sauté eggplant slices, set aside. Brown sausage meat in the skillet, drain off fat reserving 2 tablespoons, and set aside. Sauté onion in 1 tablespoon of the reserved fat, in the skillet, and add to reserved sausage meat. Brown lamb in the skillet, seasoning with salt and oregano. Add to reserved sausage mixture. In 1 tablespoon fat, sauté garlic in the skillet until just starting to turn golden. Add tomato pureé, parsley, salt and pepper. Mix well, then add wine and reserved meat mixture. Simmer, uncovered, until almost all liquid is absorbed. Butter a 5-quart casserole. Layer eggplant on the bottom of it. Cover with meat mixture. Add spinach leaves and top with mushrooms. Melt butter in a saucepan until foamy, sprinkle with flour, cook and stir for 3 minutes. Gradually stir in cream, cook and stir until smooth and thickened. Season with salt and nutmeg and pour over casserole. Top with ricotta cheese. Bake for 1 hour.

SAVORY LAMB AND SPINACH ROLL

Serves 4 to 6

¼ cup pine nuts or sliced
   almonds
5 tablespoons butter
1 pound lean ground lamb
2 large ripe tomatoes,
   chopped, peeled, and
   seeded
1 teaspoon salt
¾ teaspoon ground allspice
¼ teaspoon freshly ground
   pepper
1 tablespoon fresh lemon
   juice
1 cup chopped white portion
   of leeks

½ cup minced green onions
2 10-ounce packages frozen
   chopped spinach,
   thawed and well
   drained
¾ cup grated zucchini
2 tablespoons minced fresh
   mint
¾ teaspoon salt
¼ teaspoon pepper
1 egg yolk, lightly beaten
12 sheets of phyllo pastry
Melted butter as needed
1 egg, lightly beaten

In a large skillet, sauté pine nuts in 2 tablespoons of the butter until golden. Crumble lamb and brown in the same skillet. Drain off fat. Add tomatoes, seasonings, and lemon juice, simmer for 5 minutes. In a separate skillet sauté leeks and green onions in remaining butter and combine with meat mixture. Blend in spinach, zucchini, mint, salt, and pepper. Simmer for 7 to 10 minutes until spinach is tender, cool to room temperature. Stir in egg yolk. Preheat oven to 350 degrees. Keeping phyllo sheets covered until ready to use, place 1 sheet at a time on a tea towel and brush liberally with melted butter. Continue layering and buttering until 6 sheets are used. Spread half the lamb-spinach mixture over the sixth sheet, leaving a 3-inch border around all edges. Starting on a short side, roll like a jelly roll, folding in sides as you roll, seal seams with melted butter. Place, seam side down, on a baking sheet. Repeat with remaining phyllo sheets and lamb-spinach mixture, making 2 rolls in all. Brush tops of rolls with beaten egg and bake for 45 minutes until heated through and golden.

NORMANDY BEANS WITH LAMB

Serves 8 to 10

2 cups Great Northern white
    beans
¾ cup diced onion
½ cup chopped celery,
    including some leaves
2 tablespoons chopped fresh
    parsley
½ teaspoon dry mustard
½ teaspoon thyme

2 teaspoons salt
¼ cup firmly packed brown
    sugar
1 cup dry white wine
2 tablespoons cooking oil
1 clove garlic, quartered
2 pounds lean lamb stew
    meat

Soak the beans overnight in water to cover. Drain, and combine with onion, celery, parsley, seasonings, sugar, and wine, adding water to cover. Partially cover pot, and simmer, adding water as needed, for 1½ to 2 hours or until beans are tender but still hold their shape. Transfer to a buttered casserole and set aside. Preheat oven to 325 degrees. In a skillet heat oil, add the garlic and lamb, brown meat without allowing pieces to touch, on all sides. Add to a 4-quart casserole and deglaze skillet with a little wine. Pour deglazing liquid over meat and beans, cover, and bake for 2 hours or until meat is tender. Stir occasionally and add wine if needed to keep moist. Uncover and bake for 30 minutes longer.

PORK Á L'ORANGE

Serves 6

2½ to 3 pounds boneless loin
   of pork
Salt and freshly ground
   pepper
3 medium oranges
1 quart water
3 tablespoons sugar
¼ cup red wine vinegar
2 cups chicken stock

2 tablespoons cornstarch,
   dissolved in 3
   tablespoons port wine
½ cup red wine
2 to 3 tablespoons orange
   liqueur
1 tablespoon fresh lemon
   juice

Preheat oven to 325 degrees. Rub pork loin with salt and pepper, place on a rack in a shallow roasting pan, and roast for 35 minutes per pound. When roast is done, the meat thermometer should register 165 to 170 degrees. Meanwhile, rinse and dry oranges. Remove the rind (the colored part of the peel) with a vegetable peeler. Reserve oranges. Cut rind into thin julienne strips, and simmer them in the 1 quart water for 10 minutes, drain and dry on a paper towel. Cook sugar and vinegar in a small saucepan over medium high heat, stirring frequently with a wooden spoon, until reduced to a red-brown syrup. The syrup will start to foam as it approaches the right consistency. Remove the pan from the heat and stir in ½ cup of the stock, stirring to dissolve any caramelized syrup. Add remaining stock, simmer for a few minutes, then add cornstarch, stirring constantly. Stir in the orange rind. Simmer for a few minutes, correct seasonings, and set aside. Remove white pith from oranges and section the fruit, reserving any juice. When pork is done, transfer it to a serving platter and keep warm. Skim excess fat from the roasting pan and deglaze with the ½ cup red wine. Reduce this to 3 tablespoons. Add this to sauce mixture along with orange liqueur and bring to a simmer. Add lemon juice, orange segments, and juice, and heat. To serve, slice pork, spoon some sauce over slices, and pass rest of sauce separately.

MEDALLIONS OF PORK SAUTÉ

This rich meat dish can also be made with pork chops for a less expensive meal.

Serves 6

3 whole pork tenderloins
½ cup melted butter
1 cup fine dry bread crumbs
3 tablespoons butter
3 tablespoons vegetable oil
Salt and freshly ground
    pepper to taste

2 tablespoons cognac
3 tablespoons Madeira
2 egg yolks, lightly beaten
6 tablespoons heavy cream
4 tablespoons minced parsley

Cut ½-inch-thick medallions of pork from the large end of each tenderloin. You should get 4 from each. Reserve small ends for another use. Dip medallions into melted butter and then into bread crumbs. Heat butter and oil to very hot. Sauté pork medallions for about 10 minutes on each side. Season with salt and pepper, remove to a serving platter, and keep warm. Pour off fat from skillet and add cognac and Madeira. Simmer for 2 minutes, then remove from heat. Mix egg yolks and cream together, stir into skillet, and heat until thickened but do not boil. Spoon over medallions and sprinkle with minced parsley.

NORMANDY PORK ROAST

Serves 10

1 5- to 6-pound boneless
    pork roast, rolled and
    tied
2 tablespoons vegetable oil
½ teaspoon fennel seeds
½ teaspoon crumbled dried
    marjoram
½ teaspoon crumbled dried
    thyme
2 teaspoons salt

1 teaspoon freshly ground
    pepper
¼ teaspoon nutmeg
¼ cup all-purpose flour
Oil as needed for browning
¾ cup apple cider
1 cup dry white wine
1 cup chicken stock
2 cloves garlic, finely minced
1 cup sour cream

Rub roast well with the oil. In a mortar, crush fennel seeds with the pestle and mix well with remaining dry ingredients. Rub well into roast. In a Dutch oven brown meat on all sides in oil. Add cider, wine, stock, and garlic. Cover tightly and simmer for 2½ hours or until tender. Remove meat and reduce juices by ⅓. Return meat to pan juices, cool to room temperature, and refrigerate. Keep in refrigerator until fat congeals. When ready to reheat, skim off fat and place in a preheated 350-degree oven for 45 minutes. Transfer meat to a heated serving platter and remove strings. Keep warm. Gradually stir sour cream into juices. Warm the sauce but do not boil. Pour some of this over meat and pass remaining sauce separately.

PORC EN CROÛTE

This pork in pastry can be prepared in advance, refrigerated, then brought out about an hour or so before you wish to bake it. A beautiful and succulent pastry-covered roast. The mustard and tarragon add fine flavor to the pork.

Serves 6

PASTRY

1¼ cups flour	⅛ teaspoon salt
¼ pound cold butter, cut into pieces	2 tablespoons cold water

MEAT

3 pound boneless pork tenderloin	1 teaspoon crumbled dried tarragon
½ cup Dijon mustard	1 egg, lightly beaten

To make the pastry: Place the flour in a bowl and add pieces of butter, blending with a pastry blender until mixture has the texture of oatmeal. Add salt and water and mix lightly with your hands until dough can be gathered into a ball. Wrap in waxed paper and chill for at least 1 hour, or overnight. For the meat: In a large skillet or Dutch oven, brown roast evenly on all sides over moderate to high heat. Set aside to cool. Preheat oven to 350 degrees. On a floured board, roll out pastry in a rectangle large enough to encase roast. Spread mustard on pastry and sprinkle with tarragon. Then place roast in center and seal ends of pastry around roast, tucking them under. Place seam side down in a shallow baking pan. Brush pastry with beaten egg and bake for 1 hour or until pastry is golden.

STRASBOURG SAUERKRAUT

Donated by San Francisco radio and theater personality Scott Reach, this is dramatic to serve, since the heat from the sauerkraut causes the champagne to bubble up and spill over like an erupting volcano. Spectacular and delicious.

Serves 6

2 quarts sauerkraut
2 tart apples, peeled, thinly
    sliced
1 cup dry white wine
1 cup apple cider
1 tablespoon peppercorns,
    lightly crushed
Salt to taste
6 small new white or red
    potatoes

1 pound Polish sausage,
    sliced
6 smoked pork chops
3 tablespoons melted butter
4 tablespoons chopped fresh
    chervil or parsley
1 split of champagne at
    room temperature

Place sauerkraut in a colander and rinse well, allow it to drain thoroughly, then transfer it to a large kettle. Add apples, wine, cider, peppercorns, and salt. Cover and simmer over low heat for 2 to 2½ hours, adding more wine or cider if needed. Boil potatoes in skins and set aside. Fry sausage slices and reserve rendered fat. Set aside. After sauerkraut has cooked for 1 hour, place pork chops on top. Cover again and continue cooking. When sauerkraut is done, roll potatoes in melted butter and then in chervil or parsley. Set aside. Reheat reserved sausage fat in a skillet and cover bottom with a ½-inch layer of sauerkraut. Brown sauerkraut over high heat until crisp. Mound remaining sauerkraut in a chafing dish and arrange potatoes, sausage slices, and pork chops around the mound. Sprinkle the middle of the mound with the fried sauerkraut. Rinse the outside of the champagne bottle, ease the cork out carefully without allowing it to pop, and push it down into the middle of the sauerkraut. Present the dish immediately with champagne flowing from the bottle.

MEXICAN PORK STEW

Serves 6

3 pounds boneless pork cut into 2-inch cubes
2 tablespoons oil
1 medium onion, chopped
1 clove garlic, minced
½ pound tomatoes, peeled, seeded, and coarsely chopped
¾ cup canned tomatillos verdes (Mexican green tomatoes)
2 green hot chilies, seeded and chopped

½ teaspoon crumbled dried oregano
⅛ teaspoon sugar
½ teaspoon cumin
Salt and freshly ground pepper to taste
2 chorizo sausages, skinned, sliced, browned, and drained
1 ripe avocado, sliced

In a skillet brown pork on all sides in oil without allowing cubes to touch. Transfer to a large heatproof casserole, barely cover with water, sprinkle with a little salt, and cook over medium heat for 1 hour or until tender. Strain off stock and reserve, set casserole aside. In the same skillet in which meat was browned, sauté onion and garlic until onion is transparent. Add tomatoes, tomatillos verdes, chilies, oregano, sugar, and cumin. Cook and stir for 5 minutes. Add 1 cup of the reserved stock and season to taste with salt and pepper. Continue cooking, stirring occasionally, for 15 minutes or until thickened. Add this mixture to the pork in the casserole along with the sausages and reheat. Garnish with avocado and serve with potatoes or rice.

QUESO RELLENO DE CHIAPAS
(STUFFED CHEESE)

Serves 8

1½ pound lean ground pork
½ medium onion, minced
½ medium green pepper, minced
1 medium tomato, chopped
3 sprigs fresh coriander, chopped
3 cloves garlic, minced
1 cup tomato juice

8 pimiento-stuffed olives
1 tablespoon seedless raisins
1 teaspoon salt
¼ teaspoon pepper
Whites of 4 hard-cooked eggs, chopped
2 pounds aged Cheddar cheese, thinly sliced

SAUCE

1 28-ounce can tomatoes, drained and chopped
½ green pepper, chopped
2 tablespoons chopped onion
1 tablespoon cooking oil

2 tablespoons seedless raisins
2 tablespoons capers
2 cups beef stock
2 tablespoons butter
¼ cup all-purpose flour

Preheat oven to 350 degrees. Combine pork, onion, green pepper, tomato, coriander, and garlic. Cook over low heat for 15 minutes. Add tomato juice, olives, raisins, and seasonings. Remove from heat and add chopped egg whites. Line a 2-quart casserole with cheese slices and fill with pork mixture. Cover with remaining cheese slices and bake for 30 minutes. While baking, prepare sauce. Sauté tomatoes, green pepper, and onion in oil for 5 minutes. Add raisins, capers and stock. Bring to a boil, lower heat, and simmer for 20 minutes. Strain sauce into a bowl. Melt butter in a 2-quart saucepan until foamy. Sprinkle with flour, and stir for 3 minutes, then gradually add strained sauce. Cook and stir for 10 minutes or until smooth and thickened. Serve with casserole.

PORTUGUESE PORK AND CLAMS

The aroma of this dish is heavenly, the taste exotic and spicy. Use the best quality saffron.

Serves 6

2 pounds loin of pork, cut in
    ½-inch pieces
1 tablespoon cider vinegar
1½ cups dry white wine
1 medium onion, finely
    chopped
1 medium carrot, coarsely
    grated
2 cloves garlic, minced

1 tablespoon chopped fresh
    parsley
1 bay leaf
1 teaspoon powdered saffron
2 tablespoons oil
2 pounds clams in the shell,
    scrubbed well
Parsley sprigs for garnish
Lemon slices for garnish

Combine pork, vinegar, wine, onion, carrot, garlic, parsley, bay leaf, and saffron. Marinate for 24 hours, stirring occasionally. With a slotted spoon remove the meat cubes from the marinade. Reserve marinade. In a large skillet, heat the oil and brown the meat over high heat for 10 minutes, turning frequently. Add marinade, bring to boil, and add clams. Reduce heat to low, cover tightly, and simmer for 5 minutes or until clams open. Discard any clams that do not open. Garnish with parsley and lemon. Should be served right from the skillet or an electric fry pan as with paella.

CHINESE BARBECUED SPARERIBS

Serves 4

2 pounds spareribs
¼ cup soy sauce
2 tablespoons honey
2 tablespoons brown sugar
2 tablespoons hoisin sauce
2 tablespoons cider vinegar

2 tablespoons dry sherry
1 teaspoon garlic juice
2 tablespoons chicken stock
Condiments: hot mustard,
    plum sauce, chutney

Preheat oven to 375 degrees. Trim excess fat from spareribs and partially slice both sides in between bones so marinade can penetrate. Combine remaining ingredients in a shallow pan, baste meat on both sides, and leave at room temperature for 2 to 3 hours or in refrigerator for 6 hours, turning often. Remove meat and reserve marinade. Place the meat on a rack over a roasting pan containing a little water. Bake at 375 degrees, adding water as it evaporates and turning and basting meat with reserved marinade every 15 minutes. Bake for 1 hour or until crisp and lightly browned. Cut spareribs into individual pieces and serve with condiments.

INDONESIAN SATE

A delightfully different meal when served with steamed rice and Pikante Kool. The latter is a volcanically spicy mixture of vegetables found in the specialty food sections of some supermarkets and oriental stores.

Serves 4

7 tablespoons fresh lemon
   juice
2 large cloves garlic, minced
4 tablespoons catsup
¾ teaspoon salt
1½ pounds very lean pork,
   cut into ¾-inch cubes

2 tablespoons peanut butter
1 tablespoon butter
½ teaspoon sugar
½ teaspoon Tabasco sauce
¼ cup light cream

Combine 6 tablespoons of the lemon juice, garlic, 3 tablespoons of the catsup, and salt. Pour over pork cubes and marinate for 3 to 4 hours. Drain, reserving marinade, and thread meat on metal skewers, 4 to 5 pieces per skewer. Set aside. Combine reserved marinade, remaining lemon juice, peanut butter, remaining catsup, butter, sugar, and Tabasco. Cook over low heat, stirring constantly, until thick. Remove from heat and gradually stir in cream. Broil the skewered meat, turning once, for 15 minutes or until done over charcoal or under a medium broiler. Pour warm sauce over *sate* or pass sauce separately.

BAKED BARBECUED PORK CHOPS

Serves 4

4 chops, 1½ inches thick

SAUCE
½ cup catsup
¼ cup lemon juice
2 teaspoons brown sugar
2 teaspoons Worcestershire
    sauce

½ cup water
¾ cup chutney

Preheat oven to 350 degrees. Place all sauce ingredients in a saucepan and bring to a boil. Lower heat and simmer for 20 minutes. Place pork chops in a single layer in a baking dish and cover with sauce. Bake for 1½ hours.

STIR-FRY PORK WITH STRAW MUSHROOMS

Serves 4

1 pound pork chops
1 tablespoon cornstarch
½ teaspoon salt
½ teaspoon sugar
1½ tablespoons soy sauce
1 tablespoon dry white wine
¼ cup peanut or corn oil
1 teaspoon minced ginger
    root
2 to 3 medium carrots, sliced
    ⅛ inch thick on
    diagonal

1 15-ounce can baby ears of
    corn, drained and rinsed
¼ cup chicken stock, or as
    needed
1 8-ounce can straw
    mushrooms, drained
    and rinsed
¼ pound Chinese pea pods,
    tips and strings removed

Trim fat from pork chops and cut meat off bones. Pound the meat on a board with the side of a heavy knife or cleaver. Cut meat into rectangles approximately 1 inch by ½ inch. Mix together cornstarch, salt, and sugar, toss with meat to coat well, and add soy and wine. Toss again to mix well. Marinate, refrigerated, for at least ½ hour. Heat 2 tablespoons of the oil in a wok or heavy skillet. When oil is hot but not smoking, stir the pork again and add it to oil. Stir-fry for 2 to 4 minutes until pork is almost done but not dry. Remove pork and set aside. Rinse wok or shillet then add remaining oil. Heat and stir-fry ginger and carrots for 2 minutes or until carrots are barely tender. Add baby corn ears and stir-fry a few seconds. Return pork to mixture and add chicken stock. Stir to deglaze then add mushrooms and pea pods. Stir-fry quickly for 30 seconds until pea pods are just tender. Do not overcook. If mixture is too thick, add a little more chicken stock. Heat quickly and serve immediately.

SWEET AND SOUR PORK

Serves 6

1 teaspoon Chinese five-spice
    powder
1 tablespoon coarsely
    chopped fresh ginger
2 tablespoons soy sauce
2 tablespoons dry sherry
2 teaspoons brown sugar
1 pound boneless pork, cut
    in 1-inch cubes
3 tablespoons corn or
    peanut oil

1 medium red onion,
    quartered and sectioned
1 green pepper, cut in 1-inch
    squares
1 cup cubed fresh pineapple
1 cup canned lychee nuts,
    drained (reserve juice)
1 cup cherry tomatoes

SWEET AND SOUR SAUCE
½ cup brown sugar
½ cup cider vinegar
¼ cup soy sauce
¾ cup pineapple juice
1 cup reserved lychee juice

2 tablespoons catsup
1 teaspoon salt
1 tablespoon cornstarch,
    dissolved in ¼ cup
    water

Combine five-spice powder, ginger, soy sauce, sherry, and brown sugar. Stir in pork to coat well and marinate, stirring occasionally, for 1 hour. Drain and set pork and ginger aside separately. Heat 2 tablespoons of the oil in a wok or heavy skillet and stir-fry chopped ginger for 1 minute. Add pork and stir-fry until brown. Remove it to a baking pan and place in a preheated 300-degree oven for 15 minutes. Meanwhile, prepare the sweet and sour sauce (procedure in next paragraph). Add remaining oil to the same wok or skillet and stir-fry onion and green pepper for 30 seconds. Add remaining ingredients and hot pork, pour sweet and sour sauce over, and toss well to mix.

To make the sweet and sour sauce: combine sugar, vinegar, soy, pineapple juice, lychee juice, catsup, and salt in a 1-quart saucepan. Heat to boiling and stir to dissolve sugar and catsup. Thicken with cornstarch mixture and pour over pork.

JAMBON FARCI, SAUCE AU CHAMPAGNE

Serves 10 to 12

1 cup seedless raisins or
    currants
4 tablespoons Madeira wine
1⅓ cups finely chopped
    fresh parsley
½ cup finely chopped
    pistachio nuts
2 cloves garlic, minced
1 teaspoon minced fresh
    thyme
Freshly ground pepper to
    taste

1 5-pound Polish or canned
    ham
1 cup dry bread crumbs
2 large shallots, chopped
1 cup sweet champagne
1 teaspoon minced fresh
    tarragon
1 cup rich beef stock
¼ cup tomato paste
1 cup heavy cream
2 tablespoons butter

Soak raisins or currants in Madeira for 24 hours. Drain, chop, and combine with 1 cup of the parsley, pistachio nuts, garlic, thyme, and pepper. Using a sharp-pointed knife, make deep holes all over the ham, twisting the knife to enlarge them. Using your finger or the handle of a wooden spoon, poke the raisin stuffing into the holes. Roast ham according to directions. Thirty minutes before ham is done, coat with mixture of dry bread crumbs and remaining chopped parsley. To make the sauce, in a saucepan combine shallots, champagne, and tarragon. Reduce over high heat until almost evaporated. Add the beef stock and the tomato paste. Lower heat and simmer for 30 minutes, stirring occasionally. Add cream and cook for another 10 minutes. Pass sauce through a sieve, then stir in the butter a little at a time. To serve: Slice the ham on the diagonal so each slice has some stuffing in it. Serve the sauce over the ham slices.

HAM LOAF

Serves 10

2 pounds ham, ground
1½ pounds lean ground
    pork
½ cup milk, or as needed

2 eggs, beaten
1 medium onion, chopped
1 cup fine dry bread crumbs

BASTING SAUCE
¾ cup dark brown sugar
½ cup water
¼ cup cider vinegar

2 tablespoons dry mustard
¼ teaspoon powdered cloves

Preheat oven to 350 degrees. Combine all ham loaf ingredients, mix well, and add more milk if mixture is too dry to hold together. Form into a loaf and place in the center of a large shallow baking pan. Combine basting sauce ingredients and pour over ham loaf. Bake, basting frequently, for 1½ hours.

CALF'S LIVER URBANSTUBE

Serves 4

1½ pounds calf's liver, cut
     into strips ¼ inch wide
2 tablespoons olive oil
2 tablespoons butter
1 tablespoon chopped onion
1½ teaspoons chopped
     chives

1 teaspoon chopped parsley
½ teaspoon thyme
1 teaspoon marjoram
½ teaspoon basil
½ teaspoon sage

In a heavy skillet sauté the liver strips in heated olive oil, stirring, for about 1 minute. Transfer with a slotted spoon to a heated serving dish and keep warm. Add the butter to the skillet and sauté onion, 1 teaspoon of the chives, parsley, thyme, marjoram, and basil until the onion is soft. Return liver to the skillet and stir over high heat until heated through. Transfer to a serving dish and garnish with ½ teaspoon chives and the sage. Serve immediately.

ZURCHER LEBERSPIESSLI

Skewered broiled calf's liver served on a bed of sautéed spinach and onion.

Serves 4

1½ pounds calf's liver, sliced
     ¾ inch thick
20 small sage leaves, dried
10 slices bacon, cut in half
     lengthwise
2 tablespoons minced onion
1 clove garlic, minced
4 tablespoons butter
1½ pounds fresh spinach,
     washed, drained, and
     chopped

½ teaspoon salt
¼ teaspoon freshly ground
     pepper
3 tablespoons butter melted
     with ¼ cup vegetable
     oil
¼ cup dry white wine

Cut liver into approximately 20 pieces, each 1 inch square. Into each piece of liver press a sage leaf and wrap liver in a strip of bacon. Thread 5 squares of wrapped liver on each of 4 8-inch thin metal skewers, pressing pieces tightly together. Set aside. Sauté onion and garlic in 4 tablespoons butter until onion is transparent. Mix in spinach, salt, and pepper, cook until spinach is tender. Set aside and keep warm. Broil liver under medium heat for 10 to 15 minutes until bacon is brown and crisp, basting frequently with butter and oil mixture. Spread spinach mixture on a heated platter and arrange skewers on top. Discard fat in the broiler pan and deglaze juices over high heat with the wine. Simmer for 2 minutes then pour wine over liver. Serve at once.

SWEETBREADS AND MUSHROOMS

An epicurean's delight served with brown rice, broiled tomatoes, and garden fresh green beans.

Serves 6

2 pounds blanched
  sweetbreads,
  membranes removed,
  and separated into
  bite-size pieces
4 tablespoons butter, or as
  needed
16 fresh mushrooms, halved
¼ cup fresh lemon juice

1 cup chicken stock
¼ cup tomato paste
½ cup cream sherry
1 bay leaf, crumbled
Freshly ground pepper to
  taste
1 teaspoon arrowroot
1 tablespoon dry white wine

Sauté sweetbreads in butter in a skillet until brown on all sides. Do not allow pieces to touch. As pieces brown, remove them to a warm plate. In same skillet, sauté mushrooms, adding more butter if needed. Add lemon juice and sauté, covered, for 3 minutes. Return sweetbreads to the skillet and add chicken stock, tomato paste, sherry, and bay leaf. Simmer, uncovered, over medium heat for 15 minutes. Add pepper. Thicken slightly with arrowroot dissolved in white wine. May be prepared ahead and refrigerated. Return to room temperature before reheating.

MUSHROOM-SAUSAGE STRUDEL

This is great to serve as a brunch main course or the first course of an elegant dinner.

Serves 6 to 8

2 pounds mild Italian
   sausage
2 pounds fresh mushrooms,
   minced and thoroughly
   dried
¼ cup minced shallots or
   green onions
6 tablespoons butter

2 tablespoons vegetable oil
Salt and freshly ground
   pepper to taste
16 ounces cream cheese
8 sheets phyllo pastry
¾ cup melted butter
1 cup seasoned bread crumbs

Preheat oven to 400 degrees. Remove sausage from its casing and sauté until it is no longer pink, crumbling into small pieces. Drain and set aside. Sauté the mushrooms with the shallots or green onions in butter and oil over moderate heat, stirring frequently. Cook until pieces separate and liquid has evaporated. Add salt and pepper and combine mushroom mixture with the sausage and cream cheese, blending well. Spread a sheet of phyllo pastry on a lightly dampened towel. Quickly brush with melted butter and sprinkle with a few bread crumbs. Top with the second sheet and repeat procedure. Repeat again for the third sheet. Top with fourth sheet and butter, but omit crumbs. Spoon half the sausage-mushroom mixture along the narrow edge of phyllo pastry, leaving a 2-inch border at sides. Fold in sides and roll up pastry. Put strudel on a buttered baking sheet and brush with melted butter. Repeat procedure, using the remaining 4 sheets of phyllo and sausage mixture. Bake until brown, about 20 minutes. Cut and serve.

CELERIAC CASSEROLE MADAME MALRAUX

A variation of choucroute garnie *without the sauerkraut. A good family casserole. Use a combination of sausages or just one type.*

Serves 6

2 small celery roots
1 teaspoon lemon juice
1 medium-size tart apple
3 medium potatoes
½ pound Swiss cheese,
    grated
2 pounds sausages
    (bratwurst, weisswurst
    or Polish) sliced into
    ½-inch pieces

3 to 4 tablespoons butter
½ cup beef stock
Salt to taste

Preheat oven to 350 degrees. Peel celery roots and place in a bowl of cold water with lemon juice to prevent darkening. Peel and core apple and place in lemon water. Peel and thinly slice potatoes. Set aside. Drain and thinly slice celery root and apple, keeping them separate. Butter a baking dish and put half the sliced potatoes in the bottom. Add half the grated cheese, all the celery root, apple slices, and sausages. Top casserole with remaining potatoes and cheese. Dot with butter and moisten with beef stock. Salt lightly. Bake for 1 hour.

STUFFED CABBAGE ROLLS

Serves 8

1 large head cabbage, cored
3 tablespoons butter
2 medium onions, chopped
1 pound lean ground beef
1 cup cooked white or
    brown rice
½ teaspoon allspice

1 28-ounce can tomatoes
1 8-ounce can tomato sauce
1 6-ounce can tomato paste
1 teaspoon salt
½ teaspoon garlic salt
1 teaspoon thyme
Sour cream

Preheat oven to 350 degrees. In a large pot, steam the cabbage for 10 minutes or until the leaves are softened enough to peel away. Cool, separate leaves, gently shake off moisture, and set aside. Melt butter in a skillet and sauté onions until they are golden. Remove half the onions to a bowl containing the ground beef. Mix in the rice and allspice gently with your hands. To the remaining onions in the skillet, add the tomatoes and juice, tomato sauce, tomato paste, salt, and seasonings. Simmer for 15 minutes. Place a small amount of meat mixture on each cabbage leaf. Fold leaf over to enclose meat and, starting at the stem end, roll up. Place rolls, seam side down, in a buttered baking dish. Cover with tomato mixture and bake, uncovered, for 1 hour. Serve with sour cream.

TIJUANA TORTILLA STACKS

An excellent family supper or luncheon dish. Easy to prepare and so good.

Serves 8

1½ pounds ground beef
1 1½-ounce package
    powdered spaghetti
    sauce mix
1 teaspoon salt
1 1-pound can tomatoes, cut
    up
1 8-ounce can tomato sauce

½ cup water
1 4-ounce can green chilies,
    diced
1 pound ricotta cheese
2 eggs, lightly beaten
8 corn tortillas
1 pound Monterey Jack
    cheese, grated

Preheat oven to 350 degrees. Brown beef in a heavy skillet. Add spaghetti sauce mix, salt, cut-up tomatoes, tomato sauce, ½ cup water, and green chilies. Blend thoroughly and simmer for 10 minutes. In a bowl, combine the ricotta cheese with the eggs. In a flat baking dish, 12 by 8 by 2 inches, place about 1 cup of the meat mixture. Place 2 tortillas over the meat, side by side, and spoon some of the ricotta mixture on top of each. Then layer more meat and sprinkle with grated cheese. Repeat until each of the 2 stacks has 4 tortillas, ending with grated cheese. Bake for 30 minutes. Let stand for about 5 minutes before cutting into pie-shaped wedges.

STUFFED PUMPKIN

No one seems to think of having pumpkin except in a pie. Try this recipe and be surprised—it is as good as the best squash and the presentation is beautiful.

Serves 8

1 small whole pumpkin,
    about 10 inches in
    diameter
Boiling salted water
2 tablespoons salad oil
2 pounds ground beef
1 large onion, finely chopped
1 medium green pepper,
    finely chopped
2 teaspoons salt
2 teaspoons oregano
1 teaspoon vinegar

Freshly ground pepper to
    taste
2 cloves garlic, mashed
¾ cup seedless raisins
⅓ cup sliced
    pimiento-stuffed green
    olives
2 teaspoons capers
1 8-ounce can tomato sauce
½ cup red wine
3 eggs, beaten

Preheat oven to 350 degrees. With a sharp knife, cut a circular top about 5 inches in diameter out of the pumpkin. Save the top to use as a lid. Scoop out pumpkin seeds and scrape inside of pumpkin clean. Place it in a large kettle and cover with boiling salted water; cover kettle. Bring water to a boil, lower heat, and simmer for about 30 minutes until pumpkin meat is almost tender. The pumpkin should still be firm enough to hold its shape well. Carefully remove from water and drain well. Dry the outside and sprinkle a little salt on the inside. Set aside. In a heavy skillet with a cover heat salad oil. Add ground beef, onion, and green pepper, cook over medium high heat until beef is browned and crumbly. Remove from heat and add salt, oregano, vinegar, pepper, and garlic. Stir in raisins, olives, and capers, then gradually add tomato sauce and red wine. Cover skillet, return to heat, and simmer for about 15 minutes, stirring occasionally. Cool slightly and add beaten eggs, mixing thoroughly. Fill cooked pumpkin with meat stuffing, pressing to pack firmly. Cover loosely with pumpkin lid and place in a greased shallow baking pan. Bake for 1 hour. Allow to cool for 10 to 15 minutes before serving. To serve, carefully lift stuffed pumpkin onto a serving plate. Slice from top to bottom in flat wedges, spooning more meat filling onto each slice.

BURRITOS

Makes 24

1½ pounds lean ground beef
1 medium onion, coarsely
  chopped
1 7-ounce can green chili
  salsa
1 7-ounce can green chilies,
  seeded and diced
1 14½-ounce can stewed
  tomatoes

1 17-ounce can refried beans
Salt and freshly ground
  pepper to taste
2 dozen large flour tortillas
2 cups Longhorn cheese,
  grated
1 cup sour cream

Preheat oven to 350 degrees. Brown the beef in a skillet, crumbling
with a fork as it cooks. Drain off the fat. Add onion, green chili salsa,
chilies, tomatoes, and beans. Season with salt and pepper. Cook and stir
mixture for 5 minutes or until most of the moisture has cooked away.
Place tortillas on center rack of the oven and heat until just hot, not
crisp or stiff. Remove one at a time to plates and quickly place some
meat mixture in the center of each one. Top with 2 tablespoons of the
cheese and 1 tablespoon of sour cream. Roll tortillas around filling and
serve immediately. The burritos may be cooled, wrapped in foil, and
refrigerated or frozen.

JOE'S SPECIAL

*Nobody remembers Joe's last name, but this is still an old-time San
Francisco favorite. Mushrooms may be added if you wish.*

Serves 4

1 package chopped frozen
  spinach or ½ pound
  fresh spinach, chopped
1 medium onion, chopped
1 clove garlic, finely minced

2 tablespoons olive oil
1 pound lean ground beef
Salt and freshly ground
  pepper to taste
4 eggs, lightly beaten

Thaw frozen spinach and drain well, or cook fresh spinach and drain well. Set aside. In a heavy skillet sauté onion and garlic in oil until onion is transparent. Add beef and brown thoroughly. Sprinkle with salt and pepper and stir in reserved spinach. Keeping heat high, add eggs to the skillet, stirring constantly until eggs are blended and cooked. Adjust seasonings and serve immediately.

MEXICAN-STYLE BEEF CASSEROLE

A good family casserole and perfect to take to those potluck dinners. Spicy, and kids love it!

Serves 8

1½ pounds lean ground beef
2 tablespoons cooking oil
1 medium onion, chopped
1 cup chopped tomatoes or
    canned tomato sauce
⅓ cup chili sauce
Salt and freshly ground
    pepper to taste
12 corn tortillas, cut into
    quarters

½ cup red taco sauce
3 cups shredded Monterey
    Jack cheese
1 cup sour cream
2 10-ounce packages frozen
    chopped spinach,
    thawed and *well*
    drained

Preheat oven to 375 degrees. In a large skillet brown the beef. Pour off any fat and remove beef, set aside. Add oil to skillet and sauté onion until limp and golden. Return beef to skillet and add tomatoes, chili sauce, salt, and pepper. Dip tortilla quarters in taco sauce, covering both sides. Cover bottom of a buttered 3-quart casserole with half the tortilla pieces, slightly overlapping. Spread beef mixture over tortillas. Sprinkle beef with 1½ cups of the cheese. Layer remaining tortilla pieces on top and spread with sour cream. Sprinkle on the spinach and top with remaining cheese. Bake, covered, for 30 minutes, uncovering for the last 15 minutes. If reheating, have the casserole at room temperature and bake at 375 degrees, uncovered, until hot and bubbly.

TEXAS JACK

This quick and easy lunch or Sunday supper idea was suggested by Kathryn Crosby and was named for her native state.

Serves 6

4 slices bacon, diced
1 medium onion, sliced
1 medium green pepper, diced
2 1-pound cans red kidney beans, drained
1 8-ounce can tomato sauce
1 tablespoon chili powder

½ teaspoon salt
¼ teaspoon pepper
½ pound Cheddar cheese, grated
6 frankfurters, sliced
6 English muffin halves, toasted

Fry bacon until crisp, remove with a slotted spoon, and drain on a paper towel. Sauté onion and green pepper in remaining bacon drippings until soft but not brown. Add beans, tomato sauce, seasonings, reserved bacon, and cheese. Stir over low heat until cheese melts. Add sliced frankfurters and cook until heated through. Spoon over toasted English muffins.

"TEXAS RED" CHILI

Serves 8 to 10

3 tablespoons bacon drippings
3 pounds round steak, coarsely cubed
6 tablespoons chili powder
1 tablespoon ground oregano
1 tablespoon crushed cumin seed

1 tablespoon salt
½ to 1 teaspoon cayenne pepper
2 large cloves garlic, minced
1½ quarts water
1 cup white cornmeal, or 3 tablespoons masa harina

In a heavy skillet or Dutch oven, heat bacon drippings and brown the steak cubes on all sides. Add seasonings, garlic, and 1½ quarts water. Bring to a boil, cover, reduce heat, and simmer for 1½ hours. Skim off fat. Stir in cornmeal or masa harina and simmer, uncovered, for 30 minutes, stirring occasionally. Adjust seasonings. Serve with cooked pinto beans, warm tortillas, and beer.

KUFTA

Lebanese meat balls stuffed with herbed rice that can be served as an entree or from a chafing dish as part of a hearty buffet.

Makes 20 meat balls

3 slices white bread
1 cup tomato juice
1 pound lean ground beef
1 pound lean ground lamb
4 medium yellow onions,
    finely chopped
½ teaspoon salt
3 tablespoons olive oil
⅓ cup uncooked rice

⅔ cup boiling water
⅓ cup pine nuts
2 tablespoons chopped fresh
    parsley
¼ teaspoon crumbled dried
    basil
Allspice, salt, and pepper to
    taste

Preheat oven to 375 degrees. Soak the bread in the tomato juice. Combine beef, lamb, bread, tomato juice, half the onions, and salt. Set aside in the refrigerator. Sauté the remaining onions in olive oil until transparent, add rice and boiling water, cover, and simmer for 20 minutes or until liquid is absorbed. Fold remaining ingredients into the rice mixture and cool. Divide meat mixture into 20 pieces and form each into a ball. With your index finger make a well in each meat ball and fill with about 1½ teaspoons of rice mixture. Cover filling, reshaping meat into a ball. Place meatballs in a shallow baking dish and bake for 20 to 30 minutes.

CALIFORNIA CHILI

A favorite California rendition of this Western tradition.

Serves 8

½ pound dried pinto beans, washed

6 large onions, chopped

4 large green or red peppers, chopped

4 cloves garlic, finely minced

¼ cup corn oil

½ cup chopped fresh parsley

1 28-ounce can tomatoes, drained

2½ pounds beef chuck roast, cut in ½-inch pieces

1½ pounds lean pork butt, cut in ½-inch pieces

⅓ cup chili powder

2 tablespoons chopped, seeded green chilies

1 tablespoon salt

1½ teaspoons freshly ground pepper

2 tablespoons cumin powder

In a 1-quart saucepan cover beans with water. Cover saucepan and cook for 1 hour or until beans are tender, adding water if needed. In a heavy kettle sauté onions, green peppers, and garlic in oil until onions are transparent. Add remaining ingredients. Simmer, covered, for 1 hour; uncover and cook for at least ½ hour longer or until thick. May be frozen and reheated.

CASSOULET

This Americanized version of a French classic is an excellent one-dish meal for skiers or buffet table. It freezes beautifully, and because it is time-consuming to make, do it well ahead for use when you need it. The longer it cooks the better it is.

Serves 12

2 pounds Great Northern
    white beans
1 tablespoon salt
1 medium onion stuck with 2
    whole cloves
1 bay leaf
1 pig's foot, split
Salt and freshly ground
    pepper
1 4-pound leg of lamb
3 pounds lean pork loin or
    shoulder
1 5-pound duck

2 cups dry red wine
8 to 10 French or Italian
    sausages
4 to 6 cloves garlic, finely
    minced
1½ teaspoons crumbled
    dried thyme
1 teaspoon freshly ground
    pepper
2 tablespoons tomato paste
¾ pound salt pork, cut into
    thin strips

Preheat oven to 325 degrees. In water to cover place beans, salt, onion, bay leaf, and pig's foot. Bring to a gentle boil, partially cover, lower heat to a simmer, and cook, adding water if needed, until beans are just barely tender. Do not allow beans to boil hard. While beans are cooking, salt and pepper the lamb, pork, and duck. Roast all the meats at 325 degrees, basting with 1½ cups of the wine, for 1½ to 2 hours or until done. Remove from oven, cool meats, reserve any juices, and cut into 1½-inch cubes. Strain beans, reserving liquid, and discard onion and bay leaf. Remove the meat and skin from the pig's foot and cut into small pieces. Set aside. Poach sausages in water to cover for 5 minutes. Drain and cut into ½-inch slices. Set aside. Combine minced garlic, thyme, and pepper. To assemble: Place a layer of beans in a large casserole. Sprinkle with some of the garlic mixture. Cover with a layer of diced meats, pig's foot meat and skin, and sausages. Repeat layers until all ingredients are used, ending with a layer of beans. Combine juices from meats, bean liquid, remaining ½ cup red wine, and tomato paste. Pour this liquid over cassoulet ingredients to barely cover. Top with strips of salt pork, cover tightly, and bake at 350 degrees for 1 hour. Remove cover and bake for 1 hour longer, adding more wine if needed.

BARBECUE SAUCE FOR SPARERIBS
OR PORK ROAST

Makes 4½ cups

1 16-ounce jar
smoke-flavored
barbecue sauce
½ cup boiling water
1 chicken bouillon cube
1 cup catsup
1 tablespoon fresh lemon
juice

1½ teaspoons curry powder
½ teaspoon freshly ground
pepper
1 tablespoon Worcestershire
sauce
1 teaspoon dry mustard
6 ounces beer
½ cup dark molasses

Place all ingredients in a large saucepan and bring to a boil. Reduce to a simmer and cook for 10 minutes, adding more beer if sauce is too thick.

MARINADE FOR FLANK STEAK

Makes approximately 1½ cups

1½ teaspoons salt
1 teaspoon sugar
1 tablespoon minced onion
½ teaspoon dry mustard
½ teaspoon rosemary
¼ teaspoon powdered
ginger
1 teaspoon freshly ground
pepper

¼ cup lemon juice
½ cup salad oil
1 clove garlic, minced
¼ cup soy sauce
3 tablespoons honey
2 tablespoons vinegar

Place all ingredients in the container of a blender and blend until smooth.

ROSEMARY MARINADE FOR LAMB OR CHICKEN

Makes 1½ cups

½ cup vegetable oil
½ cup olive oil
½ cup fresh lemon juice
½ teaspoon thyme

1 teaspoon dried rosemary,
    or 1 tablespoon minced
    fresh rosemary
1 clove garlic, crushed

Mix together all ingredients. Marinate lamb or chicken for 8 to 10 hours, or overnight.

SAUCE FOR LAMB

Try this over lamb steaks or shoulder chops.

Makes approximately 1½ cups

4 tablespoons butter
1 medium stalk celery,
    chopped
1 medium carrot, chopped
½ medium onion, chopped
2 cloves garlic, chopped
1 teaspoon pickling spices
¼ teaspoon rosemary

4 ounces tomato paste
¼ cup beef bouillon
¼ cup red wine
Juice of 1 lemon
¼ teaspoon nutmeg
4 tablespoons cold butter
2 egg yolks, well beaten

In a heavy skillet melt butter and add celery, carrot, and onion. Sauté until limp and slightly browned. Add garlic, pickling spices, rosemary, tomato paste, bouillon, wine, lemon juice, and nutmeg. Simmer over low heat until reduced by half, then purée in a blender or food processor. Add cold butter and stir until butter is melted, then stir in egg yolks. Keep sauce warm until ready to use.

PIQUANT MUSTARD SAUCE FOR MEAT

Makes approximately 2 cups

¼ cup dry mustard
2 tablespoons all-purpose
    flour
1 cup brown sugar

1 cup cider vinegar
1 cup consommé
3 eggs, lightly beaten

Combine dry ingredients. Blend in vinegar, consommé, and eggs, stirring until smooth. Place in the top of a double boiler and cook over simmering water, stirring constantly, until thick, about 15 minutes. Sauce will thicken more after it is removed from heat. When cool, place in a jar, cover, and refrigerate. Serve hot or cold on ham, pork, Indonesian sates.

SAUCE BÉARNAISE

Makes approximately 1½ cups

4 tablespoons white wine
    vinegar
2 tablespoons dried tarragon
¼ cup finely chopped
    shallots or green onions

½ teaspoon salt
Freshly ground pepper
3 tablespoons water
3 egg yolks
½ pound butter

In a heavy saucepan (not aluminum) place the vinegar, tarragon, shallots, salt, and pepper. Bring to a boil and cook down until moisture almost disappears. Add the water and egg yolks and stir briskly with a wire whisk over low heat until the sauce has thickened to the consistency of mayonnaise. In another saucepan, melt the butter. Cool butter to the touch and slowly, in a thin stream, add to the yolk mixture. Sauce should be warm, not hot.

BROWN SAUCE

A classical French brown sauce, also called sauce espagnole, *is the basis for many other sauces. The secret is to use good quality, strong beef stock and to simmer the sauce very slowly. It freezes well.*

Makes approximately 5 cups

½ cup diced carrots
½ cup diced onion
½ cup diced celery
4 tablespoons diced lean
    bacon, blanched and
    drained
4 tablespoons clarified butter
4 tablespoons flour

8 cups beef stock, boiling
3 tablespoons tomato paste
4 large sprigs parsley
1 bay leaf
½ teaspoon thyme
Salt and freshly ground
    pepper to taste

In a heavy 2-quart saucepan, sauté the vegetables and the bacon in the butter until soft. Slowly blend in the flour and stir constantly over medium heat for approximately 10 minutes or until the flour is golden brown. Remove from the heat and add the beef stock all at once, stirring constantly. Stir in the tomato paste and add the herbs. Simmer very slowly, partly covered, for at least 2 hours; the longer the sauce is simmered the better it will be. Stir occasionally and skim off any fat or scum from the top. When the sauce is the consistency of heavy cream, correct the seasoning and strain through a fine sieve.

MADEIRA SAUCE

Makes approximately 1½ cups

3 tablespoons butter
1½ tablespoons flour
¾ cup beef stock

1 teaspoon Kitchen Bouquet
    or Bovril
¼ cup Madeira wine

Melt the butter, stir in flour, and cook for 5 minutes. Add beef stock, kitchen bouquet, and Madeira. Cook until thickened.

CHAPTER XII

BREADS

The Avenues

For many years nothing but barren sandhills lay between the old Laurel Hill Cemetery at Presidio Avenue and California Street and the pleasurable pastimes offered at the ocean's shore. Adolph Sutro owned much of that barren land, now known as the Sunset and Richmond Districts or, more familiarly, "the Avenues." Although the amount of real estate was vast, his developmental efforts, both creative and financial, were concentrated at the water's edge. High on the cliffs overlooking Seal Rocks and the pounding Pacific, Mr. Sutro opened, in 1896, a romantic Victorian, castle-like structure that became the destination of stylish Sunday sojourners seeking dramatic views, a lingering luncheon, or a secluded rendezvous. The Sutro Baths, a bathing establishment of incomparable proportion built in the same year, offered swimming at six different temperatures in six enclosed gargantuan pools with observation decks soaring above.

The beach itself offered tall grasses for a sheltered picnic, while abandoned cable cars, converted to roadside stands, supplied other refreshments. Later, diversions would be provided near the city's western edge: Fleishhacker Zoo, the gift of another pioneer family; Sigmund Stern Grove, where musical performances are offered free to the public throughout the summer; Playland at the Beach and Fleishhacker Pool, both now only memories.

But what of the miles of sand where horse and buggy and later the trolley traversed an empty landscape—except for a few summer cottages? Today houses march shoulder to shoulder westward across those four miles to the sea. The Avenues have become solid urban residential communities, containing a rich ethnic mix of people of Russian, French, and German descent, among others. This delightful mélange of nationalities becomes evident from the storefronts and subtle aromas of bakeries, offering freshly baked delicacies: Russian piroshki, hot and plump with meat; Swedish rye and Irish soda bread ready to be slathered with butter; German pumpernickel, dark and rich; airy French croissants; Danish breakfast pastries, laced with fruit and spices; English muffin bread ready for the toaster. Health food bakeries offer whole wheat and wheat germ bread, heavy with nutrition and social significance. And, of course, wafting from many a shop and store the heady aroma of something almost synonymous with San Francisco itself —those long crusty loafs of sourdough French bread. It is said that San Francisco's climate is the magic ingredient that makes sourdough, baked here, the best in the world. In that case, let's pick up a loaf and head for the beach.

SAN FRANCISCO SOURDOUGH FRENCH BREAD

The secret to this world-famous bread is its yeast base of "starter." You can make your own starter using the recipe following this one, or you can buy a commercial version that is available in many gift and kitchen shops.

Makes 2 oblong or 1 large round loaf

1½ cups warm water
1 cup Sourdough starter (see
   next recipe)
4 cups unsifted all-purpose
   flour

3 teaspoons sugar
1½ teaspoons salt
2 to 2½ more cups unsifted
   all-purpose flour
½ to 1 teaspoon baking soda

Combine the water, starter, 4 cups flour, sugar, and salt in a crock or glass bowl. Mix well, cover lightly with a towel or cheesecloth folded into several thicknesses, and let stand at room temperature for approximately 18 to 24 hours or until the dough has doubled in size. Mix 1 cup of the remaining flour with ½ teaspoon of the baking soda and stir this into the risen dough until it is very stiff. Turn the dough out onto a floured board and knead approximately 1 more cup of flour and a little more baking soda into it. Knead it for 5 to 10 minutes or until the dough is smooth. Shape into 2 long loaves or 1 large round loaf, place on a lightly greased baking sheet, cover, and let stand in a warm place for 3 to 4 hours or until almost doubled in size. Preheat oven to 400 degrees. Brush a little water on top of the loaves and make a few diagonal slits across the top with a sharp knife. For a crustier bread, place a shallow pan of water in the bottom of the oven. Bake for approximately 45 to 50 minutes or until the crust is a medium dark brown.

SOURDOUGH STARTER

1 package (1 tablespoon) active dry yeast	2 cups all-purpose flour, unsifted
2½ cups warm (110°) water	1 tablespoon sugar

In a 6-cup glass or ceramic container soften yeast in ½ cup warm water. Stir in remaining 2 cups water, flour, and sugar. Beat mixture until smooth. Cover loosely with cheesecloth, folded into several thicknesses and let stand at room temperature until bubbly. This may take 5 to 10 days, depending upon the temperature of the room—the warmer the room, the shorter the time for fermentation. During this time, stir 2 or 3 times a day. The starter will develop a strong "sour" odor as it ferments. When fermentation has occurred, refrigerate starter until needed.

To keep starter going: After using a cup of starter, to the remainder add ¾ cup water, ¾ cup all-purpose flour, and 1 teaspoon sugar, stir well. Let stand at room temperature until bubbly, at least 1 day. Cover and refrigerate. If not used within 10 days, stir in 1 teaspoon sugar. Repeat the addition of 1 teaspoon sugar every 10 days.

DILLY BREAD

Makes 1 loaf

1 package (1 tablespoon) active dry yeast	¼ cup finely minced onion
¼ cup lukewarm water	2½ cups unbleached white flour, unsifted
1 cup cottage cheese, slightly warm	2 teaspoons chopped dillweed, dried or fresh
2 tablespoons sugar	1 teaspoon salt
4 tablespoons butter, cut into bits	¼ teaspoon baking soda
1 egg, lightly beaten	Melted butter
	Coarse salt

Dissolve yeast in the warm water for 5 minutes. In a large bowl combine cottage cheese, sugar, and butter, stir until butter is melted. Meanwhile, add egg and onion and stir in yeast. Combine flour, dill, salt, and baking soda. Beat into yeast mixture to make a stiff dough. This is a batter bread and does not require kneading. Let rise in the bowl for 1 hour. Punch down and turn into a well-buttered 2-quart soufflé dish. Let rise for 1 hour. Preheat oven to 350 degrees. Bake for 45 to 50 minutes or until crust is golden. Brush top with melted butter and sprinkle with coarse salt. Serve warm. May be reheated in foil.

WHEAT BRAN BREAD

Makes 3 medium or 2 large loaves

2 packages (2 tablespoons) active dry yeast
2½ cups lukewarm water
1 tablespoon sugar
⅔ cup nonfat instant powdered milk
2 tablespoons dark molasses
2 tablespoons light molasses
¼ cup honey
3 to 4 cups unbleached white flour, unsifted

3 to 4 cups whole wheat flour
1½ teaspoons salt
2 tablespoons butter, softened
1 cup all bran, bran buds, or bran
1 cup unroasted sunflower seeds, hulled

Dissolve yeast in ½ cup of the lukewarm water with the sugar for 5 minutes. In a very large bowl combine remaining water, powdered milk, molasses, and honey. Beat at low speed, adding 2 cups each of the white and whole wheat flours, 1 cup at a time, until dough is smooth and well mixed. Cover bowl with a towel and let rise in a warm place for about 1 hour or until doubled in bulk. Punch down and add salt, butter, bran, and sunflower seeds. Beat in more of each flour until dough is stiff. Turn out onto a floured board and knead, adding flour as needed to prevent sticking, 10 minutes or until smooth and elastic. Place in a well-buttered bowl and let rise for about 1 hour or until doubled. Punch down and divide into 3 equal parts or into halves and form into loaves. Preheat oven to 350 degrees. Place in either 3 medium or 2 large loaf pans and cover. Let rise for about 1 hour or until double in bulk. Bake for 45 to 50 minutes or until bread sounds hollow when you tap the pan on the bottom. Remove from pans and cool on a rack.

JULEKAKE

This traditional Scandinavian Christmas bread is delicious year round.

Makes 2 loaves

2 packages (2 tablespoons) active dry yeast
¼ cup lukewarm water
1 cup milk, scalded
⅓ cup sugar
1½ teaspoons salt
¼ pound butter
1½ teaspoons ground cardamom
1 egg, lightly beaten

5 cups unbleached white flour, unsifted
½ cup currants
½ cup raisins
½ cup chopped citron
¼ cup chopped candied red cherries
⅓ cup slivered, blanched almonds

Dissolve yeast in the warm water for 5 minutes. Meanwhile, in a large bowl combine milk, sugar, salt, butter, and cardamom until sugar is dissolved and butter melted. Cool to lukewarm. Add yeast to milk mixture along with the egg and 2 cups of the flour. Beat until smooth. Add 2 more cups flour, blending well. Toss fruits and almonds with ½ cup flour and stir into dough. Add just enough of the remaining flour to make a soft dough that, when beaten, does not stick to the sides of the bowl. Turn out onto lightly floured board, knead gently 20 to 30 times, and place in a thoroughly buttered bowl. Turn the dough in the bowl to coat with butter. Cover with plastic wrap and a towel. Let stand in a warm place for 1½ to 2 hours or until doubled. Punch down, divide in half, and form into 2 rounds. Preheat oven to 375 degrees. Place in 2 9-inch round cake pans and let rise for about 1 hour or until double in bulk. Bake for 30 to 40 minutes or until a toothpick inserted in the center comes out clean and the cakes are browned on top. Cool on a rack. Cooled bread may be dusted with powdered sugar or brushed with a little melted butter and sprinkled with chopped almonds.

IRISH SODA GRAHAM BREAD

When toasted, this unusual bread is great for breakfast and is an excellent accompaniment to soup.

Makes 1 loaf

2 cups buttermilk
2 teaspoons baking soda
2 cups graham flour
1 cup unbleached white
    flour, unsifted

½ cup sugar
1 teaspoon salt

Preheat oven to 375 degrees. Combine buttermilk and baking soda and blend in remaining ingredients. Pour into a well-buttered 9-inch loaf pan and place in oven. Lower oven heat to 350 degrees and bake for 55 to 60 minutes or until a toothpick inserted in the center comes out clean. Cool on a rack.

SWEDISH RYE BREAD

Makes 3 to 4 loaves

2 packages (2 tablespoons)
    active dry yeast
½ cup lukewarm water
2 cups rye flour
¾ cup unbleached white
    flour, unsifted
2 tablespoons butter, melted
2 cups warm water
1 cup dark corn syrup

½ cup sorghum molasses or
    dark molasses
2 tablespoons fennel seed
2 tablespoons anise seed
1 teaspoon salt
2 cups rye flour
4 to 6 cups unbleached white
    flour, unsifted
Butter for pans

Dissolve yeast in warm water for 5 minutes. In a very large bowl, combine 2 cups rye flour, ¾ cup white flour, butter and 2 cups warm water. Add yeast. Mix well. Cover with a towel and let rise for about 1½ to 2 hours or until doubled. Punch down and add corn syrup, molasses, fennel seed, anise seed, salt, and rye flour. Add 4 cups white flour and turn out onto floured board and knead for at least 10 minutes until smooth and elastic. While kneading, add additional white flour if necessary to keep dough elastic. Form into a ball and place in a thoroughly buttered bowl. Turn the dough in the bowl to coat with butter. Cover with a towel and let rise for 2 to 3 hours or until double in bulk. Punch down and divide into 3 or 4 portions, depending on size of loaf pans. Form into loaves and place in 3 buttered 8-inch loaf pans. Let rise for about 1 hour or until double in bulk. Bake in a preheated 350-degree oven for 45 minutes. Reduce heat to 325 and bake for 15 minutes more, covering tops loosely with foil if too brown. Cool on rack.

ORANGE BREAD

This bread makes wonderful French toast!

Makes 2 loaves

2 eggs
½ cup vegetable oil
4 cups all-purpose flour,
  unsifted
1⅔ cups sugar
½ teaspoon salt

2 tablespoons baking powder
1 large orange, unpeeled
1½ cups milk
Butter for pans
Flour for pans

Preheat oven to 400 degrees. Beat eggs until thick and gradually add oil. Beat for 1 minute. Sift dry ingredients and add to egg mixture. Cut the orange into pieces and chop it, until fine, in a blender or food processor. Add to batter. Slowly beat in milk and continue beating for 2 minutes. Turn out into 2 8 by 5-inch loaf pans that have been buttered and floured. Let stand for 20 minutes. Bake for 20 minutes or until the dough has risen to top of the pan and started to brown slightly. Reduce oven temperature to 300 degrees and score top of bread lengthwise with the point of a sharp knife. Bake for 40 minutes longer or until a toothpick inserted in the center comes out clean. Allow to stand in the pans for 10 minutes before turning out onto a rack to cool.

ANADAMA BREAD

A rich old-fashioned bread that is well worth the effort.

Makes 2 loaves

1 package (1 tablespoon)
    active dry yeast
¼ cup lukewarm water
½ cup cornmeal
¾ cup cold water
1½ cup boiling water or
    milk

3 tablespoons butter
½ cup dark molasses
2 tablespoons salt
3 cups whole wheat flour
3 cups unbleached white
    flour, unsifted

Dissolve yeast in warm water for 5 minutes. Meanwhile, put cornmeal into the ¾ cup cold water and soak. Pour this mixture into the boiling water and stir over low heat until mixture comes to a boil again. Remove from heat, add butter, molasses, and salt. Cool to a tepid 95 to 105 degrees. Be sure it is cooled at least to body temperature—you can put it in the refrigerator, stirring occasionally, to speed up the cooling. Combine yeast and liquid cornmeal mixture. Put the whole wheat flour into a large mixing bowl, add liquid all at once, and mix into a smooth batter for 3 to 5 minutes. Gradually add white flour and beat and knead until smooth, elastic, and nonsticky. Cover dough and let rest for 2 minutes. Gently knead and form into a ball.

RISING: Place dough in a well-buttered 6-quart bowl and cover with plastic wrap and a towel. Let rise slowly for 3 hours or until doubled in bulk. Punch down, place on a lightly floured surface, cut in half, cover, and let rest for a minute.

SHAPING: Flatten dough into 2¾-inch-thick rectangles. Fold each in thirds, turn, and flatten again in the opposite direction. Roll into tight cylinders, pinching seam and ends. Roll back and forth until cylinders are the length of the bread pans.

FINAL RISING: Place dough in 2 well-buttered loaf pans (approximately 9 by 5½ by 3 inches), seam down, and cover. Let rise slowly at 75 degrees for 1½ hours or until dough has filled pans and curves above the edges. Preheat oven to 400 degrees.

BAKING: Bake for 15 minutes, checking to see that crust isn't browning too much. If so, cover with foil. Reduce heat to 350 degrees and bake for 45 minutes more. Bread is done when it pulls from the edges of pans, the crusts are firm, and a finger tapped on the bottom of a pan makes a hollow thump. Remove from pans, place on a rack, and return to *turned-off oven*, door ajar, for 15 minutes, to set the crust. Cool on a rack. When cool, place in plastic bags and store or freeze immediately.

LEMON BREAD

A marvelously fresh-tasting light bread. It's even good as a dessert or toasted for breakfast. Freezes beautifully.

Makes 1 loaf

1 cup sugar
⅓ cup butter, melted
1 teaspoon lemon extract
¼ cup fresh lemon juice
2 eggs
1½ cups all-purpose flour, unsifted

1 teaspoon baking powder
1 teaspoon salt
½ cup milk
Grated rind of 1 large lemon
½ cup chopped pecans

TOPPING
½ cup powdered sugar
¼ cup fresh lemon juice

Preheat oven to 350 degrees. Combine sugar, butter, lemon extract and juice. Beat in eggs, one at a time, until smooth. Sift dry ingredients and stir in alternately with the milk. Add lemon rind and pecans. Pour into a buttered 8-inch loaf pan and bake for 1 hour or until a toothpick inserted in the center comes out clean. Dissolve the powdered sugar in the lemon juice over low heat. Remove bread from the oven, pierce top in several places with a sharp knife blade or thin fork tongs. Pour on the topping. Cool in the pan for 1 hour. Remove from the pan, wrap in foil, and let stand for 24 hours before cutting. Will keep 2 to 3 months in the refrigerator.

PEAR BREAD

This is a light, almost cake-like bread. Very moist and good with a cup of tea in the afternoon.

Makes 2 loaves

3 eggs
1 cup vegetable oil
2 to 3 pears, peeled and
    grated to make 2 cups
1½ cups sugar
½ teaspoon freshly grated
    lemon rind

1 teaspoon vanilla extract
2 cups all-purpose flour,
    unsifted
¼ teaspoon baking powder
¼ teaspoon baking soda
½ teaspoon cinnamon
⅔ cup chopped walnuts

Preheat oven to 325 degrees. Beat eggs and slowly beat in oil. Add pears, sugar, lemon rind, and vanilla. Sift dry ingredients and add to pear mixture, stirring just to moisten. Stir in walnuts and pour into 2 buttered and floured 8-inch loaf pans. Bake for about 55 minutes or until a toothpick inserted in the center comes out clean.

ENGLISH MUFFIN BREAD

Makes 2 loaves

5 cups all-purpose flour,
    unsifted
1½ teaspoons active dry
    yeast
1½ teaspoons salt

1 tablespoon sugar
1½ teaspoons corn oil
2 cups very warm water
Butter and cornmeal for pans

In a large bowl mix dry ingredients and corn oil. Pour in 2 cups water and mix thoroughly. Cover the bowl with plastic wrap and a towel. Let stand at room temperature overnight or at least 6 hours. The dough will more than double and then may fall again somewhat, which is normal. Generously butter 2 7½ by 3½-inch bread pans and sprinkle with cornmeal. Divide dough, without kneading, into 2 portions and place in pans. Preheat oven to 350 degrees. Cover and let rise for 1½ to 2 hours or until double in bulk. Bake for 1 hour, then cool on rack in pans.

PERSIMMON BREAD

Makes 4 loaves

1 cup seedless raisins
½ cup brandy
2 cups dark brown sugar,
    firmly packed
½ cup white sugar
2 cups ripe persimmon pulp
1 cup vegetable oil
4 eggs
4 cups all-purpose flour,
    unsifted

2 teaspoons baking soda
½ teaspoon salt
1 teaspoon cinnamon
1 teaspoon nutmeg
½ teaspoon powdered
    ginger
1 cup chopped walnuts
Butter for pans
Flour for pans

Preheat oven to 350 degrees. Plump raisins in brandy and set aside. Mix together the sugars with persimmon pulp and oil. Add eggs, one at a time, beating well after each addition. Sift together the dry ingredients and add to egg mixture, blending well. Add raisins and walnuts. Pour into 4 buttered and floured 7-inch loaf pans. Bake for 1 hour or until a toothpick inserted in the center comes out clean. Cool on a rack.

ZUCCHINI PINEAPPLE BREAD

Makes 3 loaves

5 eggs, beaten until frothy
1¼ cups vegetable oil
2½ cups sugar
1 tablespoon vanilla extract
3½ cups unbleached white
    flour, unsifted
1 cup toasted wheat germ
1 teaspoon cinnamon

1 teaspoon nutmeg
1 tablespoon baking soda
½ teaspoon baking powder
3 cups firmly packed
    shredded zucchini
1 cup drained crushed
    pineapple

Preheat oven to 350 degrees. To beaten eggs add oil slowly, then blend in sugar and vanilla. Beat until lemon-colored. Add remaining ingredients and mix well. Pour into 3 loaf pans (7 by 3 by 2 inches). Bake for 1 hour or until toothpick inserted in the center comes out clean.

PUMPKIN WALNUT BREAD

This is a best-seller at any food boutique or volunteer fair.

Makes 2 loaves

1½ cups sugar
1⅔ cups all-purpose flour,
    unsifted
¼ teaspoon baking powder
1 teaspoon baking soda
¾ teaspoon salt
1 teaspoon cinnamon
1 teaspoon cloves
1 teaspoon nutmeg

2 eggs, well beaten
½ cup vegetable oil
½ cup water
1 cup cooked mashed
    pumpkin
½ cup coarsely chopped
    walnuts
Butter for pans
Flour for pans

Preheat oven to 325 degrees. Mix all the dry ingredients in a large bowl. Add the eggs, oil, water, pumpkin and beat until well blended. Add the walnuts. Pour the batter into 2 buttered and floured 7-inch loaf pans. Bake for 50 to 60 minutes or until a toothpick inserted in the center comes out clean. Cool for 5 minutes in the pans, then remove bread onto a rack. This recipe can be doubled or tripled and can be frozen beautifully.

MAPLE OATMEAL BREAD

Makes 2 loaves

2 packages (2 tablespoons)
    active dry yeast
¼ cup lukewarm water
2 cups regular rolled oats
1 cup maple syrup
1 cup hot strong coffee

⅓ cup butter
2 teaspoons salt
6 cups unbleached
    all-purpose white flour,
    unsifted
2 eggs, lightly beaten

Dissolve yeast in warm water for 5 minutes. Combine rolled oats, maple syrup, coffee, butter, salt, and 1 cup of the flour. Add yeast. Beat in eggs until mixture is smooth. Mix in remaining flour and beat until dough is smooth and elastic. Form into a ball and transfer to a thoroughly buttered large bowl. Turn the dough in the bowl to coat with butter. Cover with plastic wrap and a towel. Let rise for 1½ to 2 hours or until doubled. Punch down, divide in half, and form into 2 rounds. Preheat oven to 350 degrees. Place in 2 buttered 9-inch loaf pans. Let rise for about 1 hour or until double in bulk. Bake for 45 minutes or until a toothpick inserted in the center comes out clean. Cool on racks in pans.

APRICOT NUT BREAD

Makes 2 small loaves

1 cup sugar
2 tablespoons shortening
1 egg, lightly beaten
¾ cup milk
¾ cup fresh orange juice
4 teaspoons freshly grated
    orange rind
3 cups all-purpose flour,
    unsifted

3½ teaspoons baking
    powder
1 teaspoon salt
¾ cup chopped walnuts
6 ounces dried apricots,
    plumped in ½ cup
    boiling water

Preheat oven to 350 degrees. Thoroughly blend sugar, shortening, and egg. Stir in milk, orange juice, and orange rind. Sift dry ingredients and stir in nuts until nuts are well mixed in. Add to liquid mixture. Drain and coarsely chop apricots. Blend into batter and pour into 2 small 7-inch loaf pans. Let stand for 20 minutes. Bake for 1 hour and 10 minutes or until a toothpick inserted in the center comes out clean. Cool in pans for 10 minutes on a rack, remove from pans, and cool completely. Wrap in foil and let stand in the refrigerator for 2 days to allow flavors to blend.

BACON SPOON BREAD

A fine recipe—you'll like the addition of the bacon. It can be served instead of potatoes or rice, and it acts like a soufflé—beautifully puffed and golden when ready to serve.

Serves 6

¾ cup yellow cornmeal
1½ cups cold water
2 cups shredded sharp
    Cheddar cheese
¼ cup soft butter
2 cloves garlic, crushed

½ teaspoon salt
1 cup milk
4 egg yolks, well beaten
½ pound bacon, cooked and
    drained
4 egg whites, beaten stiff

Preheat oven to 325 degrees. In a saucepan, combine the cornmeal and cold water, cook, stirring constantly, until the consistency of mush. Remove from heat and add cheese, butter, garlic, and salt. Stir until cheese is melted. Gradually add milk, then stir in egg yolks. Crumble bacon, reserving some for garnish, and add to cornmeal mixture. Fold in stiffly beaten egg whites. Pour into a greased 2-quart soufflé dish or casserole. Sprinkle reserved bacon on top and bake for about 1 hour or until firm. Serve with additional butter.

REFRIGERATOR ROLLS

This versatile dough can be used to make hamburger or hot dog rolls, dinner rolls, hors d'oeuvre rounds—even pizza dough!

Makes approximately 5 dozen rolls

2 packages (2 tablespoons)
    active dry yeast
½ cup lukewarm water
¾ cup butter
1 cup boiling water
1 cup cold water

¾ cup sugar
2 teaspoons salt
2 eggs, lightly beaten
7 to 8 cups unbleached white
    flour, unsifted

Dissolve yeast in the warm water for 5 minutes. Set aside. Combine butter with the boiling water and stir until butter is melted. Cool and place in a very large bowl. Add the cold water, sugar, salt, eggs, and yeast. Mix well. Add enough flour (between 7 and 8 cups) to make a soft dough that when beaten does not stick to the sides of the bowl. Cover and refrigerate immediately for at least 6 hours or preferably overnight. (Dough may be kept in the refrigerator for 7 to 10 days.) When ready to use, remove any amount needed, place on a floured board, roll out about 1 inch thick, and cut or shape into any size desired. Place rolls on an ungreased cookie sheet and let rise for 1 to 2 hours. Bake in a preheated 375-degree oven for 12 to 15 minutes, depending on size of rolls.

UPSIDE-DOWN PECAN ROLLS

Makes 12 large rolls

2 packages (2 tablespoons) active dry yeast
½ cup lukewarm water
⅔ cup milk
3 tablespoons sugar

1 teaspoon salt
½ cup butter, cut into bits
5 to 6 cups unbleached white flour, unsifted
2 eggs, lightly beaten

CARAMEL SYRUP
4 tablespoons butter, melted
1 cup firmly packed dark brown sugar
2 tablespoons water
1 cup chopped pecans

4 tablespoons butter, melted
½ cup sugar
1 tablespoon cinnamon
Lukewarm water

Dissolve yeast in the warm water for 5 minutes. Scald milk and add sugar, salt, and butter. Stir until sugar and butter are melted. Cool to lukewarm and stir in yeast. Add 3 cups of the flour and stir to moisten. Beat until smooth and then beat in eggs. Add 2 more cups of flour, or enough to make a stiff dough. Turn out onto a lightly floured board and knead for at least 10 minutes until smooth and elastic, adding more flour as needed to prevent sticking. Transfer to a thoroughly buttered large bowl, turn the dough in the bowl to coat with butter. Cover with plastic wrap and a towel and let rise in a warm place for 2 hours or until almost doubled. Punch down, turn out onto a lightly floured board, and knead 10 to 12 times. Let dough rest for 10 minutes. Meanwhile, for the caramel syrup combine melted butter, brown sugar, and 2 tablespoons water, boil for 1 minute. Pour this into the bottom of a 9 by 13-inch cake pan, sprinkle with pecans. Roll and stretch dough into a rectangle 24 by 18 inches. Brush with the 4 tablespoons melted butter. Combine sugar and cinnamon and sprinkle over buttered dough. Starting from the short end, roll the rectangle jelly-roll fashion, sealing ends with a little water. With a sharp knife, cut the roll into 6 equal parts. Place rolls next to each other, cut side up, on top of syrup and pecans in the cake pan. Cover with a towel and let rise in a warm place for about 1½ hours or until doubled in bulk. Brush surfaces of rolls with water and bake in a preheated 350-degree oven for 30 to 35 minutes or until nicely browned. Immediately invert onto a serving tray, slice each roll in half, and serve warm. (Rolls will be 5 or 6 inches in diameter.) May be frozen and reheated.

BLUEBERRY MUFFINS

Makes 12 muffins

1½ cups all-purpose flour, unsifted	1 egg, lightly beaten
2 teaspoons baking powder	½ cup milk
½ teaspoon salt	4 tablespoons butter, melted
½ cup sugar	1 cup fresh or frozen blueberries

Preheat oven to 375 degrees. Sift together flour, baking powder, salt, and sugar into a mixing bowl. In a separate bowl, combine egg and milk, add butter. Make a well in the center of the dry ingredients and pour in milk mixture, stirring with fork just until dry ingredients are moistened. Fold in blueberries. Ladle batter into 12 buttered 3-inch muffin tins, filling each tin approximately ⅔ full. Bake for 20 minutes or until toothpick inserted in center comes out clean. Serve immediately or allow to cool. To reheat, wrap in foil and place in a preheated 400-degree oven for 5 minutes. May be frozen.

DATE NUT MUFFINS

Makes approximately 4 to 5 dozen muffins

1 cup chopped dates
1 tablespoon baking soda
1 cup boiling water
1 cup sugar
½ cup butter
2 eggs
2½ cups all-purpose flour,
    unsifted

½ teaspoon salt
1¼ cups bran flakes cereal
½ cup chopped walnuts
2 cups buttermilk
1 teaspoon cinnamon
1 tablespoon sugar

Preheat oven to 375 degrees. Combine dates and baking soda with 1 cup boiling water. Cool to room temperature. Cream sugar and butter until smooth. Add eggs one at a time, beating until smooth. Gradually add flour and salt, stirring until blended. Add date mixture. Mix the bran flakes cereal with walnuts and buttermilk then add to batter. Combine cinnamon and sugar and sprinkle over batter. Pour into well-oiled 3-inch muffin tins and bake for about 20 minutes or until a toothpick inserted in the center comes out clean. If a tea muffin pan is used, bake for only 12 to 15 minutes. The batter may be stored in the refrigerator for up to 6 weeks, or the baked muffins may be frozen and reheated.

ORANGE ALMOND PUFFS

Makes 2 dozen

1 package (1 tablespoon)
    active dry yeast
¼ cup lukewarm water
1 cup milk
½ cup shortening
½ cup sugar
1 teaspoon salt
3 cups unbleached white
    flour, unsifted

1 egg, beaten
Butter for muffin tins
½ cup coarsely grated
    almonds
¼ cup melted butter
Finely grated rinds of 3 large
    oranges
¾ cup sugar

Dissolve yeast in the warm water for 5 minutes. Meanwhile, in a small saucepan scald milk and add shortening, sugar, and salt. Cool to luke-warm. In a large bowl, combine milk mixture, yeast, and 1 cup flour. Beat well. Add egg and remaining flour, mix well. Dough should be smooth. Cover with plastic wrap and a towel. Let stand in a warm place for 1½ to 2 hours or until doubled. Throughly butter 24 3-inch muffin tins and sprinkle them with the almonds. Punch down dough and spoon into muffin tins. Fill ⅔ full. Brush with melted butter and sprinkle with orange rind and sugar. Preheat oven to 275 degrees. Let rise for about 1 to 1½ hours or until double in bulk. Bake at 275° for 12 to 15 minutes. Serve immediately. These may also be frozen and reheated before serving.

DANISH LOAF CAKE

Makes 2 loaf cakes

Butter for loaf pans
¾ cup finely chopped
   blanched almonds
3 cups all-purpose flour,
   unsifted
1 tablespoon plus 1 teaspoon
   baking powder

½ teaspoon salt
2 cups heavy cream
1 teaspoon vanilla extract
½ teaspoon almond extract
2 cups sugar
4 eggs
¾ cup chopped almonds

GLAZE
⅓ cup orange-flavored liqueur
¼ cup sugar

Preheat oven to 350 degrees. Thoroughly butter 2 9 by 5 inch loaf pans. Coat the sides and bottom of each pan with the finely chopped almonds. Sift together the flour, baking powder, and salt. Set aside. Whip cream in a large bowl until it holds a shape. Stir in vanilla and almond extracts and sugar. Beat in eggs one at a time. Stir in dry ingredients until just blended. Pour about ¼ of the batter into each pan. Sprinkle 2 tablespoons chopped almonds over the batter, then pour remaining batter in the pan. Smooth the top and sprinkle with remaining almonds.

Bake for 1 hour or until a toothpick inserted in the center comes out clean. For the glaze: Dissolve the sugar in the orange-flavored liqueur in a small saucepan over medium heat. Remove loaves from the oven and brush on glaze while the loaves are still warm. Let them cool in the pans.

SOUR CREAM AND ALMOND COFFEECAKE

Serves 8 to 10

8 ounces canned almond
   paste
¼ cup sugar
1 cup butter, softened
2 eggs
1 teaspoon vanilla extract
1 cup sour cream

2 cups all-purpose flour,
   unsifted
1 teaspoon baking powder
¾ teaspoon salt
Butter for pan
Flour for pan

TOPPING
½ cup chopped almonds
¼ cup brown sugar

¼ cup flour
¼ cup butter

Preheat oven to 325 degrees. Crumble almond paste between fingers into a large mixing bowl. Add sugar and beat, then gradually add softened butter. Add 2 eggs, one at a time, beating after each addition, then vanilla and sour cream. Sift together the flour, baking powder, and salt. Fold into sour cream mixture and turn into a buttered and floured 10-inch tube pan. For the topping: Mix the chopped almonds with brown sugar, flour, and butter until crumbly. Sprinkle over cake. Bake for about 1 hour or until a toothpick inserted in the center comes out clean.

BLUEBERRY COFFEECAKE

A special treat for Christmas morning.

Serves 12

½ cup butter
1 cup sugar
3 eggs, lightly beaten
1 teaspoon baking powder
¼ teaspoon salt
1 teaspoon soda

2 cups unbleached white
    flour, unsifted
1 cup sour cream
2 cups fresh or frozen
    blueberries

TOPPING
1 cup brown sugar
¼ cup butter
¼ cup flour

Preheat oven to 350 degrees. Cream butter and sugar. Add eggs, baking powder, salt, and soda. Alternating, add flour and sour cream. Fold in blueberries. Pour into a well-buttered cake pan approximately 9 by 13 by 2 inches. For the topping: Cream brown sugar and butter. Add flour to get a semidry, lumpy mixture. Spread on top of the batter. Bake for 30 minutes or until a toothpick inserted in the center comes out clean. The topping should melt and partially sink into the batter.

AUF LAUF
(German Breakfast Pancakes)

Serves 4 to 6

6 eggs
⅛ teaspoon salt
1 cup all-purpose white
    flour, unsifted

1½ cups milk
1 teaspoon sugar
¼ pound butter, melted
Powdered sugar

TOPPING SUGGESTIONS
Fruit jam, fresh berries, sliced fresh fruit, sour cream, applesauce, sugar and cinnamon

Preheat oven to 450 degrees. Lightly beat eggs with salt. Gradually add flour to milk, blending until smooth. Add this mixture and the sugar to eggs and blend well. Pour the melted butter into 2 8-inch-square baking pans. Add half the batter to each pan and bake for 15 minutes or until pancakes rise and puff and are lightly browned. Lower temperature to 400 degrees if pancakes are browning too fast. Sprinkle with powdered sugar and serve immediately with one or more topping suggestions.

EBLESKIVER

These round Danish pancakes are cooked in a special pan that can be bought in many hardware or kitchenware stores. It looks like a cast-iron skillet with golf-ball-size indentations in it.

Serves 6 to 8

2 cups buttermilk
2 cups sifted all-purpose
    flour
3 eggs, separated
2 tablespoons sugar
1 teaspoon baking powder
1 teaspoon baking soda

½ teaspoon salt
½ teaspoon powdered
    cardamom
Oil for cooking
Applesauce
Lingonberry jam
Powdered sugar

Combine buttermilk, flour, egg yolks, sugar, baking powder, baking soda, salt, and cardamom. Beat egg whites until stiff but not dry and fold into batter. Pour approximately ½ teaspoon oil into each round of an ebleskiver pan, heat, and fill rounds ¾ full with batter. Add ½ teaspoon applesauce to each. Using 2 forks, turn when bubbles appear on top of each cake. When done, keep warm in the oven until all batter is used. Each pancake will resemble a ball. Serve with lingonberry jam and powdered sugar.

SOURDOUGH PANCAKES

These pancakes, which are lighter than air, were the mainstay of the forty-niners' diet.

Makes about 28 pancakes

1 cup all-purpose flour,
    unsifted
2 tablespoons sugar
1½ teaspoons baking
    powder
½ teaspoon salt

½ teaspoon baking soda
1 egg, beaten
1 cup Sourdough Starter
    (see Index)
½ cup milk
2 tablespoons cooking oil

In a bowl combine flour, sugar, baking powder, salt, and baking soda. Combine egg, sourdough starter, milk, and oil. Stir into the flour mixture until well combined. Using 2 tablespoonfuls of batter for each pancake, bake on a hot, lightly greased griddle until golden brown, turning once.

CHAPTER XIII

RELISHES & PRESERVES

The Northern Waterfront

Domingo Ghirardelli came to California from Italy by way of Peru, where, having come upon a rich source of cocoa beans, he began his lifelong career in the manufacture of chocolate. Originally settling in San Francisco near the old Barbary Coast, he later expanded his business to include imported foodstuffs, and he moved to the northern waterfront. As business flourished, he and his sons transformed the San Francisco Woolen Works into a factory for their delectable chocolate. After Ghirardelli's death his family added other handsome brick buildings, in which mustard was manufactured, and a beautiful clock tower. Today these buildings, rescued from demolition, are the keystone for the revival of a neighborhood.

Renovation and preservation have become the theme of the northern waterfront. The preservation of the Ghirardelli factories and their transformation into an imaginative shopping and dining complex were followed by the renovation of a nearby fruit cannery. Still other old brick buildings have been changed into desirable office space and more stores and eateries. Food of all kinds abounds in these revitalized structures—Hungarian, Mandarin, Mexican, Indian, English, and Italian are only a few of the many nationalities represented within these old walls. In The Cannery an elaborate grocery store offers wines, preserves, spices, relishes, and delicacies galore. And Mr. Ghirardelli's chocolate is still being made in large vats in one corner of the Chocolate building at Ghirardelli Square.

The urge to preserve buildings as traces of our glorious past or to preserve the delectable bounty of summer's fruits and vegetables stems from the same desire to retain the best of what has come before so that we may enjoy it in the future—dare we say with relish?

CROCKED DILL PICKLES

Makes 12 to 14 quarts

16 pounds tiny cucumbers
    for pickling
¾ cup pickling spices
1½ bunches fresh dill
    (about 7 stalks)

½ pound garlic cloves,
    peeled and halved
2 cups pickling salt
2 gallons water

Wash and drain cucumbers. Place half each of the pickling spices, dill, and garlic on the bottom of a clean 4-gallon crock. Put the cucumbers in the crock. Dissolve the salt in the 2 gallons water and pour over the cucumbers. Add the rest of the pickling spices, dill, and garlic on top and cover with a weighted lid. Check every few days and skim off foam. In 2 to 3 weeks the cucumbers will be crisp and firm to the touch. Pack the cucumbers in sterilized jars. Strain and boil the brine and pour over cucumbers. Seal tightly and store in a cool place.

BREAD AND BUTTER PICKLES

Makes 5 quarts

1 gallon thinly sliced
    pickling cucumbers
4 small onions, thinly
    sliced
3 green peppers, cut into
    thin strips
⅔ cup kosher salt or rock salt

Crushed ice to cover
5 cups cider vinegar
5 cups sugar
1½ teaspoons turmeric
3½ tablespoons pickling
    spices, tied in a
    cheesecloth bag

Place cucumbers, onions, green peppers, and salt in a large glass container or crock and cover with ice. Let stand for at least 3 hours. Drain well. Combine vinegar, sugar, turmeric, and pickling spices. Bring to a boil, add drained vegetables, and return to a boil. Remove immediately and pack into sterilized jars.

SWEET AND SOUR PICKLED FIGS

Makes 8 pints

6 quarts fresh figs (about 8
    pounds)
Salt water (1 tablespoon salt
    to 1 gallon water)

8 cups brown sugar
1 quart white vinegar
8 cinnamon sticks
1 tablespoon whole cloves

Wash the figs and cover with the salt water. Bring to a boil and simmer for 15 minutes. Combine the sugar and vinegar and bring to a boil. Drain the figs and add to the boiling syrup along with the spices. Simmer for 1 hour. Pack figs into hot sterilized jars, making certain that the figs are covered with syrup and there is a cinnamon stick in each jar. Seal at once.

PICKLED ZUCCHINI

Makes approximately 5 pints

4 pounds zucchini, thinly
    sliced crosswise
1 pound onions, thinly sliced
½ cup kosher salt
1 quart cider vinegar
2 cups sugar
2 teaspoons celery salt

2 teaspoons turmeric
2 teaspoons dry mustard
2 teaspoons mustard seed
2 teaspoons celery seed
1 sweet red pepper, cut into
    thin julienne strips

Cover zucchini and onions with salt and water to cover and let stand for 1 hour, stirring occasionally. Drain well, using hands to gently press out moisture. In a large saucepan, bring remaining ingredients to a boil. Add zucchini and onions, turn off heat, and let stand for 1 hour. Return to heat and bring to a boil. Remove from heat. Fill sterilized jars to within 1 inch of top and seal. Let stand for 24 hours and tighten lids once more. Then turn jars upside down for 48 hours. Store in a cool place.

PICKLED WATERMELON RIND

Makes approximately 4 quarts

1 large watermelon
½ cup salt
7½ quarts water
1 large lemon, peeled and
    sliced
3 cups cider vinegar
6 cups sugar

3 tablespoons allspice
3 tablespoons whole cloves
1 tablespoon powdered mace
1 tablespoon whole mustard
    seed
5 cinnamon sticks, coarsely
    crumbled

Remove all pink meat from the watermelon and reserve for another use. Peel off the outside dark green rind and cut remainder into 1-inch squares. There should be approximately 4 quarts of rind. Prepare a brine from the salt and 3 quarts of the water. Place the rind in a 4-quart crock and pour the brine over it. Let stand overnight, covered. Drain and rinse thoroughly. Place the rind in a large kettle, cover with 3 quarts of the water, and bring to a boil. Reduce heat and simmer for about 10 minutes or until tender. Drain. Bring the remaining 1½ quarts of water to a boil and add all the other ingredients. Add the watermelon rind and simmer for about 45 minutes or until rind becomes translucent and liquid has thickened to a light syrup. Spoon into sterilized jars, seal tightly, and store in a cool place.

DILLY BEANS

Makes 4 to 5 pints

2 pounds tender green beans
2 cups water
2 cups cider vinegar
1½ teaspoons salt
⅓ cup sugar
1 hot red pepper

2 bay leaves
4 garlic cloves
2 medium onions, sliced
4 or 5 large sprigs of fresh
    dill

Wash the beans thoroughly and snap off the ends. Discard any that are wilted-looking or broken. Combine the water, vinegar, salt, sugar, red pepper, bay leaves, garlic, and onions. Simmer for 10 minutes. Drop the beans into salted boiling water and cook for 5 minutes. They should be very crisp. Drain them immediately and put upright in 4 or 5 well-sterilized pint jars, with a large sprig of dill in each. Pour the hot liquid over the beans to cover and seal immediately.

DILLED GREEN TOMATOES

For every one of 6 quart jars allow the given amounts of filling ingredients:

Makes 6 quarts

FILLING

1 garlic clove, halved
1 hot red pepper, cut in
    thirds
4 heads of fresh dill, full of
    seeds

6 quarts small, firm medium
    green tomatoes

LIQUID

4 quarts water
1½ cups cider vinegar
⅔ cup salt

Pack the garlic, red pepper, dill, and tomatoes into quart jars in alternating layers. Bring the liquid to a boil and pour over tomatoes to cover completely. Cover with a towel and allow to sit overnight at room temperature. Pour off the brine from the tomatoes, reboil it, and return it to the tomatoes. Repeat this process yet a third day. You may have to make more brine. On the third day, seal the jars tightly and store in a cool, dark place. Store for at least 6 weeks before using.

CHERRY TOMATO PRESERVES

Makes about 6 pints

2 quarts cherry tomatoes,
 stemmed and washed
2 cups light brown sugar
2 cups white sugar
2 lemons, thinly sliced
½ cup water

1 cup cider vinegar
3 cinnamon sticks, broken in
 pieces
5 cloves
10 ounces dried, candied
 ginger, minced

Combine all ingredients in a large saucepan and bring to a boil. Cook, covered for about 15 minutes. Reduce heat and simmer, stirring frequently, for about 1 hour or until thickened. Spoon into sterilized jars. Store in a cool, dark place.

SPICED ARTICHOKES

Makes 4 to 5 pints

40 small artichokes (1 to 1½
 inches in diameter
 across bottom)

1 quart water
1 tablespoon white vinegar

MARINADE
5 cups water
1 cup white vinegar
1 tablespoon salt
Dried red chili peppers

Bay leaves
Whole cloves
Garlic cloves
Whole allspice

Cut stalks off artichokes and remove tough outer leaves. In a kettle bring 1 quart water and the white vinegar to a boil, add artichokes, and boil for 8 minutes. For the marinade: Bring the 5 cups of water, vinegar, and salt to a boil. Fill sterilized jars with cooked artichokes. Add to each jar: 2 chilies, 1 bay leaf, 2 whole cloves, 1 garlic clove, and 1 whole allspice. Pour the second vinegar-water solution over the artichokes, filling the jars. Seal and let stand for at least 24 hours. Check seals and store in a cool, dark place up to 3 months.

ZUCCHINI RELISH

Makes 8 to 10 pints

10 cups finely chopped
    zucchini
4 cups finely chopped onion
2 cups finely chopped
    carrots
2 cups finely chopped green
    pepper
¼ cup kosher salt
2 cups cider vinegar

4 cups sugar
2 tablespoons cornstarch,
    mixed with water to
    make a paste
2 teaspoons celery seed
1 teaspoon pepper
1 teaspoon turmeric
1 teaspoon nutmeg

Combine the vegetables and salt in a large glass container or crock and
let stand for 24 hours. Drain. In a large kettle combine remaining ingredients, add drained vegetables, and bring to a boil, stirring constantly.
Remove from heat immediately. Spoon into sterilized jars. Store in a cool
place.

MANGO CHUTNEY

Makes approximately 3 pints

3½ cups sliced mangoes
2½ cups sugar
1 cup brown sugar
1 cup cider vinegar
2 tablespoons finely chopped
    garlic
4 tablespoons finely chopped
    ginger root

1½ teaspoons salt
1½ small dried chili peppers,
    seeded and chopped
1½ teaspoons whole cloves
    tied in a cheesecloth bag
½ cup raisins

Combine mangoes and sugars, stir well, and let stand overnight. Drain
mangoes in a colander, reserving syrup. In a heavy saucepan combine
the vinegar, garlic, ginger, salt, chilies, and cloves with the syrup. Simmer for 30 minutes. Remove cheesecloth bag of cloves. Add mangoes
and raisins and simmer for 20 minutes longer. Spoon into sterilized jars
and seal. Store in a cool place. DO NOT DOUBLE THIS RECIPE.

PEACH CHUTNEY

Some chutneys are best very thick and others taste better with more juice. Use your own judgment and enjoy!

Makes 6 to 8 pints

4 quarts fresh ripe peaches, peeled, pitted, and coarsely chopped
2 pounds dark brown sugar
2 cups cider vinegar
1 cup chopped onions
1 pound dark raisins
4 tart apples, peeled, cored, and coarsely chopped

2 tablespoons mustard seeds
¼ cup minced fresh ginger or 3 tablespoons powdered ginger
1½ tablespoons salt
2 tablespoons paprika
1 tablespoon cumin
Juice of 2 limes
Grated rind of 1 lime

Place the peaches in a large heavy enameled pot. Cover with sugar and vinegar. Add the remaining ingredients and simmer, uncovered, stirring occasionally, for 2 to 3 hours or until thick. Pour into sterilized jars. Store in a cool, dark place.

GOLDEN CHUTNEY

Makes approximately 6 pints

4 pounds ripe apricots, pitted and quartered
4 large mangoes, peeled and coarsely chopped
2 pounds tart apples, peeled, seeded, and coarsely chopped
4 cups brown sugar
4 cups cider vinegar
2 limes, pulp and rind finely chopped
1 large orange, pulp and rind finely chopped

2 large onions, finely chopped
1 tablespoon cinnamon
3 tablespoons salt
1 tablespoon ground cloves
1 teaspoon allspice
1 teaspoon cayenne pepper
1 teaspoon chili pepper
8 cloves garlic, chopped
½ cup chopped crystalized ginger

In a large kettle combine all ingredients. Bring to a boil. Reduce heat and simmer, stirring frequently, for 1 to 1½ hours or until thick. Spoon into sterilized jars and store in a cool place.

MIDDLERIDGE PEAR CHUTNEY

Makes approximately 12 pints

3 cups cider vinegar
2 pounds brown sugar
6 pounds firm pears, cored,
    peeled, and chopped
2 medium onions,
    chopped
2 cups golden raisins
½ cup diced preserved
    ginger, or 3 tablespoons
    chopped fresh ginger
    root

2 cloves garlic, minced
1 teaspoon cayenne pepper
4 teaspoons salt
1 teaspoon cinnamon
1 teaspoon ground cloves
4 teaspoons mustard seed

In a large kettle, bring vinegar and sugar to a boil and stir until sugar dissolves. Add all remaining ingredients and bring back to a gentle boil. Lower heat and simmer, uncovered, over very low heat, stirring occasionally. Chutney should be thick and will take 1½ hours or longer to reach correct consistency. An asbestos pad under the cooking pot will help prevent bottom from scorching. Pour into sterilized jars and seal. Store in a cool place.

PRUNE CHUTNEY

Save some time to make this delicacy in August and September when these plums are available.

Makes 3 pints

1 cup light brown sugar,
    firmly packed
1 cup granulated sugar
¾ cup cider vinegar
1 teaspoon crushed red
    pepper
2 teaspoons salt
2 teaspoons mustard seed

2 large cloves garlic,
    chopped
¼ cup chopped candied
    ginger
1 cup seedless white raisins
4 cups fresh prune plums,
    halved and seeded

In a heavy 2-quart saucepan combine all ingredients. Bring to a boil, lower heat, and simmer, stirring occasionally, for about 1 hour or until thick. Spoon into sterilized jars. Store in a cool, dark place.

TEA LANE CHUTNEY

Makes 8 to 10 pints

2 pounds tart cooking apples,
    seeded and coarsely
    chopped
2 pounds firm pears, seeded
    and coarsely chopped
2 pound quinces, seeded and
    coarsely chopped
6 cups cider vinegar

4 pounds brown sugar
1½ pounds raisins
6 large cloves garlic, minced
8 ounces crystallized ginger,
    chopped
4 teaspoons dry mustard
3 teaspoons salt
1 teaspoon red pepper flakes

Combine all ingredients in a large heavy kettle and mix well. Simmer, stirring occasionally, for 1½ to 2 hours or until mixture reduces ⅓ in volume and thickens.

RUM RAISIN SAUCE

Marvelous on ice cream or poundcake.

Makes 1 pint

½ cup dark rum
½ cup seedless raisins
½ cup sugar
¼ cup water
1 cinnamon stick, broken in
   half

½ teaspoon vanilla extract
1 tablespoon grated lemon
   rind
1 tablespoon grated orange
   rind
½ cup chopped pecans

Pour the rum over the raisins to plump. Set aside. In a heavy saucepan, mix the sugar and water together, then add the cinnamon stick. Bring to a boil and boil hard for 2 minutes. Add the raisins and any remaining rum and cook for 5 minutes more. Add the vanilla, lemon and orange rinds, and pecans. Spoon into a sterilized pint jar and seal.

SUTTER CREEK CHILI SAUCE

Makes approximately 3½ pints

3 large onions
3 medium green peppers
12 large ripe tomatoes,
   peeled, seeded, and
   chopped
2 tablespoons salt
1 teaspoon cayenne pepper

1½ teaspoons dry mustard
1 teaspoon nutmeg
1 teaspoon cinnamon
½ teaspoon ground cloves
½ cup brown sugar
½ cup white sugar
2 cups cider vinegar

Put the onions and green peppers through the coarse blade of a food grinder. In a heavy kettle combine all ingredients and stir thoroughly. Bring to a boil, reduce heat, and simmer uncovered, stirring occasionally, for about 3 hours or until thick. Spoon into sterilized jars. Store in a cool, dark place.

SALSA VERDE

Makes approximately 2 pints

3 pounds tomatillos verdes
(Mexican green
tomatoes), hulled and
coarsely chopped
½ pound jalapeño peppers,
seeded and coarsely
chopped

1 cup cider vinegar
1 pound onions, coarsely
chopped
3 large cloves garlic, minced
4 tablespoons chopped fresh
coriander (cilantro)
1 teaspoon turmeric

Combine all ingredients in a large heavy kettle and bring to a boil. Reduce heat and simmer, stirring occasionally, for approximately 1 hour or until thickened.

ARTILLERY JAM

This makes a beautiful Christmastime hors d'oeuvre when used in combination with Jalapeño Pepper Jelly (see Index).

Makes approximately 4 pints

6 large sweet red peppers
2 tablespoons salt
1 cup cider vinegar

2 cups sugar
Red food coloring
(optional)

Seed the peppers and grind them coarsely. Put the peppers in a large bowl, add the salt, cover, and let stand overnight. Drain off about half of the liquid, pour the peppers into a heavy saucepan, and add the vinegar and sugar. Bring to a boil, reduce heat, and simmer for about 1 hour, stirring occasionally. Remove from heat and add the red food coloring if you wish, a few drops at a time to make the jam a bright red. Cool slightly, stirring occasionally, and spoon into sterilized jars. Store in a cool, dark place.

OLD-FASHIONED MUSTARD

Makes 1½ to 2 pints

1 cup dry mustard
  (4 ounces)
1 cup cider vinegar

1 cup sugar
4 eggs, lightly beaten

Soak the dry mustard in the vinegar overnight. Place in the top of a double boiler and add sugar and eggs. Cook slowly, stirring constantly, for about 10 minutes or until thick. Place in sterilized jars and store in the refrigerator up to 3 months. For variety, add fresh herbs or use herb-flavored vinegar.

JALAPEÑO PEPPER JELLY

Serve this with cream cheese and crackers for a colorful and easy hors d'oeuvre, or use as a condiment for lamb or beef.

Makes approximately 6 pints

4 large green peppers
14 medium jalapeño peppers
½ cup fresh lemon juice
1 cup cider vinegar

6 cups sugar
6 ounces liquid pectin
Green food coloring
  (optional)

Seed and grind the peppers. Combine with lemon juice, vinegar, and sugar in a heavy 4-quart saucepan. Bring to a rolling boil and boil, stirring constantly, for about 15 minutes. Add the pectin and boil for 3 to 5 minutes more. Remove from heat and add the green food coloring if you wish, a few drops at a time to make the jelly a bright green. Cool slightly, stirring occasionally, and spoon into sterilized jars. Seal immediately and store in a cool, dark place.

RAW CRANBERRY RELISH

Makes approximately 2 pints

1 pound cranberries
2 apples, cored
2 oranges, peeled and seeded

1½ cups sugar
⅛ cup cognac

Clean, sort, and wash cranberries. Put the cranberries, apples, and oranges through the medium blade of a food grinder, with a pan underneath to catch the juices. Mix the fruits, juices, sugar, and cognac together and refrigerate overnight. This will keep several days in the refrigerator or will freeze well.

FREEZER STRAWBERRY JAM

This jam has the flavor and bright red color of fresh strawberries.

Makes approximately 4 pints

4 cups strawberries, stemmed
    and washed
¼ cup fresh lemon juice

1 package powdered pectin
1 cup light corn syrup
5½ cups sugar

In a large heavy kettle combine the berries and lemon juice and mix well. Add the pectin, stirring vigorously, allow to set for 30 minutes, stirring occasionally. Add the corn syrup and mix well. Gradually stir in the sugar while warming the jam to 100 degrees on a candy thermometer. Do not exceed this temperature. When sugar is dissolved, spoon into pint jars, leaving 1-inch clearance at top, and freeze immediately for at least 24 hours. After the initial freezing, jam will keep in the refrigerator for several weeks or can remain frozen for a year.

PIONEER TOMATO JAM

Makes 3 pints

3 pounds fresh ripe
    tomatoes, peeled and
    seeded
¼ cup fresh lemon juice

Grated rind of 1 lemon
6 cups sugar
6 ounces liquid fruit pectin

In a heavy 2-quart saucepan cook the tomatoes over low heat for 10 minutes. Add the lemon juice and rind. Then add the sugar and bring to a rolling boil. Boil for 2 to 3 minutes. Remove from heat and stir in the pectin. Skim if necessary, and spoon into sterilized jars. Store in a cool, dark place.

NAPA VALLEY PRUNE JAM

As an alternative to boiling your canning jars to sterilize them, place the jars in a cold oven, set to 250 degrees, leave for 30 minutes.

Makes 5 to 6 pints

7 pounds fresh prune plums
3½ pounds sugar
1 teaspoon allspice

1 teaspoon ground cloves
1 teaspoon cinnamon
2 cups cider vinegar

Pit fresh prunes and place in a large mixing bowl. Sift sugar with the allspice, cloves, and cinnamon. Add to prunes and mix well. Pour the cider vinegar into a large kettle and add the prune mixture. Cook slowly, stirring frequently, until mixture is very thick. Spoon into sterilized jars and cover with melted paraffin. When the paraffin is set, cover with a tight-fitting lid. Store in a cool place.

PEACH JAM

Makes approximately 5 pints

8 cups fresh peaches, peeled
   and chopped
¼ cup fresh lemon juice

6 cups sugar
2 teaspoons almond extract

Place peaches, lemon juice, and sugar in a large saucepan and simmer until thick, stirring frequently. Add almond extract and mix well. Spoon into sterilized jars and seal with paraffin or vacuum tops.

SUN-COOKED PRESERVES

Makes 4 to 6 pints

3 pounds berries or cherries
6 cups sugar
3 cups water

Wash and pick over enough berries—strawberries, raspberries, blackberries, boysenberries—or dark red cherries to weigh 3 pounds. In a kettle combine the sugar with the water and cook the syrup to the thread stage, or until a candy thermometer registers 228 degrees. Add the berries or cherries and let the mixture stand overnight. Skim the berries from the syrup and spread them in a single layer in shallow baking pans. Heat the syrup until a candy thermometer registers 228 degrees and pour it over the berries. Cover the pans with glass or clear plastic wrap and let them stand in direct sunlight for 2 to 3 days or until the syrup is thickened. Dampness and the lower temperatures at night can cause mold to form, so the preserves must be brought indoors each night. If the days turn cloudy, the cooking must be completed in a 225-degree oven. Pour the preserves into sterilized jars and seal them.

TANGERINE MARMALADE

Makes approximately 3 pints

4 pounds tangerines
4 pounds sugar

Peel the skin from the tangerines in large pieces. Set aside. Squeeze the juice from the pulp and discard pulp. Set juice aside. Simmer peel in water to cover for 10 to 12 minutes. Drain and cover peel with cold water. Soak overnight. Drain peel and chop medium fine. In a heavy pan combine peel, reserved juice, and sugar. Bring to a boil, reduce heat, and simmer, stirring frequently, for about 25 to 30 minutes or until thick. Spoon into sterilized jars and store in a cool place.

CURRIED FRUIT

This is a marvelous addition to brunch and a fine complement to roast pork or baked ham. Canned fruit is a must(!) for this recipe, but have a fling with all the possible combinations. We recommend the following:

Makes approximately 3 quarts

1 16-ounce can sliced
   peaches
1 20-ounce can pineapple
   chunks
1 16-ounce can pear halves,
   sliced

1 16-ounce can apricot
   halves
⅓ cup butter
1 cup light brown sugar
4 teaspoons curry powder

Preheat oven to 325 degrees. Drain the fruit well. Melt the butter with the sugar and curry powder. In a large ovenproof dish combine fruit and butter mixture and bake for 1 hour. May be served immediately or cooled and refrigerated in a tightly closed container for up to 2 weeks. Serve hot.

FRUIT CONSERVE

Serve this with roasts or game or add brandy and use as a topping for ice cream.

Makes approximately 5 pints

5 pounds pears, peeled and cut in slivers

1 grapefruit, thinly sliced, seeds removed

1 orange, thinly sliced, seeds removed

3 lemons, thinly sliced, seeds removed

5 pounds sugar

1 pound seedless raisins

1 pound shelled pecans or walnuts

Coarsely grind fruits in a food processor or meat grinder, reserving juices. Combine juices and fruits, add sugar, and mix well. Let stand in a covered bowl overnight. Transfer to a kettle and bring to a rolling boil. Lower heat to very low and simmer, stirring occasionally, for 45 minutes. Add raisins and cook for 45 minutes longer. Add nuts and cook for 1 minute. Remove from heat and pour into sterilized jars. Seal and store in a cool place.

FIESTA MIX

Great as a trail mix, lunch box treat, camping snack, or coffee table munchie. Use your imagination and add to or vary this recipe according to your fancy.

Makes 7 cups

2 cups peanuts

2 cups raisins

1 cup sunflower seeds

1 cup shredded coconut

1 cup M & M's

Mix all ingredients together in a bowl. Store in a well-sealed container in the refrigerator. Will keep for 2 to 3 months.

FRUIT LEATHER

Choose a warm, sunny day to do this project.

Makes 1 sheet approximately 12 by 30 inches

10 cups of any fruit or berries, washed and seeds or pits removed
1 cup sugar

Combine fruit and sugar in a kettle and simmer over moderate heat until a thick, syrupy consistency is reached. Remove from heat and purée in a blender or food processor. Stretch plastic wrap across a table, covering a surface approximately 12 by 30 inches. Place the table in the sun and pour fruit purée onto the plastic wrap, spreading evenly to a ¼ inch depth. Cover the purée with a single protective thickness of cheesecloth and leave in the sun for 1½ to 2 days. At the end of the first day remove the cheesecloth. The purée, which should be dry enough to peel from the plastic wrap without sticking, should be kept inside overnight and brought outside again in the morning and covered with the cheesecloth for the second day of drying. To store, remove cheesecloth, roll up fruit leather, cut into ½ inch thick slices, and place in a tightly covered container. Will keep for 3 to 4 months in the refrigerator or 10 to 12 months in the freezer.

CHRISTMAS SPICED WALNUTS

Makes 2 half-pint jars

¼ cup water
1 cup sugar
½ teaspoon cinnamon

⅛ teaspoon cream of tartar
1½ cups walnut halves
½ teaspoon vanilla extract

Bring the water to a boil. Add the sugar, cinnamon, and cream of tartar. Stirring occasionally, boil to 240 degrees on a candy thermometer. Remove from heat and add nuts. Stir in vanilla and continue stirring until all nuts are coated and mixture has sugared completely. Remove the walnuts and arrange in a single layer on a cookie sheet. Cool for 1 hour and store in an airtight container.

CANDIED FRUIT PEEL

Tie a bright bow around a jar of this for a perfect holiday gift.

Makes 10 to 12 spice-jar-size gifts

6 navel oranges
2 cups sugar
2 teaspoons light corn syrup

1 cup water
Sugar for coating

Remove the peel from the oranges in 4 large pieces. Place peel in a saucepan and cover with cold water. Bring to a boil and simmer for 7 minutes. Drain peel and again place in a saucepan with cold water. Bring to a boil and simmer for another 7 minutes. Repeat process a third time. Drain peel and cut into julienne strips. In a large saucepan, combine the sugar, corn syrup, and water. Add julienne peel and boil gently, uncovered, for 40 to 50 minutes or until most of the syrup is absorbed. Drain and cool peel. Roll strips in granulated sugar, coating well. Arange in a single layer on cookie sheets and dry at room temperature for 2 days. Store in tightly covered jars. You may also substitute grapefruit or lemon peel or combine with the orange peel for a colorful mixture.

CHAPTER XIV

DESSERTS

Nob Hill

On "The Hill of Golden Promise" dreams of the wildest fantasy became reality in the splendor and opulence of the mansions of the Comstock Kings. With Andrew Hallidie's invention of the cable car, once insurmountable hills became accessible for building. It was then that those prominent men with enormous wealth from the mines and railroads claimed Nob Hill for their own, building the most lavish homes imaginable—monuments to their position and power.

On the crest of the hill lived the Stanfords, the Crockers, the Floods, and the Hopkinses. The residence of Mr. and Mrs. Mark Hopkins stood on the site now occupied by the Mark Hopkins Hotel and, though it was not as tall, it covered about the same amount of ground. It cost three million dollars to build, starting in 1874. Architectural details were taken from all over the world, and their variety combined and blended together to create an astounding gingerbread mansion. This house and others like it were so elaborate they were referred to as "pastry chef architecture."

Just as these men built with abandon, so let us approach our grand finale with the same sense of revelry, delighting in the sublime, the rich, the elaborate. Give a cheer for those frothy, impressive, splendid concoctions—Desserts!

ALMOND MACAROONS

Makes approximately 2 dozen

1 8-ounce can almond paste
2 extra-large egg whites
Pinch of salt
1 cup sugar
¼ teaspoon almond extract

2 tablespoons grated almonds
½ cup butter, softened
Baking parchment paper
Pine nuts for decoration

Preheat oven to 325 degrees. Break up almond paste into chunks and place in a food processor. Add egg whites, salt, sugar, almond extract, and almonds. Blend until smooth. Generously butter parchment paper and place on a large cookie sheet. Drop the cookie mixture onto the paper by teaspoonfuls. Flatten tops with a knife dipped in water and place 3 or 4 pine nuts on each cookie. Bake for 20 minutes. Remove paper to a rack to cool, then carefully peel paper from cookies. If the cookies are difficult to remove, try moistening back of paper with water. These macaroons are best when served the same day. However, they freeze well.

PECAN DELIGHTS

An easy and delicious holiday gift idea! Get the children to help with the powdered sugar part.

Makes 4 dozen

1 cup butter, softened
3 tablespoons sugar
2 cups unsifted all-purpose
    flour

2 cups chopped pecans
1 teaspoon vanilla extract
Powdered sugar

Preheat oven to 275 degrees. In a mixing bowl, cream together the butter and sugar. Sift flour 3 times and blend into butter mixture. Add nuts and vanilla. Roll into balls about 1 inch in diameter. Place on a baking sheet and bake for 1 hour. While still warm, roll in powdered sugar. Roll again in it when cooled. Store in a tightly covered tin.

BROWNIE DROPS

Makes approximately 36

2 ounces German sweet
chocolate
1 tablespoon butter
2 eggs
¾ cup sugar
1¼ cups unsifted all-purpose
flour

¼ teaspoon baking powder
⅛ teaspoon salt
¼ teaspoon cinnamon
½ teaspoon vanilla extract
¾ cup chopped pecans
36 pecan halves

Preheat oven to 350 degrees. In the top of a double boiler, melt choco-late and butter over hot water. Set aside to cool. Beat eggs until foamy, then gradually add sugar, beating constantly, until thickened. Blend in chocolate, add flour, baking powder, salt, and cinnamon. Stir in vanilla and chopped pecans. Drop by teaspoonfuls onto a buttered cookie sheet. Top each cookie with a pecan half. Bake for 8 to 10 minutes. Cool slightly before removing with a spatula.

PECAN LACE COOKIES

Makes approximately 4 dozen

½ cup butter
2 cups firmly packed brown
sugar
2 eggs, well beaten
1 teaspoon vanilla extract

½ cup sifted all-purpose
white flour
1 teaspoon baking powder
2 cups chopped pecans

Preheat oven to 375 degrees. Cream butter and sugar, add eggs, and beat well. Add vanilla and stir in flour, baking powder, and nuts. Re-frigerate for 1 hour or until firm. Drop small teaspoonfuls onto foil on a cookie sheet. Bake for 5 to 6 minutes. Cool for 2 minutes and carefully remove from foil.

ICED LEMON COOKIES

Makes 4 dozen

2 cups sugar
1 cup butter
1 cup shortening
2 eggs
3½ cups all-purpose flour

1 teaspoon baking powder
1 teaspoon baking soda
1 cup sour cream
Juice of 2 lemons
Grated rind of 1 orange

ICING

2 cups powdered sugar
Grated rind of 2 lemons
Juice of 2 lemons

4 tablespoons butter,
    softened

Preheat oven to 375 degrees. In a large mixing bowl, cream together the sugar, butter, and shortening. Beat in the eggs, one at a time, mixing well. Sift the dry ingredients and add them alternately with sour cream, lemon juice, and grated orange rind. Drop by teaspoonfuls onto a buttered cookie sheet, flattening down a little with the back of the spoon. Bake for about 10 minutes or just until set and slightly browned. In a mixing bowl, beat all icing ingredients together and spread over warm cookies.

ISCHLER TORTELLETTES

These cookies are worth the trouble . . . they are rich and perfect with any summer fruit. After a big meal these, with Irish coffee, are all that are needed.

Makes 2 dozen

2 cups sifted all-purpose
    flour
1 teaspoon baking powder
1 cup sweet butter, chilled
1 cup ground almonds

¾ cup sugar
Juice of ½ lemon
½ cup jam
4 ounces sweet chocolate

Preheat oven to 375 degrees. In a large mixing bowl, place flour and baking powder, cut in chilled butter with a pastry blender until pieces are the size of oatmeal. Add almonds, sugar, and lemon juice, knead quickly until dough is smooth and forms a ball. (If dough is too hard to manage, chill for about an hour.) Divide dough in half, chill one half, and roll out remaining half on a floured board to ⅛-inch thickness. Cut into rounds with a cookie cutter and place on a buttered and floured cookie sheet. Repeat process with remaining dough. Bake for 10 to 15 minutes. Cool cookies on baking sheets and remove carefully. When cool, spread jam between two cookies until all are paired. Melt chocolate over very low heat or hot water and cover each tortellette with a thin coating.

KENTUCKY SPICE COOKIES

The recipe for these marvelous morsels migrated to California with some old Kentucky families and have become a Western favorite.

Makes approximately 7 dozen

3½ cups sugar
1 cup shortening
1½ teaspoons cinnamon
¾ teaspoon ground cloves
¾ teaspoon powdered
    ginger
¾ teaspoon allspice
2 teaspoons salt

2 tablespoons baking soda
1 cup dark molasses
5 cups unsifted all-purpose
    flour
½ cup water
Sugar
Strawberry or raspberry
    jelly

Preheat oven to 350 degrees. Cream together the sugar, shortening, spices, salt, and baking soda. Add the molasses and blend well. Gradually mix in the flour. Then add the water to make a dough of piecrust consistency. For each cookie, take 1 teaspoon of dough and roll it into a ball, then roll the ball in sugar. Place each on an ungreased cookie sheet, make a small indentation in the top of each ball, and fill with a small dot of jelly. Bake for 8 minutes. Remove from oven and immediately sprinkle lightly with sugar. Allow to cool before storing.

SPRITZ COOKIES

These are delicious—light and sweet.

Makes 6 to 8 dozen

1 pound butter
1½ cups sugar
2 egg yolks
1 teaspoon vanilla extract
½ teaspoon almond extract

1 teaspoon baking powder
4½ cups sifted all-purpose
   white flour or as needed
   to make stiff dough

SUGGESTED DECORATIONS
Candied cherries in small pieces
or
Red or green sugar sprinkles

Preheat oven to 325 degrees. Cream butter and sugar, beat in egg yolks and vanilla and almond extracts. Blend in baking powder and flour to make a stiff dough. Put dough through a large star-shaped cookie press onto ungreased cookie sheets. If dough becomes too pliable, chill until firm. Decorate if desired and bake for 15 minutes.

RAGGEDY BRITCHES

Makes approximately 6 to 7 dozen

1 cup butter, softened
2 cups sugar
6 egg yolks, lightly beaten
2 whole nutmegs, grated
Grated rind of 2 lemons

6 cups flour, sifted
6 egg whites, stiffly beaten
Hot oil for frying
Powdered sugar

Cream together the butter and sugar, slowly add egg yolks, nutmeg, and lemon rind. Stir this mixture into sifted flour and fold in stiffly beaten egg whites. The dough will be soft but manageable. If too soft, cover the bowl and chill for several hours. Roll out small amounts of dough at a time on a floured board, keeping the rest chilled until ready to use. Roll dough about ¼ inch thick and cut into strips 1 by 6 inches. Fold strips in half and twist together. Fry until golden brown in oil heated to 375 degrees. When done, remove from oil and drain on paper towels. Dust generously with powdered sugar forced through a sieve. Keep fresh in a covered tin.

SURPRISE MERINGUE COOKIES

These cookies are just the thing to do with leftover egg whites. They store in a tight-fitting tin and are delicious with ice cream, fruit, or anything.

Makes approximately 3 dozen

2 egg whites at room
   temperature
1 teaspoon vanilla extract
Pinch of salt

½ cup sugar
1 cup mini chocolate chips
1 cup chopped pecans

Preheat oven to 300 degrees. Beat egg whites until they hold a shape, then add vanilla extract and salt. Continue beating while gradually adding the sugar until mixture is thick and glossy. Fold in chocolate chips and pecans. Drop by spoonfuls onto foil-lined cookie sheets. Bake for 30 minutes. Turn off oven and leave meringue in oven to dry out until oven is cool (several hours or overnight).

THE WORLD'S BEST COOKIES

Truly the World's Best Cookies for several reasons. They stay moist, keep beautifully, are the perfect gift or food-bazaar item, and the recipe makes a huge batch. For extra sweetness, sprinkle the warm cookies with granulated sugar. Then watch them disappear!

Makes 8 dozen

1 cup butter
1 cup sugar
1 cup brown sugar, firmly
    packed
1 egg
1 cup salad oil
1 cup rolled oats, regular
1 cup crushed cornflakes

½ cup shredded coconut
½ cup chopped walnuts or
    pecans
3½ cups sifted all-purpose
    flour
1 teaspoon soda
1 teaspoon salt
1 teaspoon vanilla extract

Preheat oven to 325 degrees. Cream together butter and sugars until light and fluffy. Add egg, mixing well, then salad oil, mixing well. Add oats, cornflake, coconut, and nuts, stirring well. Then add flour, soda, and salt. Mix well and form into balls the size of small walnuts, place on an ungreased cookie sheet. Flatten with a fork dipped in water. Bake for 12 minutes. Allow to cool on cookie sheets for a few minutes before removing.

APRICOT BUTTER SQUARES

Serves 12 to 16

12 ounces vanilla wafers,
    crushed
½ pound butter, melted
2½ cups powdered sugar
2 eggs

1½ teaspoons vanilla extract
1 pound canned apricot
    halves, cut and drained
4 ounces chopped pecans
2 cups heavy cream

In a 13½ by 9-inch pan make a layer of half the crushed vanilla wafers. Mix together the butter, powdered sugar, eggs, and vanilla. Pour this over vanilla wafers. Cover this mixture with the apricot halves, then sprinkle over chopped nuts. Whip heavy cream until stiff and spread over apricots. Cover the top with the remaining half of the vanilla wafers. Refrigerate for at least 24 hours. Cut into squares to serve.

CHOCOLATE FINNS

Makes approximately 2½ dozen

FIRST LAYER

2 ounces unsweetened
   baking chocolate
½ cup butter
2 eggs, beaten

1 cup sugar
½ cup flour
1 cup chopped nuts
1 teaspoon vanilla extract

SECOND LAYER

1½ cups powdered sugar
½ cup butter, softened
½ cup heavy cream

THIRD LAYER

2 ounces unsweetened baking chocolate
1 tablespoon butter

Preheat oven to 350 degrees. In a saucepan over very low heat, melt the chocolate and butter. Set aside to cool slightly. Add the eggs, then sugar, flour, nuts, and vanilla. Spread evenly in a 9 by 13-inch pan. Bake for 10 minutes.

For the second layer, in a saucepan combine the powdered sugar, butter, and cream, and cook over low heat to the soft ball stage, about 20 to 25 minutes. Spread over baked layer.

For the third layer, in a small saucepan over very low heat melt together the chocolate and butter. Drizzle over the top of the second layer. Cool until set, then cut into squares.

NANAIMO BARS

The ultimate bars. They are rich, chewy, and positively delicious.

Makes 24 to 30 squares

CRUST

½ cup butter
½ cup sugar
5 tablespoons powdered
　　cocoa
1 teaspoon vanilla extract

1 egg, lightly beaten
1½ cup graham cracker
　　crumbs
1 cup chopped walnuts

ICING

2 cups powdered sugar
½ cup butter, softened
3 tablespoons English
　　Dessert mix or egg
　　custard mix

2 tablespoons milk
4 ounces semisweet
　　chocolate

For the crust place the butter, sugar, cocoa, and vanilla in a saucepan. Cook, stirring, until sugar is dissolved, then add egg and mix well. Remove from heat and stir in graham cracker crumbs and nuts. Pack into an 8 by 12-inch pan and refrigerate until cooled. To make the icing, combine the powdered sugar, butter, dessert or custard mix, and milk, beating well. Spread over crust and refrigerate for 30 minutes. Melt chocolate in the top of a double boiler over simmering water and pour evenly over icing. Refrigerate once more until chilled. To serve, cut into squares.

TOFFEE BARS

Makes 18 to 24

1 cup butter
1 cup brown sugar, firmly
　　packed
1 teaspoon vanilla extract
1 cup sifted all-purpose flour

Dash of salt
1 6-ounce package semisweet
　　chocolate bits
1 cup chopped walnuts

Preheat oven to 350 degrees. Cream butter, sugar, and vanilla until light and fluffy. Add flour and salt, mix well. Stir in chocolate and walnuts and spread mixture on a jelly-roll pan. Bake for 20 minutes. Remove from oven, cut into squares immediately, and let cool in pan.

PECAN SQUARES

Makes 18 to 24 squares

½ cup butter
¼ cup sugar
1 egg, lightly beaten
1¼ cups sifted all-purpose
    flour

¼ teaspoon salt
½ teaspoon vanilla extract

TOPPING

2 eggs, beaten
1½ cups brown sugar,
    firmly packed
1½ cups chopped pecans

2 tablespoons all-purpose
    flour
½ teaspoon salt
1 teaspoon vanilla extract

FROSTING

1½ cups powdered sugar
1 tablespoon fresh lemon juice

Preheat oven to 350 degrees. Cream together butter and sugar, beat in egg, and gradually blend in flour and salt. Add vanilla and spread mixture evenly on the bottom of a buttered 9 by 12-inch baking pan. Bake for 15 minutes. Combine topping ingredients and spread evenly over partially baked mixture. Continue baking for 25 minutes or until a toothpick inserted in the center comes out clean. Cool. Combine frosting ingredients and spread over the top. Cut into squares.

APPLE DAPPLE CAKE

Serves 12 to 14

2 cups sugar
1½ cups corn oil
3 eggs
3 cups unsifted all-purpose
    flour

GLAZE
1 cup dark brown sugar
¼ pound butter
½ cup heavy cream

1 teaspoon baking soda
1 teaspoon salt
3 cups finely diced apples
2 cups chopped pecans
2 teaspoons vanilla extract

Preheat oven to 325 degrees. Combine sugar and oil and beat well. Add eggs one at a time. Sift dry ingredients and stir into egg mixture. Beat in apples, nuts, and vanilla. Pour into a buttered springform tube pan and bake for 1 hour or until a toothpick inserted in the center comes out clean. Combine glaze ingredients and boil for 3 minutes. Reserving ⅓ cup, pour over the hot cake. Cool and remove from pan. Just before serving pour remaining glaze over.

CHOCOLATE BOURBON CAKE

This very rich mousse-like cake is perfect for a large crowd during the holidays. It freezes very well.

Serves 16 to 18

2 cups butter
1 cup sugar
1 cup powdered sugar
1 dozen eggs, separated
4 ounces unsweetened
    chocolate, melted
1 teaspoon vanilla extract
1 cup chopped pecans
1 dozen double ladyfingers

1 pound dry Italian
    macaroons
    (approximately 4
    dozen), broken and
    soaked in 1 cup
    Bourbon
1½ cups heavy cream,
    whipped

Cream butter and sugars until light and fluffy. Beat egg yolks until light and blend into butter mixture. Beat in chocolate, add vanilla and pecans. Beat egg whites until stiff but not dry, fold into chocolate mixture. Line a 10-inch springform pan around sides and bottom with split ladyfingers. Alternate layers of soaked macaroons and chocolate mixture over ladyfingers. Chill overnight. Remove sides of springform pan and cover top with whipped cream. If it is frozen, add whipped cream after defrosting.

CARROT CAKE WITH CREAM CHEESE FROSTING

Serves 12 to 16

2 cups unsifted all-purpose
    flour
2 cups sugar
2 teaspoons baking soda
1 teaspoon salt

FROSTING
8 ounces cream cheese,
    softened
4 tablespoons butter
2 cups powdered sugar
½ teaspoon lemon extract
1 teaspoon vanilla extract

3 teaspoons cinnamon
4 eggs
1 cup corn oil
4 cups finely grated raw
    carrots (8 or 9)

½ cup chopped pecans for
    garnish
Extra-large pecan halves for
    decoration of top of
    cake

Preheat oven to 350 degrees. Butter and flour 3 8-inch round cake pans. Thoroughly stir together flour, sugar, soda, salt, and cinnamon. Set aside. In a large mixing bowl, beat eggs until frothy, slowly beat in oil. Gradually add flour mixture, beating until smooth. Add the carrots and blend. Pour into the prepared cake pans. Bake for 30 minutes or until a toothpick inserted in the center comes out clean. Cool in pans for 10 minutes. Remove to cake racks and continue cooling. To make the frosting: Blend first 5 ingredients well, spread some frosting on each layer, also sprinkling chopped pecans over each. Assemble layers and frost top and sides. Decorate the top with pecan halves.

CHOCOLATE CHEESECAKE

Serves 12

CRUST

25 chocolate wafers, crushed
6 tablespoons butter, melted
¼ to ½ teaspoon cinnamon

FILLING,

1½ pounds cream cheese,
   softened
1 cup sugar
3 eggs
8 ounces semisweet
   chocolate, melted and
   cooled

2 teaspoons cocoa
1 teaspoon vanilla extract
2 cups sour cream

For the crust: Mix ingredients thoroughly and press into a well-buttered 10-inch springform pan. Chill. Preheat oven to 350 degrees. In a large bowl, beat cream cheese until fluffy and smooth. Add sugar and beat in eggs one at a time. Stir in chocolate, cocoa, and vanilla, beating well after each addition. Add sour cream and continue beating until very smooth and well blended. Pour into crust. Bake for 1 hour and 10 minutes. Cake may appear to be too liquid, but it will become firm when chilled. Cool to room temperature, then chill for at least 5 hours.

CHARLOTTE MALAKOFF AU CHOCOLAT

Serves 8 to 10

½ cup coffee-flavored
   liqueur
½ cup water
24 ladyfingers
1 cup sweet butter
1 cup superfine sugar
¼ teaspoon almond extract

1⅓ cups ground almonds
4 ounces semisweet
   chocolate
¼ cup coffee-flavored
   liqueur
2 cups heavy cream,
   whipped

Line a charlotte mold with wax paper. Combine the ½ cup coffee liqueur with the water in a small bowl, dip each ladyfinger in it, and line sides of the mold. In a large bowl cream together the butter and sugar until light and fluffy. Beat in almond extract and then ground almonds. Set aside. In the top of a double boiler, melt chocolate over simmering water with the ¼ cup coffee liqueur, stirring constantly. Set aside and cool slightly. Fold cooled chocolate into almond mixture, then fold in whipped cream. Pour mixture into the mold and refrigerate for 6 hours or overnight. Unmold onto a serving platter and remove wax paper.

GINGERBREAD CAKE

This cake is superb! Moist, spicy, and serves a big crowd. The applesauce gives it a marvelous flavor. Served warm, it is outstanding. Served cold, it is still outstanding.

Serves 12 to 14

1 16-ounce can applesauce	2 teaspoons powdered ginger
1 cup dark molasses	1½ teaspoons cinnamon
2 teaspoons baking soda	½ teaspoon ground cloves
3 cups all-purpose flour, sifted	4 eggs
	1⅓ cups sugar
½ teaspoon salt	⅔ cup vegetable oil

Preheat oven to 325 degrees. In a saucepan bring the applesauce to a boil. Stir in molasses, and soda. Set aside to cool. Sift flour with salt and spices, set aside. In the large bowl of an electric mixer, beat eggs until light in color. Gradually beat in sugar and continue beating until thick, then gradually beat in oil. Alternately fold in flour mixture and applesauce mixture. Pour into a greased 10-inch tube pan and bake for 1 hour and 15 minutes. Cool cake in the pan for 15 minutes, then remove to a rack to continue cooling.

CHOCOLATE POTATO CAKE
WITH FUDGE SAUCE

A rich and delectable combination. The fudge sauce is excellent over ice cream, too.

Serves 16 to 20

4 eggs, separated
2 cups sugar
1 cup butter
½ cup milk
1 cup chopped walnuts
1 cup powdered cocoa
1 cup cold mashed potatoes

½ teaspoon cinnamon
½ teaspoon allspice
2 cups unsifted all-purpose
    flour
4 teaspoons baking powder
1 teaspoon vanilla extract

FUDGE SAUCE

3 ounces unsweetened
    chocolate
1 cup brown sugar, packed
½ cup light corn syrup

4 tablespoons butter
1 cup heavy cream
1 tablespoon vanilla extract
    or rum

Preheat oven to 350 degrees. Set egg whites aside. Beat egg yolks until light and lemon-colored. Add remaining ingredients (except egg whites) in order given, blending thoroughly. Beat egg whites until stiff but not dry. Fold into batter mixture. Butter and flour a 9 by 13-inch cake pan. Pour in batter and bake for 35 to 40 minutes. Cake is done when a toothpick inserted in center comes out clean. Remove from pan and cool. To make the fudge sauce: Melt chocolate in the top of a double boiler over barely simmering water. Stir in sugar, corn syrup, and butter. Simmer, stirring occasionally, for 30 minutes. Beat in heavy cream and cook for another 10 minutes. Remove from heat and stir in vanilla extract. Allow to cool before frosting cake.

GÂTEAU GANACHE

The beauty of this delicious French meringue cake is that the chocolate hardens in the cream, and when it is served has a crunchy texture.

Serves 6

6 egg whites, room
    temperature
2 cups sugar
6 ounces ground pecans or
    walnuts

1½ teaspoons white wine
    vinegar
½ teaspoon vanilla extract

FILLING AND ICING
3 ounces semisweet
    chocolate
1 cup heavy cream

Grated semisweet chocolate
    for garnish

Preheat oven to 375 degrees. Cut 2 rounds of parchment paper to fit the bottoms of 2 8-inch cake pans. Butter and flour the parchment paper, then butter and flour the cake pans. Place a paper round in each tin. Place egg whites in a large bowl and beat until stiff. Add sugar and nuts all at once and fold in gently. Add vinegar and vanilla and spoon mixture equally into the 2 prepared cake pans. Bake meringue for 35 to 40 minutes or until crusty to the touch. Remove from the oven, run a knife around the edges, and quickly turn upside down on cake racks to cool. Remove pans and carefully peel off paper. For the filling and icing: Melt chocolate in the top of a double boiler over simmering water. Set aside to cool slightly. Whip cream until stiff. Place half of the cream in a separate bowl and add half of the chocolate. Place 1 meringue round on a serving platter and cover with this mixture. Top with second meringue and cover the top with the balance of the whipped cream. With a spatula, dip into remaining choclate and make swirls on the cream to give it a marbled effect. Grate chocolate on top for garnish. Refrigerate until ready to serve.

GRAND MARNIER CAKE

Serves 12

2 cups sugar
1 cup butter
2 eggs
2 cups all-purpose flour,
    unsifted
½ teaspoon salt
1 teaspoon baking powder

1 cup sour cream
1 teaspoon vanilla extract
1 tablespoon Grand Marnier
    or orange juice
1 cup coarsely ground
    pecans
Grated rind of 1 orange

TOPPING
4 tablespoons butter, melted
⅓ cup Grand Marnier
Powdered sugar for dusting
    top

Preheat oven to 350 degrees. Cream sugar and butter thoroughly and blend in eggs. Sift dry ingredients and add alternately with the sour cream, vanilla, and Grand Marnier or orange juice. Blend in pecans and orange rind. Pour into a tube or bundt pan that has been well buttered and floured. Bake for 60 to 65 minutes. Cool on a rack for 10 minutes. While the cake is cooling, make the topping. Melt the butter and add the Grand Marnier. Pierce the entire top of the cake and pour mixture over. Cool for 30 minutes more in the pan. Turn out onto a serving plate and cool to room temperature. Dust with powdered sugar.

ORANGE CAKE

Serves 8 to 10

2 cups sugar
½ pound butter, softened
4 eggs, separated
2 teaspoons vanilla extract
2⅔ cups all-purpose flour,
    unsifted

2½ teaspoons baking
    powder
½ teaspoon salt
1 cup milk
2 tablespoons grated orange
    rind

FILLING

1 cup sugar
1 teaspoon grated orange
    rind
6 tablespoons flour

¼ cup fresh orange juice
2 eggs, beaten
2 cups heavy cream,
    whipped

FROSTING

6 ounces cream cheese,
    softened
1 tablespoon fresh orange
    juice

2½ cups powdered sugar
2 teaspoons grated orange
    rind

Preheat oven to 350 degrees. To make the cake: Cream together the butter and sugar until smooth. Beat in egg yolks, one at a time, mixing thoroughly. Stir in vanilla. Sift flour, baking powder, and salt. Add to butter mixture, alternating with milk. Beat egg whites until stiff and fold into batter. Pour into 3 buttered and floured 9-inch cake pans and bake for 35 to 40 minutes or until toothpick inserted in the center comes out clean. When cakes are done, remove from oven and cool on racks.

To make the filling: Combine in the top of a double boiler the sugar, orange rind, and flour. Stir in orange juice and eggs. Cook, stirring constantly, over simmering water until thickened. Cool and fold into whipped cream. Spread filling between layers of cake.

To make the frosting: Combine all ingredients thoroughly and frost top and sides of cake. If desired, decorate with additional grated orange rind or small sections of fresh orange.

POUNDCAKE

Serves 8

½ pound butter
2 cups sugar
5 eggs
2 cups all-purpose flour,
    sifted
¼ teaspoon salt

¼ teaspoon baking powder
½ teaspoon mace
1 teaspoon nutmeg
1 teaspoon vanilla extract
1 tablespoon brandy

Preheat oven to 325 degrees. Cream butter and sugar until light and fluffy. Add eggs one at a time, beating well after each addition. Add remaining ingredients to butter mixture. Butter and flour a 9-inch loaf pan. Butter wax paper or parchment and line the pan. Pour batter into the pan and bake for 1½ hours or until a toothpick inserted in the center comes out clean.

BRAZO DE GITANO

This chocolate cake-rum roll is a Spanish treasure.

Serves 8

5 eggs, separated
¼ cup sugar
¼ cup all-purpose flour
¼ cup cocoa
1 teaspoon vanilla extract

4 tablespoons powdered
   sugar, sifted
1 cup heavy cream, whipped
1¼ teaspoons rum extract
1 tablespoon superfine sugar

Preheat oven to 350 degrees. Beat egg yolks and ¼ cup sugar until thick and smooth. Stir in flour, cocoa, and vanilla, blend well. Whip egg whites until stiff but not dry. Fold into yolk and flour mixture. Butter an 8 by 15-inch baking pan. Line with baking parchment paper or wax paper, butter well again, and dust lightly with 2 tablespoons of the powdered sugar. Pour batter into the pan and spread out evenly. Bake for 15 minutes. Cool for 5 minutes, then turn onto a cloth to cool. After 10 minutes peel paper off. Combine whipped cream, rum, and sugar, adjust to taste. Spread over cake and roll cake like a jelly roll, starting with long edge. Sprinkle with remaining powdered sugar. Serve in slices.

RICH CHOCOLATE CAKE

Sinfully rich, and it looks really beautiful. The chocolate must be of the best quality, therefore the recipe can be expensive but so worth it. It is addictive for any chocolate lover.

Serves 8

5 tablespoons sweet butter
1 pound dark sweet
    chocolate
4 eggs
1 tablespoon sugar
1 tablespoon flour
2 cups heavy cream

1 tablespoon powdered sugar
1 teaspoon vanilla extract
Chocolate curls for garnish
Puréed raspberries or
    strawberries, fresh or
    frozen and strained

Preheat oven to 425 degrees. Butter and flour an 8-inch cake pan. Cut a round of parchment to fit the bottom and butter and flour the paper. In the top of a double boiler, melt together the butter and chocolate over barely simmering water, stirring constantly until chocolate is shiny and smooth. Set aside. In another double boiler, place the eggs and 1 table-spoon sugar, heat, constantly stirring with a whisk over simmering water, until sugar is dissolved and mixture is barely warm. Remove from heat and beat at highest speed of an electric mixer for 8 minutes. Carefully fold in flour, then very gently but thoroughly fold in choco-late mixture. Pour into the cake pan and bake for 15 minutes. Remove from oven to cool, then place in the freezer (still in the pan) for 8 hours or more.

On the day to be served, remove cake from the freezer, let rest about 20 minutes, then remove from pan and place on serving plate. Whip cream with powdered sugar and vanilla until stiff. Pile ¾ of the whipped cream in center of cake in a mound. Decorate with chocolate curls, then pipe remaining cream around the edge. Refrigerate until serving. Pass raspberry or strawberry purée separately.

SOUR CREAM CHOCOLATE CAKE

This is a rich chocolate cake that freezes beautifully and looks as good as it tastes.

Serves 8 to 10

2 cups all-purpose flour,
    unsifted
2 cups sugar
1 cup water
¾ cup sour cream
¼ cup butter
1¼ teaspoons baking soda

1 teaspoon salt
1 teaspoon vanilla extract
½ teaspoon baking powder
2 eggs
4 ounces unsweetened
    baking chocolate,
    melted

FROSTING
½ cup butter
4 ounces unsweetened
    baking chocolate

4 cups powdered sugar
1 cup sour cream
2 teaspoons vanilla extract

Preheat oven to 350 degrees. Measure all ingredients into a large bowl and beat for ½ minute at low speed, scraping the sides of the bowl constantly. Then beat for 3 minutes at highest speed. Pour into greased and floured cake pans: 2 9-inch pans or 3 8-inch pans. Bake for 20 to 25 minutes. Remove from the oven and cool on a rack. For the frosting: In the top of a double boiler, melt butter and chocolate over barely simmering water. Remove from heat and cool. Add powdered sugar, then blend in sour cream and vanilla, beat until smooth.

SWEDISH TEA CAKE

Serves 6 to 8

1¼ cups sugar
¼ pound plus 4 tablespoons
    butter
½ teaspoon vanilla extract
1¼ cups all-purpose flour,
    unsifted

2 teaspoons baking powder
½ cup light cream
5 egg whites, beaten stiff but
    not dry
Fine bread crumbs
Powdered sugar

Preheat oven to 350 degrees. Cream sugar, butter, and vanilla until smooth. Blend in flour and baking powder, mix well, and stir in cream. Fold egg whites gently into batter and pour into a 9-inch springform pan that has been buttered and lightly sprinkled with bread crumbs. Bake for 45 minutes. Sprinkle with powdered sugar and serve warm.

9-INCH PIECRUST

This recipe will make one 9-inch piecrust. For a two-crust pie double this recipe.

1 cup unsifted all-purpose
    flour
¼ teaspoon salt
4 tablespoons cold butter

2 tablespoons vegetable
    shortening
4 tablespoons cold water, or
    as needed

Sift flour and salt into a bowl. Add butter and shortening a little at a time, blending with a pastry blender until mixture has the texture of oatmeal. Add water, a tablespoon at a time, and mix gently until mixture begins to form a ball. Continue adding water just until dough comes away from the sides of the bowl. Wrap in wax paper and refrigerate until thoroughly chilled. Place dough on a lightly floured board. Starting from the center, roll the dough into a 12-inch circle. A small amount of flour may be sprinkled on the dough if the rolling pin starts to stick. Fold the circle of dough in half and lift it into a 9-inch pie pan. Unfold the dough and press it firmly into place so that no air is trapped underneath. Trim off any excess and flute the edge if you wish (using your thumb and forefinger, pinch the dough to give it a zigzag or "fluted" appearance). Special note: Some quiches and single-crust fruit pies require high fluted sides. To make this type of edge, do not trim off excess but instead build the dough up to about ½ inch above the rim of the pie pan before fluting. For a partially cooked crust (for quiches), prick the bottom of dough with a fork to keep it from rising and bake at 400 degrees for 10 to 12 minutes. For a fully cooked crust, bake an additional 8 to 10 minutes.

10-INCH PIECRUST

This recipe will make one 10-inch piecrust. For a two-crust pie double this recipe.

1⅓ cups unsifted all-purpose flour	3 tablespoons vegetable shortening
½ teaspoon salt	6 tablespoons cold water, or as needed
5 tablespoons cold butter	

Sift the flour and salt into a bowl. Add the butter and shortening a little at a time, blending with a pastry blender until the mixture has the texture of oatmeal. Add water, a tablespoon at a time, and mix gently until mixture begins to form a ball. Continue adding water just until dough comes away from the sides of the bowl. Wrap in wax paper and refrigerate until thoroughly chilled. Place dough on a lightly floured board. Starting from the center, roll the dough into a 13-inch circle. A small amount of flour may be sprinkled on the dough if the rolling pin starts to stick. Fold the circle of dough in half and lift it into a 10-inch pie pan. Unfold the dough and press it firmly into place so that no air is trapped underneath. Trim off any excess and flute the edge if you wish (see 9-inch Piecrust for fluting, special instructions and baking).

CAROB AND HONEY CREAM PIE

Carob powder is available in health food stores and is a substitute for chocolate.

Serves 6 to 8

1 pound cream cheese, softened	3 tablespoons carob powder
¼ cup honey	1 9-inch pie shell, prebaked (see Index)
½ cup heavy cream	1 cup pecan halves
2 tablespoons vanilla extract	

Blend thoroughly the cream cheese, honey, cream, and vanilla. Divide into 2 portions and add carob powder to 1 portion. Spread the carob portion on the bottom of the baked pie shell and cover with the other portion of cream cheese mixture. Decorate with pecans and refrigerate for at least 8 hours or overnight.

COFFEE TOFFEE PIE

Serves 10

PASTRY

1½ cups all-purpose flour, unsifted

6 tablespoons butter

¼ cup brown sugar, firmly packed

¾ cup finely chopped pecans

1-ounce square unsweetened chocolate, grated

1 teaspoon vanilla extract

1 tablespoon water

FILLING

¾ cup butter, softened

1 cup sugar

1½ ounces unsweetened chocolate, melted

1 tablespoon instant coffee

3 eggs

COFFEE TOPPING

2 cups heavy cream

½ cup powdered sugar

2 tablespoons instant coffee

2 tablespoons coffee liqueur

Chocolate curls for garnish

Preheat oven to 350 degrees. For the pastry: Combine all ingredients and blend well. Butter a 10-inch pie plate and turn mixture into the plate, pressing into the bottom and sides with the back of a spoon. Bake for 15 minutes. Cool.

For the filling: Beat butter until creamy. Gradually add sugar, beating until light and lemon-colored. Melt chocolate over hot water, cool slightly, and add to butter mixture. Then stir in instant coffee. Add eggs one at a time, beating well after each addition. Pour filling into the cooled pie shell and refrigerate, covered, overnight.

For the topping: Beat cream until stiff, then add powdered sugar, coffee, and liqueur. Spread over filling and garnish with chocolate curls. Refrigerate for at least 2 hours before serving.

SOUR CREAM PEACH PIE

Serves 6 to 8

1 9-inch graham cracker crust (per directions on cracker package)

FILLING

2 tablespoons flour
½ cup sugar
¾ teaspoon cinnamon
⅛ teaspoon salt
1 egg, lightly beaten

½ teaspoon vanilla extract
1 cup sour cream
6 medium-size ripe peaches,
    peeled and sliced

TOPPING

⅓ cup sugar
⅓ cup flour
¾ teaspoons cinnamon

4 tablespoons butter,
    softened

Preheat oven to 400 degrees. Combine flour, sugar, cinnamon, salt, egg, vanilla, and sour cream. Fold in peaches to coat well, pour into prepared graham cracker crust. Bake for 15 minutes, reduce heat to 350, and bake for an additional 30 minutes. Combine topping ingredients and crumble over warm pie. Bake for an additional 10 minutes at 400.

EGGNOG PIE

Wonderful Christmas dessert.

1 9-inch pre-baked piecrust
    (see Index)

Serves 8

FILLING

1 teaspoon unflavored gelatin
1 tablespoon water
1 cup milk
2 tablespoons cornstarch
¼ cup cold water
½ cup sugar
¼ teaspoon salt

3 egg yolks, beaten
1 tablespoon butter
1 teaspoon vanilla extract
1 tablespoon dark rum,
    brandy, or Bourbon
1 cup heavy cream
Nutmeg for garnish

Soften gelatin in 1 tablespoon cold water. Set aside. Scald milk in the top of a double boiler over simmering water. Dissolve cornstarch in ¼ cup cold water and stir into scalded milk. Then add sugar, salt, and beaten egg yolks. Cook, stirring constantly, until sugar has completely dissolved, about 15 minutes. Add softened gelatin and stir until gelatin has been dissolved. Add butter, vanilla, and liquor, then cool. Beat heavy cream until stiff. Fold into filling and pour into cooled pie shell. Garnish with freshly grated nutmeg and refrigerate until serving.

LEMON CURD TARTS

The lemon curd filling keeps beautifully for weeks in a covered jar in the refrigerator for any elegant last-minute dessert. It is a great cake filling, delicious on poundcake, muffins, waffles—almost anything.

Makes approximately 20

PASTRY

2 cups flour   ½ cup cold butter
½ teaspoon salt   5 tablespoons cold water

LEMON FILLING

½ cup butter   1½ cups sugar
½ cup fresh lemon juice   5 eggs, beaten
3 teaspoons freshly grated
    lemon rind

Preheat oven to 425 degrees. To make the pastry: Combine flour and salt in a bowl. Cut in butter with a pastry blender until pieces are the size of small peas. Sprinkle the water gradually over flour mixture, stirring with a fork and drawing flour into a ball. Add just enough water to hold the mixture together and pull away from the sides of the bowl. Pat into a ball and turn out onto a lightly floured board. Roll into a circle and cut shapes to fit small tart pans or muffin tins. Prick each shell with a fork and bake for 12 minutes. Cool.

For the filling: Melt butter in a saucepan, add lemon juice, rind, and sugar. Cook, stirring, until sugar is dissolved. Add eggs and cook, stirring constantly, until thick, about 20 minutes. Cool. Fill tart shells and refrigerate until serving time.

STRAWBERRY TART

*The almond crust and garnish are a perfect complement to fresh straw-
berries. Serve cold after a spring or summer dinner.*

Serves 6

ALMOND PÂTE BRISÉE
1½ cups all-purpose flour,   1 tablespoon sugar
    unsifted   ½ cup butter
1 cup ground almonds   4 tablespoons ice water
Pinch of salt

FILLING
1 pint strawberries   1 tablespoon fresh lemon
6 tablespoons butter   juice
⅔ cup sugar   Grated rind of 1 orange
2 tablespoons cornstarch   ¼ cup Grand Marnier
3 eggs   ¼ cup slivered almonds
⅓ cup heavy cream   Powdered sugar for garnish

Preheat oven to 425 degrees. For the almond *pâte brisée:* Place flour, almonds, salt, and sugar in a mixing bowl. Using a pastry blender or 2
knives, cut butter in dry ingredients until large lumps have disappeared.
Sprinkle the cold water, stirring with a fork until dough forms a ball.
Knead with the heel of your hand for a few minutes until butter is well
blended. (The *pâte brisée* may be completely made in a food processor.
Grind the almonds first, then add the flour, salt, sugar, and butter. Then
add ice water until a ball forms. Continue as directed.) Refrigerate.
Roll out on floured board and place in a 10-inch tart pan. Place foil over
pastry, fill with beans or rice, and bake at 425 degrees for 12 minutes.
Carefully remove foil with rice or beans and cool.

    For the filling: Quickly wash berries, dry in paper towels, and set
aside. Cream together butter and sugar, then add cornstarch. Beat in
eggs, one at a time, then add cream. Stir in lemon juice, orange rind, and
Grand Marnier. Place strawberries, whole or sliced, in the tart shell.
Cover with filling and sprinkle the sliced almonds. Bake at 350 degrees
for 30 to 35 minutes. Serve chilled. Sprinkle with powdered sugar.

BLUEBERRY TART

Serves 6 to 8

PÂTE BRISÉE

1½ cups unsifted all-purpose flour

3 tablespoons vegetable shortening, cold

½ cup butter, chilled

⅛ teaspoon salt

2 tablespoons sugar

⅓ cup cold water

BLUEBERRY FILLING

2 cups blueberries

3 tablespoons sugar

2 tablespoons orange-flavored liqueur

1 tablespoon butter

6 tablespoons butter, softened

½ cup sugar

2 tablespoons cornstarch

3 eggs

¼ cup heavy cream

Grated rind of 1 lemon

Juice of 1 lemon

4 tablespoons powdered sugar

Preheat oven to 350 degrees. To make the *pâte brisée:* Place the flour, shortening, butter, salt, and sugar in a small bowl. Blend with a pastry blender until mixture has the consistency of oatmeal. Gradually add the cold water and stir until mixture forms a ball. Knead quickly a few times on a lightly floured board, form into a ball, wrap in wax paper and refrigerate until chilled.

For the blueberry filling: In a small saucepan, heat the blueberries, sugar, orange-flavored liqueur, and 1 tablespoon butter until berries are slightly caramelized. Set aside. Beat the remaining butter and ½ cup sugar in a mixing bowl until light and fluffy. Beat in cornstarch, eggs, and cream. Stir in lemon rind and juice, then fold in berry mixture. Roll out chilled pastry on a floured board and line a tart pan. Partially bake pastry for 10 to 12 minutes. Fill with berry mixture, sprinkle with powdered sugar, and bake for 30 to 35 minutes.

APPLE TART

Serves 6 to 8

PASTRY

1¾ cups all-purpose flour,
    unsifted
½ cup cold butter, cut into
    8 pieces

½ cup ground almonds
¼ cup powdered sugar
¼ cup cold water

FILLING

5 large tart green apples
½ cup sugar
1¼ teaspoons cinnamon

2 tablespoons flour
3 tablespoons fresh lemon
    juice

Preheat oven to 400 degrees. To make the pastry: Place all ingredients except the cold water in a food processor and blend to a fine meal. Or place ingredients in a bowl and cut in butter with a pastry blender until mixture has the consistency of fine meal. Add the water, a few drops at a time, until the dough forms into a ball. Place the dough in wax paper and chill.

For the filling: Peel, core, and thinly slice apples in a bowl. Sprinkle with sugar, cinnamon, flour, and lemon juice, gently mix until thoroughly coated. Remove ⅓ of the pastry and set aside. Roll out remaining dough and line a tart pan. Add filling, roll out reserved pastry to form lattice or pastry cutouts, place on top of filling. Bake for 30 to 40 minutes or until apples are barely tender and pastry is golden.

BRIE QUICHE

Brie quiche is an elegant dessert with fresh fruit. Ripe pears and crisp apples are perfect.

Serves 6 to 8

1 9-inch piecrust (see Index)
4 eggs, separated
1½ cups light cream

1 pound Brie cheese, broken
    into small pieces
⅛ teaspoon salt

Preheat oven to 375 degrees. Line a 9-inch quiche pan or pie pan with pastry. Bake for 10 minutes. Cool and set aside. Beat egg yolks and cream, thoroughly blend in cheese and salt. Beat egg whites until stiff but not dry. Stir in 3 tablespoons of the egg whites and blend to lighten the mixture. Fold in the remaining whites. Pour into the cooled crust and bake at 350 degrees for 30 minutes or until the custard is set. Allow to cool slightly before cutting.

CHERRY TORTE

Serves 6 to 8

TORTE SHELL

3 egg whites, room
    temperature
⅛ teaspoon salt
1 cup sugar
1 teaspoon vanilla extract

¾ cup chopped walnuts
½ cup saltine cracker
    crumbs
1 teaspoon baking powder

FILLING

1 1-pound can pitted red
    cherries
¼ cup sugar

⅛ teaspoon salt
4 teaspoons cornstarch
1 cup heavy cream, whipped

Preheat oven to 300 degrees. To make the shell: Beat egg whites and salt together until foamy, gradually add sugar a tablespoon at a time. Beat until stiff peaks form and the mixture looks glossy. Add vanilla. In a separate bowl combine nuts, cracker crumbs, and baking powder. Fold into egg whites. Spread mixture in a well-buttered 9-inch pie pan, making a well in the center and building up the sides. Bake for 40 minutes. Remove from the oven and cool.

For the filling: Drain the cherries, reserving the juice. Combine juice, sugar, salt, and cornstarch, mixing well. Cook, stirring constantly, until mixture boils and is clear and thickened. Cool, then add drained cherries. To assemble, spread half of the whipped cream over the torte. Spoon cherry mixture over top, then garnish with remaining whipped cream. Chill for several hours before serving.

CHESTNUT TORTE

A lovely, rich holiday dessert. It freezes well.

Serves 8 to 10

6 egg yolks at room
  temperature
1½ cups sugar
1 tablespoon vanilla extract
1 15½-ounce can
  unsweetened chestnut
  purée

1 cup ground blanched
  almonds
7 egg whites at room
  temperature

MOCHA BUTTER CREAM FROSTING

1 cup sugar
⅓ cup water
¼ teaspoon cream of tartar
4 egg yolks
5 ounces semisweet
  chocolate

¼ cup strong coffee
1½ cups sweet butter,
  softened
3 tablespoons brandy or dark
  rum

GARNISH
Chocolate sprinkles
Toasted slivered almonds

Preheat oven to 350 degrees. Beat egg yolks with sugar until thick and pale. Beat in vanilla. Add chestnut purée and ground almonds, mix well. Beat egg whites until stiff but not dry, fold into egg yolk mixture. Butter and flour 2 8-inch cake pans, then butter and flour 2 baking parchment rounds for the bottoms. Pour mixture into the cake pans and bake for 1 hour. Remove from the oven and cool in the pans, then turn gently onto cake racks.

For the mocha butter cream frosting: In an enamel saucepan boil sugar, ⅓ cup water, and cream of tartar to soft ball stage, or 235° on a candy thermometer. Beat egg yolks until pale and thick. Slowly beat hot sugar mixture into egg yolks and continue beating until thick. In the top of a double boiler, melt the chocolate with the coffee over medium heat. Add chocolate to eggs, then beat in butter a little at a time until mixure is thick and smooth. Add rum and chill until thick enough to spread, about 30 minutes. Frost torte layers generously, then frost sides and top, and garnish with chocolate sprinkles or toasted slivered almonds.

ITALIAN MERINGUE TORTE

Elegant, lovely, delicious, worth the trouble. Keeps well when made the day before.

Serves 8 to 10

TORTE

4 egg whites at room
temperature
½ teaspoon cream of tartar

1 cup sugar
1 teaspoon vanilla extract

FILLING

1 teaspoon instant coffee
4 tablespoons coffee-flavored
liqueur
2 cups heavy cream,
whipped

10 ounces milk chocolate
bar, coarsely chopped

Preheat oven to 250 degrees. For the torte: In a large mixing bowl, beat the egg whites with the cream of tartar until frothy. Continue beating, adding sugar 1 tablespoon every minute, until all sugar is incorporated. Add vanilla, beat for another 2 minutes until the egg whites hold very stiff peaks. Butter and flour 2 baking sheets, tracing an 8-inch circle on each. Spoon the meringue evenly onto the circles, using a spatula to make decorative swirls and puffs on top of one of the circles. Bake meringues for 1½ hours. Color should be pure white to faint amber. Turn off heat and leave meringues in closed oven for another 3 to 4 hours to continue drying. Remove from oven and flex pans to pop meringues free of bottom of pan. Leave in pans until meringues are at room temperature.

For the filling: Blend together the instant coffee and coffee liqueur. Add to the whipped cream, then fold in the coarsley chopped chocolate. To assemble: Place the plain meringue disk on a serving platter. Spread filling evenly over meringue. Place decorative meringue on top and refrigerate for 8 hours or overnight.

CARAMEL WALNUT TORTE

Serves 10 to 12

PASTRY

3⅓ cups sifted all-purpose
    flour
¼ cup sugar
⅛ teaspoon salt
½ pound plus 2 tablespoons
    butter, cut in small
    pieces

2 egg yolks
6 tablespoons cold water, or
    as needed

BATTER

1½ cups sugar
½ cup water
3½ cups chopped walnuts
¼ pound plus 6 tablespoons
    butter, softened

½ cup light cream
½ cup milk
2 tablespoons dark rum
⅓ cup honey

ICING

6 ounces semisweet
    chocolate
4 tablespoons butter

Pinch of salt
¾ tablespoon vegetable oil
Walnut halves

Preheat oven to 425 degrees. Butter a round baking sheet and a flan ring. Place the flan ring on the sheet and set aside.

To make the pastry: Combine flour, sugar, and salt. Cut in butter until mixture is consistency of oatmeal. Beat egg yolks with the water and quickly stir into flour mixture. Handling as little as possible, form into a ball, wrap in wax paper, and refrigerate for 20 to 30 minutes. On a lightly floured surface, roll ⅔ of the dough into a 12½-inch circle, and fit into flan ring, leaving an overhang of ¼ inch. Chill for 30 minutes.

To prepare the batter: Combine sugar and the water in a large saucepan, bring to a boil, and, shaking pan often, boil over high heat until mixture becomes a light caramel color. Remove from heat and add walnuts, butter, cream, milk, and rum. Bring to a simmer, stirring constantly, and simmer 15 minutes. Stir in honey and cool slightly. On a lightly floured board, roll remaining dough into an 11¼-inch circle.

Pour batter into the prepared flan ring on the baking sheet and brush overhang with water. With a rolling pin, place the 11¼-inch circle of dough on top of filling and press overhang of bottom shell over to close. Cut a slit in center and bake for 20 minutes or until browned. Let cool for at least 4 hours and invert onto a serving dish.

To make the icing: Melt chocolate and add butter, salt, and vegetable oil. Stir until butter is melted and mixture is smooth. Spread on top and sides of torte and decorate with walnut halves.

FROZEN LEMON TORTE

Serves 12 to 15

3 cups crushed lemon nut
   crunch cookies
1 tablespoon butter
1 cup sugar
6 eggs, separated
8 tablespoons fresh lemon
   juice

¼ teaspoon lemon extract
Grated rind of 4 lemons
2 cups heavy cream,
   whipped
4 tablespoons sugar

Reserve ½ cup of the crushed lemon cookies and spread the rest evenly over the bottom of a buttered 8 by 12-inch Pyrex baking pan. Set aside. Beat the sugar and egg yolks, add the lemon juice, lemon extract, and rind. Cook this mixture in the top of a double boiler over hot but not boiling water until thick, stirring continuously. Cool, remove to a large bowl, and fold in the whipped cream. Beat the egg whites until stiff, add the sugar, and fold into the lemon mixture. Pour evenly over the crust and sprinkle with the remaining lemon cookies. Freeze for 6 to 8 hours or overnight. Remove from the freezer 5 to 10 minutes before serving. Cut into squares.

PUMPKIN DATE TORTE

Different and tasty to serve as a fall dessert—not a bread, not a pudding, but a delicious torte.

Serves 6 to 8

½ cup chopped dates
½ cup chopped walnuts
2 tablespoons all-purpose
    flour
¼ cup butter or margarine
1 cup firmly packed brown
    sugar
⅔ cup pumpkin
1 teaspoon vanilla extract

2 eggs
½ cup all-purpose flour
½ teaspoon baking powder
½ teaspoon cinnamon
½ teaspoon nutmeg
¼ teaspoon powdered
    ginger
¼ teaspoon baking soda
1 cup heavy cream, whipped

Preheat oven to 350 degrees. Combine dates, nuts, and 2 tablespoons flour, set aside. Melt butter over low heat and blend in brown sugar until it is melted. Remove from heat and stir in pumpkin and vanilla. One at a time, beat in eggs. Sift dry ingredients and blend into pumpkin mixture. Stir in floured dates and nuts and turn into a buttered 9-inch cake pan. Bake for 20 to 25 minutes or until a toothpick inserted in the center comes out clean. Serve warm with the topping of whipped cream.

SWISS NUT TORTE

This easy dessert is good warm or cold and is not too sweet—after any meal.

Serves 8

BOTTOM LAYER
1 cup all-purpose flour,
    unsifted
⅛ teaspoon salt

¾ teaspoon sugar
½ cup butter

TOP LAYER

½ cup flaked unsweetened
   coconut
3 tablespoons flour
1 teaspoon baking powder
½ teaspoon salt

1¼ cups brown sugar,
   firmly packed
1 cup chopped walnuts
1 teaspoon vanilla extract
2 eggs, lightly beaten

FROSTING

1¼ cups powdered sugar,
   sifted
½ cup butter

2 tablespoons heavy cream
½ teaspoon almond extract

Preheat oven to 375 degrees. For the bottom layer: Combine flour, salt, and sugar in a mixing bowl. Cut in butter with a pastry blender until the consistency of oatmeal. Press into the bottom of a well-buttered 8-inch springform pan. For the top layer: Combine coconut, flour, baking powder, salt, and sugar. Add walnuts, vanilla, and eggs, blending well. Place on bottom layer in springform pan and bake for 35 minutes. Cool. For the frosting: Cream all ingredients until well blended and spread over cooled torte.

APRICOT DACQUOISE

This French cake is rarely seen in American cookbooks. It is simply layers of meringue with filling in between, but it is lighter and more elegant than flour-based cakes.

Serves 8

4 egg whites
1 cup sugar
Pinch of cream of tartar
3 ounces almonds, ground
4 ounces dried apricots
⅔ cup water

Strip of lemon rind, ½ inch
   by 1 inch
Juice of ½ lemon
1 cup heavy cream
Grated semisweet chocolate

Preheat oven to 275 degrees. Beat egg whites until stiff. Add 1 table-spoon of sugar and the cream of tartar and continue to beat for another minute. Fold in remaining sugar and ground almonds all at once. Divide mixture onto 2 baking sheets lined with baking parchment, and form into 8-inch circles. Bake for 1 hour. Remove from the oven and peel paper away. Set aside to cool. Simmer apricots in ⅔ cup water with lemon rind and juice for 20 minutes. Purée in a blender and set aside to cool. To assemble, place a round of meringue on a cake plate. Whip heavy cream until stiff and spread half of cream on first meringue. With a spatula, swirl half of apricot purée through whipped cream to give a marbled effect. Top with second meringue, cream, and remaining apricot purée. Sprinkle top with grated chocolate. Refrigerate until firm.

PAVLOVA

A delicious Australian dessert.

Serves 6 to 8

4 egg whites at room
   temperature
1 cup sugar

1 teaspoon white vinegar
1 teaspoon vanilla extract
½ tablespoon cornstarch

FILLING
Heavy cream, whipped,
   or ice cream
Fresh fruit in season

Preheat oven to 250 degrees. Beat egg whites until they begin to hold their shape. Gradually add sugar, beating constantly, until egg whites are thick and glossy. Fold in vinegar, vanilla, and cornstarch. Mound meringue on a cookie sheet in a circle, indenting with the back of a spoon, making it bowl-shaped. Bake for 1½ hours at 250 degrees, turn off oven, and allow meringue to dry out in cooling oven. Place meringue on a serving plate and fill with whipped cream or ice cream. Top with fresh fruit in season.

STRAWBERRY SHORTCAKE

Serves 8 to 10

¼ pound butter
1 cup sugar
3 eggs
1½ cups all-purpose flour,
　　unsifted

2 teaspoons baking powder
¾ cup milk

TOPPING
¾ cup butter
1 cup sugar
3 cups strawberries, mashed
　　(reserve some for
　　garnish)

1 cup heavy cream, whipped
½ teaspoon vanilla extract

Preheat oven to 350 degrees. Cream together the butter and sugar. Add eggs, one at a time, beating well after each addition. Mix flour and baking powder. Add to butter and sugar mixture alternately with milk. Pour batter into a buttered 9 by 9-inch baking pan and bake for 25 to 30 minutes or until a toothpick inserted in the center comes out clean. For the topping: In a small saucepan, melt butter and sugar together, stirring until sugar is dissolved. Add mashed strawberries and cool or refrigerate. To assemble: Pour chilled topping mixture over hot cake. Top with whipped cream, whipped with vanilla, and garnish with reserved strawberries.

PEACH COBBLER

Serves 6 to 8

3 cups sliced fresh peaches
½ cup sugar
¼ teaspoon mace
6 tablespoons butter
¾ cup sugar

1 cup all-purpose flour,
　　unsifted
1 teaspoon baking powder
1 cup milk

Preheat oven to 350 degrees. In a bowl, gently toss peach slices with
sugar and mace and set aside. In the meantime, melt butter in an
ovenproof rectangular baking dish. In a separate bowl, combine the
sugar, flour, and baking powder, stir in the milk. Pour this mixture into
the baking dish on top of the butter, then add the peaches. Bake for 1
hour. Serve warm with vanilla ice cream.

FROZEN YOGURT

Serves 6 to 8

1½ teaspoons unflavored
    gelatin (½ package)
¼ cup orange-flavored
    liqueur
1 cup fresh orange juice,
    strained

3 eggs
1 tablespoon grated orange
    rind
¾ cup sugar
1½ cups plain yogurt
1 cup heavy cream, whipped

Sprinkle gelatin over orange liqueur. Stir over low heat until dissolved.
Combine orange juice, eggs, orange rind, sugar, and yogurt in a
blender or food processor. Blend until smooth. Add dissolved gelatin
and liqueur. Chill until mixture begins to thicken. Fold in whipped
cream and put in individual serving bowls. Freeze until firm. Remove
from freezer 5 minutes before serving.

PAPAYA SHERBET

Serves 6

2 papayas
½ cup orange juice
1 tablespoon orange liqueur

½ cup sugar
½ teaspoon fresh lemon
    juice

Remove the seeds and skins from the papayas and dice them. Combine all ingredients in a food processor or mixing bowl and mix well until very smooth. Pour into a refrigerator tray or shallow pan and freeze until sherbet has the consistency of mush. Remove from freezer and stir vigorously. Refreeze until mushy again, repeat stirring. Return to freezer until ready to serve.

CHOCOLATE RUM ICE CREAM

This luscious dessert has the texture of something between an ice cream and a frozen mousse. It is the perfect finale to a grand dinner.

Serves 6

¼ cup sugar
⅓ cup water
2 tablespoons instant coffee
1 6-ounce package semisweet
    chocolate bits
3 eggs yolks

2 ounces dark rum
1½ cups heavy cream,
    whipped
½ cup slivered almonds,
    toasted

In a small saucepan, place the sugar, water, and coffee. Stirring constantly, bring to a boil and cook for 1 minute. Place the chocolate bits in a blender or food processor, and with the motor running pour the hot syrup over and blend until smooth. Beat in egg yolks and rum and cool slightly. Fold chocolate mixture into whipped cream, then pour into individual serving dishes or a bombe dish. Sprinkle with toasted almonds. Freeze. To serve, remove from the freezer at least 5 minutes before serving.

FRIED CREAM

Fried cream is a dessert with a long tradition in San Francisco. It is delicious, spectacular, and up to the final frying stage it can—in fact must—all be done in advance. It is worth the last-minute effort for the impressive results.

Serves 6 to 8

3 egg yolks
¼ cup sugar
1 tablespoon dark rum
Pinch of salt
5 tablespoons cornstarch
3 tablespoons milk
2 cups heavy cream, scalded
    and cooled

½ inch cinnamon stick
1 cup ground almonds
1 egg, beaten
1 cup zwieback crumbs
Oil for deep frying
¼ cup dark rum

Beat together the egg yolks, sugar, 1 tablespoon rum, and salt until lightly thickened. Mix cornstarch and milk into a smooth paste and add to egg yolk mixture. Stirring constantly, gradually add cream and cinnamon stick. Cook in the top of a double boiler over boiling water, stirring constantly, until thick and smooth. Remove cinnamon stick and pour cream mixture into a buttered shallow 9 by 12-inch pan to a depth of ¾ inch. Chill thoroughly. Cut cream into diamond shapes and roll in ground almonds. Dip pieces in beaten egg then roll in zwieback crumbs. Chill once more. Heat oil to a deep-fry stage and fry cream until lightly browned, then drain on paper towels and arrange on a heated serving platter. Heat rum in a small saucepan, ignite, and pour over cream. Serve immediately.

CRÈME BRÛLÉE

Serves 12

1 quart heavy cream
2 cups milk
Pinch of salt
½ cup sugar

12 egg yolks, beaten
1 tablespoon vanilla extract
¾ cup brown sugar

Preheat oven to 350 degrees. In the top of a double boiler, combine cream, milk, sugar, and salt. Heat over boiling water until sugar is dissolved. Pour cream mixture into beaten egg yolks, mix well, and add vanilla. Pour into a 9 by 12-inch baking dish. Bake in a large pan containing boiling water to a depth of 1 inch for 45 minutes. Remove from oven and chill. Several hours before serving, cover top of custard with brown sugar forced through a sieve, until sugar glaze is about ¼ inch thick all over. Place under the broiler, watching carefully, until sugar is melted, being sure not to burn. Chill once more before serving.

ENGLISH TRIFLE

This is excellent and beautiful to serve. Great after a simple boiled English dinner.

Serves 8

1 12- to 14-ounce poundcake
Raspberry jam
½ cup medium dry sherry
¼ cup brandy
5 egg yolks
6 tablespoons sugar
1 teaspoon cornstarch
Pinch of salt

2 cups milk
2 teaspoons vanilla extract
1 pint fresh raspberries
2 fresh peaches, peeled and
    thinly sliced
1½ cups heavy cream
1 tablespoon powdered sugar

Trim poundcake and cut into 1-inch slices. Completely coat each slice with raspberry jam and line the bottom of a crystal serving bowl with slices. Cut remaining slices into 1-inch cubes and place one layer only on top of slices in the bowl. Pour sherry and brandy over, cover lightly, and let stand at room temperature for 1 hour. With a wire whisk, mix yolks, sugar, cornstarch, and salt. Heat milk, stirring, until almost boiling. Very slowly, pour milk into egg mixture. Transfer to a heavy saucepan and cook over medium heat, stirring constantly, until custard coats spoon. Remove from heat, stir, and add vanilla. Blend well and let cool. Reserving 10 to 12 firm raspberries, arrange berries and peach slices on cake. Pour cooled custard over. Whip the cream until thick and gradually whip in the powdered sugar; whip until firm. Reserve ½ cup of the whipped cream for garnish and spread remainder on top of custard. Decorate with reserved berries and rosettes of whipped cream.

BLACKBERRY-APPLE CREPES

Makes 12 crepes

CREPE BATTER

¾ cup all-purpose flour,
  unsifted
1 cup milk
2 eggs
Grated rind of 1 lemon

Grated rind of 1 orange
6 teaspoons butter, melted
1 ounce brandy
Softened butter, for pan

BLACKBERRY-APPLE FILLING

3 tablespoons butter
1½ cups peeled and diced
  green apples
2 cups blackberries

½ cup sugar
½ cup white wine
1½ teaspoons cornstarch

WHIPPED CREAM TOPPING

1 pint heavy cream
Juice of ½ lemon
1 teaspoon vanilla extract

3 tablespoons powdered
  sugar

Preheat oven to 350 degrees. To make the crepes: Place the flour in a large mixing bowl and slowly add the milk, stirring with a wire whisk until combined. Beat in the eggs. Add lemon and orange rinds, melted butter and brandy. Heat a 6-inch crepe pan and brush lightly with softened butter. Ladle in about 2 tablespoons of batter and quickly tilt pan to spread batter evenly; pour out any excess. Cook until lightly browned, about 1 minute, then turn and cook until browned on the other side. Repeat until 12 crepes have been made. Keep them warm while making filling and topping.

For the filling: Sauté apples in butter until soft, add berries and sugar, and bring to a boil. Mix white wine and cornstarch and add to apple mixture. Boil gently for a few minutes to thicken. Set aside to cool.

For the whipped cream topping: Whip cream until almost stiff. Add lemon juice, vanilla, and powdered sugar. Blend gently.

To assemble: Fill each crepe with 3 to 4 tablespoons of filling, roll up, place crepes in a buttered casserole dish, and heat in oven for 15 minutes, or until hot. Garnish with whipped cream topping, or pass topping separately in a bowl.

MARINATED FIGS

Serves 6 to 8

2 cups brown sugar
1 cup water
1 lemon, thinly sliced
1 cinnamon stick

2 or 3 whole cloves
1 pound dried figs
1 cup sour cream

Bring sugar, water, lemon slices, cinnamon stick, and cloves to a boil, cook until syrup thickens or reaches 235 degrees on a candy thermometer. Add figs to the syrup and cook until just tender. Do not allow figs to split. Let stand for 24 hours to plump. Serve with sour cream.

ORANGES IN RED WINE

Serves 6

1 cup dry red wine
1 cup water
¾ cup sugar
1 cinnamon stick

2 whole cloves
2 slices lemon
6 large oranges

Combine and bring to a boil the wine, water, sugar, cinnamon, cloves, and lemon slices. Simmer for 3 minutes and keep hot. Peel oranges and reserve skins. Section oranges, discarding fibrous membranes, and drop sections into the hot syrup. Pare away the white part of orange skins and cut rinds into very fine julienne strips. Sprinkle the strips over the orange sections in red wine mixture and chill. Serve in crystal compote dishes.

PEARS ALLA ROMANA

These are good because the flavors are simple and the results elegant.

Serves 6

3 large pears, halved and
   cored
2 tablespoons butter
⅛ teaspoon almond extract

¼ cup finely chopped
   almonds
½ cup cream sherry

Preheat oven to 350 degrees. Place pear halves in a buttered baking dish, cavity side up. Cream together butter, almond extract, chopped almonds. Place a dollop of mixture in the cavity of each pear, pour cream sherry over all, and bake for 30 minutes. Serve warm or at room temperature.

POACHED PEARS IN CHOCOLATE SABAYON

Serves 6

6 ripe Bartlett or Comice
   pears, with stems
3 cups water
1 cup sugar

1 piece lemon rind
1 2-inch piece cinnamon
   stick

Chocolate Sabayon

4 ounces semisweet
   chocolate
¾ cup coffee
9 egg yolks

5 tablespoons sugar
¼ cup pear brandy or
   cognac

To poach the pears, peel them, leaving stems on. In a large saucepan, combine 3 cups water, sugar, lemon rind, and cinnamon stick. Heat to boiling and add pears. Cover and gently poach until just tender. Let pears cool in syrup, refrigerate until chilled. To make the sabayon: In a small saucepan, melt the chocolate and ¼ cup of the coffee together over very low heat. Set aside. In the top of a double boiler, mix egg yolks with sugar and beat until pale yellow. Add melted chocolate-coffee and remaining coffee to yolks, stir over simmering water until creamy and thickened. Add brandy. To serve: Place pears in a crystal dish or individual compotes and pour sauce over.

POACHED PEARS IN VANILLA SAUCE

Serves 6

1 cup sugar
1½ cups dry white wine

1½ cups water
6 fresh pears, with stems

SAUCE

4 egg yolks
1 cup sifted powdered sugar
1 teaspoon vanilla extract

¼ cup dry sherry
1 cup heavy cream, whipped

Combine sugar, wine, and water in a large saucepan, stirring until sugar dissolves. Peel pears, remove core from bottom, leaving stem on, and add pears to the hot syrup. Cover and simmer gently for 10 minutes or until pears are barely tender. Remove from heat, cool pan by placing it over a bowl of ice, and refrigerate pears in syrup until chilled. For the sauce: Beat egg yolks in the top of a double boiler and gradually add powdered sugar, beating until creamy and light-colored. Blend in vanilla and sherry, cook and stir over hot, not boiling, water for 10 minutes or until thickened. Beat until smooth, refrigerate for several hours, then gently fold into chilled whipped cream. Remove pears from syrup and serve with sauce over each pear.

CONTINENTAL PEACHES

This is also excellent as an accompaniment to meats.

Serves 6

3 large ripe peaches, peeled
    and halved
1 tablespoon rum extract

1 cup sour cream
3 tablespoons brown sugar
2 tablespoons sliced almonds

Preheat oven to 350 degrees. Arrange peaches, cut side up, in a 9-inch pie plate or baking dish. Sprinkle with rum extract. Spoon sour cream onto peaches. Sprinkle with sugar and almonds. Bake for about 20 minutes or until sugar caramelizes and almonds turn golden brown. Serve hot.

SUMMER FRUIT CHARLOTTE

This elegant and cool dessert is well worth the trouble for a special occasion, or any day! One suggestion—because the egg yolks are uncooked, keep refrigerated and serve within forty-eight hours.

Serves 8 to 10

2 dozen ladyfingers
3 tablespoons
    orange-flavored liqueur

2 to 3 cups raspberries
1 tablespoon kirsch

CRÈME ANGLAISE
1½ envelopes unflavored
    gelatin
3 tablespoons cold water
2½ cups milk
¾ cup sugar

6 egg yolks, lightly beaten
2 teaspoons vanilla extract
1½ cups heavy cream
Chopped nuts for garnish

Quickly dip ladyfingers into liqueur and line the bottom and sides of an 8-inch springform pan with them. Reserve remainder of ladyfingers for topping. Reserving ½ cup of raspberries for garnish, crush the remainder with the kirsch and refrigerate.

For the *crème anglaise:* Sprinkle gelatin over the cold water and set aside to soften. In a heavy saucepan, add the milk and sugar and bring to a boil. Remove from heat and add ⅓ of the hot milk to the egg yolks, beating constantly. Quickly whisk yolk mixture into remaining milk and stir over simmering water for approximately 15 seconds. Pour *crème anglaise* through a fine strainer and add softened gelatin and vanilla extract. Blend well and set aside. Beat heavy cream until *just* beginning to set. Place the *crème anglaise* over ice in a bowl, stirring constantly, until it is cooled. Then fold in whipped cream, reserving ½ cup for garnish.

To assemble: Pour ¼ of the crème anglaise into the ladyfinger-lined springform pan, leaving a 1-inch outer ring. Cover with half of the crushed berries. Add another ¼ of the *crème*, then the reserved ladyfingers, whole or cut up to fit the pan. Add ¼ of the *crème* and remaining crushed berries. Top with remaining crème. The mold should be filled and level. Refrigerate for at least 2 hours or overnight. Remove sides from springform pan, place on a serving dish, and garnish with rosettes of whipped cream, whole raspberries, and chopped nuts.

DOUBLE SOUFFLÉ

This is a lovely dessert—different, colorful—and it serves more people than the usual soufflé. The middle should be runny and served like a sauce over the firmer parts. Rich and good.

Serves 6 to 8

4 tablespoons butter
4 tablespoons flour
1⅓ cups milk, scalded
8 egg yolks
½ cup sugar
2 tablespoons vanilla extract
3 ounces unsweetened
    chocolate

1 tablespoon sugar
2 tablespoons strong coffee
12 egg whites
½ teaspoon salt
12 ladyfingers, soaked in
    ¼ cup rum or cognac

Preheat oven to 375 degrees. In a saucepan melt butter, add flour, and cook, stirring, for a few minutes. Slowly add milk and stir constantly until thickened, about 2 minutes. Remove from heat and set aside to cool slightly. Beat egg yolks and sugar together. Pour some of the thickened sauce into the egg mixture to warm it, then add the rest and blend. Divide this sauce into 2 bowls. Add vanilla to one bowl. In a small saucepan, melt chocolate with 1 tablespoon sugar and the strong coffee over low heat. Add chocolate mixture to the other bowl of sauce. Beat egg whites with the salt until stiff but not dry. Divide beaten whites equally between the bowls, folding in lightly. Butter a 2½-quart soufflé dish, sprinkle the inside with sugar and shake out excess. Pour in the chocolate mixture first. Then top with the ladyfingers soaked in rum. Cover with the vanilla mixture. Bake for 35 minutes. Serve immediately.

ICE CREAM SOUFFLÉ WITH HOT STRAWBERRY SAUCE

This is a marvelous blend of contrasting flavors, temperatures, and colors. Just the right dessert to complement any meal. And so easy.

Serves 8

1 quart vanilla ice cream,
   softened
8 almond macaroons,
   crumbled
3 tablespoons
   orange-flavored liqueur

1 cup heavy cream, whipped
¼ cup chopped toasted
   almonds
1 tablespoon powdered sugar

SAUCE
2 pints fresh strawberries, hulled, washed and halved
⅓ cup sugar
3 tablespoons orange-flavored liqueur

To softened ice cream add crumbled macaroons and stir in orange-flavored liqueur. Gently fold in whipped cream and pour into a 1-quart soufflé dish. Cover with plastic wrap and freeze until firm. Let stand at room temperature for 5 to 10 minutes before serving. Sprinkle with toasted almonds and powdered sugar. In the meantime the sauce: In a saucepan simmer the strawberries and sugar until berries are soft but not mushy. Remove from heat and stir in orange-flavored liqueur. Place in a serving dish and spoon over soufflé.

COLD DAIQUIRI SOUFFLÉ

Serves 12

10 eggs, separated
2 cups sugar
1 cup fresh lime juice
Grated rinds of 4 limes
Pinch of salt

2 tablespoons unflavored
   gelatin
½ cup light rum
3 cups heavy cream

GARNISH
Crystallized violets
Lime slices
Crushed pistachio nuts

Beat egg yolks until light and fluffy. Gradually beat in 1 cup of the sugar until mixture is smooth and lemon-colored. Blend in lime juice, grated rind, and salt. Cook and stir over low heat until thickened. Soften gelatin in rum and stir into hot custard to dissolve. Cool. Tie a paper collar around the top of a 6-cup soufflé dish and oil dish and paper. Beat egg whites until foamy, gradually add remaining 1 cup sugar, and beat until peaks form. Fold a large spoonful of custard into egg whites and then fold egg whites into remaining custard. Whip 2 cups of the heavy cream and fold into mixture. Pour into soufflé dish and chill thoroughly until set. Whip remaining cream. Remove paper collar and with a pastry bag decorate top with whipped cream rosettes. Garnish with violets and lime slices. Press nuts gently onto sides of soufflé.

COLD RASPBERRY SOUFFLÉ

Simply scrumptious!

Serves 6 to 8

2 envelopes unflavored
   gelatin
½ cup fresh lemon juice
8 eggs, separated
1 cup sugar

1 cup puréed fresh
   raspberries
4 tablespoons cassis
2 cups heavy cream

Prepare a 2-quart soufflé dish with a wax paper collar extending 2 to 3 inches above rim of dish. Tape into place. Oil dish and paper. Soften gelatin in lemon juice and heat over a low flame until dissolved and clear. Beat egg yolks with sugar until light and fluffy. Mix puréed raspberries with cassis and add to egg yolk mixture, then add gelatin. Cook over hot water until thickened. Cool. Beat egg whites until stiff peaks form, then whip heavy cream until stiff. Gently fold egg whites into raspberry mixture, then fold in whipped cream. Pour into the soufflé dish and chill thoroughly. Remove paper collar before serving.

FROZEN STRAWBERRY SOUFFLÉ

Serves 12

2 10-ounce packages frozen
  sliced strawberries,
  thawed
6 eggs, separated
1¾ cups sugar

½ cup orange-flavored
  liqueur
⅓ cup fresh orange juice
3 cups heavy cream
Red food coloring (optional)

GARNISH
1 cup chopped walnuts
Additional whipped cream
Whole fresh strawberries

Strawberry Liqueur Sauce
  (recipe given below)

Prepare a 2-quart soufflé dish with a wax paper collar extending 2 to 3 inches above the rim of the dish. Tape into place. Oil the dish and wax paper. Purée strawberries in a blender or food processor and set aside. Beat egg yolks and ¾ cup of the sugar until thick and lemon-colored. Stir in half the strawberry purée and cook in the top of a double boiler over simmering water, stirring, for 15 minutes or until mixture thickens and coats spoon. Remove from heat and cool. Stir in orange-flavored liqueur and set aside. In saucepan combine remaining 1 cup sugar and orange juice. Heat, stirring to dissolve sugar. Cook, without stirring, to thread stage (232° to 234° on a candy thermometer). Beat egg whites until very stiff but not dry. Very slowly pour a thin stream of hot orange syrup over, beating at high speed until all syrup is used and mixture stands in stiff peaks. Set aside to cool. Whip the cream and fold into cooled strawberry mixture along with remaining purée. Fold in the meringue and mix gently but well. Stir in a few drops of red coloring if you wish. Turn into the soufflé dish and freeze for 6 hours or overnight. To serve, remove collar and press walnuts into the sides of the soufflé. Decorate top edge with dollops of whipped cream and mound a few whole strawberries in the center. Serve with Strawberry Liqueur Sauce.

Strawberry Liqueur Sauce

Makes 3½ cups

1 quart fresh strawberries, sliced
½ cup sugar
4 tablespoons orange-flavored liqueur

Combine sliced strawberries and sugar in a saucepan and heat until berries are just heated through. Remove from heat and stir in the liqueur. Place in a saucedish and pass separately with Frozen Strawberry Soufflé.

COLD LEMON SOUFFLÉ

Serves 6

4 eggs, separated
1 cup sugar
½ cup fresh lemon juice
Grated rind of 2½ lemons,
    or 1½ tablespoons
1 envelope unflavored
    gelatin, softened in
    ¼ cup cold water

1¼ cups heavy cream
2 ounces finely chopped or
    ground toasted almonds

Tie a collar of wax paper around a 1-quart soufflé dish and oil dish and paper lightly. Set aside. In the top of a double boiler, beat egg yolks until smooth, blend in sugar, lemon juice, and lemon rind. Stir and cook over simmering water until opaque and slightly thickened. Add softened gelatin and stir to dissolve. Remove from heat and pour into a large chilled bowl. Whisk until cool. Whip 1 cup of the cream and fold into lemon mixture. Whip egg whites until stiff but not dry. Stand the bowl of lemon mixture over ice and carefully fold in egg whites. Pour into the soufflé dish and refrigerate until set. Remove paper collar. Whip remaining cream and decorate top of soufflé with rosettes. Pat almonds around sides of soufflé.

PASHKA

This is a rich version of coeur à la crème—*the almonds and lemon give it an interesting flavor. A heavy dessert, it goes well at the end of a light meal with good fruit.*

Serves 6

32 ounces cream cheese,
    softened
1 cup butter, softened
3 egg yolks
2 cups powdered sugar

2 teaspoons vanilla extract
¾ cup citron, chopped, or
    peeled and chopped
    rind of 1 lemon
¾ cup slivered almonds

Cream together the cream cheese and butter. Add egg yolks, powdered sugar, and vanilla, mix well. Blend in citron and almonds. Dampen a piece of cheesecloth and line a 5 by 7-inch clay flowerpot or any mold with a hole in the bottom. Pour in mixture and chill for several hours. Some liquid will drain from the bottom as it chills. To serve, unmold onto a serving plate and remove cheesecloth carefully. Garnish with strawberries or slices of fresh fruit.

SAILOR'S DUFF

Similar to a gingerbread, and best served warm.

Serves 10 to 12

½ cup brown sugar, firmly
    packed
2 tablespoons butter
⅛ teaspoon baking soda
2 tablespoons dark molasses
1 teaspoon cinnamon
½ teaspoon powdered
    ginger

1 egg
½ cup milk
1 teaspoon baking powder
1 cup unsifted all-purpose
    flour

SAUCE
2 egg yolks
½ cup sugar

2 tablespoons brandy
1 cup heavy cream

Cream together brown sugar and butter. Dissolve baking soda in molasses and add to brown sugar mixture, mix well. Add cinnamon, ginger, egg, milk, baking powder, and flour. Pour into a buttered pudding mold or a buttered 1-pound coffee can. To steam: Set on a rack in a large, deep kettle, add water to come halfway up sides of coffee can or mold. Bring water to a gentle boil, cover the kettle, lower heat, and steam for 1½ hours. Serve warm. For the sauce: Beat egg yolks well, gradually adding sugar. Add brandy and blend. Just before serving, whip heavy cream and fold into sauce.

GRAND MARNIER POTS DE CRÈME

Serves 10 to 12

9 egg yolks
½ cup superfine sugar
3 cups heavy cream
¼ teaspoon vanilla extract
6 tablespoons Grand
    Marnier

4 tablespoons freshly grated
    orange rind
1 tablespoon Grand Marnier

Preheat oven to 325 degrees. Place in the oven a baking pan with 1 inch of water in it to heat. In a separate bowl, beat the egg yolks with sugar until thick and creamy. Add very gradually to the cream, stirring constantly with a wooden spoon. Add vanilla and 6 tablespoons Grand Marnier, mix well. Pour mixture into *pot de crème* cups and place in the baking pan of water in the oven. Bake for 35 minutes or until a knife inserted in the center of the custard comes out clean. Remove from the oven and pan of water and cool completely. Chill in the refrigerator for at least 2 hours. At serving time, blend grated orange rind with the 1 tablespoon Grand Marnier and "ice" the tops of the custards with the mixture.

MOCHA MOUSSE

Serves 6

1 cup heavy cream
⅓ cup sugar
¼ cup toasted chopped
    almonds
1 teaspoon vanilla extract

2 egg whites
1 tablespoon instant coffee
2 tablespoons sugar
Chocolate curls for garnish
    (optional)

Whip cream until it holds peaks. Add ⅓ cup sugar, almonds, and vanilla. In a separate bowl, beat egg whites and instant coffee together until stiff. Add 2 tablespoons sugar and beat until satiny in texture. Fold whipped cream into beaten egg whites and pour into a serving dish or individual dishes. Freeze for at least 2 hours. Decorate with chocolate curls just before serving, if desired.

STEAMED CARROT PUDDING

A slight departure from traditional pumpkin pudding, but equally satisfying and delicious. Try it with a good brandy sauce or hard sauce.

Serves 10 to 12

1 cup unsifted all-purpose
    flour
1 teaspoon baking soda
½ teaspoon cinnamon
¼ teaspoon ground cloves
½ teaspoon allspice
½ teaspoon nutmeg
1 cup grated carrots
1 cup grated potatoes
1 cup grated tart apple
    without peel

1 cup chopped walnuts
1 cup raisins
½ cup finely chopped
    candied fruit
    (optional)
½ cup butter
1 cup sugar
1 egg

Combine dry ingredients. In a separate bowl, combine carrots, potatoes, apple, nuts, raisins, and candied fruit. Add ⅓ of the flour mixture and blend. In a large mixing bowl, cream butter and sugar, add egg, and then beat in carrot mixture. Add remaining flour and stir until just blended. Pour into a buttered and sugared 2-quart mold. Steam as directed in Sailor's Duff (recipe above) for 2½ to 3 hours.

STEAMED CRANBERRY PUDDING WITH VANILLA SAUCE

Excellent—serve this for Christmas or after an elegant dinner.

Serves 10 to 12

PUDDING

2 cups whole fresh or frozen and thawed cranberries
½ cup light molasses
½ cup hot water

2 teaspoons baking soda
1½ cups unsifted all-purpose flour

SAUCE

½ cup sugar
¼ pound butter, cut into bits

½ cup light cream
2 teaspoons vanilla extract

In the order given, combine pudding ingredients, stirring well. Transfer to a buttered 2-pound coffee can or pudding mold and cover tightly with foil. To steam: Set on a rack in a large, deep kettle, add water to come halfway up sides of coffee can or mold. Bring water to a gentle boil, cover the kettle, lower heat, and steam for 1 to 1½ hours or until a toothpick inserted in the center comes out clean. Be careful to keep water at a *very* low boil. Combine sauce ingredients, bring to a boil, and cook and stir until slightly thickened. Turn pudding out onto a heated serving plate and pour sauce over.

STEAMED PUMPKIN PUDDING WITH BRANDY SAUCE

Serves 10 to 12

½ cup shortening
1 cup brown sugar, firmly
  packed
¼ cup granulated sugar
1 teaspoon salt
½ teaspoon cinnamon
½ teaspoon nutmeg
¼ teaspoon powdered
  ginger
2 eggs, beaten

⅔ cup chopped walnuts
2 cups all-purpose flour,
  sifted
1½ teaspoons baking
  powder
¼ teaspoon soda
¾ cup canned pumpkin, or
  fresh cooked and
  mashed
¼ cup sour cream

Brandy Sauce

1 egg
⅓ cup melted butter
1½ cups powdered sugar,
  sifted

1 teaspoon vanilla extract
¼ teaspoon nutmeg
2 tablespoons brandy
1 cup heavy cream, whipped

Cream together the shortening, brown and granulated sugars, salt and spices. Add eggs and beat well. Stir in nuts. Sift flour with baking powder and soda, add alternately with pumpkin and sour cream, mix well. Turn batter into a well greased 2-quart mold and cover tightly with foil. Steam as directed in Steamed Cranberry Pudding with Vanilla Sauce (recipe above) for 2 hours. Let pudding rest for 5 minutes before unmolding on a warm serving plate. Serve hot with brandy sauce. For the sauce: Beat egg until frothy, then beat in melted butter, powdered sugar, vanilla, nutmeg, and brandy. Carefully fold whipped cream into egg and sugar mixture. Chill until serving time, stirring to blend just before serving.

STEAMED PERSIMMON PUDDING

Serves 12

2 eggs
1¼ cups sugar
1¼ cups sieved persimmon
    pulp (about 3 large
    ripe)
¼ cup melted butter
1½ cups sifted all-purpose
    flour
1½ teaspoons baking
    powder

½ teaspoon salt
½ teaspoon cinnamon
¾ cup milk
1 cup seedless raisins
½ cup chopped pecans
    (optional)
¼ cup brandy

SAUCE

1 cup sweet (unsalted)
    butter
2 cups sifted powdered sugar

2 eggs, separated
1 jigger rum or brandy

Beat eggs until light, then beat in sugar until smooth and lemon-colored. Combine persimmon pulp and melted butter and stir into egg mixture. Sift dry ingredients and stir in alternately with milk, beating well after each addition. Add raisins, pecans, and brandy. Transfer to a well-buttered mold and cover tightly with foil. To steam: Set the mold on a rack in a large deep kettle and add water to come halfway up the sides of the mold. Bring water to gentle boil, cover saucepan, lower heat, and steam for 2½ hours. Remove pudding from water and let cool for 15 minutes. Unmold onto foil and cool completely if wrapping and freezing. Bring to room temperature before reheating. Serve warm with sauce. For the sauce: Cream butter and sugar until soft and fluffy. Beat in egg yolks one at a time, add rum or brandy, and mix well. Beat egg whites until stiff but not dry, and fold into sugar mixture. Serve at room temperature.

AMARETTO SAUCE AND FRESH FRUIT

This sauce is delicious on any kind of fresh berries and equally good on sliced bananas, peaches, or even toasted poundcake. Very versatile, tasty, and different.

Serves 4

3 cups fresh berries or peaches
4 tablespoons Amaretto liqueur
4 tablespoons powdered sugar

SAUCE
8 ounces ricotta cheese
8 ounces cream cheese
½ cup sugar
4 egg yolks

2 tablespoons heavy cream
3 tablespoons Amaretto
    liqueur

Toss berries with Amaretto and powdered sugar. Set aside and chill. For the sauce: Using a blender or food processor, mix together ricotta and cream cheeses. Add sugar, egg yolks, cream, and Amaretto. Continue beating until smooth. Pour into a serving dish and chill. To serve: Place chilled fruit in serving dishes. Pass sauce separately to spoon over fruit.

BRANDY SAUCE

Marvelous on plum pudding, fruitcake, or as a topping for fresh fruit.

Makes approximately 4 cups

3 eggs, separated
1 cup sugar
2 tablespoons butter,
    softened

1 cup heavy cream, stiffly
    beaten
3 tablespoons brandy or to
    taste

Beat egg yolks with sugar and butter until thick and lemon-colored. Beat egg whites until stiff but not dry, and fold into egg yolk mixture. Fold in whipped cream and add brandy.

BROWN SUGAR RUM SAUCE

Serve over fresh pineapple, sliced pears, peaches, or any other fresh fruit. Creamy texture, sweet taste, lovely to look at.

Makes approximately 3 cups

2 eggs, separated
½ cup brown sugar, firmly
  packed
1 cup heavy cream

2 tablespoons rum
Freshly grated nutmeg to
  garnish

Beat egg yolks until thick, then gradually beat in ¼ cup of the brown sugar. Set aside. Beat egg whites until soft peaks form, and gradually beat in remaining ¼ cup brown sugar. Fold egg yolk mixture into meringue. Whip cream until stiff and stir in rum. Fold into egg mixture. Spoon into a sauceboat and garnish with grated nutmeg. Chill until ready to serve.

CITRUS SAUCE FOR FRESH FRUIT

Makes approximately 2½ cups

¼ cup sugar
¼ teaspoon freshly grated
  orange rind
¼ teaspoon freshly grated
  lemon rind
⅓ cup fresh orange juice

¼ cup fresh lemon juice
2 egg yolks, beaten
2 cups heavy cream,
  whipped
Fresh fruits of choice

In the top of a double boiler, combine and heat sugar, rinds, and juices. When hot, pour 3 tablespoons of this mixture into beaten egg yolks, stirring constantly. Then slowly beat egg mixture into sugar mixture and cook and stir over simmering water until thickened and mixture coats spoon. Cool to room temperature. Fold a large spoonful of the egg-sugar mixture into whipped cream. Then fold whipped cream into remaining custard. Mix well and chill. Serve with fresh fruit such as melon, papaya, pineapple, strawberries or raspberries.

EGGNOG SAUCE

Wonderful on fruitcake, poundcake, or fresh fruit.

Makes approximately 2 cups

2 eggs, separated
1 cup powdered sugar

½ cup heavy cream
3 tablespoons brandy

Beat egg yolks until thick and lemon-colored. Add powdered sugar to egg yolks and blend. Beat egg whites until stiff but not dry. Fold into egg yolk mixture. Whip cream until stiff, fold into mixture, and add 3 tablespoons of brandy.

NATILLAS SAUCE FOR PINEAPPLE

This cool and creamy sauce is the perfect foil for pineapple as well as any summer fruit . . . a platter of strawberries, peaches, grapes, bananas—anything will go with this versatile sauce.

Makes about 2 cups

2 cups light cream
¼ teaspoon salt
¼ cup sugar
1 whole egg

2 egg yolks
1 teaspoon cornstarch
1 teaspoon vanilla extract

In the top of a double boiler, scald the cream and cool slightly. In a small bowl, beat together the salt, sugar, egg, egg yolks, cornstarch, and vanilla. Add to cream and cook over hot, not boiling, water, stirring constantly, until slightly thickened. Pour sauce into a serving bowl and chill. To serve: Peel and slice pineapple into spears, reserving green top, Place green top in the center of a serving platter with pineapple spears radiating like spokes from the center. Pass sauce separately.

GRAND MARNIER SAUCE

This sauce is sublime over fresh berries or a colorful bowl of mixed fruits.

Serves 8

5 egg yolks at room temperature	¼ cup Grand Marnier
¾ cup sugar	1 cup heavy cream
	1 tablespoon sugar

Beat egg yolks until light in the top of a double boiler. Beat in ¾ cup sugar and place over simmering water, stirring constantly, until thickened, about 20 minutes. Remove from heat and beat until cool. Add Grand Marnier and refrigerate until chilled. Whip cream just until it begins to thicken, then add 1 tablespoon sugar. Continue beating until cream is medium thick but will still pour. Fold into egg sauce and pour into a serving dish. Chill until serving time, or freeze. Serve over fresh fruit.

CHRISTMAS GIFT TOFFEE

This candy is one of the great classics which the family can make together. A traditional and delicious gift.

Makes approximately 1 pound

1 cup butter	3 4-ounce chocolate bars, crumbled
1 cup sugar	½ cup chopped pecans
3 tablespoons water	
1 teaspoon vanilla extract	

In a heavy saucepan, cook together the butter, sugar, water, stirring constantly, until the mixture reads 300 degrees on a candy thermometer. Remove from heat and add vanilla. Pour into a buttered 9 by 11-inch pan and allow to cool for 5 minutes. Sprinkle crumbled chocolate bars over the top of the toffee, then the chopped pecans. When cool, break into pieces. Store in airtight containers.

Weights, Measures, and the Metric System

WEIGHTS

CONVERSION FORMULAS:
Ounces into grams, multiply the ounces by 28.3495
Grams into ounces, multiply the grams by 0.35274

POUNDS & OUNCES (most convenient approximations)	METRIC
2.2 pounds	1 kilogram (1,000 grams)
1 pound (16 ounces)	464 grams
3½ ounces	100 grams
1 ounce	30 grams

LIQUID MEASURE

CONVERSION FORMULAS:
Quarts into liters, multiply the quarts by 0.94635
Liters into quarts, multiply the liters by 1.056688
Ounces into milliliters, multiply the ounces by 29.573
Milliliters into ounces, multiply the milliliters by 0.0338

CUPS AND SPOONS	QUARTS AND OUNCES (most convenient approximations)	METRIC EQUIVALENTS
4⅓ cups	1 quart 2 ounces	1 liter (1,000 milliliters)
1 cup	8 ounces	¼ liter
1 tablespoon	½ ounce	15 milliliters (15 grams)
1 teaspoon	1/16 ounce	5 milliliters (5 grams)

Temperatures
Fahrenheit vs. Centigrade

CONVERSION FORMULAS:

Centigrade to Fahrenheit, multiply by 9, divide by 5, add 32

Fahrenheit to Centigrade, subtract 32, multiply by 5, divide by 9

FAHRENHEIT	CENTIGRADE
50 degrees	10 degrees
100	38
212	100
275	135
325	163
350	177
375	190
400	204.4
425	218
450	232
550	288

INDEX